BRITISH FOREIGN POLICY
1660 — 1672

BRITISH
FOREIGN POLICY
1660—1672

KEITH ⸰Grahame FEILING

FRANK CASS & CO. LTD.
1968

Published by
FRANK CASS AND COMPANY LIMITED
67 Great Russell Street, London WC1
by arrangement with Macmillan & Co. Ltd.

First edition   1930
New impression   1968

Printed in Great Britain by
Thomas Nelson (Printers) Ltd., London and Edinburgh

PREFACE

JUDGED by modern standards, the history of British foreign policy in the second half of the seventeenth century has still to be written. Ranke's account is seventy years old, the massive work of Gardiner and Sir Charles Firth stops at 1658, and no one has pursued the subject on anything like the same scale. To make a small contribution towards filling that gap is the purpose of this book.

The period taken is, perhaps, the most neglected in the century; the documents are uncalendared and scattered, and the detailed research which in recent years has thrown much light on the second half of Charles' reign is (with the brilliant exception of Miss Barbour's *Arlington*) still lacking for the first. For this reason, though not for this alone, I have attempted rather a general essay in policy than a diplomatic history, which requires (and is, indeed, receiving) a more intensive study of particular episodes, like the Triple Alliance. This, too, influenced the obviously imperfect choice of my material, which I should put in this order of importance, as related to the present condition of the subject: British public archives, collections in private hands, foreign printed literature, and foreign archives of which less use has been made.

I should add that dates, unless otherwise stated, are Old Style, and that where the names of both correspondents, date, and manuscript source are given, I have thought it generally unnecessary to quote folio pages. I am very specially indebted to the Marquis of Bath for generous access to the Coventry papers; to the Hon. Charles Clifford and Mr. Cottrell-Dormer for letting me see the papers of their ancestors; to the Warden and Fellows of All Souls College for leave to use some of Leoline Jenkins' manuscripts; to Dr. Japikse and his staff for helping my work at the Hague; to Senor Plaza for assistance in procuring transcripts from Simancas; and to the staff of the British Museum, the Public Record Office, and the Bodleian, for the services they render to all.

More than all, I must thank Mr. G. N. Clark, of Oriel College, for his kindness in the thankless task of reading this work in proof.

KEITH FEILING.

January 1930.

CONTENTS

CHAPTER I

CHAPTER II

CHAPTER III

CHAPTER IV

CHAPTER V

CHAPTER VI

vii

LIST OF MSS. REFERENCES
AND ABBREVIATED TITLES

(a) MSS.

1. PUBLIC RECORD OFFICE.
   State Papers, Foreign: General series. These are cited by the country and volume in question; *e.g.* France 123.
   Fr. tr. = French Transcripts.
   Archives.
   Treaty Papers.
   Roman Transcripts.
   Foreign Entry Books.
   Newsletters.
   State Papers Domestic.

2. BRITISH MUSEUM.
   Add.(itional), Sloane, Egerton, Harleian, and Stowe collections.

3. BODLEIAN.
   Clarendon, Rawlinson, Carte, and Tanner papers.

4. SIMANCAS = transcripts from the Spanish Archives at Simancas.

5. R.A. = Rijks archief, the Hague.

6. CLIFFORD = papers in the possession of the Hon. Charles Clifford at Ugbrooke.

7. LONGLEAT = papers in the possession of the Marquis of Bath at Longleat.

8. JENKINS = papers of Sir Leoline Jenkins, in the possession of the Warden and Fellows of All Souls College, Oxford.

9. COTTRELL-DORMER = papers in possession of T. Cottrell-Dormer, Esq., of Rousham.

(*b*) PRINTED

ADY. *Madame, a Life of Henrietta, daughter of Charles I and Duchess of Orleans.* 1894.

AITZEMA. *Saken van Staet en Oorlogh in en omtrent de Vereenigte Nederlanden.* 1669–71.

ARCH. *Archives de la maison d'Orange-Nassau.* 2nd series, vol. v. 1860.

ARL. *Letters of the Earl of Arlington:* ed. Bebington. 1701.

BALLESTEROS. *Historia de España*: tomo cuarto. primiera parte. 1926.

BARBOUR. *Life of Arlington.* 1913.

BLOK. *History of the People of the Netherlands.* (Eng. tr.) 1898 *seq.*

BR. *Brieven . . . gewisselt tusschen den Heer Johan de Witt ende de gevolmagtigden v.d. Stat d. Vereen. Nederl.* 1723.

BURNET. *History of My Own Time:* ed. Airy. 1897.

CAL.S.P.D. Calendars of State Papers Domestic.

CARLSON. *Geschichte Schwedens*, vols. v. and vi. 1873-87.

CHÉRUEL. *La Minorité de Louis XIV.*

CHRISTIE. *Life of Shaftesbury.* 1871.

CLARENDON. *Life of Edward Hyde, Earl of Clarendon:* written by himself. (3 vols.) 1759.

COLENBRANDER. *Bescheiden uit vreemde archieven omtrent de groote Nederland. Zeevorlogen.* 1919.

COL.S.P. Calendars of Colonial State Papers.

COMBES. *Correspondance française de J. De Witt.* 1873.

COSNAC. *Daniel de C. archevèque d'Aix: Mémoires.* 1852.

COURTENAY. *Life of Sir William Temple.* 1826.

C.S.P. *Clarendon State Papers.*

DALRYMPLE. *Memoirs of Great Britain and Ireland* (2 vols.) 1771.

D'AVENEL (ed.). *Lettres du Cardinal Mazarin.* (Coll. des Doc. inéd.)

D'ESTRADES. *Lettres, mémoires, négotiations.* (9 vols.) 1743.

DOLLOT. *Les Origines de la neutralité de la Belgique.* 1902.

DREYSS (ed.). *Mémoires de Louis XIV pour l'instruction du Dauphin.* 1860.

DROYSEN. *Geschichte der preussichen Politik.* (2nd edition.) 1866–72.

DUMONT. *Corps universal diplomatique.* 1726.

E.H.R. *English Historical Review.*

E.I.C. *Court Minutes of East India Company.* 1922, *et seq.*
ERDMANSDÖRFFER. *Deutsche Geschichte.* 1648–1740, . . . 1892.
EVELYN. *Diary of John Evelyn.*

FANSHAWE. *Memoirs of Anne, Lady Fanshawe.* 1907.
FANSHAWE LETTERS. *Original Letters and Negotiations of Sir Richard Fanshawe.* 1724.
FINCH. Report on MSS. of A. G. Finch, Hist. MSS. Comm.
FORNERON. *The Court of Charles II.* 1897.
FRUIN. *Brieven van Johan de Witt bewerkt door Robert Fruin* (ed. Kernkamp and Japikse). 1906–13.

GAEDEKE. *Die Politik Österreichs in der spanischen Erbfolgefrage.* 1877.
GREY. Anchitel Grey: Parliamentary Debates. 1763.
GROOT. *Lettres de Pierre de Groot à Wicquefort*: ed. Krämer. 1894.

HARING, C. H. *The Buccaneers in the West Indies in the Seventeenth Century.* 1910.
HARRIS, F. R. *Life of Edward Montagu, Earl of Sandwich.* 1912.
HEATHCOTE. Report on MSS. of J. M. Heathcote, Hist. MSS. Comm.
HIGHAM, C. S. S. *The Development of the Leeward Islands, 1660–1688.* 1921.
H.I. *Hispania Illustrata.* 1703.

JAMES II. *Life of James II:* by J. S. Clarke. 1816.
JAPIKSE. *De Verwikkelingen tusschen de Republiek en Engeland, van 1660–65.* 1900.
JAPIKSE, "DE WITT". *Johan De Witt:* door Dr. N. Japikse. 1928.
JENKINS. *Life of Sir Leoline Jenkins:* ed. Wynne. 1724.
JUSSERAND. *A French Ambassador at the Court of Charles II.* 1892.

KHAN. *The East India Trade in the Seventeenth Century.* 1903.
KLOPP. *Der Fall des Hauses Stuart.* 1875–88.
KRÄMER. *De Nederlandsch-Spaansche Diplomatie voor den Vrede van Nijmegen.* 1892.

LEGRELLE. *La Diplomatie française et la succession d'Espagne.* 1888.
LISTER. *Life of Clarendon.* 1838.
LOUIS XIV. *Œuvres de Louis XIV.* 1805.

MACPHERSON. *Original Papers containing the Secret History of Great Britain.* 1776.

MARVELL.   *Poems and Letters:* ed. Margoliouth.   1927.

M.H. PAPERS.   Report on the MSS. of the Duke of Buccleuch at Montague House (Hist. MSS. Commission), vol. i.   1899.

MIGNET, F. A. M.   *Négotiations relatives à la succession d'Espagne* (Coll. des Doc. inéd.).   1835–42.

MISC. AUL.   *Miscellanea Aulica.* · 1702

PAGÈS.   *Le Grand Électeur et Louis XIV.*   1905.

PEPYS.   *The Diary of Samuel Pepys:* ed. Wheatley.

PICAVET.   *Les Dernières Années de Turenne.*   1919.

POMPONNE.   *Mémoires du Marquis de Pomponne:* ed. Mavidal.   1860.

PONTALIS.   *Jean De Witt.*   1884.

PÖTTING.   *Privatbriefe Kaiser Leopold I an den Grafen Pötting.*   1903.

PRESTAGE, E.   *The Diplomatic Relations of Portugal with France, England, and Holland, 1640–68.*   1925.

PRIBRAM.   *Lisola und die Politik seiner Zeit.*   1894.

RANKE.   *History of England.*   (Eng. trans.)   1875.

REC.   *Recueil des instructions données aux ambassadeurs et ministres de France* (cited under different countries; *e.g.* "Rec. Espagne").

REV. HIST.   *Revue Historique.*

ROUTH, E. M. G.   *Tangier.*   1912.

SCHWERIN.   *Briefe aus England, 1674–78.*   1837.

SCOTT, W. R.   *Joint-stock Companies to 1720.*   1912.

SEC. RES.   *Secrete Resolutien van Holland en West Vriesland.*   1717.

TEMPLE, Sir William.   *Works:* ed. 1731 (from which his letters are quoted, save where otherwise stated).

URK.   *Urkunden und Actenstücke des Kurfursten Friedrich Wilhelm von Brandenburg.*   1864, *et seq.*

VAN DIJK.   *Bijdrage tot de Geschiednis der Nederlandsche Diplomatie.*   1851.

WICQUEFORT.   *Histoire des Provinces Unies:* ed. van Buren.   1861–74.

WILLIAMSON.   *Letters from London to Sir Joseph Williamson:* ed. Christie.   Camden Society.   1874.

CHAPTER I

THE INHERITANCE AND THE HEIR

THE last ceremonies at the Hague were over. The King's dogs were safely aboard; his aunt and sister, the wise Elizabeth of Bohemia and the foolish Mary of Orange, stepped into their barge, and with Mary's ten-year-old son William made for the shore. At four o'clock the fleet set sail, till six the crowds on the Dunes watched the sails sinking out of sight. At last Montagu, the English admiral, had performed the task for which he, like the soldier Monk, had worked since the autumn; his squadron might itself be taken as a symbol of Restoration, for Royalist exiles, Parliamentary commissioners, and politicians on the make, jostled every cabin, and the ships, whose names commemorated battle-fields and heroes of Cromwellianism, were re-baptized this day with titles more comfortable to the ear. It was the 23rd of May, a glorious evening at sea, and on the quarter-deck of the *Charles* (yesterday *Naseby*) the King paced up and down, telling of his travels and escapes.

Odysseus was returning to England, the Penelope who for him had warded off many suitors—weak Protectors, dangerous soldiers, democratic saints, specious foreign envoys. Sirens had sung to him, not wholly in vain; one indeed, Barbara Villiers, later Lady Castlemaine, had met him at the Hague and waited him at

London. But from one, the most dangerous, he had escaped—the spectre of being handed to his throne by the arms of a foreign power.

Against that danger Edward Hyde, the exile's chief minister, had long struggled, and now he was reinforced by Puritan England, for Monk had in April urged Charles to move from Catholic and Spanish Brussels to Breda, the patrimony of the House of Orange. But the English counter-revolution had moved so fast, its issues were throughout so uncertain, that to the very end foreign intervention was a real possibility. When in February Monk was ending his march at London, Charles was penniless; dependent for his bread on credit from Spain, and attracted by strong magnets towards France, both of which Powers were trying to carve the shape of the English Restoration—"to cutt him his morsels", as our agent at Brussels put it.[1] A catholic Irish clique was promising a joint Franco-Spanish *démarche* to win toleration for Catholics. The Paris circle round Charles' mother, Henrietta Maria, which had done much to destroy the father, were bent on ruining the son. Mazarin armed the Abbé Montague with funds, and Henry Jermyn was agitating for a return to Paris. Some English royalist regiments in Flanders were still in Spanish pay; Spanish authorities at Brussels had tried to keep Charles in their territories by force, and now they too begged him to take Brussels on his way to London. Rival French and Spanish dinner parties at the Hague prolonged this competition to the very eve of his embarcation.[2]

[1] De Vic to Hyde, May 8, Clarendon MSS. Cal. iii.
[2] Peter Talbot to Ormonde, May 20, Carte MSS. 214, f. 202; Chéruel, iii. 317; Jermyn to Charles II, May 1, Clarendon MSS. Cal. iii.; D'Avenel, ix. 558; Hyde to Bennet, May 6; Aitzema, iv. 595.

Happily for England, the conditions that made the Restoration a political compromise must govern also the relation of the restored King to foreign affairs. He could no more cancel Puritan foreign policy than he could their Church settlement, and for war and peace, as for the management of Parliament, he must depend on their experience, their co-operation, and their wealth. If his hands were tied by predilections dating from his exile, he was bound also by heavy commitments to the formidable Englishmen who had brought him home, and he returned, in short, to an England that was "a going concern". Such continuity was nowhere more marked than in our European relations, nor did a few superficial accompaniments of counter-revolution, the bickerings of Royalist merchants with Cromwellian merchants[1] or the like, contradict this permanence in high policy. Ex-Puritans formed half of the new Cabinet that was to prolong Cromwell's friendship with France and his hostility to Holland. The first resident ambassador it sent to Paris was Denzil Holles, twenty years earlier one of those five members whom Charles I in a fatal hour had tried to seize in the House of Commons. Cromwell's envoy at the Hague, George Downing, returned there for another four years to represent Charles II. Philip Meadowes, the Protector's envoy in 1657–58 to Denmark and Sweden, sent a minute to Clarendon as to the probable attitude of those courts in the event of another Dutch war.[2] Thurloe, Oliver's secretary and foreign minister, himself drew up similar notes on our relation with France and Holland,[3] and bequeathed the names of his secret agents.[4]

---

[1] Heathcote, 66; Finch, i. xxxvii.　　[2] Holland, 163, ff. 199 *et seq.*
[3] *Infra*, pp. 9, 56.　　[4] Carte MSS. 31, f. 67.

In a sense far wider than such personal services, English policy could not fail to be continuous, guided as it must be by continuous geographic law. The seas that bound in triumphant Britain carried upon them the means of her wealth and the power of her enemies. If, as foreigners thought, her rulers nourished the "old English error"[1] of splendid isolation, a multitude of motives must soon explode it. Even on its purely political side the struggle for the Hapsburg inheritance could not leave England unmoved, for in the Netherlands it touched her in a spot vital to her strategic and economic salvation. But the sixteenth century had entailed upon Europe two yet greater things—a new religion and a new world of commerce. Protestantism and oceanic trade were born together; for a short time making common cause, in the long run they complicated and transformed out of all recognition the original issue of Hapsburg or anti-Hapsburg predominance.

If divisions of time can ever be given to matter so liquid as diplomacy, it can be said that one scheme of alliances represented the normal British system for the century ending in 1674. A hundred years before that date Queen Elizabeth, with her wonted reservation and delay, had abandoned the traditional Spanish friendship of her family and taken the decision pressed or forced upon her by Protestant counsellors and godly pirates. The anti-Hapsburg *bloc* to which she committed her country was to survive many divergencies, that increased with each additional member. Originally it turned upon the three poles of London, Paris, and Protestant Germany; to these Holland was added by 1590, Sweden by 1620, while in 1640 Portugal was remade from the rib in the side of Spain.

---

[1] So the Brandenburg envoy, 1661; Urk. ix. 704.

But such consistency as this confederation ever possessed began to melt almost as soon as formed, and by 1648 was shaking in liquid confusion. The European grouping began to break at either end. French ambition, sheltered by the pauperism and fantasies of our Charles I, became portentous to her allies. In 1648 Austria received the sentence of lifelong imprisonment within the East, passed on her by the Peace of Westphalia, and left Spain to fight France alone; Holland, on the contrary, terrified for the Low Countries by the Peace of Münster, deserted France as an ally too powerful to be aggrandized further. During the next eleven years—exactly the life of the English Commonwealth—territorial greed, economic war, and Mazarin's diplomacy tore away more fragments of the old system. Holland fought one war with England for the carrying trade, another with Portugal for Brazil and western India. The Cardinal's machination turned to prolong English civil strife—a game to be repeated with variations till 1688—and French privateers preyed upon our commerce. Sweden's passion to master all the Baltic banded together against her the fellow-Protestants of Holland, Brandenburg, and Denmark, and a bitter contest for the customs-revenue of the Sound and Dantzig weakened the common tie of the Gospel. Within five years the militarist Charles X set glowing again the furnaces of the Thirty Years' War—Catholic Austria and Poland combining with his Protestant rivals.

In such a world stood England when at last the Protectorate put her house in order, and again she could take thought for her place in Europe. Cromwell's contribution to the reconstruction of our policy was bold in decision but characteristically conservative, and laid the base of no new system. His Protestant sword was half unsheathed to protect the Vaudois; a lucky occupation of Jamaica, the reconciliation of Barbados and Virginia, and some expansion in Acadia and New England did something to justify a neo-Elizabethan war; in Flanders and the Mediterranean the first regular English army and navy revealed a new English power. Essentially the antique alliance system lived on, though stabbed with suspicion and hopes deferred.

Of that system, amity with Holland was one cornerstone, but the Peace of Westminster, signed in 1654, was almost more wearing than battle. The ejection of the Stuarts from Holland, or the salute conceded to the English flag, did nothing to exorcise the spirit making for war. Alike uncontrolled by, and defying control from, their central governments, the traders of both countries continued their fight in every sea—wresting to their own advantage the "right of search" and the law of contraband, claiming monopoly or free trade in the tropics just as occasion suited. English parliamentary debate grew raucous with anti-Dutch declamation, not least from Secretary Thurloe; English harbours flourished on the proceeds of Dutch prizes, often captured under cover of Swedish and Portuguese commissions; Sussex farmers made themselves easy with the honey and fine linen taken from Dutch wrecks. On their side the Hollanders shipped munitions to Spain, with whom England was at war, and offered ships to convey Charles II with Spanish auxiliaries to attack the Commonwealth.[1]

In two quarters particularly the two peoples' interests directly conflicted. For both the Baltic trade

[1] Burton, iii. 462, 487; Holland, 163, f. 2; Firth, *Last Years of the Protectorate*, ii. 181.

was fundamental; "the best trade of Christendom", said Clarendon. Each depended upon it for their naval equipment—for masts, iron, tar, and hemp. Holland, in all but geography an island city, bought her cattle from Jutland, and her staple foods from Baltic ports, to which six thousand Dutch ships were said to ply every year.[1] Dutch intervention in the Northern war of 1658–60 was, therefore, suspect to the English government, who remembered the exclusive privileges in the Sound extorted earlier by the Dutch from Denmark, and when Charles X was hurling himself against the unholy coalition of Austrians and Poles, Dutchmen and Prussians, a blend of evangelical sympathy and economic fear determined the despatch of an English squadron to the Baltic. French interests so far coincided with ours, that France could not suffer Sweden to perish, and the Peace of Oliva, which with the death of Charles ended the Northern wars, was made in the main by the intervention of the two western Powers. By it the Swedes' attempt to close the Sound to foreign warships and the Dutch bid for commercial monopoly were alike frustrated, but so late as the 18th March preceding the Restoration Monk's administration found it necessary to send a strong protest against a last effort from Holland to galvanize Danish resistance.[2]

Nearer home, in Belgium, the Dutch aspirations cut across English policy. Were the masters of Amsterdam also to control Antwerp? Already by the Münster treaty they had achieved a long-cherished ambition in closing the Scheldt. Since then, faced by the French thrust upon Belgium, de Witt in 1658–59 discussed

[1] Clarendon to Downing, March 18, 1664 (Clarendon MSS. 81), Rec. Hollande, i. 183; Erdmansdorffer, i. 218, note.
[2] Gardiner, *Commonwealth and Protectorate*, ii. 82; Aitzema, iv. 447, 545; Wicquefort, ii. 643.

with Mazarin some plans, agreed upon by his predecessors and Richelieu, for a regulation of this Naboth's vineyard to their mutual advantage, whether in the shape of downright partition, or the "cantonment" of Belgium as a "free" republic.[1]

Till the eve of Restoration the possibility of a second Dutch war beset the rulers of England, who, moreover, could find no compensation in steady friendship with France. Mazarin's first instincts were, and remained, hostile. He had hoped to settle the Belgian question before England was again free to act, and in 1653 offered, at this price, an alliance to Holland. The Anglo-French treaty of March 1657 was only signed after two years of parley and hesitation, and in Mazarin's eyes was definitely a *pis aller*. Peace with Spain, preferably with Belgium thrown in, was his primary object, and only Spanish obstinacy made him resolve to take "the necessary poison" of an English alliance, or to concede what England long had asked, the possession of Dunkirk.[2]

Contemporary England, like posterity, was acutely divided regarding the wisdom of Cromwell's choice. The Republicans generally disliked it; business interests feared that we should jeopardize our Spanish markets. Sympathy for the Huguenots combined with a dread of French ambition—a dread amply justified by French schemes in Belgium and by the formation in 1658 of the League of the Rhine, the French instrument to perpetuate the "liberties", or anarchy, of Germany.

On the other side our diplomatic tradition, and many anti-Hapsburg ministers abroad,[3] pointed to the

---

[1] Dollot, 96-7; C. and P. ii. 382; Wicquefort, ii. 549.
[2] C. and P. ii. 100 and iii. 484; Rec. Espagne, 98.
[3] Waldeck was pressing the Great Elector on these lines.

Spanish Main as England's destiny. The frightful scourge of privateering and the insecurity of our trade routes were arguments to the same purpose. If Sweden could not be induced to yield Bremen, Dunkirk and perhaps Gibraltar could be extorted from Spain. And if it came to haggling between French and Spanish offers, Spanish pauperism, not for the last time, might settle the question. Most of all, a French alliance might detach the French from Holland, and dispel the nightmare of a Franco-Dutch partition of Belgium.[1]

But Dunkirk was surrendered by the French with transparent reluctance, and mutual suspicion betrayed the frailty of this friendship. Parliamentary leaders so powerful as Henry Vane attacked our ally, and even before the armistice was signed in May 1659 between France and Spain, Mazarin was accusing England of intrigue at Madrid. Finally, at the treaty of the Pyrenees in November, France abandoned us, pledging herself by a secret article not to assist England, whether directly or indirectly, against Spain. Diplomatic circles generally held that Mazarin had merely anticipated the English in a reversal of alliances; it is at least plain that commercial England was solid in urging that our truce with Spain of July should be converted without delay into a permanent settlement.[2]

Such diplomatic uncertainty was not peculiar to Cromwell or to England. Dependent on the temporary satisfaction of many intersecting interests, the balance of power had entered on that middle tract of doubt which separates the anti-Hapsburg leagues of Elizabeth or Richelieu from the anti-French coalitions of

[1] Firth, L.Y. i. 318; Harris, i. 95; France, 115, a paper headed "Foreign Affairs in Cromwell's Time, as given in by Thurloe, 1660".

[2] D'Avenel, ix. 139; Burton, iii. 490; Chéruel, iii. 251, 288; Wicquefort, ii. 530; Guizot, *Richard Cromwell*, ii. 369.

William III. Religion and commerce, dynastic and territorial motives, had cut across each other until all elements of solidity were dissolved, and unnatural antipathies and affections defied tradition, logic, and orthodoxy. A large pro-Spanish faction in Holland and Brabant weakened the Francophil policy of de Witt. Sweden and Prussia, both Protestant rivals of Vienna, had eaten of the apple of discord in Pomerania. Hapsburg unity wàs buffeted by Louis XIV's marriage to the Infanta, and until 1663 Austria was unrepresented at Madrid. A dozen legacies from the last century of war were strong enough as yet to forbid any cordial union between the old rivals, now threatened by a new danger.

Whatever decisions the new ruler of England might take in untwisting this tangled inheritance, throughout his reign they had to move within familiar, ascertainable limits, which at the risk of anticipation must here be stated. His country had, to begin with, just emerged from a twenty years' rebellion. True, a wise oblivion and political necessity reconciled to his throne the bulk of the Puritan ruling class; moreover, many alleged conspiracies of his early years reduce themselves, on inquiry, to some naked fanatic or Scottish pedlar. Yet the sediment of revolt that remained was the dregs of a cup which Europe had drunk in trembling, and the memory of it never ceased to haunt Charles' policy. The secret treaty of Dover was but the most famous of a long series, beginning in 1660, of projects for foreign assistance to crush rebellion. British rebels, so unforgetting, took pains to be unforgotten in Europe, and the visitors to the French Foreign Office in 1665–66 include the magnificent regicide Algernon Sidney and the Catholic archbishop of Armagh. Delft and

Rotterdam swarmed with Scottish exiles, whose brethren in the Lowlands prayed for a Dutch victory at sea. At Vevey and Lausanne one regicide group gathered round Ludlow, another hovered between Holland and Westphalia. And at the close of the reign, crime and misgovernment inflamed these isolated irritants into the furious fever of the Popish Plot, which created our permanent party system and destroyed for the time our foreign policy.

Still deeper reasons explain the weakness of Charles' government, if measured as a political machine. While France kept over 52,000 men on her peace-establishment, an enforced economy and popular clamour reduced our army in 1660 to the Life Guards and Monk's regiment, while any recruitment of new troops in emergency instantly produced protest against a "standing" or "Popish" army. The militia, raised under the plutocratic Act of 1663, could be trusted to deal with Quakers, but not with the regiment of Picardy. The Ordnance department, Clarendon tells us, could in these early years barely equip three battalions, or five men-of-war. But in all the services the root of evil lay deeper than mechanism—in a moral inefficiency bequeathed by the faction that supersedes merit during revolution, and in lack of funds.[1]

As an instrument for preserving peace or making war, a parliamentary structure must at all times suffer in comparison with enlightened despotism. A succession of French ambassadors noted with satisfied curiosity the English king's lack of power, and the Great Elector regretted that he could put no reliance on a country where treaties could be destroyed in the next

[1] Clarendon, *Life*, ii. 277; J. R. Tanner on the Navy in C.M.H. v.

parliamentary session.[1] It may, with justice, be retorted that later Houses of Commons loaded the
country with taxes at the bidding of William III or
Chatham, and freely entrusted to ministers whom they
trusted the prerogatives contested with the last Stuarts.
Over the historical controversy here raised much ink
has been spilled, and not a few lives laid down, for
Charles II's subjects, like his later historians, disagreed
whether he were a Romanizing despot rightfully kept
short of funds, or a patriot king driven by parliamentary niggardliness into the arms of France.

For the moment it is sufficient, and imperative, to
point out that financial poverty dogged and hampered
our policy in all its aspects and at every stage. At the
beginning of 1660 Charles was living upon credit,
based upon bills from Spain, and his expenses at Breda
and the Hague were defrayed by the States-General,
or eked out by loans negotiated in Amsterdam. Appeals
to Holland and Spain for money continued all the
autumn, for the parliamentary settlement of the revenue
removed neither the deficit nor its roots. On paper the
total assigned to the King was £1,200,000 a year, or
less than that given to the Protector, who, moreover,
had left his successor a load of debt. But this was only
half the evil, since, until the middle years of the reign,
the paper total was never realized; indeed, until 1667,
the average yield of this fixed income was not above
£740,000. From this source, too, the King was obliged
to discharge his father's debts, which Parliament would
not liquidate, and thus the disease of arrears with which
the infant Restoration was afflicted became chronic. By
1667 the Navy debt alone was £1,000,000—in 1670

[1] Comminge to Louis XIV, July 16, 1663 (Jusserand); Frederick William to
Brandt, Nov. 20, 1663 (Urk. ix.).

the total deficit nearly £3,000,000. Treasury control was senile, the collection of taxes was usurped by farmers, and peculation was rampant in every office.[1]

This sort of Richard Swiveller existence took all solidity from the conduct of foreign affairs, involved grave national danger by its effect on the King and on foreign powers, and enfeebled every weapon of policy. The sailors, whose hungry women-folk mobbed the Admiralty officials, had to be forced into this starved service by pressgangs on the Thames as far as Henley, and in time of war not unnaturally deserted to the Dutch. The dockyards were in a state of semi-starvation. Eternal arrears of salaries disheartened and prejudiced our ambassadors; if to keep up their own establishments they were forced to foreign money-lenders, they were not likely to anticipate expenditure on urgent expresses or secret service. In every capital their predicament was the same. Constantinople, being paid by the Levant company and not the Crown, was a coveted appointment, but Winchelsea had to find out of his own pocket the money he there incurred on public objects. Payment was refused him in 1661 for intelligence from Turkey, as too far off to matter, and when the next year the crew of the frigate *Anne*, cutting wood in the bay of Chiarenza, were seized by the Turks, Winchelsea produced £350 to save them from the galleys.[2] The Madrid embassy endured consistent penury. One ambassador, Fanshawe, died at his post in 1666, but arrears of £5600 were paid to his widow only in December 1669; his successor, Sandwich, dunned Charles II by personal letter; his secretary, William

---

[1] Aitzema, iv. 587; Webster to Hyde, May 20, 1660 (Clar. MSS. Cal.); Carte MSS. 214, f. 130; Cal. Treasury Books, 1660–67, xxxv.
[2] Finch, i. 119, 198, 226.

Godolphin, found it wholly impossible to live on his pay.[1] At Lisbon, Robert Southwell reckoned that his mission of 1665–67 cost him £1150 of his own. From the Hague, Downing and his subordinates reiterated, with more truth than their general character would warrant, that only punctual payment would produce decent intelligence from a Dutchman.[2]

This weak and poverty-stricken government contrasted strangely with the people whose destiny it tried to control—a people daily increasing in riches, and liable to be transported with religious emotion. On the latter of these, the two dominant motifs of our policy, nothing need here be said. Evidence of its power runs through all the reign—in parliamentary agitation against the Catholic leanings of king and duke, in the anti-Popery of Cavaliers and Whigs alike, in church offertories for Huguenots, in the flocking of volunteers to join the Dutch against France. But religious zeal had lost its first rapture, and was now subordinate to commerce.

Any statistical tests will reveal the growth of national wealth under the last Stuarts. Exports and imports, in 1662–63 some $7\frac{3}{4}$ millions, had risen to $11\frac{1}{2}$ millions in 1688, while the simultaneous increase in national savings is estimated at 100 per cent. Between 1668–77 inclusive the East India Company divided 130 per cent. in dividends, between 1676–78 the African Company, 55 per cent., and the broad basis of this speculation was politically as significant as its bulk, for in 1681 there were 181 holders of £1000, or more, in East India stock. Imports of bullion averaged £372,000 per annum from 1666 to 1680, as against £60,000 from

[1] Fanshawe, 226; Spain, 52, f. 9.
[2] Holland, 164, *passim*; Downing to Clarendon, Aug. '61 (Clar. MSS. 104).

1660–66. A machinery of credit and insurance sprang up to energize this new wealth, and by the later years of the reign 3 per cent. was a common rate of interest. Our mercantile marine doubled itself in these twenty-five years, Sir William Petty declaring that 40,000 tons were employed in the American and Guinea trade alone.[1]

In short, a century of ardent exploration and private enterprise had made England a mercantile empire, drawing upon all the ends of the earth for the necessities and amenities of life. A passion for material achievement, the earthy expression of Puritan energy, possessed the nation—"the ruling passion" on which Pope put a poetic seal, and in virtue of which we find the fairest street-names of London reproducing those of Charles' ministers. Shares in the companies that made this new wealth were held by the whole political world, from the Duke and Prince Rupert downwards, and Danby's generation watched the course of East India stock with the same devotion their fathers had given to predestination or Arminianism. During the Commonwealth an active press had argued the proper expectation of England to more places in the sun. English public economics were all this time being created, men of action like Josiah Child, Petty, or Dudley North, criticizing or expounding the nation's conduct of trade.

It was not only in the Court or the House of Commons that mercantilism had struck root. London quays were choked with the drugs and spices of the East—with pepper, alum, and indigo, with cloves, nutmeg, and ginger. "The meanest cook-maids" looked for their calicoes and Bombay chintzes; the world of fashion for silks, diamonds, taffetas, and damasks; the coffee-

---

[1] Scott, *History of Joint-Stock Companies*, i. 316-17, 298; ii. 21, 135, 142; Cunningham, 213, 361, and notes.

houses for the delicious novelty of tea. American tobacco had become a necessity to the Puritans, New England was our second base for naval stores, Newfoundland men brought fish to Sallee and the Mediterranean, and a West Indian interest was already in Parliament to voice the claims of sugar.

Life in all phases was being staged in English in all continents. In the tawdry seraglio of Algiers an English wife sat beside the Dey; out in the sun English prisoners toiled in her husband's galleys. In intervals of trade English merchants at Smyrna were hunting, and at Aleppo playing cricket. Boats' crews were searching the sweltering Gold Coast for negroes and ivory, others were freezing in the fur country round Hudson's Bay. The exploitation of black man by white was already in full blast, and the nemesis of that exploitation already launched. Across Arlington's state-papers falls the accursed word Assiento; already the French were arming the West Indian Caribs, and the English pushing the Iroquois against French Canada. Even in 1664 Charles II, who could ill afford such luxuries at home, was shipping muskets to the Moluccas for his good ally, the King of Bantam.[1]

Empires, which cannot conceivably be made in a fit of absence of mind, may come about in an absence of will on the part of governments, and the British Empire expanded in this reign by private effort far outstripping the Crown's control. Behind an official phalanx of chartered companies and consuls lay the strong arm of adventurers who were seizing ports in the Persian Gulf, the piety of New England pastors in

[1] Khan, 163; E.I.C. Minutes, 1664–67, 279; Adam Smith, *Wealth of Nations* (ed. Cannan), ii. 78; Harlow, *History of Barbados*; Routh, 140; Cal.S.P.D. 1662, Sept. 1; Teonge's *Diary*; Osgood, ii. 428; Holland, 173, f. 114.

protest against the Popery of Acadia, or the dour interlopers who were breaking through monopolies and sending single ships into the uncharted creeks of the sea.
Here, and not at Whitehall, was the real force which
made the strength or weakness of English government; in the goldsmiths who lent Charles loans to fight
Holland or refused him credit for fear of France, in
the sailors crying for revenge on the "Butter-boxes"
and the Hoghen-Moghen, in the moneyed men who
exported Bibles and Protestant chaplains so punctu-
ally to their Turkish factories. By these he might be
pushed into war, and without them he could not last
one campaign.

Save for Australasia, the incipient empire that
Charles ruled was planted in all its future ranges, and
with its wealth the vulnerability of empire was trebled.
It stood upon the sea, and there alone could it be
defended, for one day in the Channel could determine
the fate of New York and Fort George. "To the question, what shall we do to be saved in this world", said
Halifax, "there is no answer but this—Look to your
Moate";[1] and behind any manipulation of the balance
in Europe was rising the possibility of an anti-British
coalition, founded on the "fear that the dominion of
the sea should get into the hands of a Power inaccess-
ible by land".[2]

Under some such general conditions Charles' foreign
policy had to work; it remains to consider in broad
prospect the fitness of the men and the system for their
task.

Save for the occasional or violent incursions of

[1] "A Rough Draught of a New Model at Sea", 1694.
[2] Sir John Finch, resident at Florence, to Ormonde, July 17, '66, Carte MSS.
35, f. 537.

Parliament, the King in Council was still the final authority in foreign affairs, and to no part of his prerogative did Charles cling more obstinately. The members of Council, historically and actually, most nearly connected therewith were the two Secretaries of State, who of all great officers had most retained the original mark of them all—that they were the King's servants. Technically they shared equal and interchangeable powers, but in the practice of this reign one is usually found to be dominant in policy; notably so in the case of Arlington, who for twelve years wielded authority much like a minister of foreign affairs. For purposes of correspondence a method devised before the Civil War took final shape in 1662—one Secretary taking northern Europe (Germany and the Empire, the Baltic states, Holland, Belgium, Poland, and Russia), the other southern, as his province. But this division was ever mitigated, not only by the personal ratio as between the Secretaries, but through that inevitable unity of Europe, which was illustrated by ambassadors sending despatches in duplicate to both Secretaries, and by the power of the King's leading minister to interfere in all countries. From 1674 onwards the Secretary senior in standing was placed in charge of the southern department; primarily, of course, on account of the all-importance of France.[1]

Decisions in high questions of policy, if not retained by the King, were taken by the various committees of Council, which under changing names (the secret committee, the committee of foreign affairs, or the committee of intelligence) constituted the Cabinet. Ordinarily this inner ring might consist of any number

[1] Evans, *The Principal Secretary of State*, for further illustration of this matter.

from four to ten,[1] its fluctuating membership being
wholly determined by the royal will and the balance of
factions. It was here that the Secretaries brought the
outcome of their discussion with foreign envoys, or
read the despatches from our ministers abroad. Its
normal place of meeting, latterly at any rate, was in
the Southern Secretary's rooms in Whitehall, over-
looking the river; the normal time was Sunday afternoon, or evening.[2] On special occasions the meetings
were multiplied; thus from the 22nd October 1668 the
committee was ordered to assemble on Sundays and
Thursdays at 3 o'clock until further notice.[3] But, for
the conduct of negotiation or war, special committees
of Council were often appointed, only in part composed of the inner ring.[4]

In mechanical efficiency the conduct of policy improved, out of all recognition, as the reign went on. Our
earlier negotiations were prejudiced by an extraordinary ignorance of foreign languages in the case both
of ministers and envoys. Neither Clarendon, Morrice,
Clifford, or Bridgeman could understand spoken French
—Coventry could not speak it.[5] At Lisbon the consul

[1] In 1661—Clarendon, Southampton, Ormonde, Monk, Nicholas, and Morrice
(Clarendon); in November 1668 — Arlington, Trevor, Monk, Buckingham,
Robartes, and Bridgeman (French Transcripts, 117); in February 1674—Danby,
Arlington, Coventry, and Finch (Temple, i. 377).

[2] From endless illustrations I select the following: "The next day being Sunday,
the proclamation [for prorogation] was brought to the committee of foreign
affairs"—Arlington to Ormonde, Jan. 21, '79, Carte MSS. 221, f. 130; his letters
read at the committee "last Sunday afternoon"—Boreel to Fagel, Mar. 7, '71, Add.
MSS. 35,852; "Baron de Isola had his audience on Sunday last"—Carlingford to
Ormonde, July 28, '67, Carte MSS. 35, f. 582; the E.I.C. committee is to attend
the King at Coventry's lodgings on Sunday at 4 P.M.—March 7, '75, Holland, 198.

[3] Foreign Entry Book, 176.

[4] *E.g.* War committee of 1672—the King, Duke, Rupert, Arlington, Buckingham, Lauderdale, Ashley, Clifford, and Coventry; to meet on Monday and
Thursday mornings, and Saturday afternoons—*ibid.* 177.

[5] Fr. tr. 117; Aitzema, v. 552; Mignet, iii. 131. I must prefer Ruvigni to Monk
as an authority on Morrice's French.

Maynard interpreted for Fanshawe, our ambassador;
at Vienna our best Austrian expert, Carlingford,
used the Emperor's confessor for the same purpose.
Clarendon had to beg Downing not to send him
papers in Dutch, as he could not get them translated.[1]
It was more serious that a lack of co-ordination, often
due to personal pique, stultified our ministers' effort
or doubled their toil. Morrice complained that Nicholas
did not show him the despatches.[2] In 1662 the ambassador at Constantinople was ignorant of the treaties
made with Turkish vassals in Algiers and Tripoli;
Downing in 1664–65 was wholly ignorant whether his
government meant peace or war. And this raises a
larger point—that our foreign policy was still in a real
sense personal to the King. Not only ambassadors but
principal members of the administration—Clarendon,
for example, in the first Dutch war, or Secretary
Trevor in the second—were often in the dark as to the
King's real intention, and in foreign affairs, as in most
things, Charles' Cabinets contained ministers whose
objectives were incompatible.

But the amateurishness, the haphazard character, the
happy-go-lucky method of this diplomacy were derived
in part from the physical and economic circumstances
of that day. Communications both by land and sea
were precarious, whether in peace or war. Clarendon's
letter of 25th January 1666 reached Constantinople on
the following 29th October; Morrice's of 19th November 1662 only came to Fanshawe's hands at Madrid
in late March 1663. A small epic could be composed
round the commercial treaty concluded by Sandwich at
Madrid in May 1667, for a first copy was lost *en route*

---

[1] Pötting, i. 193; Clar. MSS. 75, f. 254; *ibid.* 104, 817.
[2] Finch, i. 188.

for Bilbao, a second flung overboard in the Channel to escape a French warship, a third stuck at Cadiz, and only the fourth, sent off by Vigo for Ireland and Milford Haven, reached the home government.[1] Express messengers went in perils like the Apostle Paul; Fanshawe's were robbed and beaten on the road to Alicante. Complaint of lack of home news rings in the despatches, alike from the neighbouring Hague or from distant Tangier—"so remote", as the governor wrote bitterly, "and forgot in England".[2]

Other weaknesses may be traced back to the universal lack of funds. In 1660 our sole channel for correspondence with Madrid was through merchants at Paris. In 1668, with some exaggeration, Morrice remonstrated in Parliament that he was given only £700 a year for secret service, where Cromwell had spent £70,000.[3] The appointment of consuls was vitiated by the same disease; they were often insignificant in character—ex-pursers or surgeons—and accustomed to eke out their emoluments by trading in wine.

Fundamental improvement was not to be expected in this reign, for nothing drastic could be achieved without money, and much money could not be had from a legislature that distrusted the sovereign. Yet the level of brain and integrity in the public service rose steadily; William Temple, Henry Savile, or Robert Southwell were well above Downing and Holles. Both here and in the parallel reform of the Secretaries' office the turning-point was the supremacy of Arlington, coupled with the tireless energy of his under-secretary and successor, Joseph Williamson. The latter first gave origin

[1] Spain, 52, f. 202; Sandwich to Ormonde, July 20, 1667 (Carte MSS. 35, f. 562
[2] Bellasis to Fanshawe, August 1665 (Harl. MSS. 7010, f. 372).
[3] Pepys, Feb. 14, 1668.

or adequate arrangement to the *Gazette*, the intelligence service, and the archives, and collected round
him the minor officials, like William Bridgeman and
Blathwayt, who transmitted this atmosphere of growing
efficiency to the time of William III.

We must return finally, at the end of this cursory
survey, to the exile telling of his adventures on the
Royal Charles, for he alone was to be supreme director
of this gathering machine. Of no British king is the
traditional character so firmly fixed, but of few is the
real nature so hard to describe, for his best remarks are
difficult to quote and his nearest secrets often buried.
With his private immorality we have nothing to do,
save as it affected his foreign policy, a qualification
which at once minimizes this question to the single personality of the Duchess of Portsmouth. She alone of his
many light o' loves had a touch of political *flair*. But
on one issue of first-rate importance, the Exclusion
Bill, Charles resisted her utmost pressure, and this
feminine influence has been portentously exaggerated.
There are, however, some more assured qualities of
the King, which impressed themselves upon foreign
affairs.

The poisonous, out-of-elbows atmosphere of an
exiled court had battered his character, and he had long
shown himself unable to resist the cheap pleasures
that offer themselves to princes. At seventeen years of
age he was the father of an illegitimate son; at twenty
he was plunged in the desperate cynicism of Scottish
politics. Intense factiousness among his councillors at
Paris and Brussels depraved his view of human motive,
and of anything like settled principle he became almost
uncomprehending. For this, however, he substituted
instincts and prejudices so unyielding as to surprise his

light companions—so tough as almost to merit the name of virtue. His feeling, or pride, for his family was very strong. His mother formed, perhaps, an exception, since she had made him suffer too much. Her petitions for financial relief, like anybody else's, were not received with enthusiasm, and the King was apt to turn his back and whistle when she pressed him upon politics.[1] His brother, the Duke of York, alternately amused and irritated him by a dull imitativeness, as he often complicated policy by mulish rigour. But Charles was essentially loyal to him, admitted him to his innermost counsel, and in the crisis of the reign risked his throne to save James' succession. The purest love he had to give went to his sister Henrietta, the Duchess of Orleans—"Minette", "dear, dear sister" —a love from which rose the springs of a tragic diplomacy.

To his mistresses, though technically inconstant, and to his natural children he extended an easy, constant affection; to Monmouth, who won another fraction of his heart, he allowed a share in war and diplomacy for which he was entirely incompetent. The ardour with which he hunted down his father's judges and dragged them from overseas to the scaffold illustrates rather his private affections than any zeal to avenge the Lord's anointed.

He was rarely unmindful of those who had helped him in bad times, and this in less dramatic instances than those of Father Huddleston, the Penderels, and other companions of hairbreadth days of Worcester and Boscobel. At the height of his French alliance and of the French occupation of Holland, he asked exemption from their military requisitions for citizens of

---

[1] Bartet to Mazarin, Dec. 16, 1660, Fr. tr.

Utrecht who once had assisted him. He liked, in similar fashion, to control politics through those congenial to him on other grounds. Arlington was the "Harry" Bennet with whom he had thumbed the *Gazette Burlesque* of Paris and collected new dance tunes.[1] Other confidants of his secret policies were his mother's manager (or second husband), Henry Jermyn, Lord St. Albans; Charles Berkeley, Lord Fitzhardinge, a man, save for his pandering to Charles' love of women, not wholly bad;[2] Buckingham, so vile, so dangerous, so popular, but so admirable in mimicking Clarendon, and an old Paris friend; and the ever-dependent Irish, whether the Protestant Daniel O'Neill or Catholic "Dick" Bellings, who had followed him round Europe.

But his friends, though given at least the authority which they deserved, did not rule him, and we must emphasize that Charles first and foremost meant to be King: "In all things of high concernment", wrote one of his envoys, "Your Majesty is Your own Premier Ministre".[3] He could distinguish between a necessary minister and an agreeable favourite, and his protection of Clarendon against impeachment in 1663 was as resolute as his purpose in 1667 to throw overboard his old Chancellor, now become a weakness to the Crown.

He had, no doubt, an admiration of the French monarchy, and a correspondingly hearty distrust of the House of Commons, whose interference, among other things, he judged had been fatal to his father's foreign affairs. From the first day of his return he showed his wish for a strong army, and upon reviewing

---

[1] Charles to Bennet, 1658 (MS. reference mislaid).
[2] See William Coventry's opinion in Pepys, Aug. 30, 1668; and Burnet, i. 181.
[3] Carlisle to Charles II, Sept. 13, 1664; Sweden, 5, f. 153.

his Guards, sent a malicious message to Mazarin that he was following his precepts.[1] But the Navy and our sea-power were his real political passion. He was incessantly jealous of the Dutch fleet, and his happiest relaxations, until Newmarket claimed him, were inspecting the dockyards at Chatham, or discussing naval design with Pepys and Pett. For the Navy alone he was ready to make personal sacrifice, and in 1677 paid largely from his Privy Purse to complete the ships for which parliamentary grants had, as predicted, proved inadequate.[2]

His conception of the kingly office, or at least of its trappings, was a high one. Thrice he demanded the revocation of foreign envoys—the Frenchman, Bordeaux, in 1660, the Spaniards, Watteville and Salinas, in 1661 and 1677—and in each case for the same offence, of concerting opposition to his policy among his subjects. Any respect shown to Cromwell in Europe he was determined to maintain, and his ambassadors were expected to keep up all rigours and etiquettes.

As for his intellectual power, Halifax's remark that it was fit to ride a heat, but "had not wind enough for a long course", seems unduly austere. The King's recorded sayings and epithets have something piercing in them: Judge Jeffreys was "not parliament-proof", William Coventry was *visionnaire*, or "they will never depose me, James, to make you King". His assets, considered as of the old diplomatic school, were considerable. He was a master of dissimulation, indeed of falsehood; calculated indiscretion was a weapon in which he excelled; he knew the inside of a Frenchman's

---

[1] Bartet to Mazarin, Jan. 29, 1661, Fr. tr.
[2] Beverweert to de Witt, July 1, 1660 (Japikse); Pepys, *Naval Minutes* (ed. Tanner, Navy Records Society).

mind. Nor must the love of ease justly attributed to him overshadow his ceaseless activity in business. True, he liked despatches abridged,[1] but his marginal notes are on many of them, and the cipher and the maps that lay in his study witness that he could do the spadework. He was always the most accessible of men; ambassadors could catch him as he walked from chapel to his room, and a systematic record of the audiences he gave them, more often than not apart from his ministers, would disperse for ever the legend of "sauntering Charles". Evelyn has told us how the King inspired his history of the Dutch war and personally amended the account he had compiled of the fray between the French and Spanish ambassadors; we know how "with his own hand" he framed a reply to Denmark on the thorny question of the Flag. His attendance was regular at the Committee of Foreign Affairs, Williamson noting it on ten days at least in the month of February 1673.[2]

What relation was borne by religion to foreign policy in this irreligious court is a problem too fundamental to be dismissed in this preface. It is certain that Charles died a Catholic, but then he was an unconscionably long time in dying, and no proof remains of the conversion in exile postulated by Halifax and Burnet. Indeed, the probabilities are much against it, for the giving of pledges was against his nature, and he could hope to win his Paris without a mass. On the other hand, he had negotiated in an academic way with Pope Innocent X for reunion; he was pledged by a

---

[1] Heathcote, 48.

[2] Evelyn, Oct. 1, 1661, and Aug. 28, 1670; Denmark, 8, f. 367; Meerman and Boreel (R.A.), April 4, 1668; Beuningen to States-General, June 8, 1675 (S.G. 7333, R.A.); Southwell's account of a 1½ hours' audience, Feb. 21, 1668 (Carte 36, f. 183).

treaty of 1656 with Spain to repeal anti-Catholic laws, and perhaps to his own conversion; his language about Protestantism, at least in its extremer forms, was notorious, and many of his entourage were Catholic.[1] That is as far as the pre-Restoration evidence seems to go; at the lowest it shows that Charles would never see policy through his subjects' Protestant perspective. Religious ardour was, in any case, incomprehensible to that phlegmatic serenity, and a King in whom loss of good temper was a portent would never join the army of martyrs.

And so, receiving from the mayor of Dover a Bible, which he declared he loved above all things in this world, the wanderer passed on to Whitehall, the home of his father.

[1] C.S.P. ii. 533, iii. 291; C. and P. iii. 471; Ranke, iii. 395; Airy's Note on Burnet, i. 133.

CHAPTER II

FIRST CONTACTS AND IMPRESSIONS

In the first half of 1660 everything seemed to salute an end to old warfare and the beginning of an era of peace. On the 13th February Charles X of Sweden restored the harmony of the North by his death, on the 29th May Charles II that of England by his return, and on the 9th June Louis XIV that of Europe by his marriage to Maria Theresa of Spain. But weddings, funerals, and bake-meats, with all the blare of trumpets, raised only a small dusty echo in the old corridors of national strife.

The ancient cross-divisions, of which the Spanish succession was the knot, were not planed away, and the conflicts that were leading to a new alignment grew daily more bitter. A first instalment of Maria Theresa's dowry, technically the price for renunciation of her right upon the Spanish throne, was due this June, but remained unpaid; in the royal nursery at Madrid her three-year-old brother, the precious heir, was curiously ailing. Portugal was at war with Spain and Holland, England officially at war with Spain, and unofficially with Holland in many seas. On Sunday, the 27th May, the Cathedral bells at Canterbury rang for the King's presence; that day, off Lisbon, the English ship *Experience*, bound from Brazil with sugar and tobacco,

28

was boarded by three Zealand men-of-war, her captain was killed, her cargo sold in Galicia, and the ship herself made a prize.[1] Sweden was still menaced in the Baltic by the austere Czar Alexis, and far to the southeast an illiterate Albanian, the Vizier Mohammad Kiuprili, was beating down Transylvania, the outer defence of Vienna.

From this débris of old systems and scaffolding of new the restored government of England had to construct some policy, though for the first year, loaded as they were with the liquidation of Puritanism, with resettling three kingdoms, with debt and party differences, they asked only for peace. This, and sheer lack of time, is enough to explain the faint interest shown by the King and Clarendon in Europe,[2] which aroused the French comment.

Yet even their domestic problems must drive them, sooner rather than later, to decision in foreign affairs. The King must ensure his succession by a marriage, money must be got wherewith to disband the army, and guarantees of assistance must be won against recrudescence of Puritan rebellion. English trade, obstructed in every channel by the Dutch and languishing with the Spanish war, must be restored as the condition of political salvation and solvent finance. Even the internal religious problem of England could not be settled without touching the sympathy, or susceptibilities, of foreign states.

Our government's first instincts grew, naturally, out of the prepossessions and feuds which had accrued during the ten years of exile. Throughout that time of trial Henrietta Maria and the French had brought

[1] S.P. Holland, 164, f. 108; Downing to Clarendon, Dec. 30, '61 (Clar. 106).
[2] Bartet to Mazarin, Nov. 8, '60; Feb. 10, '61, Fr. tr.

disaster on the King's cause. Her effort to drive her
sons into Popery had outraged Protestant England,
Mazarin in alliance with Cromwell expelled the
Stuarts from France, and old bitter memories separated Hyde and Ormonde from the Queen Mother.
For while they would make Charles *bon Anglais*,
Protestant, constitutional, and independent, she held
out the bait of foreign armies, autocracy on the French
model, and the Catholic Church.

St. Albans, the Abbé Montagu, and Lord Crofts
were the leading men of Henrietta's party, and the
two first were, to all intents and purposes, Frenchmen.
Both were relics of Charles I's Whitehall, and both
of them agreeable and intelligent men of the world.
"Wat" Montagu, once servant to the first gorgeous
Buckingham and court poet, had turned *dévot* and
Catholic, and suffered imprisonment and sentence of
perpetual banishment at the hands of the Long Parliament. Since those days he had taken orders in the
Roman Church, had become Abbot of Pontoise, and
was the Queen's spiritual director.

St. Albans was a far more dangerous person. Devoid
of private and public morals, for twenty years he led the
Royalists' most reckless campaigns—the Army Plot of
1641, the effort to make Charles I abandon the English
Church, the plan to eject Hyde from his post of chief
minister, and that to marry Charles II to Mazarin's
niece. He was patron to Cowley and Davenant, and
had plenty of wits to make havoc in politics. In a large
clear hand he wrote innumerable letters, commonly
on magnificent gilt-edged paper, full of meaningless
courtesy. He was large in physical build, and there is
something large, or spreading, about him. Into old age
he was a furious gambler, even when too blind to see

the cards, but he spent his winnings, and his profits as
Lord Chamberlain, with sense and advantage in laying
out St. James's Square.

As for the obedient Crofts, he belonged to a Suffolk
family who ranked with the Villiers and the Killigrews
as the familiar companions of all the Stuart princes.

The hope of this group, and their prestige, depended
on winning help from France, but hitherto Mazarin had
disappointed them. Until the Spanish peace was accomplished he was disinclined for more adventure, and
had a wholesome scepticism for British adventurers.
He had ordered Bordeaux, the French minister in
England, to be deaf to Royalist intrigue, and discouraged
the Spanish proffer of joint action; he forbade Charles
to follow him in 1659 to the Pyrenees, and when he
did so, refused him an audience.[1] He kept up friendly
relations with each successive English government,
even though he hoped to extort Dunkirk from their
necessity, and negotiated with Thurloe, with Monk,
and with the Presbyterians for a restoration based
upon France and a limited monarchy.[2] His game of
perpetuating English civil discord was inherited from
Richelieu, and descended to Louis XIV, but this time
the cards were badly played. The Cardinal misjudged
alike Monk's political elasticity and the pace of events,
and in 1660 stood exposed to the Hyde group, who for
that matter had tapped his correspondence, as their
declared enemy.[3]

In one respect, for reasons of his own, he had done
them a good turn, for he had persistently discouraged
the scheme of a marriage between Charles II and his

[1] Chéruel, iii. 290; D'Avenel, ix. 167, 315, 357.
[2] Chéruel, iii. 293; Bordeaux to Mazarin (Guizot), Dec. 29, March 29, April 19.
[3] Mazarin to Turenne, Feb. 12; to Bordeaux, May 19 (D'Avenel); Clar. MSS.
Cal. iii., f. 108.

niece Hortense Mancini, with which St. Albans and
Montagu pursued him all the winter and spring from
the Pyrenees to Provence,[1] and it was not in the
capacity of his wife that destiny reserved Hortense
for a visit to Charles' court.

But this was unknown, and upon the facts before
them the King's nearest advisers were naturally, and
strongly, anti-French. This antipathy extended to others
than the veterans, Clarendon and Ormonde. Bristol,
their rival in all else, was passionately "Spanish";
Bennet, still at Madrid, was the same; Nicholas,
the exile's sole Secretary, was so much so that the
Portuguese protested against his share in negotiation.
The Duke of York had long served in the Spanish
army, while the King himself was grateful for the protection afforded him at Brussels, as for the Spanish
money doled out to his troops, and showed his gratitude
at Breda. Before sailing to England he promised the
governor of Belgium that one of his first measures
should be a Spanish alliance, and within a week of
arriving at London his ministers asked for a cessation
of arms.[2]

About midsummer these ill relations with France
reached their climax. Mazarin and his English friends
did not abandon their effort to remodel the English
government; Bordeaux was instructed to inflame opposition in Parliament, St. Albans despatched to help
him, and further offence was given by no French envoy
being sent to congratulate the Restoration. On the
6th June Charles returned his tit-for-tat. A Council,

[1] D'Avenel, ix. 669; Chéruel, iii. 317; Mlle. de Montpensier, iii. 451 (Petitot).
[2] Mazarin to Turenne, Sept. 8, 1659 (Chéruel); to Montagu, June 21, 1660
(D'Avenel); Archives, 195; Bartet to Mazarin, Nov. 8 (Fr. tr. 108); Evans, *op. cit.*
102; Charles to Carracena, May 19 (draft), Egerton MSS. 2537, f. 44; to De Haro
(copy), Spain, 44, f. 13.

unanimous except for St. Albans, refused acceptance
to Bordeaux' new credentials, and on the 4th July gave
him his passports; no ship was assigned for his passage,
his creditors were allowed to seize his carriage horses,
and so, carrying with him, by the English account,
some of Charles I's tapestries and furniture, he passed
out of our history. Pains were, indeed, taken to water
down this strong draught, Crofts and St. Albans being
sent off with assurances that the offence was limited
to Bordeaux' person, and with expression of esteem for
the Cardinal. But Mazarin refused to take it so lightly;
England, he protested, had affronted France *de
gayeté de cœur*, and he could only view Clarendon as
an enemy. However ungratefully treated at London,
Henrietta Maria could count on being welcomed *en
famille* at Fontainebleau.[1]

In sober fact, the French had been badly advised
by Henrietta's circle, and would have to retrace their
steps unless—which the Spanish problem forbade—
they wished for an open breach. The conditions of such
a retreat would be indigestible. Schemes to upset the
English cabinet would have to be dropped, Henrietta
must be persuaded to stop her harping on the Mancini
marriage, and St. Albans forced to conceal his hatred
of Clarendon.[2]

If popular sentiment ever decided diplomacy, England would now have turned definitely against France,
but serious considerations must make the government
hesitate. Ill relations with France involved the main-

---

[1] Bordeaux to Mazarin, June 7 (Guizot), July 4 and 6 (Chéruel); France; 118,
f. 69; D'Avenel, ix. 621; Clar. ii. 145; Egerton MSS. 2537, f. 86; Carte MSS. 214,
f. 242; Mazarin to Montagu, July 3 (D'Avenel). Thurloe seems to have given
evidence against Bordeaux—Guizot, Monk, 319.

[2] Mazarin to Montagu, Nov. 19 and Dec. 8 (D'Avenel); Bartet to Mazarin,
Dec. 16, Fr. tr.

tenance of good terms with Spain and Holland, a system not easily compatible with British trade. Such an *entente* would, further, necessitate the alienation of Portugal, if not of Sweden, and thus bring dangerous repercussions to bear on our Indian and our Baltic market. Yet, if Spain and Holland could produce peace with honour, commercial benefits, a wife for the King, and political guarantees, the experiment might be tried.

This grouping, incipient or even probable in June 1660, and superficially more than really a departure from Cromwell's latest policy, had missed fire by December, and was replaced for two years by a formal understanding with France and Portugal. The grounds for this conclusion must now be examined, and the strands separated, before we try to weave English policy as a whole.

RELATIONS WITH THE HAPSBURGS, 1660–1662

The next half-century was to show that the seat of the malady poisoning Europe lay at the Hapsburg capitals, Madrid and Vienna. No coalition to resist French aggression could be formed, or, if formed, succeed, without them. Without Austria, Germany could not be stirred, and until assured of Spanish sincerity, if not of Spanish commercial concession, the maritime states, England and Holland, would hesitate to take on themselves the task of fighting the greatest war machine yet known to the western world.

But in 1660–62 the Hapsburgs were not merely pre-occupied, but divided. Spain was sore at the Austrian abandonment of her at Westphalia, and resented the pledge, wrung in 1658 by French-Electoral pressure from the Emperor Leopold, not to help Spain in Belgium. The hand of Maria Theresa, once promised to Leopold, had since gone to Louis XIV, and though it was agreed that her sister Margaret should replace her, this marriage had to wait till times were changed.[1] For the moment, France and Spain drew together in the peace and the marriage of 1659–60; financially ruined, absorbed in war with Portugal, and nervous for his succession, Philip IV made it his business to ameliorate the anti-French leanings of Vienna,[2] and gave a sullen deference to the French requests.

From the English point of view the attitude of Austria was less important. Only in one area, the Levant, did their interests intersect, and here they were divergent, for Austria naturally dreaded the Turk, peace with whom was imperative for English commerce. For the rest, Austria had disliked the English pressure for peace in the Baltic, and the consequent discouragement of her hopes in Pomerania. A formal interview given by Charles to Friquet, her veteran representative at the Hague, had been the only notice taken by the Emperor of the blessed Restoration, and the absence of an Austrian minister in London hurt the *amour-propre* of our government.[3]

The Emperor Leopold combined the high character, the taste, and the religious sense of the best Hapsburgs, with the dilatoriness and grovelling superstition of the Spanish branch. He was happier in dealing with the music of his chapel or the opera than with politicians, and a ruler who feared the use of black sealing wax as unlucky was not easily induced to truckle

[1] Engagement announced, March 1663; the marriage in December 1666.
[2] Pribram, *Venetianische Depeschen vom Kaiserhof* [1901], 610.
[3] Aitzema, iv. 593; Blok, 141.

with heretics. Like his forefathers, he was crushed with
over-centralized work, and already threatened by rebels
in Hungary. Commonly, therefore, when he took a step
in the politics of western Europe, it was taken too late,
and if, as alleged, in October 1660 he asked for the hand
of Charles' sister Henrietta, she was already pledged
to France. Nor could he count on friends of any consequence in English counsels. Prince Rupert was the
only politician reckoned pro-Austrian, and though he
lived down his old unpopularity and became a name
with the masses, he counted for little within the governing ring. He was, in fact, fonder of pheasant-shooting
and the stage door than of serious business.[1]

But Spain affected every English interest, and with
her an armistice, preliminary to a settled peace, was
a necessity. Ostend privateers were paralysing trade
in the Channel, and the clothiers of the West country
(who returned, perhaps, a sixth of the House of Commons) had lost their best market. The Spanish government were only anxious to end a war they had never
wished to begin; within a fortnight of the Restoration
the rulers of Brussels promised a truce, and on the
16th July orders were issued to all the scattered Spanish
dependencies for a cessation of arms, and for freedom
of trade to English shipping.[2] But at the first mention
of more positive approaches to alliance there at once
emerged an irreconcilable conflict.

An extraordinary envoy, the Prince de Ligne, and an
unofficial visitor, Charles' old friend General Marsin,
preceded in August and September the arrival of a
resident ambassador. To them the King revealed not
his good-will merely, but his insistent lack of money,

---

[1] Pötting, introduction; Ady, 70; Urk. ix. 704.
[2] Spain, 44, f. 47; Carracena to Charles II, June 9, Flanders, 33.

and touched on the promises he had received from France and Portugal. The Spaniards naturally recalled his professions during the exile, his undertaking to oppose Portugal, and the payments made by Spain (even in the last few months) to his troops in Flanders. No help, they intimated, could be expected until he signified his opposition to Portugal and his willingness to restore Dunkirk, and their case against him was strengthened, in that his confirmation in 1656 of the treaty of 1630 had lately been reconfirmed by Bennet, his agent at Madrid. The question of his marriage was clearly a secondary matter: married or single, Charles II, now the inheritor of Cromwellian England, could never have made good the pledges of the exile Charles Stuart.[1]

The hopes held out in some Hapsburg circles would probably in any case have broken down, for Philip IV well remembered the marriage fiasco of 1623, but it was the Portuguese offer to England which effectually obliterated them, and while the match with Catharine of Braganza was in course of negotiation (August 1660 to May 1661), Anglo-Spanish relations steadily deteriorated, until the two nations stood on the verge of war. Spanish diplomacy, always obstinate, took a new and worse direction with the advent in September of Watteville, their resident ambassador. A Burgundian by origin and a rough soldier by training, the Baron had none of the graces. He seemed to think that familiarity would pay in English society, elbowed his way at Court without ceremony, and entertained at York House with graceless profusion. His unpopularity in London reflects credit on English discernment, for,

[1] Ranke, iii. 336; Cal.S.P.D. 1660–61, 281 *et seq.*; De Vic to Nicholas, June 26, Egerton MSS. 2537, f. 86.

despite his bombastic patriotism, he became later a paid agent of France. But the stock from which he sprang was peculiar, his brother, the Abbé of Baume, having once been a Turkish pasha.[1]

The Baron argued that England, unable to avoid war with Holland, would soon need Spanish support,[2] and that loud enough vociferation would kill the Portuguese màtch. His first important memorial denounced English trade with Portugal as a breach of the 1630 treaty, and demanded point-blank the restitution of Jamaica and Dunkirk. Frequent audiences only increased Charles' exasperation, while from Madrid de Haro sent large promises, but nothing concrete.[3] As regards the marriage the Spaniards conceived that their business could be done by others, and would support, as against Catharine, any other lady of any religion, regardless of her antecedents. In the first stage Watteville seems to have pressed the time-honoured charms of the Mancini, but early in 1661 presented, in Charles' language, a whole "litany of marriages".[4] A preliminary list—a princess of Saxony or another from Denmark—was waived aside by "I hate Germans, or princesses of cold countries", but terms reached in May were more tangible and won more support. Charles, it was suggested, should marry either one of the ladies of Parma (one of whom was only twenty-one, and *de grande et belle taille*) or the Princess Mary of Orange; with either of these the Spaniards would guarantee a dowry as large as that

---

[1] Rec. Espagne, 165, note; Spain, 44, f. 96.
[2] Bartet to Mazarin, Nov. 29, Fr. tr.
[3] Bennet to Clarendon, Dec. 8, Clar. MSS. 73; Nicholas to Bennet, Jan. 3, Spain, 44.
[4] Bartet to Mazarin, Nov. 23 and Jan. 24, 1660–61, Fr. tr.; instructions for D'Estrades, May 3, *ibid*.

promised by Portugal. In return for the surrender of Dunkirk and Jamaica they offered one million crowns, but if this were refused, Watteville was instructed to threaten war.[1]

Once on a time Charles had himself asked for the hand of an Orange princess, Henrietta, elder sister of the present candidate, but his prospects had then been dark, and his proffer had been declined by the lady's mother, the formidable dowager Amalia of Solms; this time, before Watteville's arrival, it had been renewed from her side, and was backed up by the envoys of Brandenburg. The champions of the Parma scheme, on the other hand, were the Catholic Bristol and, at a distance, the cautious Bennet.[2] But the Portuguese bid was too high to be lightly refused, and by 1661 assurance of French support doubled its value. In vain Watteville rushed into print over the illegality of the Portuguese sale of Tangier, and in vain alleged the certain sterility of a Portuguese bride. Four days before his last blustering audience, the decisive Cabinet of the 9th May 1661 settled the question.

The possibility of a Spanish war must, as Clarendon said, have been "well weighed", though England had every intention to avoid it and consistently discouraged Portuguese militarism.[3] But Spain had good reason for her wrath, which eighteen months later was enormously enhanced by our sale of Dunkirk, so lately a Spanish fortress, to France, and throughout 1661–62, in consequence, we find ubiquitous Spanish pinpricks to every British interest. By their instigation the Austrian

[1] Watteville to Charles II, May 3—autograph, Clar. MSS. 74, f. 336; *ibid.* 75, f. 77.

[2] Japikse, 32 and note; Carte, ii. 182; Arch. 195; Urk. ix. 502.

[3] Clarendon to St. Albans, April 8 (Lister); Clar. ii. 154; Brandenburg despatches, May 20.

envoy designed for England was detained in Flanders, Spanish money assisted Gailan, the Moroccan prince who threatened Tangier, and Spanish troops were massed across the straits at Ceuta. Spanish attacks from Cuba began a new warfare in Jamaica, and while peace reigns officially between Madrid and St. James', Captain Christopher Mings and his men of the *Centurion* are moving by torchlight in the dark forest. From Jamaica, too, could be impelled Henry Morgan and his fellow-buccaneers as an anti-Spanish reserve.[1]

The Spanish resolution at any price to reconquer Portugal menaced English interests more seriously, and not least because Spain here met Holland on common ground. Like them, Holland was still at war with Portugal and equally irritated against England. A considerable Dutch party were Spanish partisans, among whom could be reckoned Princess Amalia, bound by her estates in Brabant, if not by Spanish money, and injured by the French seizure of the principality of Orange, while Brabançon missioners worked on the numerous Catholics among the nobles and bourgeois.[2]

A first indication of this new menace was given in the early autumn of 1661, when Sandwich was sent to attack the Algerines and take over Tangier, preliminary to escorting Catharine from Lisbon to England. The Dutch De Ruyter watched his proceedings, and Downing believed that he was ordered to help the Spaniards if Sandwich attacked them—"a thing which in Cromwell's time they durst not have thought of". All Europe was predicting war between England

[1] Pribram, *Venet. Depesch.* 650; Harris, i. 206; Routh, 51; Heathcote, 35.
[2] Archives, 170, 196; Rec. Hollande, i. 233; Downing to Clarendon, Aug. 5 (Clar. MSS. 104).

and the undeclared Dutch-Spanish alliance,[1] and had the Dutch squadron chanced to fall on a Portuguese convoy from Brazil, or the English been repulsed at Tangier, the guns might have gone off by themselves.

This August Philip IV instructed Gamarra, his experienced envoy at the Hague, to offer a defensive alliance in which, if she wished, France could also be included. Spain might thus, in conjunction with her Dutch supporters, conjure away the French threat to the Low Countries, and sink all differences in a triple grouping against England—breaking off, by hook or crook, the projected Dutch treaties with England and Portugal.[2] During the first half of 1662 the Spaniards pushed this policy along two lines. They suggested that a guarantee for Belgium should be incorporated in the Franco-Dutch treaty which was signed in April, while to France direct overtures were made of a bolder kind. In conferences with the French envoy, lasting from January till April, the Duke of Medina sketched the plan of an alliance against the common foe of all maritime Powers, as a fruit of which France should acquire Dunkirk and win a free hand to conquer Ireland. Such wild visions and grudging concession disagreed with the sober interest of Louis XIV, and woke his indignation. Much more than this *beau et futile champ de gloire* in Ireland must be paid for his alliance; nothing less, in fact, than immediate cessions in Flanders, and the recognition of his wife's claim on the Spanish succession. In October the negotiation was broken off;

[1] Harris, i. 201; D'Estrades, July 25; Downing to Clarendon, *loc. cit.* f. 222.

[2] Aitzema, iv. 792; Downing to Clarendon, Dec. 15 (Clar. MSS. 105); Holland, 164, f. 236; *ibid.* 165, f. 295, for report from "Bucquoy" (Van Ruyven), June 10, 1662; Rec. Hollande, i. 229; D'Estrades, i. 327; Louis XIV's *mémoire* of Nov. 1, 1661, Fr. tr.

for the moment it is sufficient to note the bitterness of
Spanish hostility to England.[1] In personal terms the
two peoples' relation had never been worse. Neutrals
considered Clarendon as passionately anti-Spanish,[2]
and Watteville disappeared in a trail of combustion.
His violent attacks on Clarendon and his incendiary
agitation led the English government to forbid him the
Court and ask his recall,[3] but before that took place in
February 1662, he did his best to split Anglo-French
intercourse by a notorious exploit which actually exposed the paralysis of Spain and the ascendency of
France.

Louis had ordered his ambassador, D'Estrades, to
assert his supremacy on ceremonial occasions, and
hence to claim priority for his coach in the procession
which welcomed any incoming ambassador. Despite an
English protest, D'Estrades could not disobey orders,
and the formal reception, fixed for the 30th September
1661, of Brahe, the ambassador of Sweden, gave him his
chance. He had to reckon on the hostility of London,
for Corporation and people were both irritated by
a strict maintenance of his embassy's right of asylum
—it had been necessary to detail a troop of the Guards
to protect the embassy, and a shot had already passed
through the ambassador's hat. Counter-preparations to
ensure Watteville's triumph were made, the French
said, by no less a person than Monk the English
commander-in-chief, but at any rate the protagonists
elaborately organized a battle royal in this neutral
capital. D'Estrades sent for soldiers from his command
at Gravelines, Watteville scattered money among the

[1] Mignet, i. 97; Legrelle, i. 47-55.   [2] Brandt, Nov. 28, 1662, Urk. ix.
[3] D'Estrades, July 19, 1661; draft despatch, to be carried by Moledi, n.d. 1661
—Spain, 44, f. 28; Morrice to Winchelsea, June 18, 1661, Finch, i. 129.

London mob; their coaches appeared at the meeting-place on Tower wharf encompassed by armed men, and more Frenchmen were hidden in houses on Tower Hill. Watteville won the day; at least five Frenchmen were killed, some thirty were wounded, and their horses hamstrung, while the Spaniards passed on triumphantly through Crutched Friars, next to the Swedes. A wild day in London—loose horses galloping, bullets striking innocent spectators who responded with brickbats, and English soldiers cheering the Spanish coach.

Dire was Louis' disappointment, and signal his revenge. He recalled D'Estrades, ordered the Spanish ambassador at Paris out of France at twenty-four hours' notice, and threatened to withdraw his envoy from Madrid. Spain had to lick the dust: Watteville was recalled, and in a humiliating ceremony at Paris a new ambassador admitted the diplomatic precedence of France, by a declaration tendered in presence of the diplomatic corps and later published by the French secretaries. If Spain was to count upon French friendship she was to pay for it dearly, with her remaining prestige and her defenceless territories.[1]

Publicly, Charles II's attitude was firmly correct, though in conversation he conceded the French claim. An official version of the skirmish, compiled by Evelyn and sent to St. Albans, insisted on the King's neutrality and the French provocation, and an Order in Council forbade attendance of coaches at future ambassadorial receptions. This was enforced in 1663 on the arrival of the new French minister Comminge, and Louis was content with Charles' promise that his precedence should be maintained in the palace and the

---

[1] Evelyn, Oct. 1, and appendix; Pepys, Sept. 30; Jusserand, 22-5 and 189; Louis XIV, *Œuvres*, i. 124; Wicquefort, iii. 27.

presence.[1] But it could hardly have escaped Charles'
observation, that Watteville's recall was conceded less
to his request than to the menaces of France.

In 1661–62, therefore, it became obvious that from
neither Spain nor Holland could Charles expect assistance in the obligations incurred with his marriage;
indeed, our weary and protracted negotiation with
Holland seemed every day to bring war nearer. Upon
that background—for the detail of the Dutch negotiation we reserve—we must proceed to paint the Portuguese alliance and the resulting *entente* with France.

PORTUGAL

To England, as to Holland her rival, the revolt of
Portugal in 1640 opened up prospects of commercial
empire in realms where their traders hitherto had
failed to take hold. From our side the first step was
taken by the Commonwealth's drastic treaty of 1654,
which opened to Englishmen a freedom of trade with
the whole Portuguese empire, and made the English
colony in Portugal itself almost an *imperium in imperio*.
When war broke out with Spain, successive English
governments awoke also to the political advantage to
be won from Portuguese resistance, and by a treaty
signed on the eve of Restoration, on the 18th April
1660, Portugal was permitted to enlist 12,000 English
troops.

Upon the Cavaliers Portugal had even stronger
claims. John IV, the first Braganza sovereign, not
only offered one of his daughters to the English heir,
but sent generous financial help to both Charles I and

---

[1] Cal. S.P.D. 1661–62, 104; Jusserand, 71, 204; instructions for Trevor, Feb. 17,
1663—France, 117; Charles to Madame, Feb. 16, 1663 (Ady).

his son in their adversity. His Resident in England
from 1642–46, Sousa de Macedo, a humorous and
spirited man of avowed Royalist feeling, was one of
the channels between Charles I and Henrietta Maria,
and this sympathy was one day to be important, since
he was secretary of state in Portugal at the height of the
English influence from 1661–69. Despite his diatribes
against our climate ("for five years I have not seen the
sun as God made it") he found England congenial,
and took refuge here on his final fall from power.[1]

For such reasons the rulers of England, of either
party, were ready to maintain this alliance, which
continued to be well served by another ambassador,
Francisco de Mello, better known under his later title
as Marquis de Sande, and from 1657–65 an essential
link in the negotiation. Assisted by a Jewish financier,
Coronel Chacan, he won Monk's good opinion, and
the advantages which a Portuguese Infanta would
bring were pointed out in these *pourparlers* even before Sande's interview with Charles II in May 1660.[2]
The Restoration government, determined not to be
committed to war with Spain, refused to ratify Monk's
treaty, but the terms held out in August deeply impressed them—a dowry of about £300,000, the cession
of Tangier, and liberty of trade in all Portuguese
colonies. The sailors, Sandwich and Lawson, stressed
the possibilities of Tangier as protecting our Mediterranean trade, while in response to pressure Sande
promised to get Bombay in addition, thus opening up
a window into that huge Indian empire which the
Dutch were rapidly filching away. As for religion, if

[1] For this, as for much that follows, I depend primarily on the work of Dr.
Edgar Prestage.

[2] Burnet, i. 290, and authorities there quoted; Ranke, iii. 344; Caracena to de
Haro, May 19 (Guizot).

the King could not be induced to marry a Protestant,
no Catholic bride could well be more harmless, for
Catharine, we were assured, was unobtrusiveness itself. By October the marriage was accepted in principle by both parties, and Sande went off on an English
warship to get ratification of its detail.[1] The fierce
opposition which it excited has been in part described,
and may be imagined—coming as it did from so many
quarters—from pro-Spanish Catholics like Bristol, the
pro-French Catholic group of the Queen Mother, from
Protestant Holland that feared for its East India company, and English commercial interests that dreaded
entanglement in Spanish war. When, therefore, Sande
reached England again, in February 1662, with his
adroit and portly colleague, Father Russell of the
English college at Lisbon, they found opposition in
full cry. In vain Russell won embraces from Clarendon
at the unveiling of Catharine's portrait; in vain Sande
pledged his government's acceptance of all demands,
including a partition of conquests in the Indies;[2] Watteville was poisoning the wells, the Dutch ambassadors
were spending money, and the Duke of Parma himself visited London to urge his niece's charms. Between
February and April 1661 the Portuguese hopes sank
to zero.

In these circumstances the French support may well
have turned the scale.[3] At what date it was first made
definite is dubious, but there seems no reason to doubt
Mazarin's word that he repeated in the summer of 1660
his disapproval of the Mancini match, nor Louis' later

[1] Prestage, 140; Clar. ii. 147; Harris, i. 196; Queen of Portugal to Charles II,
Nov. 29 (Clar. MSS. 73); Maynard to Nicholas, Nov. 1 (Lister).

[2] Clar. MSS. 74, f. 111.

[3] But it was neither final nor originating; it is impossible to take Louis' *Memoirs*
on this point at their face value.

memorandum that he designed this marriage as the
easiest way of continuing that help to Portugal which,
by the treaty of the Pyrenees, he was pledged to withdraw.[1] It is possible that Mazarin's assurances were
conveyed by Ruvigni even in September 1660;[2] we
know that Turenne had been organizing Portuguese
defence since 1659, and that he, whose word had
great weight with Charles, also advised the marriage.[3]
Probably the general improvement in Anglo-French
relations about the New Year decided the French on
pursuing a policy that in any event must accentuate
the weakness of Spain, and in March 1661 we reach
firm ground. Mazarin was dying—he died on the ninth
—and the business was now in the hands of Fouquet,
the gorgeous superintendent of the finances, whose
imprisonment and resounding fall soon astonished
Europe. His messenger, Bastide de la Croix, had
been Bordeaux' secretary and spoke good English;
his introductory letter, dated the 4th March, was
addressed to the English chancellor.

To counteract the various opponents in London and
the interference of Henrietta Maria from Paris, Bastide's personality was masked under an assumed name,
his letters were ciphered, the regular French envoys
were kept in ignorance, and the secret confided only to
Charles, Clarendon, and Clarendon's eldest son. The
French gave general, but satisfactory, assurances that,
though unable openly to break with Spain, they would
contribute financially to help Portugal. In August

[1] Louis XIV, *Mémoires*, ed. Dreyss, ii. 406; Mazarin to Walter Montagu, Nov. 17 (D'Avenel).
[2] Mazarin to Charles II, Sept. 2, 1660 (D'Avenel); arrival of Ruvigni by Sept. 6, Spain, 44; a curious deciphered message of Aug. 27 (Clar. MSS. 73, f. 196), that Charles waits St. Albans' arrival to hear Mazarin's ideas on "the match".
[3] Prestage, 72-6; C.S.P. Supplement x.

Fouquet promised to pay 800,000 crowns in the course of the next two or three years, and a first instalment was, in fact, paid over in January 1662.[1] Yet for some months after receiving the French promise Charles allowed the Portuguese to dread a Spanish triumph, and in April 1661 Bristol was studying in his interest the faces and figures of the princesses of Parma on their way to church, though the elder, he reported, was too ugly, and the younger too fat. It is not likely that this disappointment influenced Charles, and still less the old-fashioned view of Clarendon and Ormonde that he had gone too far to retreat with honour. Seeing that he left Bristol without information, he dallied, more probably, only to screw Portugal up to further concession, and used the time in asking for the addition of Bassein to Bombay, for the surrender of Tangier before his marriage, and the maintenance of Catharine's right to her father's throne.[2] Verbally satisfied on these points, on the 9th May, at eight in the morning, the King assembled a full Council, who unanimously advised him to proceed—a decision which the royal speech of the 21st announced to the new Parliament. One last difficulty had still to be surmounted. A betrothal in Portugal would involve a dispensation from the Holy See, a most golden opportunity for Spanish obstruction, to circumvent which Charles on the 22nd June delivered a document to Sande, declaring Catharine to be his wife.[3] By the treaty signed the next day he bound himself to equip 1000 horse and 2000 infantry, whom Portugal should pay; to make no peace with Spain prejudicing such assistance, and

[1] Bastide to Clarendon, Aug. 9, C.S.P.; English memorial for French ambassador, Jan. 19, 1663 (France, 117); Mignet, i. 88.
[2] Clarendon to Orrery, March 3, *E.H.R.* xlii.; Prestage, 145.
[3] Heathcote, 18; Prestage, 148; Clarendon, ii. 178.

never to surrender to Spain either Dunkirk or Tangier; to help Portugal against the Barbary pirates and, at need, against others, by keeping on her coast a fleet of at least ten ships for at least eight months after the Queen's arrival. He promised, finally, to mediate peace, if necessary by force, between Portugal and Holland, and to defend Portugal as though it were England itself. On her side Portugal promised payment of 2,000,000 crusados—half before the Infanta embarked and the remainder within one year; the immediate surrender of Tangier and subsequent cession of Bombay; the confirmation of Catharine's interest in the succession; and extended commercial privilege in all their territories.[1]

A great deal of water was to flow down the Channel before Catharine reached England eleven months later —a period not distinguished by a lover's romance. Sandwich, who was chosen to bring the bride to her husband, was first to occupy Tangier and embark the cash dowry, and the instructions issued to Sir Richard Fanshawe, the graceful translator of Camoens, who was despatched in August as special envoy, were more prosaic than the portrait and affectionate letters which he carried from the bridegroom. After exchange of ratifications, he was to arrange the surrender of Bombay to the English fleet, which would sail in November, and to ask that Bassein should go with it, as Sande had admitted might be possible; he must press the implementing of the facilities promised to our factories in India, and suggest that Goa should be given to England, to save it from the Dutch. Discussions were to be opened upon an English monopoly of purchasing and

---

[1] C.S.P. iii. Supplement xvi.; Prestage, 147; *Council Notes of Charles II and Clarendon* (Roxburghe Club), 28.

shipping the Brazil sugar crop; finally, a protest must
be lodged against a clause in the Portuguese-Dutch
treaty, signed on the 6th August, which gave equal
commercial privileges in South America to England
and Holland, and a request be made for the supersession of Miranda, the Portuguese envoy at the
Hague. By a later letter Fanshawe was ordered to
see the Queen aboard, and to remain at Lisbon as
ambassador.[1]

Little of this ambitious programme was accomplished
during 1661, if only for the reason that Fanshawe,
sharing perhaps his excellent wife's view that Lisbon
was a shelf, took the law in his own hands and returned
to England for Christmas.[2] For the time being there
was work enough in getting hold of the Queen, the
money, and Tangier. Portuguese patriotism resented
the loss of their fortress, while an unsuccessful attempt
on it might wreck the whole marriage, or encourage de
Ruyter, who was hovering suspiciously near, to strike
some damaging blow.[3] From the 6th September till the
3rd October Sandwich was anchored in the Tagus—
concerting details with Fanshawe, getting light craft
for his disembarkation at Tangier, securing the Brazil
fleet from fear of a Dutch attack, and in his leisure time
attending bull-fights. The next three months were
anxious. Spanish intrigue had to be countered, the
Portuguese garrison humoured, the Moor Gailan
placated. In the Straits Lawson watched de Ruyter
and the Algerines. At last, in January 1662, a Moorish
victory over the Portuguese gave Sandwich a good
pretext for landing his sailors, and Tangier was
already in our hands when the governor, Lord Peter-

---

[1] Instructions, Heathcote, 18 *et seq*.   [2] Fanshawe, 124; Heathcote, 23.
[3] Clarendon to Downing, Jan. 3, Clar. MSS. 104.

borough, arrived on the 30th with 3000 soldiers to take it over. Only an aftermath survived to plague successive English commandants, in the shape of claims from dispossessed Portuguese traders for compensation or in the propaganda of Portuguese Dominicans.[1]

Far more vexatious and disappointing was the question of the dowry. The treaty provided that, before Catharine sailed, one half of it should be put on board in specie, diamonds, sugar, and merchandise, but when Sandwich returned to Lisbon in March 1662, the Portuguese professed inability to comply, and for a large part of this instalment would only offer bills of exchange. Though against his instructions Sandwich accepted the substitute, partly moved by pathetic appeals from Catharine herself. But this was not the end. In September £47,000 of the first instalment was still unpaid, and in November the Portuguese financier, de Silva, who, according to the sanguine Sandwich, was "to make all good", was arrested by the English government for default. Even in 1668 not over £157,000 had reached the Exchequer.[2]

On the 15th April 1662 the *Royal Charles* sailed from Lisbon with the Queen and her train of 250 persons, including those elderly ladies whose plain looks and mulishness were such anathema to Clarendon. The marriage took place at Portsmouth on the 21st May—first, in secret, by the Catholic rite, and then with a mutilated Anglican service celebrated by Sheldon. A round of gaieties ended with a state entry into London in August—the Queen looking, wrote Daniel O'Neill, like a prisoner at a Roman triumph.[3]

[1] Routh, 10, 56; Prestage, 151; Heathcote, 22; Harris, i. 201-8.

[2] Sandwich to Clarendon, May 15 (Lister); secretary of the Treasury to Fanshawe, Nov. 12 (Heathcote); Harris, i. 210; Prestage, 151; Cal. Treasury Books, ii. 573.   [3] To Ormonde, Aug. 23, Carte MSS. 31.

Her marriage, not her person, was all that mattered to the English, and her influence on foreign affairs was to be wholly negligible. "Bred hugely retired", unable to speak French, and slow to pick up English, conventionally kind and mediocre, she was no match for the fair faces and quick wits who amused Charles or directed the King's policy. In time she schooled herself to put up with the infamous Castlemaine, or to be civil to the hated Spaniards, winning from Charles' better nature a sort of respectful liking, which defeated the repeated schemes of Bristol[1] or Shaftesbury to prove her sterility, or get her divorced, and finally protected her against the malignant invention of Titus Oates. But no foreign envoys courted her, as they did Castlemaine and Portsmouth; quietly gambling at her faro table and saving up money, furthering her religion by all possible means and founding therefore a nunnery at Hammersmith, she left no mark in politics—passing out of English tradition as completely as her bridal gift of Tangier.

This marriage, intrinsically a victory for Clarendon over his rivals, had been accomplished by, or coincided with, an understanding between the King, Clarendon, and the French, and to this vital aspect we must turn.

Within and around Charles II forces were always at work which drew him to intimate alliance with France —his Catholic mother and sister, his wish for unrestrained power, his admiration of a real monarchy, and his poverty. Even in 1660 a Catholic and Irish interest were building, round their hopes of a Mancini marriage, cloudy scaffoldings of a "grand design";

[1] Even in 1663 Bristol's agents were in Lisbon for this purpose—Comminge to Louis XIV, Nov. 26, Fr. tr.; the authorities for later attempts, and the facts of Catharine's life, may be found in Tout's article in the *D.N.B.*

Father Peter Talbot was profuse in promising French money; St. Albans was reported true to "our cause".[1] But more solid persons had to be won before France could count on alliance, and Charles' constitutional advisers must be conciliated, entangled, or suppressed.

Once having decided to accept the English explanation of the expulsion of Bordeaux, Mazarin had acted without delay. In August 1660 the two Courts agreed on the marriage of Charles' sister Henrietta[2] to Monsieur, Duke of Orleans, Louis' only brother. In September the Cardinal sent over Ruvigni, the Huguenot brother-in-law of the Treasurer Southampton, and in October one of his most experienced agents in Bartet— who, vain, gossipy man, was to be the last survivor of these coils, for he died in 1707 aged 105.[3] In November arrived the long-expected embassy of congratulation, headed by the Duc de Soissons,[4] husband of Olympe Mancini and father of the great Prince Eugène, whose red velvet coach, gold-laced flunkeys, and twenty pages-in-waiting were to dazzle the crowd, while real business was to remain in the hands of the Huguenot and the abbé. Their instructions were to suppress, once for all, talk of the Mancini marriage, which alienated Charles from his mother and menaced the relation of the two crowns.[5] It was recognized that, Clarendon's predominance being unshakable, reconciliation between him and the Queen Mother was important to the French interest, and, as it happened, at this moment a quarrel within the English royal house created a crisis, which must induce him to welcome the French olive branch.

[1] Anon. to Bellings, Clar. MSS. 73, f. 192; Talbot to Ormonde, Aug. 22, Carte MSS. 214; Acton, 91.
[2] The formal request for her hand is dated Oct. 6, France, 115.
[3] Rec. Espagne, 156-9.   [4] Public audience, Nov. 5; congé, the 22nd.
[5] Mazarin to Ruvigni, Oct. 1; Ruvigni to Mazarin, Oct. 2 (Chéruel).

His daughter and favourite companion, Anne Hyde, since 1654 maid of honour to Mary of Orange the Princess Royal, returned to England in July 1660. It transpired that, in the previous November, she had betrothed herself to the Duke of York, with whom she had lived, and that, if their child was to be legitimate, they must marry. The marriage took place on the 3rd September, and on the 22nd October a son was born. The arrogant Princess Royal choked at the notion of accepting her waiting woman as her sister-in-law—as her son William was later to hesitate whether he could marry this waiting woman's daughter—and the Duke of Gloucester vowed "she smelt so strong of her father's green bag that he could not abide it". The perjured calumny of Clarendon's enemies—Charles Berkeley, young Jermyn, Richard Talbot—devised for the Duke ways of escape from Clarendon's daughter. On the 3rd October the Queen Mother, with her daughter Henrietta, landed at Dover, bent on arranging the King's marriage and on breaking the Duke's.

Charles resented this neat programme. He disliked being treated, he told Bartet, like a boy of twelve, nor could he conceal a malicious pleasure in showing his mother, who had often set up York against him, that she had backed the wrong horse. He got on amicably with his new sister-in-law, and was determined not to part with his chancellor, who was the one innocent in this squalid business. King and Chancellor, therefore, gratefully accepted the good offices proffered by the Frenchmen. And if kings and queens have hearts, the affliction of the royal family this autumn probably contributed to draw the survivors together, for Gloucester died in September and the Princess Royal on Christmas Eve. By that time the new Duchess was publicly accepted. Henrietta Maria, warned that she could expect little welcome in France unless she buried the tomahawk, signified her surrender by smiling on the baptism of the York baby, and her official forgiveness of Clarendon was sealed in the nomination of St. Albans to the Paris embassy.[1]

On the 25th January 1661 the old Queen sailed again for France, defeated in all her policies, but carrying with her in the Princess Henrietta, at the moment enduring measles, a living pledge of the new *entente*. Monsieur had grown thin, it was reported, and hungered for his bride, who, poor child of sixteen, was to suffer horribly from that rouged mass of jealousy and vice. But for the day life was kind, and with her marriage on the 31st March the most brilliant of the Stuart women began her public career. Her chestnut hair, her perfect complexion (too perfect, for it meant consumption), her wit and grace, her kind heart—all this was to be sung by poets and commemorated by princes of the Church. An elderly and sour diplomat like Holles found her irresistible; from Louis XIV she extorted all the affection which he found compatible with his comfort, and forged between him and her brother a link stronger than treaties and one never after her death replaced. Except Elizabeth of Bohemia, no Stuart princess had possessed such genius for friendship, or such magic with men of power. She was patron both of Port Royal and of Molière, friend alike to Turenne, Racine, and Bossuet, and though vile men like Buckingham exploited her charm and clouded her reputation, a host of witnesses defend her intrinsic innocence.

[1] Correspondence of Bartet and Ruvigni with Mazarin in French transcripts and Chéruel; D'Avenel, ix. 679; Lister, ii. 68; Ady, *Madame*, 67-80; Clar. ii. 52; Archives, 198.

But this rare picture could not easily be fitted into an English frame. Since her second year she had lived in France, and had been bred a Catholic. She thirsted, said Bossuet in his famous funeral sermon, for the re-establishment of the faith, and devoted most of her alms to the poor Catholics of England.

The understanding which she personified rested quite as much on grounds of public interest as on the secret aspirations of princes. We have seen that, following on Mazarin's support for the Portuguese match, Fouquet's agent, Bastide, had arrived in March 1661, empowered to hold out not only money for Portugal but a common policy in the treaties which each power was negotiating with Holland, and from the bitterness of Clarendon's later disappointment it may be judged that the second motive weighed more heavily. In any case, our government's new policy would only continue the normal system of the Protectorate, which just about this time Thurloe, its last director, was describing for the benefit of his successors. Friendship with France, Brandenburg, and the Scandinavian states—Holland to be brought to reason "either by fair means or force" —on this basis England could hope to keep the peace on which our revenue and our security must depend, to preserve our trade, and to save Portugal.[1]

The objective and implications of the new understanding can, for clearness' sake, be thus distinguished: first, to renew, so far as relevant, Cromwell's public treaty and to liquidate economic and colonial rivalry; second, to establish an intimate personal alliance between the two kings; and last, to get money from France for domestic and Portuguese emergencies. This co-operation rose gradually to its climax in November

[1] Thurloe's memorandum, France, 115.

1662 over the affair of Dunkirk; from that date onwards it sagged under the stress of unsettled controversies, of a sharp difference regarding Holland, and a
new trend in English counsels.

Louis XIV was resolved, despite his treaty obligation to Spain, to continue to Portugal the indirect
assistance organized by Turenne and sanctioned by
Mazarin; yet he desired to maintain a decent secrecy.
The negotiation of 1661 was, therefore, concealed from
St. Albans, and carried on by Clarendon in direct
correspondence with Fouquet till September, when
the new French ambassador, D'Estrades, became the
channel.[1] If Portugal was to be saved, the vague
assurance which Bastide had given must be translated
into fact, for English finance was fully mortgaged; the
reconstruction of the ordnance, the upkeep of Dunkirk,
interest on the debt, provision for the royal family and
the Navy, having more than absorbed the Convention's
grant. Throughout the summer, then, the King and
Clarendon reiterated that, if France did not provide
the money, England must advise Portugal to make a
truce with Spain.[2] At last, in November, reassured
by personal discussion with D'Estrades as to Charles'
good-will in the Watteville trouble, Louis made good
Fouquet's latest promise, and in February 1662 paid
200,000 crowns to the English government.[3] But a
year later the remaining 600,000 promised were still
outstanding, despite our expostulation to successive
ambassadors, whose government seemed to be trying
to make their payments for Dunkirk a pretext for with-

---

[1] Fr. tr. 109; C.S.P. Supplement, vii. *et seq.* D'Estrades was not cognizant of
Bastide's activities till some time after his first audience on July 19.
[2] C.S.P. *loc. cit.* xi.; D'Estrades to Louis XIV, Jan. 5, 1662.
[3] Louis' memorial of Nov. 1, Fr. tr.; Louis to D'Estrades, Jan. 5, 1662.

holding the money earmarked for Portugal. Ultimately, on Portuguese initiative, Louis continued the subsidy by direct payment to Lisbon, and with this guarded assistance Charles managed to despatch Inchiquin at the head of 3000 foot and 1000 horse to Portugal, where in June 1662 they joined the French contingent of Schomberg.[1]

Poverty, the motif of which we never get rid in Charles' policy, and which allowed France thus to dominate the Portuguese question, predominantly dictated also the sale of Dunkirk. Yet on many other grounds it was a difficult possession. We were pledged to Portugal never to surrender it to Spain, but whether the French would ever give us a treaty guarantee for it remained highly dubious. Its capture had been one of the great Condé's triumphs in his palmy days, and its loss, when Condé turned traitor, still rankled; it was given to Cromwell with infinite reluctance; Mazarin's wish to recover it was unconcealed, and even in 1660 it was rumoured that France would demand it as Madame's *dot*.[2]

And if Dunkirk gave us, as Thurloe claimed, "the keys of a door into the Continent", it was a door that let through a blast of animosity.[3] Our commanders reported that the Spanish governor blockaded them with tolls and tariffs, and that Capuchin missioners, armed with English and Irish literature, tried to seduce the troops;[4] while French and Spanish officials, on

[1] Memorial for Comminge, Jan. 19, 1663, France, 117; Rec. Portugal, 95; Prestage, 81.

[2] Clarendon to Bastide, June 3, 1661 (C.S.P.); anon. to Williamson, Oct. 4, France, 115.

[3] Thurloe's note, *ibid.*; Clarendon to Downing, June 20, 1662, Clar. MSS. 104.

[4] Bartet to Mazarin, Feb. 25, 1661, Fr. tr.; De Vic to Nicholas, Aug. 5, 1660, Egerton MSS. 2537.

the other hand, accused our garrison of still exacting the Cromwellian war-taxes from neighbouring villages. Louis had already half-perfected the argument of his later "reunions", and claimed that, though England might be sovereign of Dunkirk, to France belonged *la domaine utile et la seigneurie directe*,[1] while the Dutch found its harbour the worst nest of the privateers who preyed on their merchantmen. All these things considered, it is not surprising that, both before and after the sale, many Englishmen believed that keeping Dunkirk was bound to embroil us in the event of a French-Spanish war, and entailed all the evil, with little of the advantage, of a Continental possession.

The problem, then, existed long before financial difficulty in 1662 forced the English to the sale which they well knew had never been out of the mind of France. It was now abundantly clear that our undetermined expenditure on Tangier could not be recouped from Catharine's dowry; on the contrary, Inchiquin had hardly arrived in Portugal before Alfonso demanded a naval demonstration off Galicia. Compared with the constant needs of policy, the cost of Dunkirk was out of all proportion; of £321,000 given in the year ending at Easter 1662 to guards and garrisons (and this sum exceeded the whole yield of the customs), this single fortress swallowed over one-third. And once the possibility of sale came under discussion, the technical disadvantage of Dunkirk was pressed by responsible experts: shifting sand made the harbour dangerous; without great additional expense it could neither shelter a squadron, defy a blockade by

[1] *Ibid.* ff. 120, 213; instructions for D'Estrades, May 3, 1661, Fr. tr.; St. Albans to Clarendon, May 10 (Lister); Clar. ii. 386; Harris, i. 223.

sea, nor be rendered defensible by land, and no money
could get rid of a rolling ground-swell.[1]

According to Clarendon's account the responsibility
for our decision rested in the first place with the Treasury,
next with the services as represented by Monk and
Sandwich, and last only with himself. Of the second,
at any rate, there is no doubt, for Sandwich was at all
times ready to claim credit for being the first to propose
abandonment.[2] But there are counts in the popular
indictment still worth remembering. The Cabinet
unanimity which Clarendon represents can be true
only of the final decision, for the preliminary negotiation was concealed from its secondary members, and
with D'Estrades the Chancellor took credit for the
scheme as his own. If on this head we applaud his
policy, it must be at the expense of his veracity, and
our applause will be tempered by the reflection that
two years later the same minister proposed to sell
Bombay.[3]

But, when France and England were agreed, to
dispute from whom proceeded the initiative is otiose.
It is probable that D'Estrades began the discussion
during his first embassy in July 1661,[4] but its conclusion was directed by Clarendon. His agent was Richard
Bellings the younger, whose father had been a Catholic
"Confederate" in the Irish wars, and who himself was
this autumn to carry some proposals from Charles to
the Vatican. He showed his fear of the effect of pre-

[1] Governor of Dunkirk to Charles II, May 19, 1662 (Lister); Southwell's report
of Sandwich's remarks—Leyborne Popham papers, 250; D'Estrades, i. 393.
[2] Clar. ii. 384; Sandwich, as above; Pepys, Oct. 27, 1662; Bolingbroke, *Works*,
ii. 261.
[3] Nicholas to Ormonde, July 25, Carte MSS. 47, ff. 333, 365; D'Estrades to
Louis, Aug. 17; Clarendon to D'Estrades, Aug. 9 (C.S.P.); Prestage, 161.
[4] Airy's note on Burnet, i. 303; Louis XIV, i. 175; Downing speaks of the
rumour in Feb. 1662, *infra*, p. 62, note.

mature publicity in other ways than the use of this peculiar instrument; he took steps to deceive the governor of Dunkirk, and used the certainty of outraging Parliament, whose predecessor had voted to annex Dunkirk for ever, to raise our price with the French.[1]

Early in July Bellings crossed the Channel, interviewed D'Estrades and Lionne, and by the 17th had brought back to London an intimation that France was ready to proceed. D'Estrades followed in the second week of August, and Clarendon, Southampton, Monk, and Sandwich were commissioned to negotiate, with Bellings as interpreter.[2]

In a month of hard bargaining the English descended from twelve, while the French rose from two, to five million livres; but even when the amount was agreed on, the discussions nearly collapsed over our demand for cash payment, and D'Estrades ostentatiously loaded his baggage on a Dutch ship. If either party were in earnest, there was need for haste; the Spaniards were agitating, information had leaked out, mercantile interests in London were beginning to clamour. At last, by the 25th September, all was settled, and on the 17th October the treaty was signed. Five millions was the price—two in ready money, the rest in eight bills spread over the next two years, for which Charles could get cash from the London market. England was to guarantee the French possession of Dunkirk for two years against Spain or any other aggressor; it was to be surrendered intact, with its material, within fifteen days of the French ratification. This reached London on the 4th November; on the

[1] Charles II to Rutherford, July 7 (Cal.S.P.D.); Clarendon to D'Estrades, Aug. 9.

[2] *Ibid.* June 29; Rec. Hollande, i. 194; Clarendon to Ormonde, July 17, Carte MSS. 47; Clar. MSS. 77, f. 79.

11th, 4,500,000 livres were shipped at Calais, the fortress was surrendered, and with a warm letter of thanks from Louis, and a promise to quarter York's Irish regiment in Picardy in view of trouble in England, the transaction closed.[1]

The dismay voiced by Protestant Brandenburg was deeper still in commercial England, and deepest of all among the Cromwellian diplomats. In his ardour of resentment Downing was ready to sacrifice some salary if Dunkirk could be saved: "England was never considerable, I mean to say considerable indeed, since it wanted a footing on this side the water". A tradition of humiliation sank into the long, uninstructed, but instinctive memory of the people, and as Clarendon's great new house rose at the top of St. James', men pointed with the finger to "Dunkirk House"—"la nouvelle Dunkirk".[2]

The message taken by Bellings, which set this matter rolling, intimated that the cession of Dunkirk was the best proof Charles could give of his wish to conclude the intimate alliance already held out by St. Albans,[3] and a blend of public and private motives, clouding we are bound to think his patriotic judgment, induced Clarendon to forward the proposal. Successive insurrections, real or potential, dogged his ministry throughout 1661-62. The first, Venner's rising, terrified London; there followed schemes to murder Monk and to seize the northern arsenals; in 1662, rather than face the storm, Clarendon advocated suspension of the Act of Uniformity. Foreign envoys agreed that French

[1] D'Estrades, i. 314-413 *passim*; Lister, ii. 173; iii. 222 *et seq.*; Harris, i. 221; Louis XIV to Charles II, Dec. 3, France, 116, f. 84.

[2] Downing to Clarendon, Feb. 24, 1662, Clar. MSS. 106; to Nicholas, Sept. 26, Holland, 166; Pepys, Feb. 20, 1665; Comminge to Lionne, Oct. 9, 1664 (Jusserand). [3] D'Estrades to Lionne, July 8 (Ranke).

support was essential to his personal position: failure to secure it might destroy the good results he hoped for in Portugal, would wreck his financial plans, and allow the "Spanish" section, led by Bennet, to overthrow him in Cabinet.[1]

When St. Albans proceeded to France in March 1661,[2] he was instructed not only to press for confirmation of Oliver's treaties, but to renew those private assurances carried earlier by Crofts. But though Louis professed to believe in English sincerity, St. Albans' project for "closer union" faltered and hung fire when made specific. Against foreign and domestic aggression he offered a defensive league, whereby in emergency 8000 French troops would be shipped in English transports, but when the French asked what was to be their compensation, Clarendon preached the utmost "waryness". France, he urged rather disingenuously, might expect more internal trouble than ourselves; nothing must tie us to give assistance against the Huguenots, and he would prefer French assistance in money, not in men. In private audience Charles told D'Estrades that he would await the French proposals, at the same time deploring the French guarantee promised for the Dutch fishery claims and the French negotiations in Spain.[3]

With the Dunkirk business of 1662 this project again revived, but again languished. D'Estrades stipulated that it must form part of a comprehensive treaty, and though Madame had now become their intermediary,

[1] Brandt to Great Elector, Nov. 28, 1662 (Urk. ix.); D'Estrades to Louis, Nov. 27.

[2] Instructions, France, 115, f. 193; public entry on March 20, *ibid.* 116, f. 23.

[3] Clarendon to St. Albans, April 8—St. Albans to Clarendon, May 10—N.S. (Lister); St. Albans' draft for Lionne (Jusserand), July 10; Clarendon to St. Albans, June 17, Clar. MSS. 74, f. 466; D'Estrades, July 19.

throughout 1663 each King acccompanied cordial private letters with a complaint that the other's friendship was skin-deep, or waning.[1]

A growing hardness on either side was amply represented, if not indurated, by the ambassadors who in 1663 went to London and Paris. The Comte de Comminge[2] was a gallant Gascon soldier—accompanied, though unhappily not for long, by a charming wife— but he was brusque, punctilious, and ignorant of English. He was often ill, but well or ill the English could make nothing of him. Comminge found Clarendon dictatorial; Clarendon charitably assumed that Comminge was drugged with opium, while Charles said he was "good for nothing, but to give malicious and wrong intelligence".[3]

His counterpart, Denzil Holles, lately become a peer, was now in the sixty-fourth of his destined eighty years. Having begun public life under Charles I as a companion of John Eliot in debate, fines, and imprisonment, he was to end it as a Whig leader opposing Charles II. Within him, as Burnet says, was "the soul of an old stubborn Roman"; liberty to him meant the liberties won by his caste, and he had resisted the Cromwells as he resisted the Stuarts. As one of the leading Presbyterians on whom the Restoration compromise depended, he was now, if not in favour, in the odour of political sanctity, and reckoned as one of Clarendon's supporters.[4]

Lack of public money had prevented his sailing in

---

[1] D'Estrades, Nov. 6, 1662; Charles to Madame, Oct. 26 (Ady).

[2] Reached England, Dec. 23, 1662 (Jusserand—the authority for this embassy); left in December 1665.

[3] Clar. ii. 501; Bellings to D'Estrades, May 23, 1663 (Jusserand); Charles to Madame, Jan. 18, 1664 (Ady).

[4] D.N.B. (by Sir Charles Firth); D'Estrades, i. 271.

1662, but when in July of the next year he finally
reached Paris, he seems to have decided to make up for
lost time.[1] A terrible crossing to Dieppe gave a finer
edge to his irascibility, and an attack of gout spurred
him to contest with the *douaniers* who sealed up his
luggage—not sparing his nephew Lord Clinton's silk
stockings. For the next few months he embarked with
infinite gusto on a mêlée with the French government
over his public entry—insisting, as precedent demanded,
that his coach must precede princes of the blood. On
such matters this Puritan aristocrat held decided views.
"In transactions of this nature", he told Arlington,
"between king and king and their ministers, ceremony
is substance, and who carries in that will carry it in
the essentials. All in this world is but grimace." Even
when Madame's suave peacemaking had disposed of
this preliminary, Holles' native idiosyncrasies were
undiminished. His French was execrable, and he was
almost too often at the Protestant service at Charenton,
that bare stone church where the preacher, with his hat
on, expounded the true gospel of Holles' Puritan days.
A good deal of self came into this independence. His
papers are full of his Excellency's wine (customs-free),
of his title, his salary, and speculation in Irish land.
Yet if we censure the shortcomings in the diplomat,
English liberties will always afford a laurel spray for
this dogged patrician.[2]

But the obstruction to "closer union", though not
likely to be removed by these tough racial representatives, rose from deeper causes, and when the polished
Ruvigni, with whom Charles found it a pleasure to deal,

[1] Equipage ordered by privy seal of May 31, 1662 (France, 116); Clarendon
to Downing, July 1, 1662, Clar. MSS. 104.
[2] France, 117-19 *passim*; Ady, *Madame*, 150-55; Jusserand, 80; Cottrell-
Dormer MSS. for Charenton.

came in June 1663, he could only report no progress. He, no less than Comminge, found a general suspicion, if not hatred, of France;[1] and though the commissioners selected on the English side included men with knowledge of France, or some French sympathies, they made no advance.[2]

Transcending all other problems was the relation of the two nations to Holland. Despite the negotiation in process, friction between England and Holland was on the increase, and, whether for peace or war, Clarendon had counted on French assistance.[3] These illusions were first shattered by the Franco-Dutch treaty of April 1662, the detailed provisions of which injured our most vital interest. England, like Holland, was in fact a pawn in Louis' long preparation for a new attack upon Spain; he wished to keep each dependent on himself, each to compete for his favour, without their economic competition ending in war, for each might serve his purpose. He refused, therefore, to sacrifice the tried Dutch friendship to an English alliance of more recent tradition and more doubtful prospects. With Spain he was not yet ready to break, though from Spain he kept both sea powers detached by assuring each that he was negotiating with the other. The English were, of course, not blind to these vast ambitions, and Holles was instructed to explore the French design upon Germany and the hope of a guarantee for Flanders.[4]

[1] Bellings to Lionne, July 24; Ruvigni to Louis, July 2, Fr. tr.; Comminge to Louis, May 10 (Jusserand). Ruvigni arrived by June 25.

[2] St. Albans, Buckingham, and Holles were added to the ministers Clarendon, Southampton, Monk, and Arlington. (Arlington to Ormonde, June 9, 1663; Carte MSS. 221.)   [3] Clarendon to Downing, Sept. 27, 1661 (Clar. MSS. 104).

[4] Cf. Louis to D'Estrades, at London, March 12, 1662, with the same to same, at the Hague, July 20, 1663; draft instructions for Holles, 1662, France, 116, f. 7; D'Estrades to Louis, Oct. 27, 1662.

But the gradual reversal of international relation-
ships which took place in 1663–64 was assisted, so far
as England and France were concerned, by other controversies. Some turned ostensibly upon matter of form,
for Charles was not going (in Holles' *patois*) to be
"traittez de haut en bas".[1] He felt himself to be a king,
and would not take a lower place than the usurper.
In the Watteville fracas and the matter of Holles'
audience he played a keen hand, declaring that never
would he purchase "closer union" by sacrificing his
predecessor's rights.

The everlasting question of "the flag" must be included in this category. As sovereign of the Narrow
Seas, the English had claimed, time out of mind, a
salute from foreign warships—"a feather in our cap",
wrote a later Secretary of State, "which in new conditions of sea warfare promised to prove a bloody
piece of gallantry".[2] On nothing did Charles feel more
bitterly or act, when he dared, with more vigour, and
in these years it seriously affected the budding French
friendship. But Louis made some compromise the
price of granting money for Portugal, and reluctantly Charles agreed to cede his claim south of Cape
Finisterre.[3]

A connected, but more substantial, matter was that
of the Fisheries, a venerable quarrel which entombed
the spark of many wars. Defying *terra firma* laws of
mobility, the herrings had upset the Hanse by their
migration, and were now unsettling the peace of the
Atlantic powers. Ancient feuds of the Middle Ages
still smouldered between English and French fisher-

---

[1] To Arlington, May 18, 1664, France, 118.
[2] Henry Coventry to Jenkins, Sept. 26, 1673; Add. MSS. 25,122, f. 155.
[3] Correspondence of Louis and D'Estrades, January–February 1662; Ady, 111.

men, and our state papers teem with complaint that
Yarmouth men have cut the French nets and moor-
ings, or with demands from the Cinque Ports for a
check on French poaching and the active trade
carried through Dieppe and St. Valery to the Paris
market.

A last act of the Convention Commons had been a
Bill to prevent foreign fishing within the ten miles'
limit. Louis' remonstrance reinforced Dutch threats of
war, and a year later he declared that if we attacked
Holland upon the principle of sea "sovereignty" he
would be behind her. The English suggestion of a
license system, and disavowal of any innovation,
roused him to fury, and in his treaty of April 1662 with
the Dutch he guaranteed their fishing rights—waving
aside Charles' hint of help for the Spanish succession.
The English Admiralty could only make a show of
issuing "permits", in the hope of perpetuating a principle which they dared not defend.[1]

Even if this resounding diplomatic defeat could be
forgotten, both countries were eaten up by economic
rivalry—on one side inspired by Colbert's tariffs, and
illustrated on the other by the Navigation Acts. Companies of English merchants trading to France complained, even in 1660, of excessive duties, while from
traders at Rouen and the consul at Marseilles proceeded remonstrances against Fouquet's harbour due
of fifty sous per ton on alien shipping.[2] The most-
favoured-nation terms secured by the Dutch angered
the English business world, and Colbert's tariff of 1664
tightened the screw further. A long-projected treaty

---

[1] Instructions for D'Estrades, May 3, 1661, Fr. tr.; Louis to D'Estrades, March
12, 1662; Fruin, ii. 270; *Ormonde (Kilkenny) Papers*, iii. 60; Clarendon to Bastide,
July 25, 1661 (C.S.P.).   [2] France, 115, f. 632; 116, f. 51.

of commerce, carried over by Holles,[1] insisted on fiscal equality between England and Holland, and in fiery letters to Madame Charles refused to hear of politics till the point of commerce was conceded. In November 1664 Louis replied that he could not withdraw the fifty sous duty, but that if his subjects were treated in England as in Holland—that is, on equal terms with natives—he would meet our other proposals. He asked, in short, Holles argued, "for his subjects to be all made freemen of England"; Holland, who drew the bulk of her revenue from the excise, was no parallel, and we could not be expected to shipwreck our whole fiscal system—"if the dam be never so little broken, all runs out".[2]

Impelled by the near approach of the Dutch war Charles made a last appeal, and sent his favourite, Charles Berkeley, now Lord Fitzhardinge, to treat direct, and "without public character", with the French King.[3] In a "very long audience" Fitzhardinge expounded Charles' claim for equality—"which being once consented unto and established, I am willing to enter into straighter articles, whether of union or mutual defence". His reception was disappointing, for Louis dragged in disputes touching French Canada, and referred the envoy to his ministers for detail; their reply still upheld the fifty sous, and when the English suggested a flat rate of five shillings as our equivalent, they rejected it as exorbitant. On such a note this

[1] "You carry with you a project of a treaty delivered here in your presence to the French ambassador"—draft instruction for Holles, 1663, *ibid.* 117, f. 280.

[2] Madame to Charles, Nov. 4, 1664—Charles' letters to Madame of Oct. 17 ("an extreme good one", said Holles) and Dec. 15—Ady; Holles to Arlington, Nov. 5 and 12, France, 119.

[3] Instructions, *ibid.* f. 151; first audience, Nov. 11; back in London on Nov. 20 (*ibid.* ff. 162, 178); Ady, 178.

particular problem lapsed with the outbreak of the Dutch war.[1]

Louis' allusion to Canada carries us to another group of controversies. Colbert, founder of French imperialism, was dreaming of a France reaching from the St. Lawrence and Mississippi to Aden and Singapore, and the disputes of isolated fur-trappers and diggers for gold were coming home with interest to the European chancellories. Ever since the Stuarts' accession New England and New France had filled the wilderness of their vague frontiers with petty war. By treaty of 1629 Charles I had surrendered Quebec and Novia Scotia, but New England had taken here a little and there a little more, and Cromwell's government had ignored the arbitration to which we stood committed. With D'Estrades' arrival in 1661 began forcible French protests against these "usurpations" and against our alliance with the Iroquois; by Comminge's time they acquired a new edge, and were soon whirled up in Holles' maelstrom at Paris. In fact, each government had, with royal disregard of maps, granted monopolistic privilege to its subjects, and an original confusion—that "Novia Scotia" and "Acadia" covered much the same soil—had become worse confounded by the claims of renegades, Indians, and squatters. A dim and resentful Holles found there were "other places of the same name in Novia Francia". Vainly did D'Estrades, during his second mission, invoke in Charles' presence the muse of history, and vainly hark back to 1504 or the great Champlain; the King's other ear was besieged by New England deputations and Huguenot pastors. His government steadily procrastinated—the

[1] Holles to Arlington, Nov. 12 and 17, Dec. 10—Fitzhardinge to same, Nov. 12 and 16—(France, 119).

one man who knew Acadian geography was soon
expected home, they must inquire further—for their
information showed that Nova Scotia was a promising
nursery for British seamen, and had a useful fish trade
to southern Europe. Besides, had not British subjects
been blockaded, marooned on solitary islands, forced
to live on lobsters? Louis would surely recognize the
propriety of delay.[1]

Inquiry was wanted, too, in the West Indies. In
those waters the Spanish dominion lay a huge dere-
lict, rudderless and bankrupt, tempting the buccaneer
attack of its successors in empire, the seamen of England, Holland, and France. English and French on the
spot had long joined hands against Spaniards and
savage Caribs, but from 1660 onwards this informal
alliance gave way before naval and commercial rivalry.
Royal authority and State-aided corporations superseded and absorbed the claims of private proprietors,
and surplus adventurers, swarming from English
Barbados or French Martinique on to the lesser
Antilles, now appealed with their counter-claims to
Paris and London. Between the westernmost English
base at Jamaica and the easternmost at Barbados the
French were solidly established in Martinique and
Guadeloupe, while to the north the two nations shared
St. Kitts. Between that and Guadeloupe the English
had Nevis, Antigua, and Montserrat, but north again,
round Spanish Hispaniola and Cuba, and to the south
of Dominica, others lay defenceless, exploited only by
a few Spaniards and Caribs and waiting to be won
by a strong arm. The English commander, Francis

[1] Instructions for D'Estrades, May 3, 1661—Comminge to Louis, Sept. 13 and
Dec. 27, 1663—(Fr. tr.); Arlington to Holles, Aug. 24, '63—Holles to Arlington,
April to November 1664—(France, 117-19); Col.S.P., 1661-68; D'Estrades to
Louis, Feb. 21 and March 13, 1662; C. and P. iii. 423.

Lord Willoughby of Parham, represented the experience and audacity of the Puritan adventurers, and at home the great West Indian merchants of the Commonwealth like Noel and Povey drove on Charles' new Council of Plantations.[1]

In February 1662, upon pressure from Jamaica, Charles authorized an attack on the half-inhabited island of Tortuga, which, lying to the north of the *bloc* formed by Jamaica, Cuba, and St. Domingo, was an ideal haunt for the buccaneers and privateers of all nations. The claimant in possession was French, but the title was conflicting—buried in a long trail of murder, hoards of pieces of eight, commerce in tortoiseshell. With Willoughby's arrival in the Leewards as governor in 1663 the English launched on larger ventures. St. Lucia, a dream of beauty, lay between Barbados and the major French islands. Its previous history was like others—one of English settlers wiped out by the Caribs, of French planters from Martinique, and English from overcrowded Barbados, but Willoughby alleged the superiority of our title and an invitation from the natives, and in January 1664 Charles sent him the order he desired. In the June following, St. Lucia was occupied by a Barbados expedition, led by "Indian" Warner, the ruthless product of a former governor's marriage with a Carib, and while Madame charmed St. Cloud and Charles bantered Ruvigni, Carib canoes and English sailing ships were taking the French stockades.[2]

From all the world over the two nations' jealousies returned to the centres of power. English forts on the Gambia were said to be blocking French trade; French

[1] Andrews, *British Committees, Commissions, and Councils of Trade and Plantations, 1622–75* [1908], pp. 9, 91.

[2] Col.S.P., and Higham, *The Leeward Islands, passim*; Holles to Arlington, Oct. 10, 1663, Sept. 21 and Dec. 10, 1664—France, 117 and 119.

engineers surveyed Morocco, and hoped to anticipate an English occupation of Alhucemas. The Duc de Beaufort's excursions from Toulon against the corsairs were taken to mean that France wanted a place in the African sun, and for a few months in 1664 the Picardy regiment garrisoned Djidjelli, between Bona and Bougia.[1] The same summer Colbert created the State-aided companies of the East and West Indies, chartering their conquests in seas long the province of England and Holland. Subscriptions poured in for his new venture, but "the best subscription of all", wrote Holles, "would be a warre betweene England and Holland".[2]

Such obstacles, in part of new origin, dogged the path of "closer union", and as yet the English were not ready to pay the French price. In some other respects Louis showed himself unwilling even to abide by Cromwellian treaties. Very early, and quite gratuitously, he raised the question of the English legendary title of "King of France". He tried also to replace the commercial concessions of Mazarin by the less favourable terms of 1610; demanding, for instance, the abrogation of an article which allowed our ships to pass the river to Bordeaux without payment of duty or unshipping cannon at Blaye. Though D'Estrades admitted the weakness of the French case, and at one time promised amendment in return for no restriction upon French fisheries, the Blaye matter was still disputed at the close of 1664.[3]

[1] D'Estrades to Louis, Aug. 22 and Sept. 26, 1661, Fr. 65; Picavet, *Les dernières années de Turenne*, 55; Comminge's despatches of Aug. 1663, Fr. tr.; Aumâle, *Histoire des Princes de Condé*, vii. 215; Rousset, *Louvois*, i. 79.

[2] Holles to Arlington, June 22, France, 118.

[3] Bastide to Clarendon, Aug. 9, 1661 (C.S.P.); instructions for D'Estrades, *ut supra*; D'Estrades to Louis, Sept. 26, '61 (Fr. tr.); Charles to Madame, Oct. 17, 1664 (Ady); Holles' Memorial, Dec. 20, 1664 (France, 119).

Yet all this friction had not overthrown the Clarendonian diplomatic system. Our financial and military
weakness was no secret. France knew well how far
Spanish hostility to England extended, and knew, too,
that if she shielded Holland against England, Holland
would never join Spain. But unless assured at least of
Dutch neutrality, if not of Spanish alliance, England
must adhere to the hopes pinned upon France, and
refuse the action clamoured for by those who resented
the growing French mastery of Europe. Clarendon
therefore rebuked Downing for his anti-French conversations at the Hague—he must not speak of Louis
as "only delighted in masques and dancing". The
Elector of Brandenburg was given a commercial
treaty and defensive alliance, but his activities against
Sweden, the ally of France, were discouraged, and
his request for a guarantee of the Oliva peace was
civilly refused; he was viewed as "Spanish", and sourly
advised to send envoys to Paris and Stockholm.[1] The
Anglo-Swedish treaty of October 1661 was our only
commitment, and that not a serious one, in Baltic
politics; unable financially to give guarantees involving
expenditure, we kept no diplomatic representative in
the North till the threat of a Dutch war in 1664. Elsewhere our action breathed the same tepid anti-Hapsburg air. Clarendon, in a humiliating letter, refused to
investigate the French sincerity in Portugal, and her
suggestion for mediation between Portugal and Spain;
help in that quarter could come from no one but
France, "nor can anybody imagine that the burden of
a war of Portugal can be sustained upon the weak
shoulders of the Crown of England". Good relations

---

[1] Brandt, Feb. 20, 1663, Urk. ix.; Clarendon to Downing, Jan. 17 and March
28, 1662, Clar. MSS. 104; Urk. ix. 693-702 *passim*.

were kept with the Porte, mainly in the interests of commerce—our ambassador going so far as to smile upon a Turkish war against Austria—and the Turks were encouraged to accept Portuguese friendship.[1]

It was in the course of 1663 that some first indications appeared of a changed system, and though at first minute and tentative, their ubiquity showed that they might rise to the anti-French coalition which made the hope of 1665–66. Louis XIV's correspondence revealed a growing dissatisfaction: Comminge found needless difficulty in renewing the commercial treaty, Ruvigni noted that the ministers were more hostile than the King, while the latitude allowed to Downing was found inexplicable except on the hypothesis that Clarendon's favour was vanishing or his view changed. On the other side of the lantern the Hapsburgs were slowly waking to the folly of their divisions, and to the impossibility of accommodation with France. In March 1663 the engagement was announced of the Emperor to the Infanta Margaret—a first-fruit of the mission of Leopold's personal friend Pötting, who was instructed further to press Spain to close the Portuguese war, the very object for which English diplomacy was striving. The Spaniards, stung by Louis' rejection of their alliance and alarmed at his incessant pressure, were turning to the other camp, and their overtures were not unheard. A curious spasm of enthusiasm for the liberties of the Low Countries manifested itself in Gamarra and Friquet, the Spanish and Austrian ministers at the Hague. In September Downing was, by Clarendon's order, giving them interviews, as the French discovered, while in November the Irish-Spaniard Moledi

---

[1] Clarendon to Fanshawe, April 13, 1663 (Heathcote); Winchelsea to Nicholas, June 21 and Sept. 4, 1661 (Finch); Pribram, *Ven. Desp.* 659.

appeared in London, to plead for the despatch of an English envoy to Madrid. Finally, in December, Gamarra formally memorialized the states of Holland in favour of an English-Dutch-Spanish league.[1]

So far as England was concerned, it is impossible not to connect this change with a new direction of policy dating from the last months of 1662. That October Secretary Nicholas[2] was pressed to resign; he was now hard upon seventy, and his influence on foreign policy seems to have been insignificant. He was succeeded by Sir Henry Bennet, one of the King's intimate companions in exile, who, under the title acquired the next year of Arlington, was to exercise, for twelve years as Secretary and for four more years behind the scene, an influence incomparably greater than any save the King's. This, and the fact that the common version of his personality comes from the rancour or gossip of Clarendon and Burnet, justifies a more than usually careful examination of the new minister.

Arlington, as we may henceforth call him, was born a courtier, for his grandfather had nearly become Secretary of State to James I and his mother was one of the Crofts of Saxham. He had begun public life in the following of Lord Bristol, and with him fought a campaign in 1644, the famous piece of black plaster to be seen in his portraits recalling a sabre cut over his

[1] Mignet, i. 295; Pribram, 260; D'Estrades to Louis, Feb. 1; Louis to D'Estrades, Nov. 23; Downing to Clarendon, Sept. 18 (Clar. MSS. 106); Ruvigni to Louis, June 28, Fr. tr.—all 1663; Aitzema, iv. 1110.

[2] Ormonde's fine tribute has not, I think, been printed. The King's gift of £10,000 and offer of a title were, he says, recognition worthy "of the fidelity, ability, and faithfulness, wherewith he knows, and the world with him, you have long served the King his father and him, in such tymes as might and did shake, and indeed shake off many that did not serve them upon those principles of religion and honesty that govern you. This is a testimony due to your constancy from all that know you, and love virtue and loyalty"—Oct. 15, 1662, Egerton MSS. 2538, f. 170.

nose received at Andover. In 1648 he became secretary to the Duke of York, with whom he was never at ease; gradually he drifted away from the Duke and the Queen Mother's circle, and by 1654 was high in the King's confidence. Even in 1656 there was talk that he was to be Secretary, and we have seen that from 1659–60 he was envoy at Madrid. Thence, in April 1661, he returned to England, where he promptly entered upon the strategical post of keeper of the Privy purse, and now at last, after sundry disappointments, he was promoted to the office for which Charles had long designed him.[1]

In diplomatic experience and ability he was head and shoulders above any minister of this reign. He was now a man of forty-four, matured during fifteen years' exile by incessant missions—to Ireland, France, Germany, Rome, and Spain—and his mastery of French and Spanish was a rare accomplishment in contemporary British politicians. Over many years there was only one opinion among foreign envoys as to his ability, dignity, and effective power.[2] Sir William Temple, who reserved a much harder version for his *Memoirs*, was glad to write in 1674 that "the man has never yet been in my eyes that can fill your station, especially as to what concerns the foreign affairs, in any degree near what I am sure you can do, if you please".[3]

To him, and his under-secretary, Joseph Williamson, was due the first decent organization of the secretaries' office, with the systematic docketing and filing of foreign correspondence. It was he who brought forward

---

[1] Barbour, cap. ii.; Cal.S.P.D., 1660–61, 580; Clarendon to Ormonde, Nov. 1, 1662 (Lister).

[2] Heathcote, 50; Brandt (1663), Urk. ix. 707; Mocenigo (1670), Add. MSS. 10,171; Colbert to Pomponne (1672), Forneron; Schwerin (1678), 252.

[3] Aug. 4, 1674, Add. MSS. 35,852, f. 109.

some of the best diplomatists and public servants of
the reign—in Temple, William and Sidney Godolphin,
Leoline Jenkins, and William Bridgeman.[1] The for-
mality and punctiliousness, which foreigners admired
and his countrymen ridiculed, had their good side in a
minister of State; his own despatches were clear and
cogent, and he made it a matter of complaint when he
received them from others couched in slipshod English.[2]
His industry at least was undoubted: as he dressed the
Gazette was read to him by one of Williamson's clerks,
and his endorsement is on thousands of papers. He was
not an exalted character, for to be on the winning side
and with the big battalions was his preference, and he
shared the mercenary mind of Restoration politicians.
His style of living was sumptuous, and his palaces—
Euston with its conservatories, waterways, and library,
or in London, at Goring House—were filled with royal
guests and high festival. His greatest ambition was to
be Treasurer, where remuneration was most easily won,
and, as it was, his pickings as Secretary and later as
Lord Chamberlain were very considerable. But both
Arlington and his servant, Williamson, seem always to
have refused the French bribes; the bribes taken so
cheerfully by his rival Buckingham, for himself, his
mistress, and his followers.

The new Secretary was unmoved, whether in foreign
or domestic policy, by the common motives of a Clarendonian Cavalier. Dartmouth, Queen Anne's minister,
with good opportunities of knowing, has said that
Arlington was essentially a Whig;[3] he certainly kept up
a curiously friendly relation with Shaftesbury in the
epoch of the Popish plot, and his constitutional timidity

---

[1] M.H. Papers, i. 433, 455; Heathcote, 219.   [2] Holland, 169, f. 146.
[3] Dartmouth's note on Burnet, i. 181.

was little less valuable than a valour for the constitution.
As for religion, charges of Popery hung about him, as
about his master, from the exile onwards, and we may
guess that, like Charles, he believed the Roman Church
was best, if one had to have a church at all. Of a death-
bed conversion there is fairly decisive proof,[1] though
none of anything earlier, and throughout his period of
office he took the oaths of the establishment, just as he
built the Anglican church at Euston. On the other hand,
he consistently opposed the "Clarendon" code, supporting, partly on the ground of national unity, a toleration
for Protestant dissenters, while among the authors to
whom he played Maecenas were the learned sceptic
Vossius, and Edward Phillips, a nephew of Milton.[2]
His leading preconceptions on foreign politics have
already been before us. His ambition in 1662 to get the
Paris embassy had been resisted by a French protest
against this "pensioner of Spain", and his anti-French
feeling was avowed both to foreigners and to English
colleagues.[3] It was, we shall see, long to continue.
"Espagnol par lui-même", wrote Ruvigni, "et Hol-
landais par sa femme";[4] this second and vital link
was welded in 1666 by Arlington's marriage, during the
Dutch war, to a Dutch woman—Isabella van Beverweert, granddaughter (with a bar sinister) of the great
Maurice, and sister of Lady Ossory. Styled from this
date *mon frère* by members of the Orange house,[5]
Arlington thereby attained a place in Anglo-Dutch relations rather above that of a subject, and one differing

---

[1] It is stated categorically in a conversation of James II with Bishop Francis
Turner (see extracts from the Bishop's memoirs—Add. MSS. 32,096—a reference
I owe to my pupil, Mr. C. Emmott, of Queen's College, Oxford).

[2] Barbour, 42, 156, 261; Lister, iii. 201; *D.N.B.*; my *Tory Party*, 130.

[3] D'Estrades to Louis, Feb. 6, Louis to D'Estrades, Feb. 12, 1662; Brandt,
May 1, 1663; Arlington to Ormonde, May 26, 1663. Carte MSS. 46.

[4] Oct. 21, 1667, Fr. tr.   [5] Holland, 180, f. 27.

alike from typical English mercantilists and from Louis XIV.

Such was the minister called to lead British foreign affairs. We shall meet him more and more, with his goggle eyes, his fair wig, his perpetual headache, and his pipes of port; we shall see him outlive his power and survive impeachment, to die in the next reign. No contrast could be sharper, few antipathies more inevitable, than those between him and Clarendon. Superficially, by St. Albans' agency it was thought, they were reconciled after a first attempt to oust the Chancellor failed in the spring of 1663.[1] But if so, Clarendon won a respite in part because his real power was waning, and nowhere more than in foreign affairs, for neither in the crucial negotiations in the Spanish peninsula, nor in the inception of the Dutch war and the efforts to close it, did the King's titular chief minister play a chieftain's part.

The Clarendonian era of foreign policy may, then, at this stage be judged upon its merits. Justice must record that the weight laid on his shoulders was crushing, and that the cheerful-sounding term "Restoration" involved a dozen herculean toils. The church, the army, the finances, an Irish settlement, a Scottish settlement, the King's marriage, the embers of civil war—the brunt of them all fell on him. Physically, he collapsed. He was often, for weeks at a time, bedridden with gout, and on this count alone his touch with envoys abroad grew less intimate. A valid criticism of his policy, no doubt, is that he grossly exaggerated the danger of rebellion, an obsession which explains both his anxiety, at almost any price, for peace, and his repeated application to France for guaranteed assistance against rebellion. But then

---

[1] Ruvigni to Louis XIV, June 25, 1663, Fr. tr.

the critics have not fled before Puritan arms from island to island, or for ten years climbed the cold stair of exile.

His readers will not doubt his English heart. If he possibly took money from the Dutch, or some of those lacquered cabinets which they sent to tempt our ministers, such persuasions did not govern his policy, and he refused much greater gifts from Louis XIV.[1] Yet he can, justifiably, be described as unfitted to deal with the foreign politics of that age. His views were not so much false as irrelevant; the factors to which he gave weight belonged to Civil War England and an older Europe. His count against de Witt was not his radically anti-English bias, but his alleged share in excluding the Stuarts, and he still reckoned the Huguenots as a weighty international force. Whatever the need of peace and economy, he made undue diplomatic sacrifice to them; he allowed Charles to support a French marriage for the Portuguese King,[2] and seemed to miss the danger in a French mediation between Portugal and Spain; provided that France paid, he did not heed. Two characteristics, marked in other sides of life, did damage here. He gave too much weight to personal slights or resentment; Watteville's boisterousness, or the Austrian incivility, rankled too long. With this he had a natural credulity, or sanguineness, which made it hard for him to hold back his cards. He expected to find in the French court an almost altruistic sympathy with the prosperity of the English monarchy, and it can rarely be wise to tell a foreign prince that on him hangs your country's finances, or that you value nothing in comparison with this friendship. Ardent alliance, or hostility to the edge of war—between these he seemed to

[1] Mignet, i. 87; Clarendon, ii. 175; Fruin, iv. 188; Japikse, 77; Urk, xii. 619-22.
[2] Prestage, 83.

have no middle, and to be ignorant of the art of diplomatic preparation. The envoys of his own choice were, like Holles and Fanshawe, old-fashioned and insular; over others, and even over them, whether from illness, overwork, or conscious diminishment of power, he gradually lost control.

But the virtues and vices of his system were now to be tested, for England and Holland, despite their treaty of September 1662, were drifting into war.

CHAPTER III

THE ORIGINS OF THE DUTCH WAR

CHARLES II's first Dutch war sprang from those
national antagonisms which defy the most pacific of
governments. Feuds and conflicts accumulated for half
a century were pressing for solution, and to solve them
without recourse to arms would have asked, on either
side, a rare magnanimity coupled with absolute power.
But magnanimity could not be expected from mercantilism, and both Charles II and de Witt depended for
political existence on mercantile support.

Neither government originally desired, nor at any
stage manipulated, the outbreak. Domestic sedition
and the implications of the Portuguese marriage made
peace imperative for England, and Clarendon's pacifism shines through the London negotiation or his
correspondence with our minister at the Hague. Our
isolation in Europe alarmed him. A peace with Holland
would "disappoint the Spanyards' expectation of a
rupture betweene us, as likewise that of the seditious
and discontented party at home"; it would "compose
the minds of men who do still apprehend new troubles",
revive the "deadness" of trade, and encourage foreign
investment. In such assurances Clarendon associated
the King's name with his own, and on the eve of
the struggle Charles accurately described himself to

Madame as "almost the only man in my kingdom who doth not desire war".[1]

Peace was also the plain interest of Holland. Their magnificent civilization was at its zenith. Ships of all nations crowded their ports; their own were the world's carriers. The arts of peace and war had reached among them a height hardly surpassed since Periclean Athens, or the Venetian golden age, and the young Pensionary de Witt and the sailor de Ruyter had the mental strength and plain civic virtue of the classical republics. Rembrandt, Cuyp, and Vermeer were in their prime, Amsterdam was still the financial centre of the world, Leyden a capital of the European mind. But all this glorious fabric, the Hollanders' daily bread and their continued power, hung upon peace, for even their highly organized credit had been strained by the last age of war. They paid a yearly interest of £500,000 on war debts, and Downing persistently reported that they were "not in a condition to have warre with anybody".[2] Moreover, while war must always excite an effervescence of Orange sentiment, and raise the taboo question of military command for Nassau princes, peace with the Stuarts might lay this bogey, and seemed more likely from a stable monarchy than a warlike Commonwealth.[3]

It was, at least, urgent to clear up the unsatisfactory state of Anglo-Dutch relations obtaining in the spring of 1660, if the unofficial trade war of the East was not to strike home to Europe. Our government's first approaches faltered with the internal revolutions of 1659, but in February 1660 Downing renewed them, and the

[1] To Madame, Sept. 19, '64 (Ady); cf. Comminge to Lionne, May 12 (Japikse, app. xiv.).
[2] Japikse, 159; Downing to Nicholas, Aug. 22, '62 (Egerton 2538, f. 116).
[3] De Witt to van Thielt, May 30, '61 (Fruin); Japikse, 46-7.

States professed their general readiness for discussion. When Charles reached the Hague he declared his personal wish for an alliance, and the despatch of a Dutch embassy was resolved on before he sailed.[1]

Their leading envoys well typified the permanent antipathies of this Republic. Van Hoorn, a burgomaster of Amsterdam and a director of their East India company, stood for the triumphant merchant aristocracy. On the other hand, Louis of Nassau, Heer van Beverweert, was a natural son of Prince Maurice. He was now a man of sixty, a born courtier and an enemy of the Princess Dowager, but reckoned to be pro-French and to be drawing nearer to de Witt. A year before this, his daughter Emilia had married Ormonde's heir, the ever-lovable Ossory; if this gave Beverweert a good introduction in English society, his hard driving over the marriage portion showed that even Orange princes were not devoid of the Dutch business aptitude.[2]

The embassy reached England in November,[3] and began in high hope their conferences with the English commissioners, of whom, not unfittingly, a majority were Cromwellians,[4] since it was precisely the legacy of Cromwellian England that was in question. There was, indeed, one extraneous matter, interesting rather the Royal family than the nation—the position of Charles' nephew, William of Orange; and we deal with it here, that we may eliminate it once for all as a cause of the war, or as a directing motive of Charles' policy.

[1] Fruin, ii. 151 and note; Aitzema, iv. 579, 583, 603; Urk. ix. 481; Japikse, 41.
[2] Rec. Hollande, i. 177; Burghclere, *Ormonde*, i. 517; Japikse.
[3] First audience, Nov. 19; conference, Dec. 7.
[4] Monk, Robartes, Annesley, Ashley, Morrice, with the royalists Nicholas and Berkeley.

For ten years, as though obedient to one law, the star of monarchy seemed to have waxed and waned in England and Holland together. Charles I's daughter Mary had married William II in 1641, when England was falling into the Civil War, and to her husband's Court her father's friends went thereafter for money, arms, and cities of refuge. In 1649 the English republicans brought Charles to the scaffold, and in 1650 the Dutch Republic rose again from the premature grave of William II. The Protector's treaty of 1654 with Holland tried to bury the very name of monarchy in both countries. Not only did the Dutch undertake to expel the Stuarts, but the State of Holland contracted a further obligation, by the Act of Seclusion, to exclude the infant William III from succession to his ancestors' prerogatives as stadtholder or captain-general.

The republicans whom William II had tried to extirpate now fixed themselves in power, and found in John de Witt, elected Grand Pensionary in 1653, not only a political genius, but the spirit incarnate of civic revenge. In talent and resolution he surpassed any contemporary Englishman, having a mind moved as on wheels of poised, chilled steel, cleaving an even way with smooth precision through wide seas of policy or infinite executive detail. Among its by-products were theses on curves, conic sections, and chain shot; deeply versed in economics, a shrewd investor on the Bourse, he was also master of the whole process of political action, from the organizing of alliance to commanding a fleet. His father had been one of the deputies encaged at Louvestein by William II, and something exceeding party passion breathes in the son's determination to slay for ever the Orangist monarchy. Did he not tell Downing, "If there were not one man more in the

country of his mind, yet that he must oppose the restitution of the Prince of Orange"?[1]

Just as his share in the Act of Seclusion had been
dominant, so his attitude to the Stuarts hitherto had
been unrelenting, and even when at war with the Commonwealth he had declined to entertain approaches
from Charles II.

He had been fortunate in his opponents, for the
Orangist party was torn by faction, and in the spring
of 1660 lay deep in the mire. The mother and grand-
mother of the young Prince had fought like tigresses
for his person and his powers. Mary, his mother, was
one of the least wise of the Stuarts. She treated the
Dutch with insolence, had never troubled to learn their
language, and, judged by the high standard of her
aunt Elizabeth of Bohemia, she was "deadly lazy";
she was certainly feather-headed, and unlucky in her
confidants—high among them her lady-in-waiting,
Lady Stanhope, who was accused of making her mistress Anglophil and of accumulating a fortune for herself into the bargain.[2] Against this light, lissom princess
loomed up her massive mother-in-law, Amalia von
Solms, widow of Frederick Henry. As a girl, far off in
Prague days, she had been a waiting lady to the Winter
Queen, and the parvenu stamp is on her dealings.
Wherever Mary moved, Amalia countermoved. To
Mary's England she opposed another son-in-law, the
Great Elector, and while Mary's leanings were French,
Amalia's sympathy and, report said, her financial
interest lay with Spain. Their mutual grief had not
mitigated the two ladies' feud, which had long irri-

---

[1] Downing to Clarendon, June 21; for the Act of Seclusion and de Witt's share
in it, see Clar. MSS. 104, during Oct. 1661; Archives, 119; Pontalis, i. 186; and
de Witt's letter of Oct. 1, 1660, to Beverweert (Combes).

[2] *D.N.B.*, sub Kirkhoven; Arch. 169; Everett Green, 354, note.

tated, and now disgusted, western Europe; they had carried their litigation into the highest court of Holland, which vainly invited them to share the guardianship of William in peace.

A central point for their rivalry lay in the principality of Orange, far distant between Nîmes and Geneva, surrounded with the glamour of Nassau origins, and yielding in tolls and taxes some revenue for the cause. By 1658 that petty state was distracted between Mary's and Amalia's partisans, each of whom appealed to the ready Mazarin to intervene. Having failed to bribe Mary, the Cardinal succeeded better with the governor, Amalia's nephew Frederick von Dohna, who surrendered the city for 200,000 livres in March 1660. A tornado of recrimination broke out in Holland and Zealand, and from these days we hear of those followers of Mary who so long formed the link between Orange politics and the English government—Oudart, her secretary, a pleasant, cultivated, horsy old Etonian, who became Latin secretary in England; Zulestein, natural son to Frederick Henry and governor to the Prince; and Gabriel Sylvius, an intimate friend of Arlington, who had a long score running from these French politics against Dohna.[1]

Such was the scandalous state of the once great Orange dynasty when the English Restoration, which restored so many causes, promised an Orange revival. Charles was bound, it might seem, at least to make that party a make-weight to the republicans, who had excluded his nephew from power and himself from their hospitality, and Mary might hope for the long arrears of her dowry and the consolidation of her sole authority

[1] Arch. 185 *et seq.*; Aitzema, iv. 624-33; Chéruel, iii. 310; D'Avenel, ix. 522; Arl. i. 388; de Beer in *Bull. Inst. Hist. Research*, June 1928.

over her son. In taking leave of the States in May, Charles therefore declared that whatever they would do for his nephew he would reckon as service done to himself.

Yet his avuncular zeal was temperate, for conversation with de Witt had convinced him that he must not go too fast. He damped down Mary's pressure to get an immediate designation of William as stadtholder, and advised her to accept, with a show of moderation, the compromise that he had discussed with de Witt—that Holland should educate William as "a child of the State" and improve the financial provision for the royal family. On the 30th September Holland revoked the Act of Seclusion, de Witt asking meantime for the return of the original transmitted to Cromwell, as a guarantee that the dead might bury their dead. To the indignation of Amalia and of Orangist Zealand, Charles and Mary seemed prepared to transact with the evil thing.[1] In late September Mary set out to England, to plead her case in person, for there were many incidental matters left over for settlement; the States, for instance, wanted to bring William's court to the Hague and to supersede Zulestein by a more orthodox governor.

But death, sudden, hideous, premature, death by small-pox, carried her to the grave on the 24th December, and her inheritance of troubles others did take. Her French cook was paid off, some of her jewels went to the "waiting woman", Anne Hyde, whose marriage she had done her best to shipwreck, and a share of £250, which she left in the "Royal Adventure for Guinea",

[1] Memorial of Mary, July 20—replies of States of Holland, Sept. 15 and Oct. 29—Holland, 163, ff. 35, 50, 72; *ibid.* 164, f. 29; Combes, 150 *et seq.*; Arch. 206; Aitzema, iv. 635, 656; Japikse, 26, 31.

was the residuary irony of fate on the peace of the two nations blended in her son.[1]

That son, her greatest and indeed her sole legacy, was left by her to the guardianship of Charles II, who by this time had changed his opinion of the Dutch and was describing them to French envoys as *coquins*. By renewing the Navigation Act and introducing a Bill to protect the fisheries the Convention Parliament's expiring activity stung the Dutch, who answered by refusing the loan of two millions for which Charles had asked, while the Orange question must emerge, by Mary's death, into a harsher light, for the rôle of guardian would permit the English king to keep for ever ajar a door of interference into the politics of Holland. Letters from Amalia and an embassy from Brandenburg goaded him to champion his defenceless ward, and to instal Amalia as acting guardian on the spot.[2]

Later evidence will show the determination of the English court at this time to finish their treaty with Holland, and the acerbity clothing the Orange problem in 1661 must certainly not be debited wholly to the English side of the account. De Witt's tone was high, his contempt for English weakness was marked, and he was determined to keep foreign influence out of the Prince's guardianship and the regency of Orange territory. He meant to force a recognition, or tacit admission, that the guardians derived their authority only from the sovereign court of Holland.[3]

The rival view was forcibly put in England from March onwards by the Brandenburg envoys—John

[1] Oudart's statement, October 1661, Holland, 164, f. 116.
[2] Bartet to Mazarin, Feb. 7, '61, Fr. tr.; Amalia to Charles, Jan. 14 (Holland, 164); Great Elector to Clarendon, Jan. 21 (Clar. MSS. 74); Urk. ix. 497.
[3] Fruin, ii. 277; Combes, 299.

Maurice of Nassau, the former governor of Brazil, and his prolix colleague, the Rhinelander Daniel Weiman—who passionately advocated an Anglo-Prussian alliance as the one salvation for Orange, and won the warm regard of Clarendon. The treaty consequently signed in May constituted Amalia as executive guardian, though in large questions and permanent appointments both King and Elector were to have a say; but de Witt's reply was, in short, "all or nothing"; he denounced the treaty as offensive to the honour of Holland, and in September the provincial Estates by a majority disavowed all responsibility for William's upbringing.[1]

But such recrimination was the effect, not the cause, of the ill relations between Holland and England, and though the English would nurse Orange sentiment for future use in emergency, they would not let it impede the making of peace. Clarendon discouraged the propaganda of Oudart and Sylvius, and relied on diplomatic offices with France to obtain restoration of the principality.[2] This, indeed, was optimism, for, as against an English dominance of Holland through the Orange interest, three elements of opposition existed which inevitably would coalesce—the republicans, Amalia, and the honest brokers in France. By midsummer 1662 Amalia was clear that she could expect neither military nor money assistance from England, who, moreover, from deference to Holland discouraged a marriage she had at heart for one of her daughters to the King of Portugal. She was ready, therefore, to eat

[1] Aitzema, iv. 760; Wicquefort, iii. 54, 62; Clarendon to Downing, Nov. 9—Downing to Clarendon, Sept. 13—(Clar. MSS. 104); Urk. ix. 534-40; Japikse, 150; Holland, 164, f. 50.
[2] Clarendon to Downing, Sept. 6 and 27, Nov. 22, Clar. 104; St. Albans to Clarendon, Feb. 28, '61, France, 115; D'Estrades to Louis XIV, Sept. 5, Fr. tr.

the leek, and to plead with the States of Holland to
reconsider their decision. The weakness, or the pacifism, of English policy was exposed by Charles supporting her application, and all hope of a split between
the provinces vanished in September with the agreement of Holland and Zealand to suspend decision of
the stadtholdership question until William's eighteenth
birthday.[1]

But neither the situation of William, nor the relations between his guardians, perceptibly improved.
The States of Holland, not unmoved by French pressure, refused to commit themselves, and merely promised to use their influence to protect the Prince's
rights and domains, while Amalia drifted in the same
direction as the best chance of getting Orange State
and improved finances, and the Dutchmen highest in
favour in England were her particular enemies. Not
English influence, but the French wish to please
Brandenburg, achieved a nominal restoration of the
Orange principality in 1664, and the Orange problem
had no influence upon the English decision in that
year to make war on Holland.[2]

But on the Dutch attitude that problem exerted a
tremendous weight. Since Orangist restoration would
destroy all that made up life for de Witt, and since
the English could not be expected to banish the project for ever, he must find his security elsewhere. In
December 1662 D'Estrades, ornamented with fifty years
of love and war, and endeared to the Dutch by long

---

[1] Amalia to States of Holland, July 17, '62 (Holland, 166); Arch. 214; Clarendon to Downing, Dec. 13, '61 (Clar. 104); Downing to Clarendon, Jan. '62 (*ibid.*
106); Charles to Amalia, Japikse, app. xi., and to the States, Aitzema, iv. IIII,
both of Feb. 28 '63; Aitzema, iv. 966.

[2] D'Estrades to Louis, Feb. 22 and March 22, '63; Aitzema, iv. 1112; Downing's correspondence, *passim*; Urk. ix. 597; Pontalis. i. 503; Japikse, 259, 329.

service in their interest, returned to the French embassy at the Hague. He was instructed to cultivate and protect de Witt's party, and at any symptom of Dutch approaches to Spain to brandish the threat of an Orange *revanche*. He was assisted by the generally pro-English or pro-Spanish leaning of the Orangists, and his assurances found in the Grand Pensionary a natural welcome.[1] But all this, both chronologically and in political fact, was far inferior to the breakdown of negotiation with England on other and more combustible matter.

Trade was the life-blood of both countries, and economic causes extinguished the wide hopes and good intentions with which both had entered on the peace conferences of December 1660. The Dutch envoys were empowered to sign a defensive alliance of mutual guarantee which, by simultaneous action at Paris, should be made a triple bond.[2] In this particular, a favourite scheme of Holland, neither London nor Paris showed any interest;[3] and even the notion of a dual defensive alliance, which Clarendon hoped might be achieved before the new Parliament met in May, long before that had vanished also. The Dutch proposals for reciprocal military assistance—12,000 men from England as against 4000 from themselves—were perhaps not equitable, but the English objection took wider ground, protesting the insignificance to England of a Dutch alliance, and challenging the whole idea of an equiponderant guarantee. Further, and going to the heart of the controversy, they asked that any

[1] Turenne's note of 1662, Rec. Hollande, i. 244; Arch. 209; Mignet, i. 261; D'Estrades, March 22, '63–7, February '64; Japikse, 247

[2] Dutch instructions in Aitzema, iv. 612; powers to treat with England and France, in Treaties, 302.

[3] Fruin, ii. 154; Arch. 191; Wicquefort, ii. 211–iii. 3; Aitzema, iv. 727.

guarantee should be extended to possessions outside Europe.[1]

By March 1661 the two projects were still further apart, for while the Dutch declared an extra-European guarantee too wide and impracticable, the English were claiming another to cover Dunkirk. On vital points, like the fisheries area, the English projects were vague in the extreme, while Holland was emphatic that no mention could be made of Dunkirk except in return for trading advantage, and instructed their envoys to suspend talk of guarantees till satisfied on commerce and marine.[2] A war against Spain in defence of Dunkirk, of which the English were increasingly nervous, was anathema to the Dutch—the States of Holland having, indeed, privately decided that in no event would they be a party to it. All chance of wider agreement having thus vanished, in June the Dutch suggested a more modest scheme of "a treaty of amity", based on previous agreements.[3]

The controversy thus at last reached bedrock, for it was rooted in the English mind that both the theory and practice of Dutch trade were expressly designed to ruin our own, whether in peace or war. In a note submitted in this March to our government,[4] which deserves to become classic, the ex-Secretary John Thurloe declared that on this rock had broken all negotiations of the previous ten years; that the Dutch maxims of *mare liberum*, of free trade, of "free ship, free goods", and no right of search, would destroy our sovereign right of the fisheries and the flag, ruin the

[1] Japikse, 81, 98; Aitzema, iv. 611.

[2] English *projets*, before March 11, in Japikse, app. iv.; Dutch instructions of March 19, Aitzema, iv. 745.

[3] Japikse, 106-10; Aitzema, iv. 747.

[4] Printed by Sir Charles Firth in *E.H.R.* xxi. 319.

fabric of the Navigation Act, shatter our insular advantages in war, and give Holland the carrying trade
of all nations. He pointed out that these champions
of freedom had closed the Scheldt, barred our exports
by high tariffs, excluded British shipping from their
plantations, and proclaimed a system of monopoly in
India.

Practical commentary on this belief will be found
only too abundantly hereafter, and here we need only
note that men of a type far removed from chauvinism
found in the Dutch pretensions the supreme obstacle to
what they considered our legitimate expansion. "Coûte
que coûte", Monk told one Dutch ambassador, "England must be allowed its share in world trade". Henry
Coventry wrote that the Dutch declared themselves
sovereign of the South Sea; Holles, with reference to
West Africa, told Downing, "the truth is they would
have all that trade, and will try a bloody nose before
they quit their pretensions".[1]

Charles' government had showed their pacifism by
suppressing the Convention's Fisheries bill, but it was
totally beyond their power to hold up the renewal of the
Navigation Act,[2] or to resist pressure from the City.
Exporters to Spain and her colonies were particularly
urgent, for the Navigation Acts were a dead letter on
the Main, and the Dutch were capturing most of the
West Indies trade. In October 1660 the East India
Company petitioned the King to examine the havoc
wrought in their market, and to enforce reparation and
security, and in November asked leave to occupy the
island of Pulo Run, which had been ceded to England,

[1] Van Goch to de Witt, July 20, 1664, Pontalis; Coventry to Ormonde, Feb. 13,
Carte, 47, f. 420; Holles to Downing, Oct. 17, Add. 22,920, f. 51.
[2] Dutch protest of Dec. 17, 1660, Holland, 163; Japikse, 57, and app. ii.

but never yet surrendered, under the treaty of 1654. Some months earlier Charles had invited the East Indian, Turkey, and Eastland companies, and other mercantile interests, to nominate representatives for membership of his new Council for Trade and Plantations, and it was to this body—composed of politicians so realistic as Ashley and William Coventry, thinkers as independent as Robert Boyle, merchants so weighty as Povey of the West Indian trade or Nicholas Crispe, the Hammersmith merchant prince who had founded the market in Guinea—that the East Indian petition was referred.[1]

Their report, dated the 3rd January 1661, underlined with concrete instances the view which we have just heard from Thurloe. The Dutch, it postulated, owned "no other right than might" in the East. They made war on natives who dared to trade with the English, confiscated our vessels on pretext of an imaginary blockade, persecuted offending natives in the Moluccas "with extravagant cruelty", and "barbarously murdered" the Banda islanders. An invested capital of £800,000 was at stake, and they endorsed the Company's demand that, before a treaty was signed, reparation be exacted, and security given for the future.[2] Even inside the Council chamber the wrongs, real or alleged, of fifty years ago were revived—once more "Amboyna" was on all lips, and the suffering of British seamen, bound in misery and iron and half-starved on rice and water, which had been commended to King James, rose from oblivion with cries to his grandson for vengeance.

[1] Higham, 36; Japikse, 55; E.I.C. Court Minutes, 60-63, pp. 40, 48; Col.S.P., 1574–1661, p. 492.
[2] Minutes, *loc. cit.* 56, 69; Khan, 107.

With this sort of clamour out of doors, the commissioners addressed themselves to the negotiation, in an atmosphere thick with suspicion. External events repeatedly threatened to cut it short. There was talk of Dutch espionage in the Woolwich and Chatham dockyards. Charles warned their envoys that, both for himself and for Portugal, he must resent their sending a squadron to India, and, if they persisted ("je vous dis franchement cela, et en ami") he must break with them. In May the Dutch countered with the "dangerous consequences" of the impunity allowed to our privateers, and in July sent in a furious protest against Captain Holmes, who, with five ships flying the Union Jack, had seized Cape Verde and some Dutch settlements in the Gambia. Faced with gigantic claims for damages from our East India Company, they in their turn refused to surrender Pulo Run till such claims were waived, and furbished up absurdities like alleged loans of twenty years earlier to Scots rebels. In August the envoys were instructed to come home if not promptly satisfied, and early in 1662 Clarendon was resisting a move in Council to issue letters of reprisal.[1]

A comparison of the treaty, as finally signed on the 4th September 1662,[2] with the *projets* and despatches of the eighteen months preceding, reveals the purely negative nature of a peace which was achieved only by agreeing to suppress, or to slur over, every acute difference. An examination of particular controversies will reveal even more—the seeds of the ensuing war.

[1] Holland, 163, ff. 47, 61, 91; Aitzema, iv. 748, 756; Khan, 115; Japikse, 163-5, 189; Downing to Clarendon, Oct. 4, n.s. 1661 (Clar. 105).
[2] Text in Aitzema, iv. 915; signed "yesterday afternoon", Clarendon to Downing, Sept. 5, 1662 (Clar. 104); ratified Dec. 14 in England and Nov. 21 in Holland.

FREEDOM OF TRADE

The Dutch aspiration to be treated on the same footing as denizens of Britain was promptly quashed by the Navigation Act, and by another Act forbidding the export of wool. Any such equalization of duties the English were unwilling to accept, nor would they proceed upon the basis of the *Intercursus Magnus* of 1495, which was one source of the Dutch envoys' instructions. Neither party would, in short, abate any of their vantage ground; de Witt's next suggestion for tariff stabilization met with a frosty welcome, and a hint from England that wool might enter Holland duty-free vanished in silence. The negotiators fell back, therefore, on the drab generalities of Cromwell's peace—the ninth article of the new treaty merely providing that, subject to the laws and statutes of either country, their merchants should freely ply their traffic, paying no heavier duties than other aliens.[1]

The Fisheries were the main European artery of Dutch existence, and of this artery the herring trade in British waters was a parent stream. Each year, between June and January, 1000 or more herring busses, convoyed by cruisers, sailed out of the Zuyder Zee and the Meuse for the Shetlands, whence they worked steadily south to Yarmouth, and twice a year the catch went back to Holland to be salted and cured for export. On this central wheel their artificially contrived wealth turned and depended. Getting salt from Languedoc, Portugal, and Spain, they paid with the salted fish for the Baltic grain, Spanish oils, or

---

[1] *Parl. Hist.* iv. 167; Aitzema, iv. 612; Japikse, 64 and 100; English concept of April, *ibid.* app. iv. C.

French linen, brandies, and wine, and this when most English ships sailed for these markets in ballast. From Raleigh's time onward Englishmen had grudged this loss to the realm, and tried to enforce on the Dutch a limitation of area or payment of license, while from the Orkneys to the Cinque ports our fishermen poured in complaints of armed guardships, forcible poaching, and cut nets.[1] The publication in 1635 of Selden's *Mare Clausum*, by royal command, instantly connected this matter with our claim to "sovereignty" of the narrow seas, the ground upon which Thurloe in 1652 had rejected the claim for "free fishing".[2] But against any reopening or definition of this indefinable proposition de Witt set his face like flint, and won in so doing, it has been seen, the keen support of Louis XIV. While he, then, would admit no phrase more binding than "the old customs" of the sea, the English refused to hear the teaching of Grotius, which would make ubiquitous fishing a common right of man, and by rejecting the *Intercursus Magnus* implicitly rejected the fisheries claim also. But the guarantee given by France, after long hesitation, to Dutch fishing rights in their treaty of April 1662 altered the aspect of this question. For England, and particularly for Clarendon, it was a heavy blow, as Morrice said, to find their confidence in France so "ill laid". Diplomatically they could only, with some caution, show their teeth by approaches to Spain, but from the present treaty the problem disappeared, to await a not distant posterity. For in December 1663 the Council of Trade reported that one

---

[1] Edmundson, *Anglo-Dutch Rivalry, passim*; Khan, 28; Downing to Clarendon, July 8, 1661 (Lister); Japikse, 70.

[2] Thurloe, *E.H.R., ut supra*; Holland, 163, f. 145—note endorsed by Williamson, "communicated to me by A[rlington?]".

indispensable preliminary to revival of our fisheries
would be war with Holland.[1]

The same chronicle, and a like impotent conclusion,
surrounds the parallel question of *the Flag*. In what
precise seas foreigners must salute English ships was
controverted, even among English Admiralty judges;
to what ships—whether to a single vessel, or only to a
fleet in force—was disputed by the Dutch, and in 1672
was to be the pretext for a war. But, provided the issue
of sovereignty was left in oblivion, the States-General
raised no objection to the salute in vague terms as conceded to Cromwell, and the tenth article of the treaty
therefore provided that the flag should be dipped and
topsails lowered to British men-of-war encountered in
British seas, as heretofore had been the custom.[2]

RIGHT OF SEARCH AND CONTRABAND

Liberty of movement as middlemen and carriers
being vital to their economic life, the Dutch had never
ceased to contest the interpretation of maritime law enforced by England and, less rigidly, by France.[3] Under
cover of their doctrine of "free ship, free goods", they
had made their fortune as neutrals during the English-
Spanish war, and even now were damaging our ally of
Portugal by shipping munitions to Spain. Denying as
they did any "right" of search, they held the English
navigation system at arm's length, and defied it by a
large illicit trade with English colonies, while contraband

[1] Japikse, 100, 186, 203; Morrice to Downing, March 27, 1662 (Add. 22,919,
f. 203); Clarendon to Downing, Dec. 13, 1661 (Clar. 104); S.P. Holland, 165,
ff. 46, 131; Andrewes, 83.

[2] Edmundson, *Anglo-Dutch Rivalry*, app. B; Aitzema, iv. 917; Japikse,
110, 163; *The Petty Papers* (1927), i. 234.

[3] Rec. Hollande, i. 153; Pomponne, ii. 390.

they would water down to the minimum, of munitions and instruments of war, insisting especially that money and foodstuffs must not be included. Such were the main points outlined in the Dutch instructions of October 1660 and argued during the first six months of conference.

But Cromwell's government had already rejected them in their entirety, and the differences were too wide to bridge. The English refused to take a system of passports in lieu of the right of search, which was therefore omitted from the treaty, and the definition of contraband was left to a less prejudiced but distant future—illumined only by Downing's comforting comment that "what you can catch you will confiscate".[1] Save for some restriction on acceptance of privateering commissions from each other's enemies, and an increased period of delay to precede the issue of letters of marque, the conflict of maritime law remained after the treaty, as before it, in the clouds. We may be permitted to descend to those matters terrestrial which outweigh in importance, yet illustrate, these disputed principles.

Amboyna was the word of shame, the Fontenoy or the Khartum for that generation of Englishmen, evoking that passion for revenge which dies last and hardest in international relations. Oliver's treaty had given official burial to this draggled body of 1623, but in June 1661 the English commissioners exhumed it. The Dutch, strongly instructed by their East India Company, demanded that it should be left in "the tomb of forgetfulness", and, if evil spirits could be entombed in treaties, they got their way. But Amboyna continued to haunt them, and at the height of the second Dutch

[1] Aitzema, iv. 608; Japikse, 60, 81, 100; Downing to Nicholas, April 25, 1662 (Egerton, 2538, f. 59).

war, ten years later, Dryden's worst play exploited once more for the London theatre the suffering of tortured Englishmen and the fiendish cruelty of Dutch officials.[1]

To the *English East India Company* must be assigned the greatest share of responsibility for the Dutch war, which in the annals of Eastern trade formed only an episode, and from a company point of view was merely reparation for years of bad dividends. Cromwell's treaty of May 1654 had nominally closed the account on either side to that date, but had begged the largest of questions, in that, while stipulating for freedom of intercourse in Europe, it implicitly forbade each nation to trespass on the other's plantations.[2] Since that date the Dutch, already masters of the Moluccas, had carried almost to completion their destruction of Portuguese power in India. Cannanore, Nagapatam, and Ceylon had fallen, the whole Malabar coast looked like sliding into their hands, and their garrison was planted at the half-way house, the Cape of Good Hope.

Dutch conquest involved a Dutch monopoly, and the Company's first petition to Charles II presented a long list of confiscated vessels, ranging in date from 1654–1659 and valued at nearly £300,000. The Dutch, it was true, had paid an indemnity of some £50,000 in respect of three specified ships under an agreement of 1659, which, they contended, must extinguish all previous claims, but this interpretation was hotly denied both by our Company and by Downing, the agent who had negotiated the very agreement of the 6th February 1659 to which the Dutch appealed.[3]

---

[1] Japikse, 110, 164; Dutch memorial of Oct. 4, in Holland, 164; further instructions of Dec. 6, n.s., in Aitzema.

[2] Text in Aitzema, iii. 920; Thurloe's comments, *E.H.R., ut supra.*

[3] E.I.C. Minutes, 1660–63, 77, 123, 140; Downing to Nicholas, April 11, 1662 (Egerton, 2538).

In April 1661 our commissioners advanced as their own a series of proposals already propounded by the Company. English ships were to trade freely within the limits of their charter, neither side were to enforce monopoly contracts with native states, and the Indians, even if hostile to the Dutch, were not to be prevented from trading with the English.[1] This was to ask the Dutch nothing less than to abdicate from a vantage ground won by years of sacrifice, and needless to say the treaty is silent on these demands. But from two cases under discussion at the moment of ratification we may seize in action the gist of the English case and the Dutch method of resistance.

In October 1662 Dutch ships were besieging Cochin, one of the best pepper ports on the Malabar coast. Forty miles to the south, at Porakad, the English had lately set up a factory by invitation of the local Rajah, who, we contended, was vassal not to Cochin but to the Zamorin of Calicut. Our Presidency governor at Surat, in the same month, despatched the Company's ship *Hopewell* to discharge gold and opium at Porakad and to embark the pepper collected by our factors; but she was stopped by the Dutch and turned back, on the ground that the whole coast was under blockade. Surat then tried the effect of the royal flag, but just as vainly. H.M.S. *Leopard* was held up at Cochin, the captain being told that, since Cochin had surrendered, all its dependencies, including Porakad, were under Dutch dominion, and that Cochin had contracted to deliver the whole pepper crop to them. Incidentally, they could hardly make retrospective the contracts made in March 1663, or confiscate without warning English factories established two years earlier, but the

---

[1] Japikse, app. iv. C; Minutes, *loc. cit.* 57.

sting of our grievance lay deeper—in the plain resolution to achieve a monopoly through warfare on the
natives, and so to interpret the "laws" of this war as to
suppress all neutral trade.[1]

English merchants and public opinion further
charged the Dutch with downright violation of treaty,
and the Pulo Run case gave most substance to the
charge. South-west of New Guinea lay the Banda
islands, headquarters of the nutmeg trade. One of
them, Pulo Run, ceded to the English by the natives
in 1616 and now the sole relic of our aspirations in
the Spice islands, had become ours officially, or so
we claimed, by the treaty of 1623; subsequently,
as a sequel to Amboyna, we had been forcibly
evicted. But this was ancient history, for by the
treaty of 1654 it was clearly stipulated that our East
India Company should recover "their little vinyard".[2]
Nothing had followed; the Company's embarrassed
finances forbade them to try force, and the Dutch,
they alleged, were deliberately ruining the island by
destroying the nutmeg trees. But the profits to be won,
and the demand for spices, were enormous; so much
so that a proclamation of 1662 allowed their wholesale
importation, despite the Navigation Act, pending the
recovery of Pulo Run.

After months of recrimination with the Dutch envoys, Charles in January 1661 authorized the Company to occupy the island, and an expedition sailed that
spring. In October it encountered a blank refusal from
the Dutch officers at Batavia, and an effort in March
1662 to cajole the men on the spot at Pulo Run failed

---

[1] Minutes, *ut supra*, xl. and 364; Khan, 119; Japikse, 282; Downing to Clarendon, Dec. 18, 1663 (Clar. 107), March 18, 1664 (*ibid.*).
[2] Aitzema, iv. 748; Minutes, *loc. cit.* 230.

likewise. It is, indeed, clear that from the first the Dutch were determined to make Pulo Run their lever wherewith to extort other concessions.[1] They would ask as their price the English acceptance of a clean slate in the East, up to and including 1659, and until such acceptance they would issue no orders to the Pulo Run officials. How much they valued the island was shown by their offer—sternly rejected by the English Company—to buy or lease it.

It is impossible not to sympathize with the indignation of our East India merchants. Pulo Run was theirs by treaty; now, before it could be won, they were being asked to waive all claims for damages, however legitimate, incurred since 1654. And though the fifteenth article of the treaty records a Dutch diplomatic victory [2]—their promise to surrender Pulo Run on condition that all other claims in the East were cancelled up to January 1659—it was dearly won, reflecting neither the consent of our Company nor the equities of the question, but the English government's resolution to make peace. To this resolution, manifest in the long-drawn controversy over the "pretensions", we turn.

As to Pulo Run, it was not until March 1665, after the outbreak of war, that the English occupied it, and at the peace of Breda, two years later again, they officially recorded this question to be "the true cause of the war".[3]

All chance of agreement having vanished regarding those matters of principle that would influence the

[1] States-General's resolutions of Jan. 28 and July 28, 1661 (Japikse).
[2] "Et quod per restitutionem illius insulae Pula actiones et pretensiones omnes . . . exstinguentur"—Aitzema, iv. 917.
[3] Instructions for Holles and Coventry, April 18, 1667 (printed, so far as relevant, in E.I.C. Minutes, 1664–67).

future, the crux of the treaty from the English point of view was the degree of material satisfaction that could be obtained for the past, and the reality of the method adopted to carry that satisfaction into effect. The Dutch asserted that claims for Europe before 1654, and for the East before 1659, were barred by the agreement of the latter year; the English Company were decided to go at least behind 1659, and claimed £300,000 in damages accruing since 1656. Downing hotly supported them, not merely, it may be granted, because the Company remunerated his services, but because he held that the Indian interests at stake far transcended in value those of Europe.[1]

Clarendon's attitude was wholly different. He wished for peace, partly in the interest of Portugal, but even more emphatically because he wished to prevent Holland cementing an alliance with France. He was more interested in matters affecting the King's honour in Europe, as compared with Cromwell's, than in questions of trade, and admitted that the losses of Cromwellian merchants left him cold. He left most of the direct negotiation to subordinate commissioners, among whom Cromwellians predominated, and his spasmodic intervention was thus apt to unravel Downing's over-ingenious arrangements.

Early in September 1661 the English accepted in principle the obliteration of Indian pretensions before the 20th January 1659, and to this very considerable concession Clarendon adhered, despite a three-cornered misunderstanding with Downing and de Witt, and despite protests from Downing, whom he rapped over the knuckles with some ironical humility as to his own "want of understanding". An English note of April

[1] Khan, 100, note 2; Downing to Clarendon, May 24, 1662 (Japikse, app. ix.).

1662 stipulated for 1654 as the corresponding "term" for Europe, and with the Dutch acceptance of this in July this knot was unloosed.[1]

Final settlement was delayed, not only by particular policies and events—de Witt's personal wish to break off negotiations,[2] a spate of unofficial English "pretensions", and friction over privateering—but by radical disagreement as to the means of liquidating these claims and pretensions. Nothing would induce the English to accept the Dutch Admiralty courts. The King personally told their envoys that on this point he dare not face public opinion; settlement by special commissioners had been conceded to Cromwell, and why not to him?[3] It was Downing's peculiar boast that he had enforced this method during the Protectorate, and his view was pressed upon all and sundry: "I never yet knew that case so just wherein a Holland Admiralty did not upon one pretext or other give sentence against the English", he wrote, nor had they since the Restoration discharged a single English ship.[4] The Dutch, on the contrary, refused the scheme of commissioners sitting at London to dispose of all causes submitted, and professed to entertain visions of a swarm of unsifted and unsubstantiated claims going behind the "terms" of 1654 and 1659. Up to January 1662 there seemed no hope of breaking this deadlock. The English Cabinet were still adamant on appointing

[1] Japikse, 169, 200 *et seq.*; Downing to Nicholas, April 25 (Egerton MSS. 2538) and July 11 (Holland, 164); Clarendon to Downing, Sept. 27, 1661, April 25, July 31, and Aug. 8, 1662 (Clar. MSS. 104).

[2] In September 1661 (Clar. MSS. 105, f. 647) and in June 1662 (Japikse, 214).

[3] Conference of the King (part of the time alone) with Dutch envoys, Oct. 4, 1661 (Aitzema).

[4] Downing to owners of ship *Experience*, August 1661 (Holland, 164); to Clarendon, Jan. 27, 1662 (Clar. MSS. 106); to Nicholas, June 13, 1662 (Egerton MSS. 2538).

commissioners in the treaty itself, and had tried to hurry decision by hoisting the Dutch with their own petard—that is, by refusing to release Dutch ships under detention except by process of our Admiralty courts—while the utmost that Holland would concede was the reference to commissioners of a previously sifted, and merely residual, list of damages.[1]

At last, in February, de Witt and Downing found a way out, and in May their *projet* was accepted at London and incorporated in the fifteenth article, our East India Company to the last protesting. The English formally secured their point—that the last word should lie with joint commissioners sitting at London; the Dutch theirs—that such commissioners should have no cognizance of events previous to the two "terms" nor of events subsequent to their appointment, while the lists they were to consider should be framed *à l'amiable* by the two governments, and be sifted for a year previously between Dutch deputies and the English ambassador at the Hague.[2]

To this hardly won basis for the settlement of pretensions there was to be one exception—the owners of the ships *Bona Aventura* and *Bona Esperanza* were to be free to pursue the litigation they had begun. To dismiss these two almost mythical vessels would be grateful but historically indecent, for the space they occupy in the state papers is exorbitant, and the circumstance not unhumorous. Their story begins with the wild speculation of William Courteen, who began

[1] English proposal of July '61, Japikse, 110; conference of Aug. 15, Aitzema; Dutch protest of Oct. 4 and Privy Council reply of Nov. 6, Holland, 164; Clarendon to Downing, Sept. 27 and Oct. 25, '61, Clar. MSS. 104; E.I.C. Minutes, 60-63; Dutch report of Jan. 20, '62, Holland, 165; Order in Council, Nov. 8, '61, *ibid.* 164.
[2] Downing to Clarendon, February '62, Clar. MSS. 106; Holland, 165, f. 90; 158, 204; Clar. MSS. 104, ff. 55 and 61; Aitzema, iv. 898.

life as son of a Flemish refugee in Pudding Lane and ended it as rival to the East India Company, financier of Barbados, Northamptonshire squire, and money-lender to the Stuarts. Like others who enjoyed the last capacity, he died bankrupt; hence his son's enforced assignation of many effects to Sir Paul Pindar, and among them these ships of tedious memory; the which, while plying their lawful occasions in 1643—one in the Straits of Malacca and the other off Mauritius—were captured by the Dutch. Briefly, from 1647 onwards, Courteen and Pindar representatives were struggling against each other at the Hague for compensation; in 1649 the Dutch paid something to the Courteen syndicate, but sturdily refused to pay for the same ships twice over; this was not congenial to the Pindar group, who included gentlemen of political weight like Anglesey, from 1660 Lord Privy Seal. Perhaps for the very reason that the Pindar claim had been presented to Cromwell's commissioners, or partly, perhaps, moved by the old financial relation of the Courteen firm to the Crown, Charles II declared his honour affected, and in March 1662 demanded that the two ships be excepted from the general amnesty. The Dutch, by a majority of provinces, thought it wiser to give way, at least on paper, than to break, Downing having announced in the Gazette of Holland that if their envoys were re-called he would leave for England. War on this flimsy ground seemed, besides, intolerable to a minority of the English Cabinet, who disliked Downing's style of diplomacy, Clarendon was bent upon peace, and Charles was convinced that the Dutch would yield.[1] After weeks of tension in July and August, and days of

[1] Downing to Clarendon, Aug. 22, '62, Clar. MSS. 77; Morrice to Downing, July 4, Add. MSS. 22,919, f. 234.

search for a formula by Downing and de Witt, a sesame was at length devised — that the *lis incepta* might be pursued.

Wearisome *lis* and grossly intangible *incepta*! For who the owners were, when the "lis" had "incepted", whether *prosequi* meant the Dutch courts or diplomatic action—these were the very matters in dispute, which (as Downing immediately discerned)[1] the treaty left in the air. All through 1663, till evening, Downing was still belabouring the old points—that Courteen had been bankrupt, that Charles I had been in duress when he endorsed the Courteen claim, that the *Esperanza* had not carried contraband—still in 1664 the "lis" was renewing its youth, its external accompaniments getting more sprightly, Charles granting letters of marque to the Courteeners and Pindars, and the Dutch with tongue in cheek suggesting the *Parlement* of Paris as referee. Faint yet pursuing, the creditors opened their revolving jaws again in 1669, but no Dutch money fell into them, and with a skirling pamphlet warfare the "lis" faded away.[2]

This wretched business, upon which closed the treaty signed on the 4th September 1662, is a fair index to its rooted insincerity. The questions at stake had either been wholly omitted, blurred over in meaningless generalization, or left dependent on executive action, the hopelessness of which could be gleaned from the past history of the arbitrations, Admiralty jurisdictions, and commissions on either side. On the 18th September the Dutch envoys reached Holland again after their two years' exertion, leaving only a secretary behind,

[1] Downing to Nicholas, Sept. 19, Holland, 166.

[2] Aitzema, iv. 902, v. 78; Wicquefort, iii. 81, 126; Japikse, 216 ff.; Lister, iii. 247, 264, 518; Temple, ii. 192; Holland, 166, ff. 1 and 113; Downing's papers, *passim.*

and in October Sir George Downing returned to England, leaving no one—not to return till September of the next year.[1] A year of silence, which we may use to study this loquacious ambassador, in whose mouth hovered, it may be, the arbitrament of peace or war.

George Downing, our ambassador at the Hague from December 1657 till August 1665, may be admitted to have been what the French diplomat Comminge called him, "un assez désagréable personnage", but his culpability as a public man has been exaggerated, and the father of Downing Street was a man of native force, charged with the thrust and enterprise of Puritanism on its material side. He was nephew to Governor John Winthrop of Massachusetts, spent his formative years in New England, and had even (though neither his English nor his Latin were convincing testimonials) graduated at the infant college of Harvard. His fortunes were made in the days of trouble after 1645, and we find him in turn schoolmaster at Barbados, a chaplain in Okey's regiment, scoutmaster to the Cromwellians in Scotland, and a member of Parliament. In 1654 he planted himself in the aristocracy by marrying Frances Howard of Naworth, and now he rose by parallel steps with his brother-in-law Charles Howard, captain of Cromwell's life-guard and one of his major-generals, in 1659 a Royalist conspirator, and at the Restoration Earl of Carlisle. And so the scoutmaster, who had three years before led a movement to crown Cromwell, in April 1660 made his peace with King Charles, obtaining confirmation of his dual appointments as ambassador and teller of the exchequer.

[1] Morrice's letter of recall, Sept. 12, Add. MSS. 22,919; Cal.S.P.D. 1663–64.

Like Monk, he approved his new rôle by zeal against his old comrades, and as Monk won eternal infamy by producing letters which led to the execution of Argyll, so the blackest blot on Downing's scutcheon is the unholy energy with which in 1662 he hunted down the regicides in hiding at Delft—Corbett, Barkstead, and Okey, the colonel under whom he had preached the holy war—shipping them off to die at Tyburn, as die they did that April, looking (by Pepys' surprised formula) "very cheerful". But Downing had another twenty-two years of life in him, wherein to think, if he so pleased, of Okey. Glimpses of him crackle in the memoirs; his alarming loquacity, his upright, ill-educated, legible hand, his stinginess and pride in saving his pennies, his kid gloves, and that grim house-full in Cambridgeshire—his old mother, his half-witted son, and on the hearth the still young scout-master, with £80,000 in the funds.

As a diplomat his shortcomings were portentous, and yet his rugged rascality strikes like the east wind after the scented languor of Whitehall. From personal arrogance even considerable diplomats have not always been immune, nor was Downing: "I concluded all the wars of the North", he once informed Clarendon, whom he deluged with accounts of the slights cast on His Majesty's representative at the Hague. His impertinence was unimaginable. He was good enough to assure de Witt that he would try to get good terms for him in the event of an Orange restoration, proposed to arrest in this friendly country the printers of tendencious pamphlets, and demanded the removal of certain Portuguese attachés. For all foreigners he had a contempt, but especially for Dutchmen, any one of whom he conceived could be bribed—a conviction in which he was to some extent warranted by his experience. In a public fracas with the Duke of Holstein nothing pleased him so much as the proper spirit of his footmen, to each of whom he gave a new hat and sword, "to encourage them to demean themselves like men".[1]

His diplomatic method was to be always on the offensive, to keep the sledge-hammer going, to push our case up to the verge of rupture, to fill the indictment. He lamented the poverty of the East India Company's list of "pretensions"; why did not the merchants of Scotland and the West country help to swell the London figures? We must render tit for tat, and force for force: "This mealie way", he told Arlington, "is not the means to hinder a warre". The African company must act; "God helpe them if they depend upon paper releifs, . . . what ever injuries the Dutch doe them, let them be sure to doe the Dutch greater". In fact, he despised the legitimate weapons of his craft. The "paper bullets" of Dutch propaganda in Scotland left him unmoved—but "I will not give 2d. for any paper security if they once finde themselves His Majesties masters in point of men of warre". His rôle, as he conceived it, was to apply this never-ceasing fomentation to Holland, but the one condition for success must be unfailing royal support. If that lapsed, the King's ministers abroad might as well "shut up shop"; "all I can say will be looked upon but as barking", but "if the King will stand by me, I make no doubt but to make them weary as well as I did formerly".[2]

[1] To Clarendon, June 21, '61, Clar. MSS. 104; April 8, '64, *ibid.* 107.
[2] To Nicholas, Feb. 24 and June 20, '62, Egerton MSS. 2538; to Arlington, Sept. 18, Holland, 167; and to Williamson, Sept. 11, '63, *ibid.*; to Clarendon, Nov. 18 and Sept. 30, '64, Clar. MSS. 108; Nov. 11, '61, *ibid.* 105.

He asked, in short, a free hand as the royal attorney, professing as he did that "it is not worth a rush to treate with any of their ministers here, or ambassadors abroad". His programme was to storm de Witt in his own country, by corrupting and dividing the States-General, by stirring up provincial feud, and playing upon Orangist passion. He demurred strongly to Clarendon's policy of 1661–62—that is, to drop the Orange cause until the treaty was safe—and his obstinacy in believing what he wished to be the fact contrasted in all this badly with the Chancellor's own moderation.[1]

Nevertheless, it would be unjust hastily to conclude either that Downing was wholly wrong-headed, or that he was in all ways anti-Dutch. He was full of the zeal for efficiency and belief in action, characteristic of the Puritan business man. Chartered companies and monopolies were suspect to him, for they meant routine, idleness, and high prices. His highest ambition was to make England the commercial leader of the world, and he had studied commerce like no other of our ambassadors. Our merchants, he repeated always, must be given convoy, without which their ships had to sacrifice freight to space for guns and crew, and if only we could get cheap navigation, "good-night Amsterdam". The Navigation Acts had hit the enemy hard in the West Indies and challenged them in the Baltic, but Swedes and Danes still held most of the latter market. We should encourage Dutch fishers to settle at Yarmouth, cut off Irish wool from Holland, use some energy in establishing the linen and china-clay industries, and overhaul our weights and measures. And

[1] To Clarendon, July 2, '61, *ibid.* 104; Clarendon to Downing, Aug. 16, '61 (Lister).

though he retained from old days something of the Puritan tradition, more than once recommending the cause of the Vaudois, his instinct reacted more keenly to any upsetting of the European balance as it affected his country, specially on its economic side. We must beware, he argued, how far we guarantee the Sound settlement of 1659–60, which might result in equal privileges for France, or how we show sympathy with Austria, or let our subjects take service with her, lest it embarrass our market in the Mohammedan world. He saw the supreme opening of the future in Spanish markets; France was getting too strong—"It's high time His Majesty were upon better terms with Spain"; we should nurse Scandinavia against Holland, and the German princes against France.[1] It is, perhaps, a lesson of history that ambassadors should not be kept in one place too long, and it may have been his Cromwellian experience as much as his temperament that led Downing to his rooted fallacy, that under no circumstance would de Witt fight us. He would continue "sailing between Scylla and Charybdy", "shuffle and cutt capers", but never make war; and the nearer the certainty of war, the more unhesitating became Downing's asseverance of its impossibility. The Dutch "dread a warre as the Divell", "their hearts goe pit-a-pat", it would break them financially, the fishing interests would not sacrifice themselves for directors of the East Indian Company, and so forth.[2] But the pitcher he shouldered so aggressively was to go to the well once too often.

Yet if we distinguish the man's method and men-

[1] For the above the sources are volumes 104-108 of the Clarendon MSS. *passim*, and Holland, 173.

[2] To Clarendon, Jan. 6, '62, Clar. MSS. 106; April 8, April 29, May 6, '64, *ibid.* 107; May 13 and Sept. 16, *ibid.* 108.

tality from his inmost policy and heart's desire, it can be said confidently that he neither desired this war nor consciously devised it. More particularly, after his return in September 1663, did he argue that if, as was our bounden duty, the Spanish Netherlands were to be saved from France, Holland was our natural rampart, since her own interests made her so, and that she would, if assured of support, resist the onward sweep of France.[1] The policy was an obvious one, and was in many Englishmen's minds; already the young enthusiast Temple was pressing it upon his early patron, Ormonde.[2] But whether this alternative policy was a real one—real, that is, on the facts of the international situation in 1663–64—deserves such examination as we can give it, for it goes to the root.

Steadfast resistance to France in the Netherlands must involve the league for which Gamarra was moving at the Hague, between England, Holland, and Spain, and nothing that transpired in these years made it probable. In spite of heavy defeat, in spite of peace tenders from London and Vienna, Spain was still mulishly fighting Portugal, and still her ill-paid infantry were being scraped together from Lombardy and Flanders to be thrown into that morass. Not only beyond the Line, but in the Mediterranean also, the ancient Anglo-Spanish feud burned merrily; still the Spaniards were helping Gaylan to blockade Tangier, still refusing our ships food or water at Port Mahon and Valencia, and the English were still foraying from Jamaica. The Hapsburgs were still at cross-purposes, and no Spanish envoy had yet reached Vienna. Nothing could be expected from the Emperor, for this

[1] To Clarendon, Feb. 10, '62, Jan. 8 and April 22, '64.
[2] Jan. 19, '63, Carte MSS. 47, f. 250.

summer the Turks advanced along the Danube to harry Styria. The payment of Austrian tribute to Constantinople, the presence of French troops to help Austria against the Turk and to back the Elector of Mainz against his rebel subjects, showed up the fatuity of German power.

But the deciding fact was the attitude of John de Witt. Of the diplomatic exchanges in process between the Hague and Paris from March 1663 to April 1664, this only need here be said, that the French alliance, so vital to the Pensionary's personal and political existence, was driving him to the wall. His *mémoires* for D'Estrades rang the changes upon cantonment of Belgium as a free republic, instigation of revolt against Spain, and outright partition with France. Try though he did to make Louis drop his claim of "devolution", and dreading the contiguity of a French frontier, he returned more and more to the conviction that only some arrangement with France, prior to the King of Spain's death, could save Holland, for whom a bold policy might win Ostend and the complete mastery of the Scheldt. A European league of resistance appeared to him a chimera; Spain he thoroughly detested, and her alliance would mean a crushing financial burden. He could not believe that England would ever oppose France; what good could come out of England, that monument of caprice, false to all expectation and even to her own interest, as the sale of Dunkirk and the Portuguese marriage showed?[1] It is, then, impossible to detect in de Witt's proceedings any serious intention of meeting half-way the tentative approaches which, at the end of 1663, Downing brought from Clarendon.

---

[1] Mignet, i. 184-270; Legrelle, i. 83-97; Dollot, 155 *et seq.*; Fruin, ii. 539 and appendix; D'Estrades, ii. *passim.*

True, he surprised our minister by a new cordiality, but he none the less passed Clarendon's points on to the French, and was bitterly resisting among his own colleagues the scheme of an *entente* with the Hapsburgs which he commended to Downing.[1]

The growing coldness between England and France, noticeable (as we have seen) since Arlington's advent to office, would require stronger stimulants than this if it was to grow into an anti-French system. As it was, the news from Spain was lamentable, and it was conceived that we were not pressed for time, for our envoys reported that France was disbanding her troops and had postponed the idea of war. In view of the Flemish problem it also seemed incredible that Louis would be loyal to Holland, and we still had hopes that he would restore Orange.[2] Finally, any alternative policy had to reckon with the controversies dividing England from Holland, and the growing concentration of English opinion on that single issue.

Twenty-year-old *Bona Aventura* and *Esperanza* were still skipping like young rams, reinforced now by the *Leopard*, the *Hopewell*, and other comparative infants. The Dutch had not fulfilled their pledges; Pulo Run was still in their hands, and the English were ceasing to believe in the existence of the "orders" sent to the governor of Batavia. The East and West Indian Companies of Holland had already condemned out of hand the English "pretensions", and when in August 1664 their own list at last appeared, not only was it found to be stuffed with absurdities — like damages done by Cromwell's ships off Ostend — but

[1] Downing to Clarendon, Oct. 23, Clar. MSS. 107, and Jan. 8, '64, *ibid.*; D'Estrades, Oct. 11 and Nov. 28, '63; Legrelle, i. 83; Mignet, i. 265, 261.

[2] B. Gascoyne to Arlington, March 9, '64, France, 118; Arlington to Holles, May 9, '64, *ibid.*; Downing to Clarendon, March 18, Clar. MSS. 107.

the atmosphere had grown far too hot for "amicable conference".[1]

At least as regards their attitude to a *règlement* for future trade, it is impossible to acquit the Dutch of calculated insincerity. The conferences held with Downing in February 1664 staged the same principles as those which Thurloe had resisted. The cases of *Leopard* and *Hopewell* from the East, and of *Charles* and *James* from the Guinea coast, involved the Dutch monopoly contracts and their abuse of "blockade"; their rule, said Downing, was *"mare liberum* in the British seas, but *mare clausum* on the coast of Africa and in the East Indies". His own proposal to assign monopoly ports to each side being dropped, he reluctantly accepted de Witt's proposal to frame a *règlement* to avoid future controversy, and in the draft which he submitted in September challenged the whole Dutch fabric. That the English should, as he proposed, be free to trade with Indians who were at war with the Dutch, and be wholly immune from search in those waters, would be worse for Holland than losing a campaign; with the demand, refused by Downing months earlier, that any marine treaty should apply to Europe also, they terminated a farcical negotiation which they had not meant to succeed.[2]

A swarm of minor complications heated each side still further. The absence, for two years, of any Dutch ambassador not only offended the King but removed one check on the commercial warfare which covered the globe. There were fishery Bills in Parliament, bounties for herring boats, and safeguarding of linen, while the

---

[1] Aitzema, iv. 1114; E.I.C. Minutes, 347; *ibid.* 164-7, 52; Charles II to Downing, Oct. 30, '63, Lister; Downing to Clarendon, Aug. 26, '64, Clar. MSS. 108.

[2] Japikse, 325, 378, and app. xvi.; Lister, iii. 286; Downing to Clarendon, Oct. 7, '64, Clar. MSS. 108; Khan, 121; Colenbrander, i. 126.

Dutch in Downing's absence prohibited the entrance of our dressed cloth. One struggle raged for control of the Persian Gulf customs, and another in the concessions at Constantinople. The Secretary's office was inundated with reports from our spies, moving uneasily from taverns at Middelburg to taverns at Antwerp, turning a dishonest penny by denouncing rebels. Orangist agents applied their stimulus as of old, and Van Ruyven, most experienced of our secret-service men, forwarded copies of the debates that showed up the divisions in the States-General. Nervously our government watched the least move of the exiles. Was not Cornet Joyce, best known as of Holmby House, at Rotterdam? Desborough was at Arnhem; Ludlow was somewhere, but where? Arms were being shipped for Scotland, and godly ministers arriving at Yarmouth.[1]

The clash of two racial ambitions, as of two economic systems, ranged from these small matters of obstruction and jealousy to the large-scale collision which we are now to see in Northern Africa, Portugal, America, and the Gold Coast.

In Constantinople, Aleppo, and Smyrna, English and Dutch consuls and merchants were fighting for supremacy—a balanced fight, where the English had the greater volume of trade, the Dutch the larger ships and the lower freights. But the oils, wines, or currants of the Levant were bought dear, any Mediterranean trade being hazardous while the sea-rovers of Algiers, Tripoli, and Tunis were left immune. Our small craft were pounced upon at dawn by Mohammedan dhows; even East-Indiamen were held up and robbed of their silver, and the Algerines' "right of search", nominally

[1] Aitzema, iv. 1119; Japikse, 271; Holland, 177 *passim*; Downing to Clarendon, May 7, '64, Clar. MSS. 107.

for renegades, extended in fact to anything they fancied. Treaties wrung from them by naval commanders, Lawson or de Ruyter, and duly ratified by the Porte, were found to be worthless, and if ever commercial peoples should have combined against a common scourge, here was the time, But the English refused all suggestion for common action, believing that the Dutch had instigated the Algerines, a belief akin to the advice tendered by Arlington and Downing that we could damage the Dutch with the Turk by hinting at their readiness to assist Austria.[1] The Portuguese problem embraced more vital British interests— a check on the Dutch conquest of Portuguese India, and on their exploitation of Brazil—and even before his marriage added an obligation of honour, Charles warned Holland he would resent an attack on Portugal and offered his mediation. The Dutch accepted this in March 1661, and promised to keep him in touch with the negotiation which had been for eighteen months proceeding with Miranda, Portuguese envoy at the Hague.[2]

This was the situation when Downing reached the Hague in June 1661, to find them on the eve of concluding a treaty detrimental to British interests and inconsistent with our treaty with Portugal just approved and signed on the 23rd of the same month. He made two particular objections—the grant of pre-emption to the Dutch over the salt supply from Setubal (twenty miles south of Lisbon) and the concession in general terms of the same commercial privileges as those given to England; for Cromwell's treaty (now confirmed) had

[1] *Finch Papers*, i. *passim* ; Harris, i. 198; Downing to Clarendon, Nov. 27, '63, Clar. MSS. 107; to Nicholas, Sept. 19, '62, Holland, 166; Clarendon to Winchelsea, Dec. 29, '63, Clar. MSS. 81; Japikse, 300.

[2] Japikse, 92, 115; E.I.C. Minutes, xvi. 93, 107.

secured priority for English shipping.[1] Our ambassador rose to his full activity, and aided by an angry
autograph letter from the King[2] wrung from Miranda a
pledge to sign nothing without his concurrence. Merely
to suspend the negotiation, without an armistice, would
give Holland more time in which to swallow up Portuguese India, and Downing's recommendation was a
truce, "whereby the Portuguese will for the present
save their moneyes, the English their trade, and the
designs of the Holland East Indye Company be
stopped". It was too late; on the 6th August, in full
concert with de Witt, Miranda signed. All that
Downing had been able to win was a separate article,
providing that clauses found to be at variance with the
Anglo-Portuguese treaty should be nullified, and this,
he hoped, would "cutt out some work" for Fanshawe at
Lisbon. English indignation was heaped on the head
of Miranda, but Fanshawe reported the condition of
Portugal as so hopeless, that in January 1662 Charles,
expressing an academic hope of compensation in
other quarters, withdrew his objection to ratification.
Renewed war between Portugal and Holland would,
Clarendon said, bring "a thousand mischiefs", and
with infinite reluctance, with disobedience to orders
that called down a sharp reproof, Downing had to
co-operate.[3]

But his forebodings found their echo in India, where
the long delay involved by this English pressure,[4] and

[1] Downing to Clarendon, June 6 and 14, '61, Clarendon to Downing, Jan. 3,
'62—Clar. MSS. 104.

[2] Corrected draft, June 14, Egerton MSS. 2537, f. 347.

[3] Correspondence of Downing and Clarendon, Clar. MSS. 104; Prestage,
passim; Japikse, 233 ff.; Aitzema; Downing to Nicholas, Aug. 12, n.s., Egerton
MSS. *loc. cit.* f. 368.

[4] The treaty was ratified by Portugal, May 24, '62; at the Hague, Nov. 4;
published at Batavia, March '63.

by Dutch provincial divisions, gave the Dutch Company their chance. While the diplomats at Lisbon and the Hague were haggling, they finished off the coast of Malabar; Quilion, Cranganur, Cochin, and Cannanore fell between November 1661 and February 1663, the pepper ports and pearl fisheries were in their hands, and they were said to be inciting the great Mogul Aurungzebe against Goa. Despite annual protests Portugal could never get her losses in India recouped; in Europe Holland was ready to stock her with munitions against Spain, but in Western India they closed the door. The maxims of trade they there applied we have seen in the case of the *Leopard* and *Hopewell*, and henceforward our interest in the Portuguese settlements was caught up in the wider grievances accumulating in every sea.[1]

The conquest of the New Netherlands, rechristened in May 1664 as New York, was planned by Cromwell, and only deferred by the peace made in the Protectorate's first year. Virginia, New England, and Maryland had all received charters from the Stuarts embracing the banks of the Hudson and Delaware actually in Dutch possession, and no English government yet had admitted the Dutch title; it was "only in the mapps", Downing blandly told de Witt, that any such country as "New Netherlands" existed. It was, indeed, a case rather of penetration than conquest, for New York had been from the first a most cosmopolitan colony, from 1640 the growing element being the English, who spread over the border from Connecticut and now held about half of Long Island. An "English secretary" in the Dutch government implicitly admitted this Anglicization, and by the Restoration many town-

[1] Clar. MSS. 75, f. 404; Holland, 167, f. 146; Rec. Hollande, 1, 281.

ships were divided between English and Dutch factions. From murderous adventurers like John Scott
and New England experts like Samuel Maverick,
advices reached Clarendon and the Plantations committee that the time was ripe.

The English ministry clearly viewed the question
less as one of attacking the Dutch than as part of a
much-needed reorganization of the American colonies,
whose boundaries were uncertain, their politics rabid,
and their administration weak. The Navigation Act
could not be enforced while the Dutch held Manhattan
Bay, which separated New England from the southern
colonies; our customs officers reckoned that £10,000 a
year was lost by Dutch shipments of tobacco; New
Amsterdam, so Clarendon heard, was in undesirable
communication with the regicides' refuge at New
Haven. It was not contemplated that the conquest
would be difficult, for the Dutch West India Company
had scandalously neglected New Amsterdam, and
in January 1664, just when the States-General were
waking to the danger, a committee of Council, including William Coventry, recommended immediate action.
In March the Duke of York was named proprietor of a
huge belt between the Connecticut and the Delaware,
and in the middle of May the royal commissioners left
Portsmouth, empowered primarily to correct the administration of all the colonies, but incidentally to expel the
Dutch "encroachers". Their leader, Richard Nicolls,
was a Scots cavalier of the best type—humane, hard-
headed, and competent, and on the 29th August he
received the surrender of New York without trouble,
rather from its civilian inhabitants than from its plucky
governor, old one-legged Peter Stuyvesant. The
rumours of this exploit, long current and gathering

weight, were officially confirmed in Europe half-way through October.[1]

WEST AFRICA

"And pray, what is Cape Verde? a stinking place",[2] said Charles II to the Dutch ambassador; "is this of such importance to make so much ado about?"

The Guinea question which Charles alluded to so airily was, in point of fact, the proximate cause of war, and embraced most of the controversies which made it inevitable. Here, as in India, English and Dutch were contesting the spoil of an ancient Portuguese dominion, but with roots in this case going deeper, and with a history older and more involved. Since Henry VIII's later years, French, Dutch, English, Danes, and Swedes had been struggling in West Africa for mercantile empire, which here found in full perfection the two bases of its system—slaves and gold. On a regular stream of African slave labour hung the very exist-ence of the West Indies, of Brazil, Guiana, and the tobacco and sugar industries; at this moment English and Dutch diplomacy were competing at Madrid for Assiento contracts which would cement the trade wrung from Portugal by their adventurers. As for the gold, let alone its cash value, it made the nucleus of a dual trade to India *via* the Gold Coast.

The facts of title to this El Dorado were as vague as in America or in India, resting upon contracts with illiterate savages or the *obiter dicta* of corrupt factors, and the claims from either side were correspondingly portentous. Our Royal African Company was thus

[1] Doyle, *The Middle Colonies* (1907); Osgood, *The American Colonies in the Seventeenth Century*, iii.; Channing, *History of the U.S.A.*, ii.; Cal. Col. 1661–68; Colenbrander, i. 125; Japikse, 397.

[2] "Using these very words"—interview of Charles II and Van Goch, 6 P.M., Oct. 11, '64—Eng. copy, Holland, 172, f. 298.

in 1662 granted the whole coast from Sallee to the Cape of Good Hope, and twice the next year the Dutch governor-general warned off our naval officers, claiming the whole coast for his country in virtue of conquest.[1]

Actually the right to either section of what was loosely called Guinea was intricate and antique, for in each the two nations had planted factories simultaneously, and side by side. The northern area, a hundred miles south of Cape Verde, turned on the great Gambia River, which was navigable for two hundred and fifty miles from the sea. Off Cape Verde the Hollanders had in 1617 fortified the island of Goree; in the Gambia they had occupied during 1659–60 some forts belonging to the Duke of Courland, while twenty miles up-stream the English had long settled at Fort James.

Seven hundred miles south, on a harbourless surf-lashed shore, the gold-bearing reefs ran down to the sea. Here, just east of Cape Coast Castle, an English factory rose in 1618 at Cormantine, to be followed in 1624 by the Dutch next door at Mouree, and in 1637 to the west at Elmina, henceforward their seat of government. All title to "Cape Corso" itself was soaked in contradiction. The Dutch said they had bought it from Denmark, which the Danes denied; our East India Company swore that the Dutch had twice over, in 1659–61, burned their godowns and factories. It was one of Downing's favourite schemes to make common cause with Denmark, perhaps by buying the Danes' right, and in 1664 he was in conclave with their foreign minister, Hannibal Sehested.[2]

[1] Cal. Col. *loc. cit. passim.*; Holland, 167, f. 279—Valkenburg's protest to Captain Stokes of the *Marmaduke*—Sept. 13, 1663.

[2] Cal. Col. *loc. cit.*, July 26, '62; Downing to Clarendon, Aug. 19, n.s., '61, Clar. 104; Oct. 23, '63; March 25, '64; and memorial of Feb. 8, *ibid.* 107; Downing to Arlington, Dec. 4, '63, Holland, 168; for Sehested, *ibid.* 169, f. 71; Aitzema, v. 213, 364; Japikse, 365; E.I.C. Minutes, 25, 78, 287.

On this rich carcase, riddled by damp heat, rains, and fever, where dividends were won at the price of young factors' lives, an undeclared war of peculiar atrocity raged without ceasing. Nowhere was so marked the weak hold of seventeenth-century governments over their agents; nowhere so transparent the artifice whereby they shuffled off their responsibility on to trading companies; nowhere blacker guilt. A long series of "regrettable incidents" dragged West Africa into the light. In March 1661 Robert Holmes first came on the scene — a swaggering, bickering Irishman, friend of York and Buckingham. His challenge to Cape Verde and firing on the Gambia forts were disavowed, with technical veracity, by our government, but when a Secretary of State was writing of the "good news" to be expected from Guinea, Holmes neither had reason to fear, nor did he incur, anything more drastic than nominal reprimand.[1] But the Dutch took speedy reparation. In May their negro allies sacked the English factory at Capa Corso. In August the East-Indiaman *Merchant Delight* was seized off Elmina, and her crew turned adrift—an epic ship, rechristened now the *Arms of Amsterdam* and later recaptured by the English in the West Indies. At the new year, 1661–62, Dutch factors of Cape Verde tried bribery on our forts in the Gambia, and stimulated the chief of Barra to the attack by gifts of linen and brandy.[2]

The next case became classic. In the autumn of 1662 the African Company's ship *Charles*, master, William Crowford of Wapping, was forcibly prevented from

---

[1] Clarendon to Downing, July 26, Downing to Clarendon, Aug. 5 (Clar. 104); Holland, 164, f. 102; Aitzema, iv. 756; Japikse, 168, note.
[2] E.I.C. Minutes, 286; Cal. Col. 65, 91, 213; Holland, 169, f. 82.

trading by Dutch warships, who followed her from port to port, and drove off the native canoes. The later Dutch defence at the Hague comprehended, first, a claim of sovereignty, and second, a doctrine of blockade; no forces, they argued, could act continuously in that climate by land, and hence no blockade could be complete. In April 1664 de Witt was suggesting that the matter be referred to the treaty commissioners, and when at last he mentioned reparation, it was hopelessly intertwined with graver conflicts.[1]

Our effort to break this monopoly system, which we had earlier met with in India, grew more intense with the full development of the Royal African Company in 1663. Its president was the Duke of York, the King himself had £5000 invested, its shareholders included the City princes—Backwell and Povey, Crispe and Noel—and most of the rising politicians like Arlington. Its active secretary was Ellis Leighton, with whom we shall meet in a more sinister field, and contact was close between Whitehall and its office in Broad Street. Its directors declared later that they had organized eighteen factories in 1663–64, sold £150,000 worth of goods, and secured a Spanish assiento for 3500 slaves a year. But when their convoy reached the Coast in the summer of 1663, they found Cape Coast Castle, their destined centre, in Dutch hands, and Cormantin beleaguered. The English bulwark among the natives, John Cabessa, was treacherously betrayed; a remarkable negro, whose ambition was to visit King Charles, and who cut his throat a year later rather than fall into the hands of de Ruyter. From every point came the

---

[1] Affidavits of Crowford, Holland, 166, and Cal. Col. 113; Downing's memorial of Sept. 17, '63, Holland, 167; Downing to Clarendon, April 1, '64 (Clar. 107); Japikse, 287, 383.

same story, that the Dutch were firing on all canoes that traded with the English.[1]

Our Company determined to strike hard. Borrowing three royal ships, late in September they sent out the redoubtable Holmes, armed with orders to protect British traders, if need be by force. The result might have been predicted. Cape Verde and Goree fell to us in January 1664, and by mid-May the whole Gold Coast, save the Dutch capital Elmina, was ours. It is true that, under later examination, Holmes declared that he had respected private property and only acted in self-defence; true, too, amid all the hard swearing, that he had no orders from the Crown[2] to take the offensive. But the precise channel of offence hardly mattered to the Dutch, and it is certain that our official circles had expected some such event.[3] It was the middle of July when certain intelligence of Holmes' exploit reached the Hague—the stage when Downing had just returned (after two months' leave) to urge the "pretensions", and when Nicolls was on the Atlantic bound for New York.[4] The task of statesmanship, loaded now with the arrears of ten years' rivalry, was proving too heavy to be carried further. There were signs that war would be welcome in England, if not with enthusiasm, yet with resignation to unavoidable necessity. The Commons' committee on trade, acting upon the great Companies' petitions, found unani-

[1] Cal. Col. *passim*; Downing's memorial, Aug. 4, '64 (Clar. 108).

[2] So Clarendon, Clar. 104, Oct. 28; Coventry, Nov. 27, Cal.S.P.D., 1664; Coventry in conversation to Pepys, May 29; Charles to Madame, Jan. '65 (Ady).

[3] "We expect to hear what is done between us in Guinea—something material no question, and we hope the best"—Williamson to Fanshawe, April 28 (Heathcote).

[4] Dutch memorials of May 13 and July 9, Aitzema; Holland, 169; Downing to Clarendon, July 22 (Clar. 108).

mously that the Dutch were the chief obstruction to
commerce, and claimed damages of some £1,200,000,
and its composition fairly reflected the "country" as
well as the Court.[1] French and English evidence agrees
that the pressure for war, or at least signal reparation,
from Parliament, merchants, and seafaring classes,
was extreme; the old Cromwellian captains volunteered for service, and by the autumn, despite the
monstrous corruption of the pay and victualling de-
partments, and the hated pressgang, we find something
like national passion. Young Michael Pack, otherwise
unknown to us, sticks in the memory; he asked to go
as midshipman, for "the Dutch did slay his father with
a cannon shot, and he hath some mind now to see if
he can have his pennyworths of them for it".[2] It was
thus amid applause from seamen, "transported with
animosity, hope, and drink",[3] that the joint resolution
of the two Houses was taken to the King on the
27th April. It should have disabused de Witt of the
fallacy that Downing's corrupt malignity accounted for
the perverseness of his government, while it assured
Charles that he could find a national backing. Yet it
is certain that the rulers of England in the summer of
1664 neither expected nor desired a war. Their envoys
and spies in Holland continued to delude them; to
represent that the north-eastern provinces would not
fight in the interest of Holland and Zealand, that
Münster and Brandenburg would invade the Dutch,
and that the mailed fist would bring them to concession. "Go on in Guinea," cried Downing—"if you

[1] C. J., March 26, April 21-2; *Parl. Hist.* iv. 292; Pepys, April 1-2;
Japikse, 314.
[2] Charles to Madame, June (Ady); Comminge to Lionne, Feb. 28 (Jusserand);
Cal.S.P.D., 1664–65, 11 and 44; Clarendon, ii. 422.
[3] Brodrick to Ormonde, April 23 (Carte MSS. 215).

bang them there they will be very tame." The peace
could thus be kept, at Dutch expense.[1]

Our politicians, too, were well aware that war would
again cripple our convalescent budget, and bring
grave risks of Puritan trouble and Scottish rebellion.
The veterans Clarendon and Southampton opposed it
with vehemence at all stages, emphasizing the danger
of isolation and the better opening that would come
when Spain and France renewed their contest.[2]
Ormonde and the bishops were in the same category.
William Coventry, blamed in later years by Clarendon,
in fact faced war with uneasiness, predicting our merchants' losses and asking ruefully, "when all the poor
of London are starving for want of fuel, what then"?[3]
Nor does there seem to be any evidence, except Clarendon's posthumous prejudice, to connect Arlington with
the outbreak; all his diplomatic inclination must have
gone against it, and in July anyhow his attitude was
conciliatory.[4] The royal response to Parliament tends
to the same conclusion; not only were their offers of
May to live and die in His Majesty's service so curtly
received that Dutch East India stock rose 15 per
cent, but they were promptly prorogued, and repro-
rogued by successive stages till the 24th November.
When in June a Dutch ambassador finally appeared,
in the shape of the weak and vapouring Van Goch,
he received assurances that Downing would soon

[1] D'Estrades to Louis XIV, June 5, n.s.; Downing to Arlington, Sept. 23
(Holland, 172); "Bucquoy's" reports, *ibid.*; Downing to Clarendon, April 15
and Sept. 16 (Clar. 107-8).
[2] Pepys, March 20, 1669; Clarendon, ii. 373-435; so Clarendon to Ormonde—
"what I think of the warr, you know; I pray God put an end, or take me out of
the world"—Dec. 11, '65 (Carte, 47, 101).
[3] Pepys, April 13 and May 29; his memorandum for Falmouth, Dec. 10, Add.
MSS. 32,094.
[4] Aitzema, v. 88.

return, and that Holmes, if found guilty, would be punished.[1]

While Van Goch confirmed in Charles the impression stereotyped by Downing, that Holland would not fight, across the water de Witt harboured, till the end of August, a like delusion. But his was not a mind that left things to chance, and whosesoever the primary responsibility, the Dutch took the decisive step which made retreat towards peace almost impossible. Their fleet was first at sea this year, and their armament ahead of ours. Our admiralty noticed in April that de Ruyter greatly outnumbered Lawson in the Straits; Tromp went off to meet the East-Indiamen returning by the Orkneys: their dockyards were working on Sundays, and working overtime. In May the States resolved to put thirty ships in the Channel, while Sandwich's squadron that issued in July was little more than the ordinary "summer guard", and on the 25th of that month, after hearing about Holmes, the Dutch promised to lend twelve men-of-war to their West India Company. Following on this, inflamed by reports of English reinforcements for Cape Verde and by Downing's refusal to treat Guinea in isolation from older grievances, on the 11th August they took an action which was to prove in Coventry's words "the cause"—the proximate cause, that is—of the war, by ordering de Ruyter from the Mediterranean to Guinea to recapture by force what Holmes had taken.[2] This resolution was long hidden from the English; the fact was denied point-blank by de Witt to Downing, more

[1] Aitzema, v. 87, specially Van Goch's interview with Arlington, July 2; Japikse, 345, 423; Ady, 163.
[2] Fruin, ii. 540, note; Pontalis, i. 332; Pepys to York, Add. MSS. 32,094, April 24; Downing to Clarendon, May 6 (Clar. 107); Japikse, 355; Coventry to Arlington, Nov. 24, Cal.S.P.D.

circuitously by Van Goch to the King, and only
brought home to our government by Lawson's warning in October.[1] Our step of the 13th August, to equip
twelve ships for Guinea, was thus taken in ignorance
of the enemy's decisive measure; it was meant, Charles
explained to both Dutch and French, as a reply to
their alarming armaments and their resolution to
support their West India Company. Nothing, at least,
could have been more open than the warnings given
to Van Goch by Charles, York, and Archbishop
Sheldon, that if their squadron sailed for Guinea, we
should take it as a "rupture". Forcible reprisals of this
sort, the English argued, would violate the fourteenth
article of the treaty of 1662, and were, in Arlington's
words, "no other than club-law".[2] The stage reached
in late September was, then, a serious one. De Witt
demanded unconditional restoration in Guinea—without which he would not hear of our older "pretensions"
—and a pledge of naval inactivity. England, on the
other hand, declared the sending of a Dutch fleet
to Guinea as tantamount to war, stuck to their old
grievances, insisted on "freedom of trade", and would
not condemn Holmes unheard; that, Downing told de
Witt, was "the way of treating their footmen".[3]

In October the deadlock hardened further, with
news of our seizure of New York and of de Ruyter's
voyage. On the 11th Lawson reached Portsmouth, to
confirm his intelligence that de Ruyter, whom he had
spoken off Cadiz, had sailed south, it was thought for

---

[1] Downing to Arlington, Sept. 23 (Holland, 172); Lawson to Fanshawe, Sept.
27 (Heathcote).

[2] Arlington to Fanshawe, Sept. 29 (Arl. ii.); Downing to Arlington, same date,
Holland, 172; to Clarendon, Aug. 5, Clar. 107; Aitzema, v. 87.

[3] Interviews of Charles and Van Goch, Sept. 21—of de Witt and Downing,
Sept. 23 and 28—(Holland, 172).

Guinea, with full stores, and on the 18th Charles told Van Goch that, if this were true, he would be "juggled with" no longer. Upward movements on the Amsterdam Bourse and gloom in English naval opinion introduced Downing's definite message on the 6th December, that de Ruyter's orders were to reconquer Guinea, and then cross the Atlantic to attack Barbados and North America.[1]

There is a stage that follows diplomatic feverishness before it touches the crisis of war, and this had been reached. Only negation came out of the November-December conferences at the Hague. Neither de Witt nor Clarendon, the head of the English peace party, could yield on the major questions of Guinea and New York, and little reality marked the Dutch attitude on minor matters. Their demand that the commercial *règlement* should be extended to Europe consisted ill with de Witt's suggestion that war should be confined to the colonies, as both these proposals did with the orders sent after de Ruyter to attack the King's ships if they impeded him—the Dutch refusing to accept the plea that Holmes had acted without authority from the Crown. Their final conditions, drawn up early in January, were complete restoration in America and Africa, even of Holmes' captures of 1661, and a *règlement* embracing Europe.[2]

Allowing for the greater precision and purpose of de Witt, the sentiment of each government was much the same, and the successive steps taken by the English tell sufficiently the whole story. By November we may assume Charles to have decided that neither honour nor

---

[1] Heathcote, *loc. cit.*; Pepys, Oct. 12; Japikse, 412, 460; de Witt to Downing, Oct. 21, Holland, 172; Clarendon to Downing, Oct. 28, Clar. 104; Downing to Clarendon, Nov. 4 and Dec. 6, Clar. 108.

[2] Japikse, 420, 432, 469; Charles to Comminge, Oct. 16 (France, 119).

pocket could stomach a retreat, and that the Dutch must pay his expenses—either through an indemnity in peace, or war forays on their trade.[1] Some fighting would now, as Clarendon put it, be "the better husbandry", and in such an underhand, wasting war, it was believed that we could last the longest. But the door would not finally be closed while hope lasted of any remunerative settlement. The royal speech on opening Parliament in November argued that the real culprit was the Dutch West India Company, and when the hero Holmes reached London he was imprisoned for two months pending examination.[2]

Yet it was certain that the English would not make peace, save on terms which no Dutch government could accept—the liquidation of the pretensions, an indemnity, even the surrender of Sluys and Flushing as guarantee towns.[3] From November onwards the steps taken on each side indicated that the pressure was reaching its maximum. Each cancelled sailing orders for Guinea, massed their fleet in home waters, and laid an embargo on shipping. In November the English began a war of reprisals, justified by reference to de Ruyter's seizures in Africa, and at the New Year had taken over one hundred ships, whose miserable crews besieged Van Goch's house at Chelsea. December brought decision nearer still. Commissioners for the sick and wounded took over the Savoy Hospital; the Forest of Dean and Alice Holt heard their best timbers crashing; pressgangs were redoubled. Warnings

---

[1] Downing to Clarendon, Sept. 30 (Clar. 108); Clarendon to Downing, Oct. 28 (Lister); Sandwich to Arlington, Oct. 31, Cal.S.P.D.; Aitzema, v. 94.

[2] Downing to Arlington, Jan. 24, '65 (Japikse, appendix); Arlington to Downing, Feb. 6 (Barbour).

[3] Japikse, 436; Urk. xii. 622; Treaty Papers, misc. 73.

not to touch Holland goods issued to Hamburg and the Hanse, and on the 19th our admiral, Allin, began war in Europe by attacking their Smyrna convoy off Cadiz.[1]

Before this state of things was regularized by the English declaration of war on the 4th March, another long interval elapsed. It is not to be ascribed to the King's effort (a rôle in which Charles depicted himself to the French) to escape from a warlike Parliament; for his nearest counsellors were hoping to "blind the Dutch a little longer", and if the Dutch actually tried bribes on Clarendon and Downing, they cannot have expected anything better than delay.[2] On the major issues neither nation budged an inch, though the Dutch well knew that Parliament had given two and a half millions, and though the English might well dread both diplomatic isolation and internal disorder. On the contrary, both supported the stakes already played overseas by their advance guard of sailors and traders. By February it was known that de Ruyter had taken every port on the Gold Coast except Cape Coast Castle. Meantime the English induced the Duke of Courland to surrender his interest in the Gambia, "in exchange" for the island of Tobago in the Antilles, half occupied though it was by Dutch settlers. Modyford, our governor at Jamaica, was commended for his plan to root the enemy out of all the islands, and was issuing commissions to buccaneers, who proposed to pounce on Curaçao. Governor Nicolls of New York was holding a convention to frame laws for our new colony.

[1] Downing to Clarendon, Dec. 23, Col. i. 148; Aitzema, v. 334; Allin to Fanshawe, Dec. 25, Cal.S.P.D.

[2] Comminge to Louis XIV, Dec. 22 (Japikse); Louis to D'Estrades, Feb. 13; W. Coventry to Arlington, Nov. 24, S.P.D.

England, like Holland, employed the lull of winter to sow propaganda and seek alliances. To put ourselves right with Europe, and in particular with France, it was vital to prove that Holland was the aggressor, and Downing's exposition of our case in the questions of Guinea and Amboyna was therefore issued in translations at Madrid and Paris. A new era in our diplomacy began with the despatch of Fitzhardinge to Paris in November, with the enlarged powers sent the same month to Henry Coventry at Stockholm, with the renewed urgency of Fanshawe at Madrid for a truce with Portugal, and the invitation pressed upon Brandenburg to form a German league and avenge the wrongs done to the Orange house.[1]

Upon the success of this preparation the moment of declaring war, its scope, and its fate, must depend. But the war itself, involving the future of two maritime empires, could be staved off no longer; the guns, levelled so long and so often in hope of intimidating the enemy, were going off of themselves. Poor humanity was already being caught up and broken in this whirlwind. Black John Cabessa was cutting his throat rather than surrender to de Ruyter's black allies. Hundreds of British seamen were starving at Amsterdam, or taking Dutch service to keep body and soul together. Lawson's flagship, the *London*, blew up in the Thames on the 7th March with three hundred men; fifty widows already to wring the kind heart of Mr. Commissioner Evelyn.

Both King and people were engaged; "the world", said Henry Coventry, "will take us either for very weak

---

[1] Downing to Arlington, Holland, 172, f. 107; Holles to the same, Dec. 31 and Feb. 11, France, 119-20; Arlington to Fanshawe, Dec. 22, Arl. ii.; Coventry to Arlington, Nov. 30, Sweden, 5; Brandt to Great Elector, Dec. 30, Urk. xii.

soldiers or very strong Christians if we make peace with them".[1] Such a peace had for the time being passed out of possibility, despite the efforts of Louis XIV, the strongest Christian king.

[1] To Arlington, March 15 (Sweden, 5).

CHAPTER IV

THE DUTCH WAR AND THE SEARCH FOR ALLIES
1664–1666

THE outbreak of war was delayed till the middle of 1665 while either party sought to win the alliance of France. War came, but still France hesitated, and for yet another year flatly contradictory reports from our ambassadors at Paris and the Hague reflected a conflict within the mind of Louis XIV.[1] Beyond, and embracing, this collision of Anglo-Dutch commerce lay two dangers to the peace of Europe—left in process of solution by fifty years of war—the Spanish Succession and the Baltic balance of power. The settlement made five years earlier, by the treaties of Oliva and the Pyrenees, already showed signs of collapse. Friendly relations between France and Spain had proved impossible to maintain; on the other hand, Madrid and Vienna were at last coming together. In November 1664 a new and chauvinist governor, Castel Rodrigo, took over the Spanish Netherlands, and his first action was to ask the loan of Austrian troops. That same autumn the warlike Bishop of Münster, representing the territorial enemies of Holland, appeared at Vienna to discuss with Leopold, who was seeking to dissolve the League of

[1] Downing to Clarendon, Jan. 27, Clar. 108; Holles to Arlington, Dec. 3, France, 119.

the Rhine, the basis of an anti-French coalition. A few months earlier the Peace of Vasvar had for the moment relieved Austria of her Turkish war, and to the undisguised nervousness of France and Holland the princes of Germany were free to look to the west. To the north Sweden was fretting at French patronage of Catholic Poland, and offended at the French arms sent to help the Elector of Mainz against the Protestant city of Erfurt; it was as yet uncertain whether the Great Elector's claim upon certain Dutch fortresses would swamp his zeal for the Protestant religion; and both these rival Powers were looking askance at the Russian pressure upon Poland. So the circle widened, as the stone thrown into the torrid waters of Guinea sent a last ripple into ice-bound Archangel.[1]

Charles II, deceived perhaps by the very intricacy of French interests, was convinced that the worst he need expect from Louis was neutrality. His envoy, Fitzhardinge, reckoned by the French as their best friend in England after St. Albans, had returned in November delighted with the civility shown him in Paris, and Madame, ever sanguine, contributed to the same impression. Charles argued that, since the Dutch were so transparently the aggressor, Louis was freed from his treaty obligations; if France made difficulties he hinted that other Powers were ready to help us.[2]

He should, before this, have been disillusioned by the mediation offered by the French in July 1664 and repeated, more sharply, in October; though holding out hopes of reparation for proved damage, they invited him to restore Holmes' African captures and to confine

[1] Mignet, i. 323; Urk. ix. 61, 614; Pagès, 104; Downing to Clarendon, Oct. 7, Clar. 108; Holles to Arlington, Oct. 12, France, 119; Carlisle to Charles II, Sweden, 5, f. 152.

[2] Colenbrander, i. 205; Charles to Madame, Jan. 5 (Ady).

the war, if it must come, to the colonies.[1] Late in November the wise Ruvigni[2] came to shatter the day-dream infused by Fitzhardinge, and to explain that Louis would protect Holland against aggression; in December Comminge presented the first of a series of complaints against our seizure of French goods on Dutch ships, accompanied by an insistent demand for the formulation of our terms of peace.[3]

Indeed, the contemporary correspondence of the French ministers, like Louis' later memoranda, show that he felt himself to be on the horns of a cruel dilemma, from which nothing but peace could save him.[4] He was thinking of Madrid and Brussels, not of these wretched bickerings in the tropics. If he joined either belligerent, he risked driving the other into the extended arms of Spain, while neutrality would not merely violate his pledges to Holland but mean economic ruin, since Holland was the carrier of France in the infancy of the French marine. He must, then, struggle for peace even beyond the eleventh hour; but if choose he must, he could hardly hesitate. For an English victory might involve reinstatement of the Orange family as an English tool, and our obnoxious doctrines of sea sovereignty and the right of search would be revived to the destruction of French exports. As to the Spanish succession, much though he resented de Witt's latest criticism of his Queen's "rights", the fact remained that de Witt had more than once accepted the idea of partition, and, when the great

[1] Louis to D'Estrades, July 11; Comminge to Louis, July 21 (Japikse); Comminge's memorial, Oct. 7, and Charles' reply, Oct. 16, France, 119; *Rev. Hist.* xcviii. 62.

[2] Landed Nov. 25; left at end of January.

[3] Japikse, 445; France, 119, f. 212; 120, f. 11.

[4] I refer once for all to the articles by Japikse and Pagès in the *Rev. Hist.* as the last word on this matter.

moment came, would surely prove his gratitude for the loyalty of France. Could he count upon England showing a like complacency? True, Charles had sent through Ruvigni a magniloquent offer of *carte blanche* for France in Belgium, if England were left alone to attack the Dutch, but nothing more came of it. Madame was clear that no pledge had been given. Moledi's presence in England was suspect, and this threat of an Anglo-Spanish *entente* took on greater substance from Arlington's well-known Spanish sympathies and Downing's conversations at the Hague with the Austrian Friquet. Nor was it easy to see anything, outside the Dutch alliance, to deliver France from a British "empire of the seas", a menace of which found offensive expression in the very terms of our declaration of war.[1]

It was thus in an uncheering atmosphere that in February 1665 Louis launched his final effort for peace in the *célèbre ambassade*, which he composed by adding to the resident, and unliked, Comminge two persons of greater usefulness or of more acceptance. The dignified member of the embassy was the Duc de Verneuil, a natural son of the great Henri, and so, after Henri's fashion, Charles' uncle—a rather gouty ornament, it is true, most in his element at Newmarket; his working partner was to be Courtin, not only a diplomat of a high order, but a jovial sinner who could understand Charles' ruling passion.

Their stay in England, from April till December, was extremely disagreeable. The plague drove them from London to Kingston, and thence to Oxford and Salisbury, and the most trained diplomat found it hard

---

[1] D'Estrades to Louis, Nov. 20; Louis to D'Estrades, Dec. 19; Japikse, 461, note; French protest at Madrid, Feb. 8 (Mignet); Barbour, 81; Charles to Madame, Jan. 22—Madame to Charles, April 8—France, 120, f. 74.

to keep a smiling face; everywhere the bells ringing for
the cart to fetch away the unwanted dead, torchlight
burial processions, a grave-digger's paradise. Moreover,
the Frenchmen's task was hopeless, for with the first
English success and the consequent passion for war,
their rôle as mediators became increasingly unpopular.
They were refused lodging, the Londoners expected
them to provide illuminations for English victories,
their windows were broken, and their doors chalked
with the plague cross. For once in its history Restoration England was a united nation. Harwich, the base
of the fleet, was packed with Court ladies. Blake's surviving comrades, Sandwich, Penn, and Lawson, were
serving under York and Rupert, while Buckingham
and the mob of gentlemen at ease came to help, or
obstruct, the "tarpaulins"; we hear of an English ship-
wright, exiled in Holland, begging to return if only his
conscience may be free. Both King and ministers were
decided that the fleet must be given its chance, and
their demand to see the French proposals in writing
only meant that England was playing for time.[1]

On the 3rd June came the English victory off Lowestoft, one of the heroic fights between two nations of the
sea. A calm, cloudless day, the towers of the rich
Suffolk churches almost in sight, and here they fought
all day, from four in the morning till darkness covered
the Dutch retreat and hid the sea, now defiled by
bodies and smoking wreckage. Five thousand of the
Dutch were killed—among them two admirals, Opdam
and Cortenaar—twelve of their ships destroyed, and
nine taken. Two only need we name of the thousand
English casualties: Falmouth, the dashing ally of

---

[1] Ambassadors to Louis XIV, April 23 and 27, May 24 (Jusserand); Barbour,
84; *Rev. Hist.*, *loc. cit.*

France, who was killed by the Duke's side, and Lawson, that tough Yorkshireman, mortally wounded, of whom the ballad-maker sang:

> Lawson, whose valour beyond Fate did go,
> And still fights Opdam in the lake below.

But even if England had been pacific or despondent, the breach with France was opening wide. For while we had accepted mediation in the hope of gaining time or French neutrality, their envoys had orders to hear no word of alliance until England and Holland were at peace. By parallel steps, then, we see Louis advance in the terms he would make Holland concede, and yet resist our diplomacy all over the globe, but the English fast hold to their swollen notions of an honourable peace, and tilting over to the anti-French camp in Europe. The French embassy's offer of May merely repeated the Dutch terms of January, which had been contemptuously ignored; our reply, three weeks after the victory of Lowestoft, was practically a manifesto against Holland, declared that the British navy had better prospects of winning a peace than French diplomacy, and passed over in silence the request for our terms.[1] Still Louis persevered. His pressure on the Dutch, at London and the Hague, resulted in a second offer on or about the 5th August, which reflected, or indeed over-represented, the concessions he had been able to wring from Holland. England should keep New York, Bonavista, and St. Andrie on the Gambia, Cormantin in Guinea; Cape Coast Castle should be razed; commissioners should draw up commercial regulations for the future; Holland should keep Pulo

---

[1] *Rev. Hist., loc. cit.*; Aitzema, v. 374; de Witt to D'Estrades, May 2 (Combes); Downing to Clarendon, May 5 (Clar. 108); Charles to Madame, May 29; Add. 22,920, f. 143.

Run. But of any weakening on the Orange and fisheries questions de Witt refused to hear, and the English reply, given at Salisbury on the 19th August, was uncompromising. New York and Cape Coast Castle were ours by right, Pulo Run was ours by two treaties, reparation must be given for our ships and pretensions—there were hints of a war indemnity.[1]

Hitherto the labours of his envoys, a direct petition to Charles that "for his sake" he should make peace, and all the pleadings of Henrietta Maria and Madame, had availed Louis nothing, and at midsummer there were symptoms that he realized the peril of losing Holland by further delay. A storm had risen from the East, ridden by that bird of ill-omen, the Bishop of Münster, in whose visit to Vienna the previous October and in whose treaties with Brandenburg and Neuburg for reconstruction of the Westphalian circle Louis saw a German revival which might wreck his dearest hopes. When on the 3rd June the Bishop's envoy signed a treaty in London · it became clear that these two threats might end in an Anglo-Hapsburg alliance, and D'Estrades sent word that Münster troops were massing on the Frisian border, preparatory to joining hands with the English coming from the sea. On the very day that the Englishman Temple had audience of the Bishop, Louis wrote that he would defend Holland. Two weeks later he informed both London and the Hague that, if England persisted in her refusal of terms, he would declare war.[2]

[1] D'Estrades, May 1 to July 23; Clar. 108, f. 310; Aitzema, v. 385 *et seq.*

[2] Colbrander, i. 217; Madame to Charles, June 22; Holles to H. Coventry, Sept. 7 (Longleat); Urk. ·xii. 610; Pagès, 110; Louis to D'Estrades, July 7; Holland, 177, f. 45; Flanders, 33, f. 220; Downing to Clarendon, April 28, Clar. 108; W. Coventry to Ormonde, Aug. 26, Carte MSS. 47; Aitzema, 598; *Rev. Hist., loc. cit.* 65.

Two other causes contributed to this sharpening of the French tone. Their dread of a British supremacy at sea rose after the battle of Lowestoft almost to an obsession. Alike to Sweden and to Brandenburg Louis dilated on the insufferable prospect of "the seas dominated by a single nation", while Lionne suggested a blockade of the Baltic and Mediterranean to bring England to her senses.[1]

A second prospect, if more unlikely, was infinitely more alarming; it was a reconciliation of England with Holland, with or without Spanish mediation, on the basis of the defence of Belgium. "That serpent" Downing, as Louis crisply called him, had all his old nationalism aroused; he had long pressed Arlington for authority to sound the Dutch, and declared he would "rather contribute to the last penny than be menaced by France into a peace". Assisted by Oudart, once Mary's secretary, he was inciting the Orange partisans, and intriguing for a special meeting of the States-General.[2]

Arlington, in whom the French saw the real culprit, was for the moment merely striving to separate the two enemies. France, it was clear now, would not give way, and our continued negotiation with her had only one purpose—to give the Bishop of Münster a little more time in which to perfect his invasion of Holland. But a second string, of direct approach to Holland for peace, could either be used for the same limited purpose or, if other factors fitted in, might develop into

[1] Courtin to Lionne, June 22 (Colenbrander); D'Estrades to Louis, July 30; instructions for Terlon, June (Rec. Suède), and Moulin, Nov. (Rec. Prusse); Rev. Hist., loc. cit. 65.

[2] D'Estrades to Louis, July 23; Downing to Clarendon, July 14 (Clar. 108); Wicquefort to Lionne, June 25 (Colenbrander); Downing to Arlington, Aug. 15, Holland, 177.

something serious. Profiting by de Witt's absence at sea, in July Arlington at last responded to Downing's repeated request for our conditions. He was instructed to underline the French threat to Flanders, and to paint in rosy hues our negotiations with Spain; positive overtures must come from the Dutch side, but if they would pay an indemnity, grant "good conditions" in the East with reparation for Guinea, and act decently towards Orange, we should be glad to hear more.[1]

There were ample reasons, apart from the abysmal folly of Spain, for the total failure of this tepid courtship. *Bonaventura* and *Esperanza* still whined in the background their Indian incantation, but the root cause was de Witt's purpose, with which he fired all his party, to make no peace except through victory. No chance existed, Downing had to report, of getting an indemnity or anything for Guinea, and late this same August de Ruyter's triumphant return from his travels and escapes set Dutch patriotism in a blaze that consumed this chatter of a separate peace. In September Downing was recalled. He had long felt the strain of life in an enemy capital. His house required police protection, his secretary was arrested, and he had asked that Van Goch might be kept in England as a hostage for his safety. And so, leaving (so the Dutch said) his creditors unpaid, he returned home to take up duty in the English Exchequer.[2] His home-coming coincided with an outbreak of warlike passion, violent enough in itself to extinguish the

[1] Courtin to Louis, June 1 (Barbour); Lionne to D'Estrades, Aug. 29; Arlington to Temple, Aug. 24 (Arl. i.)—Arlington to Downing, July 7—Holland, 177, and see appendix; Downing to Arlington, July 14, *ibid.*—to Clarendon, July 7—Clar. 108.

[2] Downing to Arlington, Aug. 1 and 8 (Holland, 177); to Clarendon, July 14 (Clar. 108); Coventry to Arlington, Aug. 26, Cal.S.P.D.; Colenbrander, i. 192, 210; Wicquefort, iii. 204.

negotiation he had just attempted. The good people of London were ready to fight France and Holland combined. Sandwich had just taken twenty prizes in the North Sea, and two of them were large East-Indiamen, the loot from which was changing hands in Thames-side taverns. Londoners had given up doffing their hats to the French envoys. York, Monk, Ashley, and Lauderdale were loud for war, and at the October meeting of Parliament at Oxford the Commons cheered Clarendon's harangue, and voted blithely another one and a quarter millions. Holles reported from Paris the French military unpreparedness and Colbert's attack upon our trade, the Münster forces crossed the Dutch frontier late in September, and Temple was confident that Holland must soon be forced to a "truckling peace".[1]

On the 7th September a much greater event brought the collision nearer, for that day Philip IV of Spain died, leaving only a sickly boy of four to interpose a mite of legality between Louis XIV and his heart's desire. An immediate state of tension in Belgium reinforced the English belief that France must soon be engaged in a Spanish war; Louis, on the other hand, rejecting the temptation of glory, discerned that it was all the more imperative to get the Anglo-Dutch business out of the way, and pushed more strenuously his earlier decision to break with England if she refused resonable terms.

His wish for peace, and our determination for war, were proved to the hilt in late October, when Louis, without telling the Dutch, proffered his final terms. In effect they were what the English themselves had asked in August, less the indemnity and the "pretensions";

---

[1] Arlington to Ormonde, Nov. 30, Barbour; Coventry to same, Aug. 26, Carte, 47; Temple to Arlington, Oct. 16, *ibid.*; Holles to same, October (Jusserand).

despite his pledge to Holland, he was still ready, it
seemed, to promise us possession of New York, Pulo
Run, and nine-tenths of Guinea. Our refusal was declared on the 7th November; representing the unanimous view of the Committee of foreign affairs, it
offensively hinted that Louis' impartiality was doubtful, and announced that we could act only in concert
with Münster, Sweden, and our other allies.[1]

What wisdom there was in this weighty decision will
be more discernible hereafter; for the time being, it is
safe to suggest that the precise terms of peace were no
longer the governing factor in the English mind. The
war-fever against Holland had been transferred to
France; it was the ubiquity of the French offensive, in
Germany and the North, in anti-Orangist moves, in
seizure of our ships—it was resentment at this armed
"mediation" and anger at their abandonment of
"intimate union" which fired the English government,
rather than the merits of Cape Coast Castle, razed or
fortified. Clarendon and Arlington, usually divided,
were for a season agreed; both were looking towards
Spain, and both were ready to discuss direct with
Holland. The part to be played was still the same—to
keep France and Holland apart—but now the foot was
pressing the other pedal. As for Louis XIV, a declaration of war with England was now the only means left
him wherewith to make Holland share with, or leave to,
him the making of peace; there were signs that he might
hark back to the idea which had already struck him, to
leave the two sea Powers engaged in a lingering war.[2]

---

[1] *Rev. Hist.*, *loc. cit.*; Pomponne, ii. 9; Rec. Suède, 82; Aitzema, v. 395, 602;
Jusserand, 176.

[2] Arlington to Ormonde, Nov. 30 and Feb. 17 (Barbour); to Fanshawe, Nov. 4
(Arl. i.); Clarendon to Temple, Dec. 28 (T. ii.); Arlington to Ormonde, Jan. 20
(Carte, 46); Louis to D'Estrades, Aug. 21, Rec. Suède, 82; Pontalis, i. 367.

At any rate, within three weeks of the English reply, he recalled his envoys; on the 6th January 1666 he declared war, and on the 10th February England followed suit. And now, whatever might come of the peace feelers at the Hague, England had seriously to bethink herself of allies.[1]

MÜNSTER, GERMANY, AND AUSTRIA

The ideal constitution of a league against France and Holland was clear enough to its potential members:[2] England, the Hapsburgs, and Sweden should be able to contain them, and to stave off the danger to the Spanish succession. Yet vast must be the difficulty of forming such a league, involving as it must the sinking of religious passion and colonial jealousy, of Spain's antagonism to Portugal, and of Sweden's to Denmark. And between the centres of alliance lay the great hiatus of northern Germany, that soil fertile in hungry princes and stout mercenaries.

Hence emerged the first British ally, indeed the only one who ever took the field—an alliance welcome, says Clarendon, "as if it came from heaven", but in truth liable to almost every earthly drawback. Christopher Bernard von Galen, Bishop of Münster from 1650 to 1678, united in himself the *Realpolitik* of his own with the warrior-priestliness of former ages. In one capacity a reforming Catholic, in a second a lieutenant of that high-minded trimmer the Archbishop of Mainz, he was known best of all as a mighty, incessant fighter. He had fought against the Turk, fought in Cologne service, fought his own rebellious city. War was his hobby,

---

[1] Aitzema, v. 607, 913; Carte, 46, f. 221, and 47, f. 436; *Rev. Hist., loc. cit.* 43.
[2] Clarendon to Coventry, Oct. 4, 1665 (Longleat MSS.); Austrian protocol, Jan. 2, 1666 (Pribram, 275); Arlington to Fanshawe, Nov. 4, 1665 (Arl. ii.).

bombs and siege artillery his specialized art, and this pillar of the Church, whose Latin was as good as his shooting, was preceded by a guard of "Heyducks", armed to the teeth with poleaxes and carbines. Round this ardent spirit clustered the volunteers of many countries, Scots and Irish included, who partook of the conviviality, and presumably of the gout, which encompassed him, and he indulged his taste with a large disregard of immediate results, promising himself that his investments at Venice would bring a Cardinal's hat to soothe old age.[1]

In 1664, when nearly sixty, he was, not for the first or the last time, at war with Holland, whose citizens he habitually corrupted and whose frontier he menaced. The proximate causes are now remote and trival; one, touching the fief of Borkelo, and running back to 1406, involved him with the province of Gueldres; another, over East Frisia, was more serious, for here he was acting as administrator for the Empire. Early in 1665, when war with Holland was certain, Clarendon was surprised to receive a messenger from a Westphalian abbey, an English Benedictine whom he had met in exile, bringing an offer of the Bishop's alliance. To him rapidly succeeded an avowed, and effusively genial, envoy, the Baron von Wreden, with whom without more ado a treaty was made.[2] Münster was to produce a force of 30,000 men within two months; for this to receive 500,000 dollars, payable in three instalments by the end of August, and small monthly payments thereafter—such payments to be diminished *pro rata* if Brandenburg, Neuburg, or either of them, joined the

[1] Pomponne, i. 375; Wicquefort, ii. *passim*; Pontalis, i. 361; Courtenay, i. 37; Temple, i. 4, 22.
[2] June 3: Brinckmann, "Charles II and the Bishop of Münster", *E.H.R.* xxi., and Aitzema, who here had personal knowledge.

confederacy. And no peace was to be made, save by common assent.[1]

At first all went well. Helped by recruitment in Belgium, the Bishop's men broke in two waves upon Holland, overran most of Overyssel, and in November were fighting through Groningen to join the English on the coast. Already Swedish troops had reached Pomerania, and visions rose of Holland beleaguered by a great coalition. But then they faded in the light of day.[2]

The British diplomat in charge of this Münster affair was to be the most famous of the reign—William Temple, who won out of it his baronetcy and a good deal of disillusion. He alone of that unsuccessful school has remained tolerably familiar to our own day, chiefly because fortune endowed him with three choice gifts —a delightful wife in Dorothy Osborne (of whom he was unworthy),[3] a secretary of genius in Jonathan Swift, and an excellent prose style. His abilities were, indeed, solidly meritorious. Son of a Cromwellian and nearly related to the Sidneys, he had little original claim upon the Court, but by 1663 he had won powerful patrons and a safe niche in Restoration society. He stood high with the two ablest directors of policy in the reign, Arlington and Danby. The first, presumably through Ormonde, introduced him to the public service, and much as they deviated afterwards, Temple did not abandon, until Arlington lost power, a tone of clientship which originally was adulation; but if Arlington thought of him as a possible fellow-secretary in 1667, it was Danby, with whom he had travelled abroad in youth, Lady Temple's kinsman, and at one

[1] Text in Arl. i.; ratifications, July 5, Flanders, 33, f. 220.
[2] Blok, 322; Aitzema; Urk. xii. 62; Clarendon to Coventry, December '65 (Lister).
[3] *Clarendon Corr.* i. 629, and many of his letters.

time her courtier, who twice pressed that office on him. Macaulay's famous essay has overpainted Temple's love of ease.   Sir William did not undervalue himself, his declamations on the charms of retirement must not be antedated, and just as the old high priest of the anti-Bentley party in the Phalaris controversy can hardly be acquitted of vanity, so the young diplomatist liked to direct things in his own way. To young men kind, to sovereigns candid and courageous, human and humane, fond of his game of cards and his gardens, he was often jealous of his colleagues, often disdainful to his official masters, and his self-portraiture as "the plain man" will not bear examination. To be industrious, uncorrupt, and single-minded was not uncommon in that service, nor was his early distrust of France exceptional in Arlington's followers; nor, again, do his immense letters, so rotund in form and orthography, mostly sensible and always exhaustive, give any impression of genius. What really distinguished Temple from others was a wild and sanguine ardour, carried away by any imaginable combination of the moment, and bearing the successive imprint of stronger personalities. In six months he travelled from a credulous belief in the Bishop of Münster's integrity to suggesting the composition of a pamphlet scarifying his breach of faith; in 1666 he was holding out for no peace without power for the Prince of Orange; in 1669 the Prussians wrote of him as "de Witt's *familiarissimus*"; from 1674 and onwards he was almost Orange's man.[1]

His mission in 1665 being to make Münster the

[1] For some suggestion of this view of Temple, though it depends rather on scattered MS. correspondence, see Fruin-Japikse, ii. 70; Courtenay, i. 42; Temple, ii. 379, 390; Urk. xii. 899. I have taken some hints from the MS. journal of Charles Cottrell-Dormer, who saw much of him in 1675.

cement which would bind the German princes to
Britain, he was instructed[1] to urge the Bishop to take
the field and to act on his advice in approaching
Brandenburg, Mainz, and Neuburg. But his pleasure
and optimism in this employment rapidly diminished.
A first blow was the entrusting of the German business
to two special envoys, Lord Carlingford and Sir
Walter Vane, and Temple's complaints show how he
felt it: ironically admitting that he could neither drink
deep nor speak German, he suggested that he should
be made resident at Brussels, where, we must understand, the language and habits of cultivated society
obtained.[2] Meantime, the question of subsidies for
Münster went from bad to worse. In the lack of bills of
exchange we shipped specie and tin, but the tin ships
were wrecked off Ostend (they were still being fished
for, years later), and good Alderman Backwell's duca-
toons were refused. Through such ill-fortune, and
through the plague-stricken poverty of London, the
subsidy got ever deeper into arrears—the June quota
was only paid in August, and the August payment not
till the following spring. And then in November the
Bishop cried out for troops to be sent from England or,
this failing, the doubling of his allowance.[3]

This bishop of ill-fame, economically so thirsty and
in a military sense so impossible to help, was also
diplomatically so ruinous that all Europe hungered
to suppress him. Louis XIV, worried by his talk of
"German loyalty" and Westphalian leagues, turned
on him both barrels of his political weapon. With one,
he despatched six thousand troops to eject the Münster

[1] June 22, Courtenay; original in Add. 9796.
[2] Temple to Arlington, Sept. 12, Flanders, 33; Sept. 15, Courtenay.
[3] Flanders, 33, ff. 218-279; Carte, 47, f. 258; E.H.R., loc. cit. 691; Carte, 46,
f. 223; Arl. i. 45.

army from Holland; with the other he begged the
Dutch to yield something, and promised the Bishop
an easy fall.[1] The Germans were even more forcible.
Münster separated Brandenburg from its Rhenish
duchies, and threatened the Hanoverians at Osnabruck; his past record and his present proceedings
raised the spectre of religious war, and the voice of
German Protestantism in alarm reverberated to Holland and Sweden. This very year religious passion had
inflamed a succession dispute among the princes of
Brunswick, and the victors, George William of Lüne-
burg and Ernest of Osnabruck (husband of our excellent Princess Sophia), were hiring out their troops to
Holland; their arch-adviser was George Frederick of
Waldeck, most long-sighted of politicians and most
inveterate in dislike of the Hapsburgs.[2]

And if religion and territorial feud kept Sweden
apart from Münster, fear of Sweden and France impelled patriotic Germans to stamp out the Münster
flame before it set light to the Empire. To embarrass
France by detaching her Rhenish "protectorate", the
Emperor Leopold had encouraged the Bishop's diplomacy, but he recoiled at the prospect of war in
Germany; he would explore the notion of an Anglo-
Swedish *entente*, but not till Sweden ceased to threaten
the imperial city of Bremen. In truth Austria's enemy
was not Holland but France, which was bent at this
moment upon dangerous schemes in Poland, and if so,
then not only the Münster but the English pressure
must be taken off Holland. But a German impetus
could come only from the Hapsburgs; as Temple

[1] Rec. Prusse, 108; Aitzema, v. 319, 597; Pagès, 114.
[2] Temple to Castel Rodrigo, Dec. 2; H. Coventry to Arlington, Aug. 30,
Sweden, 5; Vane to Arlington, Dec. 8, Add. 16,272; Aitzema, v. 642; Ward, 163;
Wicquefort, iii. 222.

wrote, "none of the German princes will make France an enemy, without the House of Austria to back them in their alliance with us upon this Münster quarrel".[1] Yet Vienna would not budge without Madrid, and from Madrid there was only irritating negation. Arlington was just about repudiating a commercial treaty which Fanshawe, our worthy man on the spot, had bungled, and though at Brussels the governor Castel Rodrigo was profuse and sincere in good-will, he could produce nothing more solid till our league with Spain was made.[2]

It was bad enough that our Münster cement was turning into high explosive; it was worse that our government were handling it with fumbling, half-hearted courage: worst of all that, in 1665–66, as almost always, a radical inconsistency cursed our counsels. For Germany rang with rumoured intrigue at Paris by the "Popish" St Albans, even while ostensibly our energy was directed to peace feelers at the Hague and the formation of an anti-French system. To such a system Clarendon was only a temporary convert; its chief inspiration came from Arlington, who concluded sardonically that, if adequate terms could be won by direct negotiation, we should "be furnished with a good message to the King of France, that at his recommendation we have at last made the peace".[3] And if this were possible, the Münster feud with Holland became secondary and tedious. Assurances must go out to Protestant Europe that we had no wish to crush Holland; the German princes must know that Münster

---

[1] Temple to Arlington, Dec. 1, Flanders, 33; to Ormonde, Jan. 5, 1666, Carte, 47; H. Coventry to Arlington, Nov. 29, Sweden, 5.

[2] Arlington to Fanshawe, Dec. 10, Arl. ii.; Temple to Arlington, Aug. 4, Flanders, 33; to Ormonde, Sept. 18, Carte, 47.

[3] S.P. German States, 57, ff. 1-20; Clarendon to Coventry, December (Lister); Barbour, 90; Arlington to Ormonde, Jan. 20, Carte, 46.

would be restrained, and that German unity was dear
to the English heart. To adjust this line to the encouragement we were giving Sweden would be delicate
work, but a risk eminently worth running if the peace
were made under the presidency of England, and not
of France. In any case Münster stock had sunk low;
it was only in the Oxford Gazette, our Frankfort
correspondent said, that its prospects had ever looked
bright. In March 1666 Temple therefore received
orders to inform the Bishop that peace with Holland
was not impossible—or, in other words, that he might
expect to be thrown overboard.[1]

The Bishop, we know from other sources than
Temple, had already decided to go in his own time. He
was in a tight corner; Dutch and Prussian troops held
the keys of his territory, and he had descended to the
sale of his jewels. On the 16th March his envoy told
Arlington that his master was pressed to make peace
by his German enemies, who, moreover, proposed to
mediate between England and France; much about
the same date he sent a second agent to Paris, and even
earlier he had committed himself to make peace without England, if England were obstinate. This pledge
had been extorted by pressure from Berlin,[2] the nodal
point in all this tangle, and the heavy diplomatic defeat
which England had to endure in 1666 reflected the
acumen and the realistic craft of the ablest ruler of the
day. Upon the Great Elector turned, as de Witt saw,
the decision whether Germany would take the field
against France, or no.[3]

Nowhere in Europe was the absence of a competent

---

[1] *E.H.R.*, *loc. cit.*, and xxiv. 254; Arlington to Temple, March 23.
[2] *E.H.R.* xxi. 694; Pagès, 134; Arlington to Temple, March 16, Arl. i.
[3] De Witt to Vivien, Nov. 17, '65, Fruin, iii. 153.

English minister more deplorable, for the Elector was not only a man of strong passions but a statesman balanced upon clashing and uncertain paths. Though a militant Protestant, he hated Sweden, his Protestant neighbour in Pomerania, with a perfect hatred, and though a loyal servant of Germany, he was filled with hereditary and well-grounded suspicion of the Hapsburgs. He had been educated at Leyden and had loved his first Dutch wife; moreover, he looked to Holland as the citadel of the faith. Yet from his mother-in-law, the vindictive Amalia, he had acquired an Orange partisanship, and he had inherited an ancient feud touching the Dutch garrisons kept in some Rhenish fortresses. Again, no one save France could discipline Sweden, offset the Austrian weight in the Empire, and help him to juggle with his rival in Jülich and Cleves, the Catholic Palatine of Neuburg; but must he therefore let Poland and Belgium fall to Catholic France?

The northern settlement of 1660 had antagonized him, and fear of a French-Polish-Swedish group had explained his anxiety to make an English alliance, through which he hoped also to assist the chaotic condition of the Orange House and get some return for the money he had sent to Charles as an exile. The treaty signed in May 1661[1] was not greatly to his mind. He had hoped for a unilateral pledge from England; on the contrary, the treaty was mutually defensive, committed him to protect our interests in the Baltic and North Sea, and by an article obliging him to seek extension of the defensive clauses among other German princes, promised to be fertile in trouble. Subsequent negotiation

---

[1] For this mission of Weiman and John Maurice of Nassau, see Urk. ix. 465 *et seq.*; they arrived, March 10, and had audience of congé on July 17; ratified by Brandenburg, July 27; copy in Holland, 164, f. 50.

showed that the English were either ignorant of his feel-
ings or weighed them lightly in the scale. His zeal for
the Protestant interest visibly counted for little with
Charles, who ironically brushed aside his suggestion of
suitable Protestant brides, and betrayed no interest in
the suffering Lutheran pastors of Cleves and Jülich.
Besides this, their suspicion of Spain drove the English
government during 1661–63 to follow the French lead
in the north, while they refused to offend Sweden by
including the city of Bremen in the league, or even to
guarantee the Peace of Oliva. Morrice, the "northern"
Secretary, was believed, like most ex-Puritans, to be
Swedish in sympathy, but the Elector's capable envoy
Brandt was equally emphatic as to the factiousness of
the council as a whole and the inveterate tendency of
Englishmen to behave as if they lived in a world of
their own. It is, then, natural enough to find Frederick
William, opposed by negation at Vienna and by Francophil insouciance at London, gradually turning himself towards Paris, that he might be safe from isolation
in Poland or from sudden attack by the Swede.[1]

And now Holland, on so many counts his enemy, was
at war with England and Münster, and the English,
tardily adopting Downing's advice, were suddenly
deluging him with objurgation and favour: the Westphalian enemies of Holland must combine, the Prince
of Orange should be restored, and Charles, on his word
"as King and gentleman", would make his nephew's
cause his own. The first olive branch produced by this
dove, cooing after three years' silence, was the long-
asked guarantee of the Oliva peace.[2]

It says much for the Elector's restraint that, in the

---

[1] Urk. ix. 693; *ibid.* xii. 607; Pagès, cap. i.; *E.H.R.* xxiv. 1, c.; Droysen, 15.
[2] Downing to Arlington, March 4, 1664, Holland, 169; Urk. *loc. cit.*

teeth of his counsellors, he refused these stimulants, declined the Münster promise of a league against France, and by November 1665 had taken his course. The Papist bishop must be suppressed; Holland should have an alliance, and should pay high for it; in one policy he would combine the immediate wishes of France and the ultimate salvation of the Empire. In this autumn of 1665 his troops moved to the Rhine, and he himself in mid-November to Cleves, which for six months became the centre of Europe. There gradually collected some of the quickest brains of that age: Beverning from Holland, William of Fürstenberg, who may be called the French master-key to Germany, Colbert de Terron, Austrians, Brunswickers, and Danes.

Sir Walter Vane, whom the English government selected to confront them, was a younger brother of the executed Sir Henry, and was later to serve—indeed, at Seneffe to die—in the service of the Prince of Orange.[1] But diplomatic experience he had none, and, save for the fact that John Locke went with him as secretary, his embassy might be left in oblivion. Dreary work the sociable secretary found it to be, in particular to be deprived of letters from home; but intrinsically it was more melancholy for Vane, whose mission was hopeless from the outset and always bungled from home.[2] Despatches received during November from Temple and Carlingford had already declared it impossible to win the Elector, whose anti-English symptoms were inflamed at this moment by a controversy over our prize courts. Two of his best ships were first detained at Falmoûth, then released, only to be recaptured by

[1] Papillon papers (*H. MSS. Comm.*), 258; *D.N.B.*, *sub* "Henry Vane" (the elder); Hatton Corr. i. 98.   [2] German States, 57, f. 30.

English cruisers off the Lizard; hence the despatch of lading papers to the Court at Salisbury and other ceremonial, humiliating to the parent of an infant mercantile marine.[1]

The auspices were thus unfavourable when, on the 1st December, Vane reached Cleves. His instructions were to ask assistance under the terms of the 1661 alliance and to propose a triple league of England, Brandenburg, and Münster: a Protestant aside intimated that the Bishop was well under our control. The Elector was warned against the ambition of France, and promised a guarantee against Swedish aggression in Pomerania.[2] On paper Vane's further suggestions sounded well enough: no peace was to be made that did not restore the house of Orange, the Elector should recover his fortresses on the Rhine, and receive a subsidy of £100,000. But Frederick's resolution remained unshaken, and it was not due to Vane that he tarried till February to sign a subsidy treaty with Holland; on the contrary, the English name was used only as a lever to bring de Witt to the Elector's terms, for Frederick had abandoned the Orange cause already, and his adviser in such matters, the Princess Amalia, had been listening to the advances of D'Estrades.[3] Nor apparently had Vane any authority for his offer of a subsidy in return for neutrality. Clarendon rode his highest horse—"God forbid the Crown of England should fall so low as to give the Elector of Brandenburg money to do us no harm". Nothing but tiffs with Colbert, whose Anglophobia was excessive when in wine, relieved the tedium of the last few weeks, and early in February Vane

---

[1] Vane to Arlington, Jan. 5, 1666, German States, 57; Temple to same, Nov. 6, n.s., 1665, Carte, 47; *E.H.R.*, *loc. cit.* 254; Urk. xii. 623.

[2] Vane's letter book, Add. 16,272, f. 5

[3] Pagès, 112; Stowe MSS. 191, f. 6, instructions dated October.

returned to England, accompanied by a Prussian charged with two most ungrateful errands—to explain away Frederick's Dutch alliance and to offer his media-tion. But the Prussians could cheerfully disregard our reproaches and the charge of perfidy to Orange, realiz-ing as they did that our threat to make terms with Holland was childish, and that Frederick was reinsured both at Paris and Stockholm.[1]

In effect the Münster episode was ended, for France and Brandenburg combined—with whatever difference of motive—dispelled any hesitation lingering in the satellites Mainz, Neuburg, and Cologne; as the Prus-sian troops drew near, our ally's last scruples of loyalty faded, and on the 19th April he accepted the bitter pill of almost total disarmament. To stop this humiliation, if not to our arms at least to our prestige, Arlington sent Temple off post-haste for Münster; to such base uses, to disguise as a Spaniard, to sleep snatched in barns, to eluding German troopers, had the optimist Temple descended. The Bishop's excuses rained from "all points of the compass"—he spoke of a "pax vio-lenta, et nullam violentam perpetuam", and did, indeed, pack off another baron to England with suggestions for another try. But all real fight had left him, and a final spark flickered out in last efforts to get another subsidy. We had had enough; "His Majesty is of your opinion", wrote Arlington, "that the less we speak of it the better".[2]

[1] Vane to Arlington, Dec. 5 and 15; to Morrice, Jan. 10, n.s.; Clarendon to Vane, Jan. 4, Add. 16,272, ff. 8-31; Prussian protocol, Dec. 19, in *Publik. aus der preuss. Staatsarchiv*, 1919; Achen's account of his mission, Urk. xxi.; Arlington to Vane, Dec 21, *loc. cit.*; Prussian-Swedish treaty of March 31, Urk. ix.; Morrice to H. Coventry, Jan. 6 (Longleat MSS.).

[2] *E.H.R.* xxi. 695; Arlington to Temple, March to May; Temple to Arlington, April 17 (Carte, 47); to Sir J. Temple, May 10; for the Münster communication of the terms, German States, 5, f. 81.

Even so, the Great Elector had not completed the diplomatic edifice begun in his Dutch treaty and the peace of Cleves. Fixing his eyes on the ultimate ambitions of France in Belgium and Poland, and determined to offset them by peace within Teutonic Europe, in May he concluded a defensive treaty with Denmark, in June secured understanding with Neuburg by admitting his claim in Poland, and in October completed a quadruple alliance with Holland, Denmark, and the Brunswick dukes. These swift steps, of which France and England from different angles disapproved, made the nucleus at least of a central and mainly Protestant *bloc*, able both to check French dictatorship and to guide Dutch, or at least Orangist, opinion in the direction of peace.[1] For the immediate purposes of England, however, they only accentuated a diplomatic defeat, which already was sore to bear, and daily gathering soreness (as we shall see) from Hapsburgs and Scandinavia. And this effort to combine two systems in one offensive was bringing out the dilemma latent in Arlington's scheme. Only if they were concentrated against Holland would Sweden engage; German and Hapsburg support, on the contrary, was conditional on Holland being spared and a diversion of the war upon France. Our diplomats were insistent that for the second purpose the key lay with the Hapsburgs, without whom neither Germany nor Sweden would move.[2]

But in 1665 our relations with Austria, still officially suspended, were further damaged by our refusal to join in the Turkish war, visibly because we prized our

[1] Urk. xii. 69, 643; Pomponne, i. 273; Louis XIV, ii. 129.
[2] Clifford's note of Nov. 16, 1665 (Ugbrooke MSS.); Coventry to Arlington, Aug. 23 (Lister).

factories in the Levant above the interest of "Christendom".Yet the hour of decision was near, and not least
for Austria, who was finding in Poland, the Rhine, and
Hungary a suffocating belt of French influence between her and the outer air. In September 1665 the
eleventh hour sounded, on the death of Philip IV of
Spain. His will placed next in the succession to the
poor infant Charles II the Infanta Margaret, Leopold's
affianced bride, and a secret article in the marriage contract promised Belgium to her second son. This slight
to the Queen of France was soon, like most diplomatic
secrets, public property; already the friends of peace,
and the Francophils of Germany, had taken alarm;
already Mainz and Cologne were sounding Paris and
Vienna on the chance of an agreed settlement; already
a Franciscan envoy had laid this explosive proposition
before the Court of Spain. Through the corridors of
pacifism and the coarse world of ministerial feud at
Vienna percolated the notion of a partitioned Spanish
empire.[1]

Yet Leopold himself made no sign that he would
abandon his wife's inheritance or his German faith, and
in many quarters during 1664–65 his attitude had been
grateful to England. He had exhausted exhortation to
Spain to make peace with Portugal, he had stood by
Castel Rodrigo's effort to make Belgium defensible, he
sympathized with the notion of an English-Hapsburg-
Swedish league. But in a demand for action against
Holland to protect Münster his pace could not be
entirely his own. Whether as head of the Empire or
heir to Spain, he ran risks immeasurably greater
than the English, and though he welcomed the
idea of an English envoy, commended to him by

[1] Gaedeke, i. 9; Pribram, 328; Legrelle, i. 196; Pötting, i. 92 *et seq.*

Medina,[1] that was a long step still from offensive alliance.

In September 1665 he opened contact with Arlington, using as intermediary one Father Donellan who, good man, showed as much interest in favours for his Irish kindred as in *la haute politique*, but whose letters did, at least, repeat that to expect Austrian help for Münster was moonshine.[2] Serious business began with the mission of Lord Carlingford, whose instructions, dated the 22nd August, reveal the threefold German policy of his government. With two parts of it—the launching of Münster, and the scheme to bring in Brandenburg, Mainz, and Neuburg—we have already dealt; the third related to the Emperor, to whom he was to take our congratulations on his Turkish peace and his Spanish bride, a justification of our Dutch war, and an exalted version of the "union and alliance" now in course of making between England and Spain.

Theobald Taafe, first Earl of Carlingford, one of the more attractive of Charles' envoys, was, like several of them, an Irish loyalist, and, like "Dick" Bellings, had been one of the moderates among the confederate Catholics—"a Papist dog", to use his own reproachfully smiling expression. The present mission continued a family connection with the Austrian royal house which, *plus* some experience of Imperial diplomacy during the exile, perhaps determined Charles' choice, and his son Francis later became an Austrian field-marshal. In character, despite Temple's sarcasm, Carlingford showed himself well fitted for his appointment. His convivial gifts were, perhaps, superabundant, and gout is the master key of his coming in and his going out; outward bound, he had ten days of gout

---

[1] Pötting, i. 180; Germany, 11, f. 177.   [2] Empire, 11, ff. 30-51.

in bed at Cassel, while his last word a year later from
Vienna echoes, "I cannot get quitt of this damned
gout". On his own account it came from misfortune,
not misconduct—"Upon my word", he protests, "I
was not near drunk since I left the Bishop of Münster"
—but a cavalier of his type was made very happy by
Leopold, who gave him fine Transylvanian horses and
"the best hawking in the world". The one dark blot on
his private contentment proved the public decrepitude
of his government; he was penniless. With a natural
competence that deceived the Emperor he had to
feign to be bedridden with gout on his arrival; Father
Donellan's credit was used but soon exhausted,
butchers and bakers dunned him—"for God's love",
he broke out finally, "let me live decently, or call me
home". His diplomatic year seems to have cost his
private pocket some £5000.[1]

Every line of his sensible despatches emphasized
our diplomatic embarrassment. To the English a
bare defensive league could be only an encumbrance.
It might so turn out that a persistent French-Dutch
offensive, or an attack on Flanders, would make a
Hapsburg alliance essential, but if so, they must put
in full stakes; Spain must produce her promised treaty
of commerce and end her war with Portugal, Austria
stop her "coldness" to Sweden and her pinpricks to
Brandenburg. Arlington was ready to promise, "we
will not forsake them if they do not forsake themselves",
but he was not going to offend France past recall
without an assurance that the Spaniards meant business.[2] At midsummer, 1666, he merely asked Leopold

[1] Pötting, i. 179, 189, Carte MSS. 47, ff. 268, 314; Carlingford to Arlington,
Jan. 6 to July 7, 1666, Empire, 11; Oct. 27, *ibid.* 12.
[2] Draft instructions for Carlingford (endorsed "sent in cipher"), June 22,
Germany, 11; Arlington to Sandwich, Aug. 2 (Arl.).

to send an envoy to England with proposals, and since
Leopold, with much the same hesitation, in July ordered
Lisola to proceed to London, only an academic importance attaches to the conferences at Vienna which
Carlingford, popular and gouty, maintained till October. Exceeding both his instructions and his information, he told Leopold that England would join an
offensive alliance, and told Arlington that Leopold
would attack France if any Hapsburg territory were
violated. Unhappily, neither was in the least likely,
and not half so probable at the moment as an *entente*
between France and Spain.[1]

In Spain, then, was the root of the tree of apathy,
blighting all the fruits of endeavour against France,
and to the Peninsula we must descend. But before
doing so, we may once more delimit and test the problem of our government's sincerity in these approaches
to the Hapsburgs. What truth was there in the common
impression of Spaniards that England would prefer
good terms with France—what substance in the complaint of Charles' vagueness that came from the patriotic Sophia of Hanover?[2]

Now the instructions given to Sandwich on his
departure for Spain clearly contemplate a coalition,
based on England, the Hapsburgs, and Scandinavia,
one effect of which must be that Holland would, sooner
or later, join it; if satisfied on other matters, we would
bind ourselves to make no peace with France for three
years. Arlington's intention of dividing Holland from
France, by fair means or foul, was sharpened in the
spring of 1666 by the breakdown of the "peace conference" engineered at Paris, which he interpreted only

---

[1] Pribram, Pötting, and *E.H.R.*, *loc. cit.*; Empire, 11, f. 169; 12, f. 3.
[2] Sophia to Carlingford, Sept. 26, 1666, German States, 57.

as designed to divide us from the Hapsburgs, and as built on nothing stronger than the "credulity" of the Queen Mother and St. Albans.[1] Our acceptance of Swedish mediation in July 1666, our appeal to her Protestant passion, our offer at Madrid to drop assistance to Portugal, all fit in with the Prussian conviction that the English scheme was to win, at almost any cost, a separate peace with Holland.[2]

How far this Gallophobia would be translated into action must depend, as ever, upon the response we could get from our prospective allies, and there lay the rub. But three conclusions may be drawn with tolerable certainty: first, despite a free use of menaces to galvanize Hapsburg lethargy, that there is no evidence, from March till October 1666, of any resolution to accept the French advances; but second, that the ministry was divided—Clarendon leading a section who would "deal roundly" with Spain, and not dislike peace through the French medium;[3] and, third, that this section was gaining ground by the autumn.

A bitter strain of war, plots, and tangled negotiation shape and confuse this process; we have to search in the Hague, in Norwegian and Irish harbours, and in the eddies swirling round the embassies of Stockholm, Lisbon, and Madrid.

SPAIN AND PORTUGAL

It is some presumption of diplomatic incompetence when salvation can come only by a diplomatic revolu-

[1] "Additional instructions for Sandwich", Feb. 22, Carte, 274, f. 11; Arlington to Temple, April 10 and Aug. 27—to Sandwich, March 22—to Ormonde, April 21—Carte, 46.

[2] Arlington to Temple, July 27 and Oct. 29; instructions for Thynne, Sweden, 6; Urk. xii. 636.

[3] Clarendon to Sandwich, Aug. 7, Carte, 75; Brandt to Great Elector, Sept. 17, Urk. xii.; St. Albans to Ruvigni, Nov. 22, Fr. tr.

tion, and that was the case with our Spanish dealings
of 1665–66. We had embarked upon war with France
before we had weaned Spain from the bitterness of our
past relations, and no legerdemain could swiftly super-
impose Spanish friendship on a Portuguese alliance.
To close that historic feud would demand the finesse of
Mazarin and the resources of Louis XIV; the task
was committed by Clarendon to Sir Richard Fanshawe.

Fanshawe, ambassador at Lisbon from July 1662
to August 1663 and at Madrid from June 1664 until
May 1666, was one of those loyal Cavaliers who, with
the Restoration, reaped, perhaps unhappily for their
country, their loyalty's reward. He and his heroic wife,
whose memoirs have painted a halo of affectionate prejudice round his diplomacy, had followed the Stuart
cause over hills and sea, leaving behind them pledges
of devotion in their children's graves at Oxford, Paris,
Madrid, and Lisbon. As a type of the purest of this
school Fanshawe deserves commemoration, for he was
a competent master of the Latin tongues, a perfect
gentleman, whose letters were never more perfect than
when he was superseded, and a God-fearing son of the
Church. But he was now ageing; his experience had
been limited to a few years, before the wars, in the
Madrid embassy, and his correspondence betrays a
lack of diplomatic sense. "I beat a hundred bushes to
start one hare", he once wrote to Clarendon, and attractive though we find his letters, or his naïve pleasure
in small pomps of office, or his interest in portraits,
Brazil birds, and seed pearls, that attractive prolixity
usually enfolded a fantastic or contradictory recommendation. Thus, between July and October 1662, his
alternative policies range from a triple league of England, Spain, and Portugal, based either on a Spanish-

Portuguese marriage or a migration of the Braganza dynasty to Brazil, to a war against Spain that would win for us guarantee ports in Portugal and the Spanish Indies; in 1665 he was poising a similar scheme as against alliance with Spain to reopen the Scheldt. He was, in fact, a creature of impulse, in nothing better shown than in his repeated practice, or threats, of returning to England without leave, which did serious damage.[1]

When he returned to Portugal the alliance which he had helped to make, and which England was pledged to defend, was labouring in heavy seas. Catharine's dowry was still unpaid. The Viceroy of Goa still refused to surrender Bombay, and only by a lucky sequence of events did the East India Company get hold of it in 1665. A worse corollary of these ill relations was the wretched fate of the British auxiliary troops. It was not their gallantry that was at fault: at the sight of their red and blue caps the Spaniards fled, but they were ground between the millstones of English and Spanish poverty. They "moulder away daily", we are told: were used up in forlorn hopes and small detachments, and dwindled, despite reinforcement, to a bare 1300 men. Thus misused, and starved of their pay, they rapidly deteriorated and deserted; some of these "Cromwell's whelps" refused to serve under Inchiquin and the O'Briens put over them, swearing that "if Jesus Christ was an Irishman they would not obey Him". Both governments behaved badly; for if we tried to palm off the scum of our Irish recruits, Portugal belied her treaty obligations and asked more

---

[1] Memoir of July 30, 1662, Clar. MSS. 77; Fanshawe to Clarendon, Oct. 28, 1662, Heathcofe; to Charles II, Feb. 8, 1665, Spain, 48; Arlington to Fanshawe, July 25, 1663, Portugal, 63; and March 16, 1665, Arl.; Warwick to Fanshawe, Oct. 21, 1664 (Fanshawe letters).

subsidies for the period of the war. Our firm refusal
to accept a further responsibility, or to entertain the
notion of war against Spain, represents the stage
reached when Fanshawe departed in August 1663,
leaving the consul Maynard to fill the gap till Southwell's arrival in January 1666.[1]

Maynard, an old stager dating from the Commonwealth, heaped a little more fuel on the flame. Arbi-
trary valuation of British goods, excessive tariffs on
wine and oil, impounding of debts by the Inquisition—
such dry husks choke his sycophantic letters; so much
so, that the Portuguese minister, Castel Melhor, asked,
and eventually obtained, his recall.[2]

But in Portugal, as elsewhere, the tension between
ourselves and France was the matter of importance.
Not only was France rich and England poor, not only
did her troops accept a lower rate of pay, but France
was ready to prolong the Spanish war, which England,
not on financial grounds only, was doing her best to
end. Before his departure, Fanshawe noted that Portuguese peace leanings ebbed with the coming of a
French agent, whose mules panted under bills of exchange, and he deprecated transferring the command
of our men to the French marshal Schomberg: he
noted, too, that French influence persistently blocked
our effort to mediate peace with Spain. Gradually
Clarendon's philosophic content, that France should
do our work for us, disappeared in Arlington's acuter
suspicion, and our blessing upon Alfonso VI's desperate effort to wed a French princess was replaced,
late in 1665, by an instruction to Southwell, that if not

[1] Heathcote, 32 *et seq*.; Portugal, 6, f. 23; Prestage, 158; Arlington to Ormonde,
Jan. 30, 1664, Carte, 221; D'Ablancourt.
[2] Maynard to Clarendon, June 8, 1664, Clarendon MSS. 81; Portugal, 6,
ff. 190, 292; Add. 34,336, f. 28.

too late (which was the case) he should stress the charms of an Austrian Hapsburg.[1]

So deep a rift was still distant when, in September 1663, it was decided, partly at the Portuguese request, to send Fanshawe to Spain. Yet wrangles with Comminge and the smooth promises of Moledi had already affected our view, and the tone of Fanshawe's instructions rang definitely against France. He was to impress the fact that France only waited her opportunity to fall upon Spain—to which end she was making advances to England, and spinning out the Portugal war. That war he must endeavour to close, by a promise to withdraw assistance to Portugal if she refused reasonable terms. With regard to an alliance, he must play for safety till a regular Spanish ambassador was sent to England, but meantime he should keep well to the fore the opening of freer trade, even, perhaps, an English monopoly in the Indies, and an assiento for the African Company; in a favourable atmosphere he might moot the coining of Spanish bullion in our Mint, and a pre-emption on Spanish wool.[2]

Fanshawe's rehearsal of business done, after nearly a year's work, is sad reading. Here and there a bright spot lighted the background: Tangier was profiting from more open trade, both sides released prisoners in the Indies, and in July Molina was designated for the embassy at London. But Spaniards were still helping the Moors, they had not ceased talk of regaining Tangier and Jamaica, and any commercial concession was made contingent on the capital point of Portugal.

[1] Fanshawe to Clarendon, March 2, to Arlington, March 20, 1663, Portugal, 6; Arlington to Fanshawe, May 14, Heathcote; Clarendon to Fanshawe, April 12, *ibid.*; FitzHardinge to Arlington, Nov. 12, 1664, France, 119; instructions for Southwell, Dec. 20, 1665, Add. 34,336; Prestage, 83, 156.

[2] Instructions of Jan. 14, 1664 (Fanshawe letters).

A new difficulty arose on the outbreak of the Dutch war, in the sale of Dutch prizes at San Sebastian and Cadiz. In short, Fanshawe felt himself "driven to a dead wall", and only express orders stopped him returning home.[1]

Molina reached England in April 1665, but the popularity of his chef's ollas and blanc-manges did not get over the indigestible grievances of Jamaica and Portugal. If in the autumn the negotiation became cordial, that was due to the collapse of Anglo-French conversations, to the danger threatening Belgium, and to the crushing defeat at Monte Claros inflicted on Spain by the Portuguese. Lisola was pressing the dying Philip to make certain his daughter's inheritance and close the ranks against France, with the effect that in early September Fanshawe was at last empowered to approach Portugal. In November Molina dropped the sticking point of commerce, and agreed to discuss our project of an offensive alliance, on the basis that we should abandon Portugal if she adhered to France or refused reasonable accommodation, that Spain should not demand Tangier or Jamaica, though an "equivalent" was not excluded, and that Spanish subsidies should be forthcoming to engage Sweden. Simultaneously, and in concert with Portugal, it was arranged to send Southwell to Lisbon, thence to meet Fanshawe half-way in his negotiation.[2]

But this edifice of hope trembled and fell at the death, on the 17th September, of Philip IV; the "happier

---

[1] Fanshawe to Arlington, Aug. 28, Nov. 4, Nov. 8, *ibid.*; Feb. 12 and March 15, 1665, Spain, 48; Arlington to Fanshawe, March 16 (Arl.), Aug. 2, 1665 (Harl. MSS. 7010); Heathcote, 168.

[2] Fanshawe to Arlington, Aug. 2, Harl. MSS. *loc. cit.*; Arlington to Fanshawe, April 6, *ibid.*; May 25, Aug. 22, and Nov. 4, Arl.; Jusserand, 151; Evelyn, June 23; Pribram, 265; Pötting, i. 165; Prestage, 159.

days", which from his dying bed he wished to wife and son, were never to be. He left the once superb empire smitten, like that son, with hopeless disease. Starving soldiers in flight from Portugal, the bullion from the Americas dwindling and intercepted, the fortified cities in Flanders unmanned and mouldering, Catalonia lapsing into chronic conspiracy, bread tumults in Madrid—such is a section of the picture of ruin, of "Babylon", painted by Venetian envoys and despairing Austrians. All the web woven by Lisola was rent in pieces, faction seized on the Council of Regency, and Medina de las Torras, in spite of his lethargy the allies' best hope, lost his ascendency. Peneranda, the monarchy's most experienced and able servant, was a "Gallican": convinced from old days at Münster of the evil done his country by the Austrian connection, he systematically ignored Fanshawe, and kept touch with the dangerous Auersperg, the French tool in the Vienna government.[1] And if he, with most Spaniards, hated the widowed Austrian Maria Anna for her alien blood, her folly soon presented them with reason for contempt. She abandoned a scandalous degree of power to her confessor Nithard, a Tyrolese, a Jesuit, and a bigot; and outraged nationalists, or defeated intriguers, turned to the one surviving man of the Royal house, Don Juan, Philip's son by the actress Maria Calderon, whose showy gifts and proved contact with France henceforth overshadowed the rights, or the life, of his young brother. The first, and perhaps the basest, stage of that Spanish paralysis, which for another half century kept Europe unresting by a death-bed, thus began with the first years of this wretched Charles II—a

---

[1] Ballesteros, 258; Lisola's character-sketch in Pötting, and the Venetian reports—Barozzi e Berchet, *Spagna*, vol. ii.

stage ended only in 1669 with the forcible expulsion of Nithard and his relegation to a Roman cloister, there to pursue at leisure his studies in the Immaculate Conception of our Lady.

Before this concatenation of weakness and folly fully evolved, Fanshawe had staked his diplomatic life, and his country's credit, on a desperate attempt to cut the Portugal knot; and this episode we must examine, since it largely explains the collapse of English hopes from the Peninsula during 1666–67, with all the resultant effects on our diplomatic scheme. Not till midsummer 1665 had he been able to send home a draft commercial treaty, and on this Arlington, Clarendon, and Molina set to work. Though aware of these discussions,[1] Fanshawe late in October accepted a Spanish protocol, providing that, if not completed by a given date, the whole treaty should be void; a final draft reached Arlington on the 13th November, but a letter from him, of the 5th, reporting that the commercial articles were being drastically revised, had not reached Fanshawe when he, on the 7th December, signed the treaty.

The joy of the Spaniards, testified by large presents to the Fanshawes, and the displeasure of Fanshawe's government, are both intelligible upon studying the treaty terms. The first, or commercial, articles simply confirmed in essentials those of 1630. They made no provision for free trade in the Indies and no mention of the Navigation Act, obtained no exemption from the right of search, defined contraband in a sense unpopular in Whitehall, and secured us only a bare equality with Holland. By a second, and secret, set of articles touching Portugal, Fanshawe undertook to try for a settlement at Lisbon, but only a thirty years' truce, not a

---

[1] Harris, ii. 41; Arl. ii. 88, 93; Harl. MSS. 7010, f. 417.

definite peace, and without granting Alfonso the royal
title. It was equally serious that, though we were mediator and had not yet heard the Portuguese terms, Fanshawe pledged us to ratification within four months.[1]

That Arlington found some things "inconvenient" in
this treaty, and "others impossible to be ratified", is not
surprising, but actually Fanshawe's recall had been
determined before. The government found him tactless
and unbusiness-like, particularly lamenting his zeal in
pushing, at this moment, a feud with the Madrid police.
With a French war looming, it was imperative to clear
up the Spanish problem, and receipt during November
of Fanshawe's disquieting despatches seems to have
decided them to act. Arlington's letter of the 10th
December informed him that Sandwich was named as
his successor, and on the 17th another issued to bid him
suspend his negotiation.[2]

Clarendon's view, that Fanshawe was recalled as a
"Clarendonian", would have been tempered if he had
read Lady Fanshawe's letters, and is untenable. It was
Southwell's opinion—and he was a moderate man well
acquainted with the facts—that the ambassador was
rushed into signature, which concurs with other evidence of the exultation in Hapsburg circles, and with
Lady Fanshawe's ingenuous exposure of her pleasure
in their congratulation.[3] Some excuse could be found
in the delay of important despatches from England,
but what is one to think of an ambassador who, after
signing a treaty as described on the 7th December,
receives on the 4th January a letter telling him that a

[1] Text in Arl. ii. 114; Arlington's criticism in Sandwich's "additional instructions", Feb. 22, 1666, Carte, 274, f. 11; Fanshawe's defence in Carte, 75, f. 486.
[2] Arl. ii. 76; Harris, ii. 40.
[3] Southwell's correspondence, Add. 34,366; Pötting to Leopold, i. 197;
Embrun to Louis XIV, Jan. 14, Mignet.

new draft discussed with Molina is nearly ready, yet acknowledges it with the observation that it leaves him "nothing disanimated"?

Ignorant of the blow impending, and undismayed by the knowledge that negotiations in England were near completion, good Sir Richard took up his next task, the making of a truce with Portugal.

On the day that he drove out of Madrid, 16th January 1666, a second English diplomat reached Lisbon in the excellent Sir Robert Southwell; the quarantine tests extorted from him and his company, to "cutt capers and drum upon our bellyes", might be deemed symbolic of what awaited him. Southwell, like William Temple, was one of the many Irish Protestants who came at this time through favour of Ormonde and Petty into high office, and of that active generation he was an honourable type. His instructions ordered him to suggest, as Portugal had earlier herself, a truce during the minority of the Spanish king, and to indicate that our military position made agreement with Spain vital. If he received satisfaction, he should report to Fanshawe.[1]

Two brief interviews with Melhor, before Fanshawe reached Lisbon, were enough to show Southwell that no concession would come from Portugal; the minister was adamant on the kingly title, and "eternall in the panerguirick of the Portugeeses". And, with Fanshawe's arrival on the 27th January, the fat was in the fire, the Portuguese at first refusing to see him at all. Behind them stood the new French ambassador, arrived this very week, St. Romain, than whom none could be more formidable; for his experience was great, his spirit both sceptical and resolute, while his general

---

[1] Dated Dec. 20, 1665, Add. 34,366, f. 6: whence most of these details.

endowments satisfied even the exacting standard of
Saint Simon. It was, then, a minor triumph for the
Englishmen when Melhor at last, on the 11th February,
was induced to detail the terms he would accept, and it
says a good deal for his partiality that he promised to
suspend negotiation with France till the end of March.
None the less, his demands were portentous—a definite
peace and the royal title, fortresses on the frontier,
and the surrender of Ceuta—and with this heavy load
the two Englishmen set out for Madrid, which they
reached on the 26th.[1]

There the storm broke from the other quarter of
this obstinate firmament, and heavily on the unhappy
Fanshawe. Had he not promised them peace, and had
they not, in consequence, begun to disarm? His friend
Medina was sore at being exposed to his enemies,
among whom Southwell notes Peneranda as "abomin-
ably sour", and no one except the Queen and Nithard
appeared to be inclined to peace. On the 13th March
the Spaniards accepted in principle an offer from
France of mediation at Lisbon, and before Sandwich
reached Madrid on the 18th May, after weeks of delay
at Corunna over quarantine and transport, Fanshawe's
sun was set. His failure had broken him; he abandoned
business to Southwell, and he had hardly with his
unvarying hospitality welcomed Sandwich, before he
fell an easy victim to fever. We must hope that some
kind words in Charles' letter of revocation may have,
as he said, "broken the blow". On the 16th June,
waving aside the priests and relics with which Spanish
friends besieged him, he died, a true Cavalier, leaving
a fragrant memory, a chequered diplomatic reputation, an adoring family, and a mountain of debt due

[1] *Ibid.* ff. 27-33; Mignet, i. 458; Prestage, 164; Rec. Portugal, 88.

from the Crown. A week later his body set out on its
long journey home to Hertfordshire.[1]

Sandwich, his successor, now a trifle grossened from
the young Puritan sailor, sweltered the rest of this
summer in the Council room at Madrid, where a long
line of Rubens' portraits gazed on his wrangling, maintained in mixed Spanish, Latin, and French, with
Medina, Nithard, and Peneranda. As compared with
his predecessor he had two advantages—one in his
secretary, William Godolphin, who in time succeeded
him, "one of the most accomplished, worthy, and
generous friends that ever I met with", as he said, and
again in that, though for the moment under a cloud,
he had swum in the inner circle at Whitehall and could
speak with more assurance than poor Fanshawe that
his views would be weighed. But the situation itself
was intrinsically worse; the Fanshawe fiasco would
need time to blow over, and the French declaration of
war against us was more fatal still.

Yet the note struck by his instructions was aggressive and grandiose. He was to outline a general league
between England, Spain, Sweden, and Denmark,
which could allow Germany to intervene, unhampered
by fears from the north, and would inevitably bring
Holland in, sooner or later, as a partner. If Spain
would attack France, we would guarantee no peace,
save by common assent, for three years, and he was to
hint that we could at any time win France for ourselves
by sacrificing Belgium. Fanshawe's treaty could not
be accepted, unless Portugal were satisfied and its
commercial clauses revised. Though an exchange for
Tangier was not excluded, and though we would

[1] Fanshawe, *Memoirs*; Harris, ii. 58; Pötting, i. 234; Embrun to Louis XIV,
March 16, Mignet.

consider giving a monopoly of English tin, in return
we should ask the Spanish wool, and free trade from
British America to the Spanish Indies.[1]

The Spaniards felt, not unnaturally, that they might
well get better terms when England was fighting Holland and France. Making the huge assumption that
the Portuguese knot could be cut, what could induce
Spain to enter yet another war? Southwell was explicit
that they "will never league with England if France
will let them be quiet", and could only suggest that
we should either feign understanding with France, or
force France to expose her Flanders design.[2]

Louis XIV's game in these circumstances was easy.
His purpose to attack Belgium at the first opportunity
was unshaken—late this year Vauban was surveying
the frontier—but until the English war shaped clearly
he would dissemble. Wherever a nucleus of union
against France gathered he poured in a dissolving
mixture, and though as yet unsuccessful at London
and Vienna, at Lisbon and Madrid he triumphed. Not
only Portuguese vanity, the spot which St. Romain
was bidden to attack, but their common sense told
them that they held strong cards. In February Sande
had at last arranged a marriage between Alfonso VI
and Mlle. d'Aumale, and in August he and Ruvigni
escorted the flaxen-haired Queen to Lisbon, while
Beaufort's squadron lay outside the Tagus. In May
St. Romain produced a final bribe to overcome the
popular wish for peace and Melhor's Anglophil sympathies; if Portugal would maintain the war, Louis
promised to attack Spain immediately he was at peace

[1] Carte MS. 274, ff. 5 et seq.; ibid. 35, f. 468, for Southwell's narrative for
Ormonde; Add. MSS. 34,336, f. 211.
[2] To Arlington, April 28, ibid.

with England, and to make no settlement that did not
secure the Portuguese monarchy; meantime, even for
one more year of war, Portugal should receive subsidies on a royal scale. Hopes at Lisbon grew high of
an alternative solution which would make the best of
all. worlds; Ruvigni pleaded for reconciliation of England with France and Holland, while Sande, by Southwell's account now the "oracle in all foreign affairs",
was planning a partition of the Spanish empire, giving
England the Indies. Early in September the tireless
Southwell, uninstructed by his government and on
Portuguese insistence, rode post to Madrid, carrying
an ultimatum that the Portuguese royal title must be
admitted within the month, or they would sign the
French treaty.[1]

His mission was useless, and most unwelcome to
Sandwich, whose egoism was not diminishing. Embrun
had dangled before the Council of State visions of
a French league against "the tyrant of the seas", of
winning back Jamaica, of Catholic unity, and he horrified Nithard with the picture, which had done duty in
1662, of the faithful Irish groaning under a heretic yoke.
Upon Medina his rivals heaped opprobrium for Fanshawe's perjured treaty and new complaints of English
privateers, and though some concession was made on
the point of a long truce, not an inch would they yield
on the Portuguese title. Vainly Sandwich invoked
the Austrians' assistance; Southwell's appearance
with the Portuguese terms inflamed the Spaniards
more, and an English scheme for a sixty years'
truce, with a vague recognition of the Portuguese

---

[1] Prestage, 95; Mignet, i. 476; Rec. Portugal, 97; Southwell to Arlington,
Aug. 23 and Nov. 6, Add. MSS. 34,336; Sept. 19, Spain, 52; Add. MSS. 34,337,
f. 2.

"corona", was in November abruptly rejected by both parties.[1]

So hopeless was the difference between the two governments that early in 1666 Carlingford was recalled, but in mid-April he received from Arlington a countermanding letter—written under pressure from Molina, and connected with the Secretary's view that, for the time being, France and de Witt were determined to prolong war.[2] Yet even now our envoy's powers were not enlarged nor did the Imperialists ever come to grips with reality. Leopold's intimate Pötting was, indeed, instructed to back up Sandwich, and from the despatches of his second, far greater, representative at Madrid, Lisola, Leopold was well aware that, if the Hapsburgs rejected our alliance and our mediation with Portugal, both would be engrossed by France. Still, without Spain he would not move, nor if she did would he make the treaty against France an offensive one. His empress only arrived in late July, and till then he dared not further excite Spanish feeling, which was already sore at rumours of partition and at losing the heiress to their throne. The fatality of Carlingford's mission was precisely that it coincided with this inter-Hapsburg tension, and with a corresponding revival of pro-French influence at Madrid.[3]

In fact the scheme of Portuguese peace had once again broken, and Arlington ordered Sandwich to drop it, concentrating for the time being on a commercial treaty with Spain. Hope of a wider league must be suspended till the Hapsburgs met us half-way; as for

[1] Louis to Embrun, May 30 (Mignet); Fanshawe and Southwell to Melhor, March 14 (Heathcote); Arlington to Sandwich, Aug. 2; Sandwich to Arlington, Spain, 52, and to Clarendon (Lister), both of Sept. 1.

[2] Arlington to Sandwich, March 22, to Temple, March 16 (Arl.).

[3] Pribram, 281-6; Lisola to Leopold, March 29 (Klopp); Pötting, i. 256-7.

Portugal, it must be left "to support itself in its own humour by an alliance with France".[1]

So ended another phase of the Hapsburg negotiations. With the rejection in November of Sandwich's last offer both at Madrid and Lisbon, with Lisola's simultaneous arrival in Brussels *en route* for London, and with Carlingford's departure from Vienna, this ambitious plan broke new and heavy ground in another field.

SCANDINAVIA, 1664–1666

Hapsburg Europe held this priority of importance for any grand alliance, but in order of time our diplomacy had first sounded the powers of the North. Here too the waters ran deep, lashing round the permanent rock of Swedish-Danish hostility, and taking their rise from far-off springs of the Middle East. Thanks to the great Gustavus and to Charles X, Sweden held the Weser through Bremen and the Elbe at Stade; her client Holstein formed the top half of the shears that threatened to squeeze the life out of Denmark, her fortresses commanded the northern coast of the Sound, she held Stettin, Riga, and the site of Petersburg. Her soldiers had twice in ten years occupied Warsaw, and now the Polish succession, a prize tempting (like that of Spain) the avarice of half the Continent, was falling open. Longer and more easterly ran the threads of fate; the fortunes of war, as seen from London, came to hang on the outrages of Polish crusaders against Cossacks of the Ukraine, or on invocations murmured before the ikons of holy Russia against the Polish Jesuits.

---

[1] Prestage, 167; Harris, ii. cap. ix.; Arlington to Sandwich, Aug. 23, to Ormonde, December—Carte MSS. 46, f. 425; instructions for Carlingford, June 22, Germany, 11.

In 1664 the immediate purpose of our government was a Northern league against Holland. Since the Restoration our relations with both Sweden and Denmark had been friendly but distant, and restricted to the interests of commerce. Treaties to this end had been signed with both in 1661, which gave us most-favoured-nation terms, kept open the door into the Sound, which Cromwell had forced, but politically only bound us by vague defensive clauses to maintain the Baltic *status quo*. Yet if compelled to make a choice between our allies, we could hardly hesitate. Denmark could, indeed, give us useful quantities of masts and hemp, tar from Stavanger, train oil and stockfish from Iceland, but both political tradition and commerce fast tied her to Holland. To Sweden, on the other hand, leaned all the sympathies of the surviving Cromwellians, and the vital demand for our staple naval supplies,[1] while Clarendon hoped to make good relations with Sweden one of his bridges for keeping the peace with France. But at present we still hoped to combine both in one system, and in September 1664 sent off in one ship Gilbert Talbot and Henry Coventry as our envoys; at Kronsburg they parted, and the several threads of their negotiations must for a time be taken apart.[2]

Sir Gilbert Talbot was yet another relic of the exile and *persona grata* at court, but some experience twenty years before as resident at Venice had neither warmed his ability nor cooled his temper. On the whole he

[1] Meadowes' minute, Holland, 163, f. 199; Urk. ix. 618; Clarendon to Coventry, Nov. 4, 1664 (Longleat); orders to Clifford, Aug. 1665, Carte MS. 46; Denmark, 17, ff. 147 *seq.*; Talbot to Arlington, March 21, 1665, Rawlinson MS. A. 252.

[2] Talbot's first audience, Sept. 23, *ibid.*; Coventry's, Oct. 3, Sweden, 5, f. 156.

reads as a peppery and sanguine Cavalier, hankering to "cudgel"* Dutch envoys, jealous of Coventry's larger powers, and on ill terms with Morrice, the northern Secretary. Quite early in his time at Copenhagen he convinced himself that Frederick III, and, with even less reason, that his chief minister Hanibal Sehested, were preparing to come down on the English side of the fence. More knowledge of Sehested's career would have warned a stupider man. This adroit politician, the husband of one of Christian IV's many morganatic daughters, was a survivor of the old school of Danish magnate, and had bought continuance in power by disgorging nearly half a million of his gains. He had visited England this very year, had offered, it was said, a daughter to Clarendon's son with £40,000, and effused plenty of anti-Dutch sentiment. But despite his professions about concord in the north, he had in 1663 come to terms with France, whereby Denmark entered the league of the Rhine and partook of the subsidies hitherto monopolized by Sweden.[1]

The demands presented by Talbot on the 17th October included the provision of free ports in either country, a fixed annual quota of tar, copper, and the like, certain rights of pre-emption, and the recall of Norwegians serving in the Dutch fleet. All this, Denmark urged, meant a break with Holland, and for that they required an English squadron of fifteen ships in the Sound, subsidies during and after the war, a pledge of concerted peace terms, and the removal of the English factory at Hamburg, not to Stade as Sweden had asked, but to Glückstadt. As to co-operation with

[1] Talbot to Arlington, Oct. 22 and Nov. 4, *loc. cit.*; Rec. Suède; Urk. ix. 710; Clifford's note of Nov. 8, 1665 (Ugbrooke MSS.); Bain, *Scandinavia*; Denmark, 17.

Sweden, they would not renew the treaties which had sealed their humiliation in 1658–60, but were ready to consider a new guarantee.[1]

Thus far Talbot's report up to March 1665, and although some commercial articles were signed on the 29th April, they were limited and cloudy. His government found much to criticize, and Morrice took umbrage at corrections made in his French. The Danes, fearing the loss of their cattle and grain trade to Holland, stuck at our views on contraband, and the Navigation Act played havoc with the notion of free ports. Without sanction Talbot had accepted a secret article, committing us to protect Denmark against offended commercial Powers, while the subsidies projected as compensation for war damage to the Sound tolls were also found exorbitant. Meanwhile, Denmark was playing a waiting game, with her eyes on Paris and Stockholm. Terlon arrived in October as French envoy, and though Talbot could not see what was in "the bottom of his bag", he was plainly working "like a feed solicitor" for the Dutch, who in their turn reproached Denmark with her treaty obligations; certainly promises were reaching Paris that nothing would be settled without French approval.[2]

Our victory off Lowestoft, which spurred Louis XIV to take more pains in the North, for the moment tilted the needy Frederick towards the English end of the scale; his poverty was so serious, Talbot wrote, that he was selling crown lands "to have bread to eat". Within a fortnight of the battle he accepted Talbot's

---

[1] Talbot to Arlington, Oct. 8, 1664, to May 6, 1665; to Clarendon, Jan. 21 and March 25, *loc. cit.*; Frederick III to Charles II, Denmark, 17, Nov. 22, 1664.

[2] Talbot to Arlington, April 22 to Nov. 4, Morrice to Talbot, June 30, *loc. cit.*; Rec. Suède, 52; Aitzema, v. 558.

suggestion[1] that a happy moment to declare war would come when de Ruyter, known to be homeward bound from America, touched with his prizes and the East Indies convoy in some Norwegian port. Thus began the inglorious exploit of Bergen. Frederick still refused to be hurried into an offensive war, and he was to be protected against a charge of treachery to neutrals or allies, but in fact he agreed to sell the Dutch harbouring in Bergen at the price of half the spoil. By the 10th July the Danes had received Arlington's word —"the spoil shall be fairly divided", and Talbot was certain we should "have them all in a net". The spoil expected was great; Clifford, an eye-witness, valued it at six million sterling.[2]

This precious scheme miscarried in every particular. Ruyter slipped past Sandwich in the fog and reached the Texel, and our assault of Bergen on the 2nd August was a fiasco. We pass over that nightmare of muddled orders and false faith; over the fiord serrated by rocks, the bombardment from the Danish forts, the withdrawal in the summer morning leaving six captains and four hundred able seamen dead; Clifford's midnight conversations with the governor, disguised as a sailor and searching for a second chance in mixed Latin and French—all this, the event upon which both Northern Powers waited for decision, had gone against us.

Clarendon, recognizing in Talbot's "extreme folly" a chief cause of this humiliation, was still anxious to make it clear that we had not broken the law of nations, but the majority of the government were determined

[1] So Talbot to Arlington, June 17, contrary to the later official English versions, which put the initiative on the Danes.

[2] Ugbrooke MSS.: Arlington to Talbot, June 30, Denmark, 17.

to mark in more drastic fashion the Danes' breach of faith. Clifford, the new emissary sent to Copenhagen in September, was Arlington's choice,[1] and his impetuous character was matched with some rough instructions. If he failed to get full satisfaction, he was at once to proceed to Stockholm, to strike up an offensive alliance against Holland, and to invite Sweden to "join us in our revenge" against Denmark.[2] Though Sehested "with deep execrations" denied his intrigues with Holland and France, it took Clifford a month to extract even a paper decision, and only after delivering a threat of war was a treaty signed on the 18th October. In addition to £100,000 a year during the war, England was to provide twelve ships at her own expense for one year; Denmark was to declare war on Holland, close her ports to Dutch trade, make no peace save by our consent, and exempt our ships during the war and five years thereafter from the Sound dues. Armed with this triumph, on the 21st Clifford set out for Sweden; and here was the crux—that unless Sweden declared war also within six weeks, the Danish treaty was to be void.[3]

Void it was like to be in any case, and suspicion was universal[4] that the Danes merely played for time, raising a market with which they always meant to close. In early November the voluble Sehested set out for the Hague, and in February 1666 signed the treaty

[1] "Whom I love and esteem so much", Arlington to Coventry, Aug. 29, Longleat.

[2] Arlington to Ormonde, Aug. 22, Carte MSS. 40; Harris, i. 331; governor of Bergen to Clifford, appendix; Clarendon to Coventry, Dec. 7, Clifford to same, Dec. 21 and 30, Longleat.

[3] Clifford's note of Nov. 8, Ugbrooke MSS.; his first audience was on September 15; see also Talbot to Arlington, Oct. 7 and 21.

[4] Crockow to Great Elector, Feb. 21, Urk. ix.; Pomponne, ii. 22; Arlington to Clifford, Nov. 7, Longleat.

which expanded, as we have seen, into the Quadruple Alliance and involved a breach with England. A French subsidy greased the wheels, and it was to France, not to England as he had promised poor Talbot, that Sehested passed onward from the Hague.[1]

As Sweden was the more important scene, so Henry Coventry was a man more massive and meritorious than the choleric Talbot. "Hector Harry" was both staunch royalist and born House of Commons man, and the brain most politics-proof of all his able family. Long in the confidence of the Crown, always genial and shrewd, to a fierce party opponent like Marvell he seemed "honest and wise", and in thirty years of public life, eight of them as Secretary of State, kept his unclouded reputation, his empty pocket, his Rabelaisian speech, his taste for hunting, and his gouty frame. He was to find his eighteen months in Sweden inexpressibly tedious; Stockholm was more expensive than London, while to one who was a victim to gout the climate was awe-inspiring; a fur coat was wanted in September, and Easter was indistinguishable from Christmas—"the same fires, the same snow, and the same drinking".[2] Apart from the barometer, the conditions of his work were curiously like those at Madrid, in which Fanshawe and Sandwich alternately shivered and sweltered. Here too was a regency, and a queen mother balancing two factions; here too a knot of great nobles, dilatory, carousing, rural, and corrupt. Magnus de la Gardie, head of the French party, would have shone in any court, for he was son to a national hero, brother-in-law to the Queen, "born eloquent", says the

[1] Talbot to Morrice, Nov. 11; Dreyss, i. 16, 109; Wicquefort, iii. 277; Beuningen to de Witt, Feb. 2, Br. ii.
[2] To Arlington, March 15 and Sept. 6, 1665, Sweden, 5.

great Pomponne, in many tongues, and once deemed worthy of Queen Christina herself. But he was French in descent, a courtier by temperament, a spendthrift of the public purse, and this could end only in one way. Against him was a floating body, not so much Anglophil as anti-French, with only one solid man among them—the parvenu, prolix, and passionate Bierenclau.[1]

Sweden at this date was an obvious target for any in search of an ally against France and Holland. The Dutch navy had robbed her of Copenhagen in 1658, and Dutch pressure had forced on her in 1659 that hated revision of the Elbing treaty under the name of "elucidations", which, she contended, bound her tariff to the Dutch chariot wheel. There were, too, venerable claims for arrears of subsidy, allegation of Dutch encroachment at Cape Corso and in America, for all of which Sweden had long been demanding redress. As for France, her treaties of 1662–63 with Holland and Denmark, and her reduction of the old subsidy to the Swede, seemed to indicate a new departure in the North, while both Protestant feeling and political fears set Sweden in opposition to the matured design of the French Queen of Poland to settle the succession of her husband's crown on Condé's son, or some other French princeling. Sweden was still a member of the league of the Rhine, but in enlarging it the French had weakened its cohesion, and in warfare in 1664–65, both at Erfurt and Hanover, the religious cleavage had reappeared which spelled the end of French supremacy.

One other factor, vital to Sweden, was involved.

---

[1] Wicquefort, ii. 62; Firth, L.Y. ii. 24; Aitzema, v. 248; Pomponne, ii. 15, 65; Rec. Suède, 45.

At the back of the Baltic, threatening to enfilade her straggling empire, was the new spectre of Russia, with whom England already did a very considerable trade, exchanging cloth and textiles against their tar and furs, caviare, iron, and timber. A year previous to Coventry's mission, Downing's unlikeable brother-in-law Lord Carlisle had been sent to Moscow on what turned out a most empty errand; he was gratified by seeing the Czar on a silver throne, but was refused the restoration of the trading rights confiscated during the Commonwealth, and badgered for English loans. When in September 1664 he reached Stockholm on his way home, he found the Swedes nervous and annoyed: they pressed him and Coventry to get a squadron sent to blockade Archangel and to divert the Russian trade to Riga.[1]

Our treatment of this promising situation was slow and clumsy. Even the minimum objects of Coventry's mission, to get a lower tariff and pre-emption over naval stores, would involve a new treaty, and though he was empowered to discuss a defensive alliance, the Clarendon section of the ministry had neither given him power to conclude—"impotence", he wrote scornfully, "naturally attendeth a Bedchamber man"—nor clear instructions.[2] The short treaty[3] which he sent off to England in March 1665 provided for mutual defence, allowed us (but not the Dutch) to sell prizes in Swedish ports, declared the "elucidations" treaty void, and stipulated that Plymouth and Gottenburg should be free ports during the war, but left the larger questions

---

[1] Carlisle to Clarendon, March 12 and June 14, '64, Clar. MSS. 81; to Charles II, Sept. 13, Sweden, 5; Coventry to Arlington, June 14, '65, *ibid.*; *Rev. Hist.* September 1926.

[2] Coventry to Arlington, Oct. 12 and 29, Nov. 30, '64, to Williamson, Nov 16, Sweden, 5; to Fitzhardinge, Oct. 18, Rep. iv. 279.

[3] Ratified by Charles II, June 9 (Longleat).

unsettled. The permission given him in March to promise money was revoked by August; we had swallowed their colony of New Sweden, but repelled their ambitions on Bremen; we asked large powers for an English trading corporation, a monopoly of iron furnaces and cloth imports, but abruptly refused the guarantee they asked for Holstein.[1] We had met their passion for the Protestant interest by alliance with the Bishop of Münster, and their scheme against Archangel with vague anti-Russian platitudes.[2]

Meantime, while our diplomats hesitated upon which leg to stand in the North, the French induced their ally to make concessions at Stockholm. In March 1665 Holland compromised the Swedish claims on Guinea for cash down, and in October, compelled by the pressure from Münster, promised to cancel the "elucidations".[3] Coventry had predicted this state of things; he had reiterated that Sweden did not want to see Holland obliterated, that she must receive the promised money, and be assured of protection against Denmark and Hanover. Feeling himself thus impotent, he asked permission to retire; the request was refused, but in flattering terms, for with Clarendon he was on terms of close affection.[4] But in September new orders to wait the arrival of Clifford filled him with despair; not so much, one concludes, because it looked like supersession as that the added delay gave France the very opening of

[1] Clarendon to Coventry, March 24, Lister; Coventry to Charles II, March (Longleat); to Clar., Oct. 19; Arlington to Coventry, Nov. 4 (*ibid.*); Coventry to Arlington, March 15 and Aug. 30, Sweden, 5; Queen of Sweden to Charles II, March 9 (*ibid.*).

[2] H. to W. Coventry, Nov. 2 (Longleat); Clarendon to H. Coventry, Nov. 4 (*ibid.*); Urk. ix. 808.

[3] Aitzema, v. 538; Pomponne, ii. 20; Wicquefort, iii. 230.

[4] "God bless thee, dear Harry, and bring us again well together"—to Coventry, Sept. 4 (Longleat).

which Arlington had warned him, "to cut the ground under our feet at Stockholm".[1]

When, finally, Clifford arrived in November with the Danish treaty, Coventry made serious objections. He was forbidden to divulge, though it would be impossible to conceal, that the subsidy hitherto withheld from Sweden was actually promised to the Dane; Clifford was instructed to refer to himself, though he was still neither instructed nor empowered. At a price, he insisted, it would be still possible to get Swedish co-operation with the Hapsburgs and make a league.[2]

If paper promises could meet the case, the new instructions sent to Coventry round the New Year of 1665–66 should have moved mountains. We would offer subsidies ourselves up to £100,000, not to be withdrawn even if Spain, as we hoped, contributed others; if Denmark played false, we asked an offensive alliance against her, but the "foolish discourse" of sea sovereignty was to be repudiated, and so far from meaning to obliterate Holland, our scheme was ultimately to include her in a quadruple bond with Spain and Sweden.[3] But the Swedes wanted action, and that came from all quarters except England. In February 1666 Denmark, Holland, and France agreed upon joint action, Brandenburg and Holland completed their understanding, Russia threatened the Swedish frontier, and Pomponne, greatest of French envoys, reached Stockholm. Receiv-

[1] Coventry to Clarendon, Sept. 13 (Lister); to Arlington, Aug. 30 and Nov. 1, Sweden, 5; to Clifford, Sept. 23 (Longleat); Arlington to Clifford, Nov. 9, Ugbrooke MSS.

[2] Talbot to Morrice, Oct. 21, *loc. cit.*; Coventry to Clarendon, Nov. 8 (Lister); to Arlington, same date, Sweden 5: "it is our duty to tell you, as your factors, what commodities here are to be had, and at what price, but it belongeth to you to tell us whether or not you will give us that price for them."

[3] Clarendon to Coventry, Oct. 4 and Dec. 7 (Longleat); December n.d. (Lister); Morrice to same, Dec. 23 and Feb. 23 (Longleat).

ing no reply to appeals for English troops, and intimidated by the peace of Cleves, the Swedes decided for delay, which would at least get subsidies from one side or the other, and let them continue their profitable export of munitions. Making the Russian threat their plea, they repudiated the draft treaty made with Coventry, and, even before the Dutch naval victories of June, gave a pledge to France not to attack Denmark. With the acceptance in July, by the four Powers at war, of Swedish mediation, ended for the time being any chance of a Northern league or a Swedish-Hapsburg alliance.[1]

One last episode in the autumn of 1666 roused English hopes to a twilight flicker. For years the reduction of Bremen to full obedience had been a Swedish ambition, and the arrival of Wrangel's army outside it meant that Sweden hoped to recover the year's loss and stake out a ground for subsidies. They had underestimated the distrust that they inspired in Germany. Brandenburg and the Brunswick dukes leaped to arms, the Dutch massed troops in East Frisia; in October the definitive making of the Quadruple Alliance put the seal on this resistance, and in November Wrangel was forced to a peaceful compromise. Arlington's disappointment and the French joy were both significant; from the German, as from the Baltic, flank it had proved impossible to shake the Dutch diplomatic system.[2]

Yet the case of Sweden must be distinguished from the despairing situation in Hapsburg Europe. Her mediating ambassadors had reached London in May,

[1] Coventry to Arlington, Feb. 21, Sweden, 5; Pagès, 132; Pomponne, ii. 49; Aitzema, v. 726; Urk. xii. 63; Arlington to Temple, July 27, Carlson, iv. 479-488.

[2] Pomponne, ii. 264; Erdmansdorffer, i. 395; Arlington to Ormonde, Nov. 10, Carte MSS. 46.

Pomponne could extract no pledge of permanent neutrality, and Charles still counted on Sweden to drive Holland to an honourable, or a decent, separate peace.[1] The French hold on the north was visibly shaken, and already the Swedes, Neuburg, and Brandenburg were feeling their way towards a non-French settlement of Poland. From the general failure of our diplomats this at least had emerged, that if the Dutch side of the war could be eliminated, and the French aggression in Belgium set against a clear sky, there was still artillery to be wrung by a skilful leader from the scattered ordnance of heaven.

THE AFFAIR OF BUAT

Arlington had made one serious attempt, in conjunction with this wider issue, to force peace upon Holland from within; an attempt only with difficulty to be distinguished from direct approaches to the Dutch government, since the same agents were often employed in both, and the line was a fine one between schemes for compromise with de Witt in the Orange interest and an effort to overthrow him by an Orangist revolution.

Two consequences in Holland could be predicted with certainty from any period of war strain, a pacifist movement and an Orange revival, and in 1665 the naval battles and the Münster campaign provided an occasion. From Zealand came a renewed pressure for giving the young Prince a military command or a seat in the Council of State, and from Overyssel a resolution that he be sent on a mission of peace, while Beverning's withdrawal from office was taken to mean

---

[1] Brandt's audience with him, reported Oct. 8, Urk. xii.

that the Pensionary's own supporters were beginning to despair.[1]

Until assured of French military support, de Witt must at least listen to talk of peace, and the Dutch despatch of the 1st December 1665 offered Charles the choice of two alternatives, the *status quo ante bellum* or that of *uti possidetis*. Our reply of the 16th not only protested Charles' desire for a just peace and his Protestant zeal; it was a manifesto against France and against the province of Holland as the true authors of war. The dove would clearly be more welcome if it came decked in Orange colours.[2]

Downing's precipitate retreat from the Hague in September 1665 had not removed the last English representative. There was Sir William Davidson, long the leader of the Scottish merchants at Amsterdam. From Frisia our old acquaintance, the informer Van Ruyven (*alias* "Bucquoy"), was issuing his ill-informed letters. There was that curious old gentleman William Macdowall, once of St. Andrews and since professor of philosophy at Groningen. Temple was conducting a negotiation of his own from Brussels. Oddest of all, the broad-minded woman Aphra Behn was in Antwerp, bent on extracting information from the colony of English regicides. Arlington, it will be recalled, was just a-marrying Isabella von Beeverweert, the preparations for whose safe transport were engaging our harbour officers round the New Year of 1665–66.[3]

The English government were not inclined to any

---

[1] Vane to Arlington, Dec. 15, Add. MSS. 16,272; Wicquefort, iii. 40; Aitzema, v. 494.

[2] *Ibid.* 397-8; de Witt to Beuningen, Nov. 12, Br. ii.

[3] Colenbrander, i. xxi.; Arl. i. 56, 102; Fruin, iii. 233 and notes; Cal.S.P.D. 1665-66, 222.

policy of war *à l'outrance*, or to make, as the impulsive Temple advised,[1] peace conditional upon an Orange restoration, but had this autumn opened a secret negotiation with the Republic. Gabriel Sylvius, the Huguenot refugee of Orange, was now in our service, and through him we established contact with Henri de Coulant, seigneur de Buat—once page to Frederick Henry, and now the recipient of an English pension, a plucky soldier, and a boon companion.[2] Others of the Cabinet besides Clarendon may well have disliked Arlington's choice of agents, for Sylvius was a hot-headed enthusiast, Buat gossiping and over-convivial.[3]

In December, and again in January 1666, Sylvius went *via* Belgium to the Hague, and put before Dutch-men of Buat's selection the English suggestions for a separation of Holland from France. The shrewd and influential Beverning, whom Arlington asked to England, found them too vague, but Buat was insistent that Orange interests demanded peace, and would find support in those, like the Zealand fishermen, who were ruined by war. Sylvius returned with prediction of a counter-revolution, and rumours of a vast Orange movement were communicated by the Great Elector to Walter Vane.[4]

Our next steps were more real, and the terms conveyed through Sylvius were more reasonable. We asked the full execution of the last treaty and £200,000 by way of indemnity—this, however, to be reduced, if we could be guaranteed an alliance against France, and

[1] Temple to Arlington, Jan. 23 (Courtenay); Arlington to Temple, Feb. 9.

[2] Siccama's sketch of Sylvius in *Rev. d'hist. diplomatique*, xii.; Japikse, "Buat als diplomaat", Bijd. voor Vad. Gesch. 4th Ser. iv.; Holland, 165-6.

[3] Clarendon, iii. 637; Urk. xii. 636.

[4] Sylvius to Arlington, Dec. 5 *et seq.*, Flanders, 33; Japikse, *loc. cit.*; Vane to Arlington, Jan. 12, German States, 57; Arlington to Buat, Jan. 23, *Br. aan de Witt*, ii. 277.

could be assured that the Prince would be given office
after peace was signed.[1] On or about the 5th February, Buat put these proposals, with Beverning's previous objections, before de Witt, who asked more detail
and suggested that an indemnity, with the cession of
Pulo Run, might cancel out any claims under the
former treaty. In the same twenty-four hours Beverning and Vane were conferring at Cleves.[2]

It is incredible that the Pensionary was sincere. Not
only did he refuse to treat apart from France, and
stand fast on the Dutch alternatives offered in December, but he transmitted to France these and all subsequent approaches from Buat. It might be well, of
course, to soothe down the Orangist excitement, and
this probably explains the step taken in April, in concert with Princess Amalia, for adoption of the young
William as "child of the State". But the Pensionary's
diplomatic position, as events at Cleves and Copenhagen showed, was daily improving, and hesitation
must have vanished with the war-resolution of France,
which must oppose an Orange party depending on a
speedy peace. French money tempted the members of
the State of Holland, and D'Estrades made it clear
that the only Holland which Louis would save was a
Republic.[3]

In short, one and the same fact, the patent weakness
of the Orange cause, determined both de Witt and
Arlington. Buat had, indeed, dined genially with
William's uncle Zulestein (who this April lost his
appointment as William's governor); Fagel, the

[1] "Instructions for Monsieur Sil", Jan. 23, Holland, 179, f. 79; Japikse, *loc. cit.*
[2] Sylvius to Arlington, Feb. 6, *ibid.*; Vane to Arlington, Jan. 8, n.s., Add.
MSS. 16,272; Pagès, 137.
[3] De Witt to Beuningen, Feb. 8, Br. ii.; to Fannius, Sept. 4, '66, Fr. iii.;
Wicquefort, iii. 215; Blok, iv. 330; Louis XIV, ii. 42.

adviser of later days, was incriminated; Kievit,
Tromp's brother-in-law, was deeply involved. But
despite desperate efforts to prove the contrary, both
William and Amalia seem to have stood aloof, and
there was no sign, not even in Zealand, of a general
rising. Buat's own correspondence shows his despair,
and a report from Sylvius at the end of February ex-
tinguished Arlington's hopes.[1]

The full extent of sterility in this Buat business was
exposed by the conference held in April 1666 at Henrietta Maria's Paris house, between the French ministers,
Beuningen, and Lord Holles. The Queen Mother and
Madame hoped great things, and there were the others
involved—Ruvigni, Sande, and St. Albans—who
planned an English-French understanding, to combine with Portugal against Spain, and to divide us from
the Dutch. But with the principals it was merely a
manœuvring ground. De Witt, though deaf to Buat's
plea for a mission to England, would act with his allies
in exploring the English intentions, and incidentally
smother the peace agitation. Holles was merely authorized to listen to the proposals, for Arlington was convinced that the French were only trying to block our
league with Spain; at this moment Sandwich was
approaching Spain with instructions for such a league,
while, at Lisbon, St. Romain was bidding for alliance
against her. It looks, indeed, as if our government
wearied of this contest in insincerity, since they recalled Holles even before the conference began.[2]

[1] Fruin, Versp. Geschriften, iv. 288 (1901); Japikse, loc. cit.; Arlington to
Ormonde, Feb. 20 and 24, Carte MSS. 46, ff. 257-9; Buat to Arlington, March
(Aitzema); Droysen, iii. 584.

[2] De Witt to Beuningen, April 12 and 19, Br. ii.; Holland, 179, f. 154; Holles
and Arlington letters, France, 122; Arlington to Sandwich, March 22, and
Temple, April 10; to Ormonde, March 24, Carte MSS. 46.

We are entitled, then, to be brief over its proceedings. Holles was broken by his wife's death, could scarcely bear a boot owing to gout, and was disinclined to agree with anyone, least of all with the wordy Van Beuningen. Not only did we object to the Dutch terms as fit, in Arlington's words, to be accepted only "after our loss of a battle", but we still counted on the tide turning and on the Dutch coming to realize the advantage of a peace without France. After much recrimination the conference was mutually broken off, and Holles, grumbling at what he called a *Parturiunt montes*, proceeded home.[1] The conference, and its fiasco, reacted seriously, however, upon the Buat conspiracy and all other circuitous approaches to de Witt. The gulf between the two peoples was dug deeper by the great battles of June and by Holmes' destruction of the merchantmen in the Vlie during August. In July Buat and Sylvius had their last interview, and it was made clear that our action would depend upon something "solid" in the way of rebellion from the Dutch side.

It was this letter, sent about 29th July, after Sylvius' return to England, which sealed the Rittmeister's doom. His habits were unfortunate. He would attack patriotic sermons in churchyard conversation, and vapour in taverns to the effect that he held the keys of peace. Warmed by one such occasion, on the 8th August he left with de Witt the last packet he had received of courteous inanity from Arlington, and in it Sylvius' letter, inscribed *Pour vous-même*. That night he was arrested; he had taken no pains to burn his papers, and under examination named some sixty

---

[1] Aitzema v. 921 *et seq.*; Holles to Arlington, March 3 onwards, *loc. cit.*; Charles to Madame, May 2 (Ady); Pomponne, ii. 165; Arlington to Ormonde, April–May, Carte MSS. 46.

accomplices. The bubble had burst. His lieutenants fled—Kievit to England, there to acquire a new reputation in brickmaking and land drainage, and the spy "Bucquoy" to Brussels; and the historic hatred of Louvestein against Orange flared up again. Louis XIV asked for an exemplary sentence, de Witt pressed it, Prussian remonstrances were waved aside. On the 1st October the scaffold ended the intrigue, or the idealism, of Buat. If the French interpreted it as a special favour to their King, nothing certainly could be a more violent affront to England.[1]

So we reach the close of the second year of war. Our one ally, the orthodox and bomb-making Bishop of Münster, had been castigated, and we were at war with three Powers instead of two. Hapsburg league, Northern diversion, and Orange conspiracy had all alike failed. Save for some signs of tension between France and Holland, we were, diplomatically, worse off than ever, and other reasons than this cried clamantly for peace.

[1] Beuningen to de Witt, April 20; de Witt to Davidson, Aug. 20; Japikse, *loc. cit.*; Arlington to Ormonde, Aug. 25, Carte MSS. 46; Aitzema, v. 839; Fruin, iii. 213; Pontalis, i. 392; Dreyss, i. 78; Williamson's Journal, 1669, S.P. Dom.

CHAPTER V

THE CHOICE OF SYSTEMS, 1666–1667

THE hand of God Himself seemed outstretched against England—of "the great and the terrible God" evoked by the naked madman whose voice, Defoe tells us, horrified the survivors of the Plague. In 1665 some 68,000 persons died of plague in London; in the next year it was ravaging the provinces, killing trade and demoralizing energy. Outside Portsmouth dockyard the crows and ravens pecked at shallow graves. Less tragic, but in its effect on the war more potent, was the great Fire which, in the morning of September 2, 1666, began to obliterate the capital. The loss of the Customs House and its records, and of the cloth ware-houses, was almost the last blow to an already falter-ing economic fabric; £60,000 worth of rents were ex-tinguished in London, and no more sinews of war could be expected from the City members who picked their way to Westminster over smouldering heaps of ruin.

Crowds on the heights of Kensington listened wearily for the sound of guns, with none of the exultation of two years before: "let not a '66 come these hundred years again".[1] In home waters there had been bloody but indecisive fighting. The division of the fleet in the June battles had left behind bitter controversy. Holmes'

---

[1] R. Burgoyne to Ralph Verney, Dec. 31 (Verney Papers).

commerce-destruction had not been followed by fleet actions, and with the winter it became clear that we were losing command of our own sea. French pica-roons were picking up prizes in the Humber, in the Bristol Channel, and off the Lizard, and their men-of-war appeared in rivers of Kerry.[1] Our casualties in ships and men had been heavy; in June alone we had lost nearly 5000 of all ranks, and thirty-nine flag officers, by Pepys' reckoning, had been killed by the end of 1666.[2] Courtiers and "tarpaulins" blamed each other, and some cases of irresolution had added a sting of shame to defeat. Seamen's pay was in arrears—in some ships up to twenty months; only the press-gang could keep crews up to strength, and this was so severe that hackney coachmen in London refused to face the streets. Much desertion, execution for mutiny, weeping women round the Navy Office, were signs of the misery which was rotting the wooden walls of England. Of the commanders, Lawson, Myngs, and Berkeley were dead, Rupert and Monk had quarrelled, Sandwich and Penn were under a cloud.

The siege tightened on this island. The winter of 1666–67 was hard; the Thames was full of ice, but coal sold in London at three guineas a chaldron, for the Newcastle colliers could not get convoy. A clamour for rent-remission flustered the landlords in the House of Commons. Newsletters breathed of invasion—even in the Secretary's office there were rumours of flat-bottomed boats building in Normandy and Holland—and not only were the militia embodied, but the country gentry had been called on for troops of horse. In the outer fringes of the Empire the year had been as bad. In

---

[1] Orrery Papers (1742), 141.
[2] Colenbrander, i. 254, from Rawlinson MSS. A. 191.

April the French seized the English half of St. Kitts with every atrocity of negro warfare, expelled our settlers, and closed the Protestant churches. In July Lord Willoughby, the heroic governor of the Lee-wards, disappeared in a hurricane. Antigua and Montserrat fell to the French in November, and Surinam to the Dutch in February 1667. Meantime, French troops and Canadian irregulars had fallen on the Mohawks and threatened Albany, and Governor Nicolls of New York was labouring to extract from Massachusetts a contribution to imperial defence.[1]

Such losses at the extremities could have been re-trieved if the heart of the Empire had not been flabby and congested. Ireland, needless to say, was a sheer weakness, and the "old saying", as quoted by Arlington, "he that will England win, with Ireland must begin",[2] was well appreciated at Paris. There were to be seen the hungry faces of Irish priests, and French muni-tions found a way to Connaught.[3] Scotland simul-taneously rose in the rebellion long provoked by Lauderdale and Archbishop Sharp. Her markets were hit hard by war, her liberty of soul was dragooned, and the Covenanters' field meetings were broken up by Drummond and Dalziel in the style learned in Russian service. Four thousand Covenanters marched on Edinburgh in November 1666, and if their easy dis-persal consoled the government, the executions and outrage meted out to the West exposed yet another limb of Empire in face of the enemy.

It was not only in Scotland that a Dutch war re-

---

[1] Cal.S.P.D. *passim*; Arlington to Ormonde, Jan. '67, Carte MSS. 46, f. 316; Portland, iii. 300; Osgood, ii. 127; Brodrick to Ormonde, Carte 35, f. 239; Pepys, Dec. 8, '66.

[2] To Ormonde, Aug. 25, '66, Carte MSS. 46.

[3] Fr. tr. note of Aug. 5; Carte MSS. 47, f. 315; Burnet, i. 449; Dreyss, i. 175.

vived "the old cause". Puritans were found longing
for English defeat, Whitehall filled up again with the
alarms and "informations" which had poisoned the
first years of the reign, and our secret agents reported
intense agitation among the exiles at Arnhem and
Rotterdam. Sidney betook his grandiloquence to Paris,
where also were hatched schemes to rouse the lion
slumbering at Vevey, Edmund Ludlow. Richard
Cromwell, good soul, was painting water-colours in
France or Switzerland, but his letters were intercepted,
while Desborough was sent to the Tower.

Misfortune and misgovernment had made this
anarchy in England. Treasury control had collapsed
under the honest but unready Southampton, and each
department was fending for itself, scrambling for any
credit it could get from goldsmiths and tax-farmers.
The funds given by Parliament were inadequate, and
later examination showed that from other sources
Charles had given nearly £1,500,000 for the war.
Whosesoever the fault, by the close of 1666 credit was
dead, the ordnance firms and shipwrights would work
no more.

Without large grants no fleet could now be put out
to sea, but Parliament met in October, after nine
months' absence, in an ungiving mood. Their debates
ran on the Papists who had so unquestionably fired
the City, or on the evil counsellors who had divided
the fleet. To their vote of £1,800,000 they tacked
another for a commission to examine the royal
accounts since the outbreak of war—"a manifest distrust", as Arlington naïvely put it, "of the management thereof"[1]—and the consequent argument with
the King and the Lords delayed the passage of the

[1] To Ormonde, Dec. 7, Carte MSS. 46.

money bill till mid-January. For practical purposes this was late, and it was later still that the money could come in, and hence sprang a decision destined to be fatal. By the 1st February the Cabinet (York dissenting) had resolved to lay up the big ships, and use cruisers only for protection of commerce, among the various reasons given being not only the lateness of the year and the number of our enemies, but the necessity to "drive as much trade as we can".[1]

The government's followers deplored the lack of management which left the Commons to "drive at random",[2] and this touched on the root of all evil, that the Cabinet was honeycombed with faction. Except on their one destructive purpose, Clarendon's rivals —Buckingham, Arlington, and Coventry—were disunited. Buckingham had dislocated the session by his feuds, but his dismissal from all his offices in February merely enhanced his repute as the champion of toleration and reform. This scandalous factiousness, the despair of honest Englishmen, was unhappily clear to foreigners,[3] and a broken foreign policy naturally emerged from this Cabinet of atoms. In Piccadilly the chancellor's new palace was rising, the King and Duke outraged society by their vices, and the illogic which associates public misfortune with private ill conduct was gathering into a dark storm. Faction, money-getting, lust, corruption—and the issue thereof—defeat and invasion; on all sides we hear the angry voices, the thick-coming drops before the thunder crash. It was a portent in the England of 1666 that two constituencies

---

[1] *Parl. Hist.* Jan. 18, 1667; Arlington to Temple, Jan. 14; to Ormonde, Feb. 1 and 5, Carte MSS. *loc. cit.*; James, i. 425; Barbour, 107.

[2] Brodrick to Ormonde. Nov. 3, Carte MSS. 35; Pepys, Dec. 15.

[3] Southwell to Arlington, Feb. 3, n.s., Portugal, 8; Brandt, Sept. 28, '66, Urk. xii.

refused the King's pander "Bab" May and Arlington's under-secretary Williamson.[1]

Peace was the universal cry, but the way was to be
difficult and weary. The principle of an early peace had
been granted in the last summer; we had accepted in
July the Swedish mediation, and their envoys noted
that the English were now ready to drop their grotesque
claim for cautionary towns, would accept the Paris
basis of *uti possidetis*, and stipulate nothing for Orange.[2]

But peace is, after all, as much a step to avert, or to
be protected against, the next war, as a means to extinguish one now raging, and the long manœuvring
from October 1666 to the Peace of Breda the following
August would be meaningless if we did not look to the
future. After, as before, that peace we must determine
our attitude to the balance of power, and on that decision would turn the very means we took towards
peace: whether the satisfaction of France or of Holland
—whether we staked all on French friendship, or based
all on resisting France, or stood aloof from either side.

The troubles of Europe, so far transcending Anglo-
Dutch commercial quarrels, rose to a climax just as the
congress assembled at Breda. On the last day of April
1667, with a resigned *ergo moriendum*, Queen Marie of
Poland, so long the advanced post of Latin policy in the
East, ended her last struggle; just at the same time, on
the banks of the Somme, Turenne was putting the last
touch to the army mobilized to invade Belgium. Before
the phase of the Dutch war closes we thus reach the
next, which begins with the war of Devolution, and
ends in the Triple Alliance and Peace of Aix-la-
Chapelle. It was under the pressure of these great im-

---

[1] Cal.S.P.D. 166-7, pp. 198, 308; Marvell, Jan. 12, 1667.
[2] Swedish despatch, Aug. 31, R.A.

pending events that the English government took its
steps towards peace, and if their vacillation proceeded
in large part from their own disorders, we must also
admit the real difficulty of holding a straight course in
this misty and incalculable sea.

Our enemies shared at this stage our pacific intention. Holland was financially exhausted, and divided
by party quarrels which hampered even their navy, the
very condition of their making war. But this Orangist
excitement meant that de Witt, to win peace coupled
with party security, must depend upon France, and up
to the spring of 1667 we need not suspect Louis' fidelity
to his bond, or his desire to clear the decks for his
Spanish war by terminating this troublesome struggle
with England. His fleet, if carefully husbanded, had
given an important distraction, his diplomacy in the
Baltic had saved Holland, he had resisted temptations
to treat separately.[1] There is, however, substantial proof
that from about May onwards he reverted to an older
notion, of leaving England and Holland engaged in a
drawn-out war;[2] the negotiations which we are about
to describe revealed in either of these countries an
antagonism to France stronger than he had supposed,
and may well have convinced him that he could not
safely embroil himself in new undertakings if Holland
and England were at peace with each other and detached from France. It was one of the paradoxes of this
topsy-turvy time that the Hapsburgs long opposed the
peace which alone could save them. Despite Lisola's
efforts, till the French were actually on Belgian soil

[1] So far, I venture to agree with the case put forward by Dr. Japikse and M.
Pagès (*Rev. Hist.* 98), as against Blok and Pontalis.

[2] Louis to Lionne, June 3, n.s. (Droysen, iii. 587), and Lionne's intercepted
letter of August, Wicquefort, iii. 358; Beuningen to de Witt, April 22, Br. ii., still
emphasizes French pacifism.

Castel Rodrigo and the Spaniards generally conceived that prolongation of the Anglo-Dutch war would best serve their turn. France, they argued, would not dare to strike while England had a fleet at sea, and the pro-French de Witt was best kept employed.

Such being the tangled skein of the forthcoming year, we can take up the English threads from the autumn of 1666. Till October there was no change. In spite of the Buat fiasco we did not relax our effort for a separate peace, or the pressure put upon de Witt from within Holland. Temple printed a pamphlet, inspired from Whitehall—*The London Merchant's Letter to him of Amsterdam*—to expose the French insincerity, and explored various private channels to bring about a meeting with some Dutch representative.[1] Simultaneously, round the body of Admiral Berkeley, killed in June and waiting a last journey to the Abbey, began an exchange of courtesies which developed into negotiation. The English still made much of Holland being the "aggressor", but dwelt (as also to Sweden) on the danger besetting Protestantism; Dutch mediation would be accepted with Denmark, but they must define more narrowly the alternatives, and they would surely render to Charles what they had to a usurper and send their negotiators to Westminster. They might, however, rest assured that there was no intention of foisting the Prince on them, or claiming a new-fangled sovereignty of the sea; we should be content with faithful performance of the 1662 treaty, a moderate indemnity, a disavowal of the offensive proclamations issued in Africa, and a binding settlement of East Indian commerce.[2]

---

[1] Courtenay, i. 90 *et seq.*; Arlington to Temple, Nov. 5 and 16; de Witt to Beuningen, Nov 8, Br. ii.; Brandt's interview with Charles, Oct. 8, Urk. xii.

[2] Charles to States-General, Aug. 4 and Oct. 4, Aitzema; instructions for Thynne, Sweden, 6, f. 103.

Elsewhere also this anti-French complexion coloured our policy. We applauded the Brandenburg-Neuburg *entente* over Poland, and encouraged their good relations with Sweden; Sandwich and Southwell were bidden not to relax their efforts for Spanish-Portuguese peace, and Lisola's arrival was anxiously awaited.[1]

But a convincing series of rebuffs forbade us to put our whole dependence on this single strand. The Dutch republicans would have been mad to drop the French alliance, and naturally insisted on a neutral place for the peace congress. Frederick William refused to be cajoled and, worst of all, the Spanish news was hopeless. Arlington had long since predicted that Spain would turn us French "contrary to our inclinations", and now if Sandwich's last attempt failed we must take ourselves to "new measures".[2]

Of these new steps the middleman was the old villain of the piece, St. Albans, who this autumn opened a negotiation with Ruvigni, known in the first instance to Charles alone. Louis refused a proposed conference in England and communicated our first advances to Holland, but in November Charles agreed to accept a neutral place for the congress and the Dutch basis of *uti possidetis*, if France would restore our West Indian islands. By December it was understood that France would use her good offices, though for the present it was decided to conceal the negotiation lest publicity should jeopardize Parliamentary supply.[3]

[1] Brandt, Oct. 29, Urk. xiii.; Arlington to Temple, Sept. 21; to Southwell, Nov. 6; to Sandwich, Dec. 6.

[2] States-General to Charles, Sept. 6 and Nov. 25; Arlington to Ormonde, Dec. 8, Carte MSS. 46; to Temple, Aug. 27 and Nov. 30.

[3] Arlington to Ormonde, Dec. 7 and 18, Carte MSS. 46; *Rev. Hist.* 98; St. Albans to Ruvigni, Nov. 12, Fr. tr.; Ruvigni to St. Albans, Nov. 14, D'Estrades; Br. ii. 396, 403; Pomponne, ii. 365; St. Albans to Clarendon, March 6, 1667, Clar. MSS. 85.

A long lull followed before St. Albans returned to France: to the French it seemed suspicious,[1] and not irrationally they connected it with the arrival in London of their greatest living enemy, the Austrian Lisola,[2] who was instructed to offer mediation with Holland and, if Spain were still passive, a defensive league. It was not his first visit; once before, as an untried man, he had been here in 1640 to energize Charles I against Richelieu, and for two years had been an uninterested spectator of our civil war. Uninterested, because while Hampden and Falkland fell for insular ideals in village skirmishes, the Burgundian's eyes followed that greater chessboard upon which England was but a pawn. To him she must be a destined weapon against France— France the upsetter of balances, the ravisher of his own Franche-Comté, the destroyer of Austria. He was now fifty-three, worn by years in Warsaw, Berlin, and Madrid, and a man of one idea. Fantastic he was often, apt to see a mirage of rebellion in France, or to read his own passionate hopes of Anglo-Dutch union in the calculated utterance of de Witt, but great and inspiring he never ceased to be. It was his misfortune that he was too big for his employers, and that the brakes from Vienna were always grinding against this impulsive, vehement machine.

From the new year 1667 our government plunged into a web of contradictory policies, and seem to have thought, like earlier Stuarts, that adroit balancing would win the place in Europe conceded to an armed and ready nation; forgetting, to quote Temple's potent reminder, that peace "as well as war is made with force and with arms, how much soever some men may trust to

---

[1] Louis to Embrun, March 6, Mignet.
[2] Private audience, Dec. 20.

arts and address".[1] Lisola indeed thought that not only
Parliament, with which he instantly established contact,
but Charles himself was ready to break with France,
and in later days even suggested that Charles deliberately set out to prove the French perfidy to the Dutch.[2]
It is hardly necessary to refine thus far to explain the
English passivity in January, and their sudden embracing of two inconsistent policies in February. Without
more solid guarantees than those raised by Lisola and
Molina that de Witt could be made a "good Hollander", we could not light-heartedly offend France, a
Power armed to the teeth, and one which, in any event,
must play a great part in the congress; there would be
a virtue in dilatory negotiations at Paris, which would
allow us to discover the real intentions both of France
and Spain.[3] Nothing short of necessity could justify us
taking a hand in another war, and an optimist might
see in the break of France with Spain a golden chance
for England, which would give a breathing space for
our commerce, and allow us to intervene as umpire at a
later stage.[4]

But the Cabinet's indecision proceeded, unhappily,
from causes less valid than the genuine difficulty of the
case, and represented the daily acuter cleavage between
the Clarendon and the Arlington wings. Vainly the
King asked Lisola not to listen to stories of the Chancellor's "Gallicanism",[5] and vain it would be to ignore
it. Clarendon's first motive was, doubtless, the public

[1] To Ormonde, April 15, Carte MSS. 35.
[2] Lisola's despatches, Jan. 21 and June 12, Klopp, and March 8, Pribram.
[3] Arlington to Temple, Dec. 10 and Feb. 28; to Sandwich, Jan. 24, Spain, 52;
Carlingford to Ormonde, Jan. 15, Carte MSS. 35.
[4] Temple to Holles, March 29, *ibid.*; to Arlington, May 27; Arlington to
Ormonde, April 20, *ibid.* 221; W. Coventry to Sandwich, April 25, *ibid.* 75.
[5] Lisola, Feb. 7, Sept. 12, Klopp; Urk. xii. for Brandt's letter of May 24;
mémoire for Ruvigni, Aug. 1.

and honourable one of peace, and hence, alive though
he was to Charles' French leanings, he learned to dislike Lisola as a man of war; he saw in St. Albans'
mission the one chance of getting his desire, and looked
upon Sweden, not as a counterbalance to France, but
as a lever to force Holland into concession. But private
reasons influenced him too; Henrietta Maria, he hoped,
would assist the position of his daughter the Duchess of
York, and at the end of a life, half of which had been
spent in deadly conflict with the Queen Mother, we find
him hoping for her return to Somerset House, "never
to travel again".[1] On the other side Arlington, perhaps
for the very reason that his nature was more timorous
or less set, made no such mistakes; his tone to Holland
was more cordial, his suspicion of St. Albans deeper,
and his hopes from Lisola were more real.[2]

The confusion of the issues, like the duplicity or
dualism of the Cabinet, was exposed by the first positive steps taken in the new year. On the 24th January
Sandwich was instructed to play for time. On the 28th
St. Albans was despatched to Paris. On the 30th Charles
invited the Dutch to open the peace congress at the
Hague; simultaneously Lisola was asked to get into
touch with de Witt, and a suggestion made that Hapsburg money should arm the Swedes.[3]

St. Albans' instructions, drafted by Clarendon, did
not empower him even to sign preliminaries, and he
was, in Arlington's version, "only to answer the question France has asked us these two years—'tell us but
what you would have of the Dutch, and we will try to

---

[1] Clarendon to St. Albans, April 11 and 20, Lister; March 22, Clar. MSS. 85;
St. Albans to Clarendon, *ibid.* March 6.

[2] Arlington to Ormonde, Feb. 1, Carte MSS. 46; to Lisola, May 18, Klopp.

[3] Spain, 52, f. 133; France, 123, f. 10; Aitzema, v. 9; Klopp, ii. 144; Brandt,
Feb. 11, Urk. xii.

get it for you'": If satisfied as to French sincerity, he should accept the *uti possidetis* basis; from Holland we must also have performance of the last treaty, security for oceanic trade, and £200,000 indemnity; France must surrender the English part of St. Kitts, and rest content with our neutrality in regard to Spain.[1]

But though St. Albans was not the man whom even this weak government would employ in business which involved decision or protracted consultation, in diplomacy even limited powers may end in unlimited liability, and the choice was a fatal one. He could "neither choose well, nor buy cheap", Charles had once said of him (in regard to old furniture); "full of soup and gold", he repeated on gilt-edged paper the formulae drafted by Lionne, sank cosily into the French atmosphere in which he felt at home, and staked his life on the pacifism of France.[2]

Within three days of his arrival Lionne produced the bait. France would admit a distinction between her conquests and those of Holland, but on one condition alone: if Charles would send a written declaration to Henrietta Maria that, with the peace, he would return to the "closer union" so long sought or, at the lowest, give a pledge that neither had he nor for a year would he contract any alliance against the French interest. All the old private batteries were employed. Turenne spoke of assistance to Charles' internal security, Abbé Montagu assured Arlington that "Flanders will not be swallowed up in a year's time", Henrietta swore never again to set foot in England if her prayer were rejected, and again we heard how the

---

[1] Arlington to St. Albans, March 4 (copy), France, 123; Clarendon to the same, March 25, Lister; Clarendon's draft instructions, *ibid*.

[2] Clarendon, iii. 760; Beuningen to de Witt, Feb. 18, Br. ii.; Clar. MSS. 85, f. 184.

royal authority and our empire in the Indies should be increased.[1]

These terms, backed by St. Albans' word that France would effect peace with Holland, were before Charles and Clarendon on the 11th February, and the next evening Charles put his signature to the momentous pledge demanded, adding that Sandwich's negotiation at Madrid was purely commercial. But if our Cabinet imagined that the certainty of a French-Spanish collision made our peace assured, they were promptly undeceived.[2] The proposition of the Hague as the congress place, suggested (it seems) by Arlington and Coventry, was accurately interpreted by de Witt's party as designed to bring us into touch with his domestic rivals, and by Louis XIV as proof of our intention to divide him from Holland.[3] Both therefore independently and sharply rejected it, the Dutch putting forward either Breda, Maestricht, or Bois le Duc, and Louis suggesting Dover. A distinct growth of tension between Paris and the Hague showed that in part we were succeeding, but this was a game at which two could play. From this moment, perhaps, Louis fanned the flame between us and Holland, for while to de Witt he deplored the wish of Orangist Zealand to accept the Hague, to us he intimated that the Dutch alone were responsible for refusal.[4] By fair means or foul he would keep the making of peace in his own hands; to our immense detriment, a report from Paris

[1] Lionne's draft, Feb. 6, Fr. tr.; Montagu to Arlington, Feb. 8, France, 123; Ranke, iii. 443; St. Albans to Clarendon, March 13, Clar. MSS. 85.

[2] Arlington to St. Albans, France, 123, and to Ormonde, Carte MSS. 46, both Feb. 12; Charles to Henrietta Maria, Arl. i. 139.

[3] Clarendon, iii. 767; Clarendon to St. Albans, March 2, Clar. MSS. 85; Arlington to same, March 4, France, 123; Pomponne, ii. 368.

[4] States-General to Charles, Feb. 14; Louis to States, Feb. 15; mediators to Charles, March 7, Aitzema; Mignet, i. 522.

covered Europe that St. Albans had full powers to
conclude, and that preliminaries signed at Paris would
merely be ratified at Dover.[1]

Pained but futile, the English government fell into
another spasm of indecision, for weeks attempting to
shake the French on the question of the Hague and
absorbing their peaceful professions. A resolution
taken on the 18th March to accept the Dutch proffer
of Breda represents, no doubt, a victory for the Arlington section, who had long urged the intrigue encom-
passing any negotiation in a neutral place; since France
ruled out Spanish territory, and since to treat at Paris
would be read as surrender, it might be best to take
Breda with the hope of further dividing our enemies.[2]
But such a policy could only march if positive approaches were made to Holland, and here the failure
of Lisola's mission is illuminating.

The communication between Lisola and our government reached its maximum in the first half of March,
when anger over St. Albans' juggling was keenest.
King and Duke dined with Arlington to meet him, and
at a conference about the middle of the month[3] the
scope of his mediation was agreed. De Witt had given
some sort of undertaking to hear proposals, even for a
separate treaty, according to Clarendon, and Charles
now asked Lisola to say that he wished the Pensionary
to be the channel of a solid peace. Clarendon's tone was

---

[1] Lionne, March 3, n.s., Fr. tr.; Aitzema, vi. 17; Arlington to Ormonde, March
9, Carte, 46; to Sandwich, Feb. 28; Thynne to Clarendon, March 28, Sweden, 6.

[2] Arlington to Ormonde, Jan. 5 to March 19, Carte MSS. 46, and April 2,
ibid. 221; Temple to same, April 2, *ibid*. 35; Arlington to Temple, Feb. 15; Louis'
conclusion (*Œuvres*, ii. 288) that we took Breda to please him is certainly
wrong.

[3] Before the 18th; it was held at Clarendon's house—proof in itself of the in-
accuracy of his later account. Its proceedings, in Lisola's hand, are in Sweden, 6,
f. 135.

stiffest;[1] Pulo Run and the West Indies must be restored, and if an indemnity could not be got for the
two historic ships, it must be thrashed out between the
two East India Companies. In consequence of Lisola's
pleading it was finally settled that compensation
would be accepted for Pulo Run, and that he might
offer Holland a defensive alliance, which should include a guarantee for Belgium; Clarendon's last request was that he should disbelieve rumours to our
discredit.

Urged on by Charles, the ambassador set out in-
cognito for Brussels, arriving there on the 25th March,[2]
and after three weeks' stay saw de Witt on the 21st
April. From the English point of view nothing could
be more hopeless. Though profuse in generalities as
to the danger from France, he refused to discuss Pulo
Run, or to hear of an indemnity for our "pretensions",
and hinted not obscurely that, with a fleet ready and
superior to ours, Holland need not listen to talk of
concession.[3]

No thesis, then, could well be further from the truth
than that of a de Witt aspiring to a separate peace
with England, to be followed by a league against
France; on the contrary, the terms that he meant to
exact from England were fixed in his mind, and he was
already suggesting to France the surrender of Belgian
territory. The English ministers might, again, well
ask why we should jeopardize ourselves for the Hapsburgs, who had looked on "unconcernedly" during our
struggle, and though Sandwich was authorized to go

[1] This, I think, is clear from Lisola's sarcasm that the Chancellor's "discourse"
would be admirable if the world were ruled by reason.
[2] Sweden, 6, *loc. cit.*; Klopp, i. 144; Pribram, 306; Arlington to Sandwich,
March 11, Carte MSS. 75; Clarendon to H. Coventry, May 27, Add. MSS. 32,094.
[3] Lisola, April 23, Klopp; Temple to Holles, May 19.

so far as a treaty of commerce with a pledge of non-assistance to each other's enemies, we were still without Spanish news, and not prepared to go beyond this gilded neutrality.[1]

But unfortunately neither legitimate disappointment nor statesmanlike caution can wholly explain our facile descent to the terms of Paris, where all was over long before we could have heard from Lisola. Clarendon seems, with his eyes open, to have swallowed the Queen Mother's plea that only France could get us peace; "you will never be able to look us in the face", he wrote to St. Albans, "if France does not thoroughly stick to us in treating". One by one the barriers to a dictated peace fell down; Pulo Run and the two ships were withdrawn, while Clarendon pooh-poohed Lisola's errand and asserted he had no powers. He even urged France to strike quickly in Belgium—a high price to pay, one might think, for our peace with the Dutch—and blindly accepted their promise to stop the Dutch fleet sailing. By the 8th April the secret agreement was made, whereby neither party should for one year make alliances to the other's prejudice; Acadia should be exchanged for St. Kitts, and "closer union" be further investigated.[2]

"I look upon the peace as made" was the cue taken from St. Albans, and as May passed into June our blind dependence grew more marked. Lisola was told that, unless he brought full powers for an alliance, his return to England would be embarrassing, and recruiting for Spain was stopped in Ireland. The Con-

[1] Witt to D'Estrades, May 1 and 13, Combes; to Beverning, June 4, Fruin, iii.; Arlington to Temple, May 10; Leopold to Lisola, May 20, Pribram; Harris, ii. 96.

[2] Clarendon to St. Albans, March 22, Clar. MSS. 85, March 25 and April 11, Lister, April 15, Fr. tr.; Lionne to Louis, April 6, *ibid.*; Louis to Henrietta Maria, April, 8, Mignet.

tinent, our Olympians argued, could gang its own gait, while England, propped by the Grand Monarque, sat on the clouds. Arlington seems the exception; he remarked to Lisola that nothing but words had yet come from France, and imparted to Coventry that "to this day we have not seen a copy of what counter security the King of France gave the Queen Mother". Only a dreamy note of his in reply to Temple gave hope of a change: "the cards are strangely shuffled—I agree with you that, if it please God, we may yet have a fair game dealt us".[1]

In ignorance, naturally, that the Lisola and St. Albans missions had both been mutually betrayed by France and Holland,[2] our government despatched its envoys to Breda. To his immense chagrin Downing had been excluded, but to some extent the choice reflected our divided counsels, for Holles was a Clarendonian, while Henry Coventry (who seemed to the French to be more in his government's confidence) was getting nearer to Arlington. On the 2nd May they reached Flushing, and on the 14th made a costly entry into Breda, trumpeters in crimson riding, and blue-laced lackeys running alongside, so that years later Englishmen still heard Holles' coaches "talked of with wonder". Here collected East India merchants, domestic chaplains, and young gentlemen making a bowing acquaintance with diplomacy. The foreign envoys were men of mark: Beverning, bibulous but experienced, led for Holland; France sent a dangerous pair in Courtin and D'Estrades; while the Swedish

---

[1] St. Albans to Clarendon, April 20, Clar. MSS. 85, and May 4, France, 123; Arlington to Ormonde, April 20, Carte MSS. 221, and May 18, *ibid.* 46;—to Sandwich, May 9 and 17;—to H. Coventry, June 7, Sweden, 6;—to Temple, June 7;—to Lisola, May 18, Klopp.

[2] Barbour, 107; Arlington to Temple, *loc. cit.*

representation was balanced between Fleming, whose Scottish extraction was thought hopeful, and the pro-Dutch Coyet.[1] With them our representatives had to shake down and overcome the preliminary etiquettes of that age of procedure, for only Gresham College, Coventry said, could "make a room and a table where every one should have the right hand and be furthest from the door".[2]

The Englishmen's instructions, drafted by Clarendon[3] before hope had been lost of meeting at the Hague, represent the better mind of our government. An immediate armistice was the first point, and no bones must be made of the points discussed at Paris; we could not break the peace for Pulo Run, though we might try for Cormantine in exchange, and the claimants to the two ships must get compensation by efforts of their own. Any approaches from France should be reported to London, but the envoys were to impress on Holland the desirability of a triple alliance with England and the Swedes. Spain, it was certain, would try to obstruct the peace, and the Swedes should be told that till assured of Spanish sincerity we could not proceed in Lisola's schemes. They should intercede between Holland and Portugal, and must try to reconcile de Witt (whom Lisola should have rendered more pacific) with the Orangists.

Had all this been faithfully followed, the Triple Alliance would have been anticipated, and a squalid page in our history spared. But it takes two to make a tragedy, and the obstacle came rather from the Dutch side than from ours. Every word and move of de Witt

[1] Downing to Arlington, Feb. 21, Holland, 182; Aitzema, vi. 34; D'Estrades, June 11; Sweden, 6, f. 225; Clarendon, iii. 755; Charles Cottrell-Dormer's Journal.
[2] To Arlington, June 3, n.s. (Longleat).
[3] Autograph draft, Clar. MSS. 85, f. 441; copy, Holland, 182, f. 95.

proves his fear of France and his distrust of England. He vigorously controlled our envoys' communication with England, made them pay rent for their quarters, and tied their suite down to Breda, while to the mediators he declared that at the end of one month Holland would not be bound by previous offers. With or without France, he was bent on continued war rather than a bad peace, and so far his persistence had triumphed, that by the 25th April he had received the promise of a French squadron. Before Holles' coach rolled up to Breda castle, he was making the last preparations with de Ruyter, and while the first conferences frothed and differed, he was seeing sailors who knew the neighbourhood of Chatham. On the 27th May the fleet sailed, with his brother Cornelius representing the Republic; "you", wrote the Pensionary, "will be our best plenipotentiary".[1]

And de Witt demanded not peace speedily only, but a conclusive peace. *Uti possidetis* was to be interpreted literally, and not weakened in principle by making an exception of Pulo Run, which, though surrendered by Holland in 1665, had been recaptured. The 1662 treaty must be bared of its dead wood—the clauses touching the two ships and extradition of rebels must go, and that on the Flag be freed from obscurity. If the Navigation Act were not repealed, it must at least be amended so as to allow the Dutch carrying trade in middle Europe, and a marine treaty must be made an integral part of the settlement.[2]

Meanwhile, unconscious of the cloud hanging over them in the French-Dutch naval agreement, the English government abandoned the whole spirit of their

---

[1] Fruin, iii. 296; Aitzema, vi. 110; Combes, 293; Longleat MSS. lxxxi.
[2] De Witt to Beverning, May 3 and 13, Fruin; Dutch instructions, Aitzema.

envoys' instructions, and revived every demand most
galling to Holland. Our envoys asked an indemnity for
the two ships, a pardon for Buat's accomplice Kievit,
and the punishment of our own rebels; some of whom,
like Dolman, were actually engaged on a better errand
in the Thames. We refused to make any concession on
the Flag, and, counting on French support, put in a
claim for the islands of Tobago and St. Eustatius,
which we had taken from Holland and the French
had later taken from us. Clarendon was insistent on
the treaty of 1662, and looked to Sweden less as a
mediator than as a possible ally, instructing the envoys
to seek her help against Holland and Denmark, while
at Breda Holles' new, and French, wife was chattering
about Dutch obstinacy.[1]

The profound insincerity of Louis XIV, patent alike
to neutrals, to de Witt, and to Arlington,[2] was finally
exposed in early June, together with the Dutch resolution and our own weakness. By the 8th it was known in
England that the Dutch fleet were off the Thames
estuary, and the French in Mounts Bay; on the 10th,
that the Dutch were up to the Nore; on the 11th, that
despatches from Cornelius de Witt had been intercepted, which called for French assistance. Toping Sir
Alan Brodrick, with other more sober persons, reflected that we "had trusted the promises of a faithless
prince, and the credulity of my lord St. Albans".[3]

There followed two dark and bitter weeks for England. On the night of the 10th smoke came from the

[1] Clarendon to Holles and Coventry, May 27, May 31, and June 14, Add.
MSS. 32,094; de Witt to Beverning, May 29 and June 4, Fruin; Clarendon to St.
Albans, April 29, Lister; D'Estrades, June 3, n.s.; Aitzema, vi. 45, 253.

[2] Wicquefort, iii. 311; Brandt, May 24, Urk. xii.; Arlington to Southwell, June
5; *Rev. Hist.* xcviii. 60.

[3] Arlington to Ormonde, June 11, Carte MSS. 46; Brodrick to same, June 11,
ibid. 35.

yards at Sheerness; on the 12th the enemy broke the
Chatham boom, fired six men-of-war, and carried off
the *Royal Charles*; at London Bridge one could hear
the enemy guns. For another fortnight they held the
river, while a second squadron threatened Devon and
landing parties alarmed East Anglia. With defeat rose
the phantoms of panic and rebellion. There was a run
on the banks, bills of exchange were refused, and Mrs.
Pepys, like many others, was packed off to the country
with £1300 in gold. Clarendon was insulted in Westminster, his trees were cut down and his windows
broken, seamen were deserting, wild rumours spread
of armed Papists, fuel was running out in London.
Judith Singleton, widow, was sent to Newgate for
wishing the King were hung on the highest tree in
England—but drunk, says she, at the time. A black and
squalid time; yet with one luminous point in it, for this
month *Paradise Lost* stole into the world almost un-
perceived.

Charles' first impulse to recall his envoys soon evaporated, for peace, as Clarendon wrote, was essential "for
composing the mind of the people".[1] Even now one-
half of this vacillating apology for a government still
clung to France and would not trust Holland; Charles
angrily dilated to Molina on French perfidy, but refused to hear Lisola's active suggestions. An express
with appeals for peace went to St. Albans on the 15th,
and Clarendon, at the risk of wrecking resistance to
France in any quarter, instructed our envoys that they
might tell Sweden of our secret Paris agreement, and
that, if other terms with France were settled, they might
undertake to surrender Acadia. Since this was his conception of peace, it is not surprising that with all his

[1] To Holles and Coventry, June 21, Add. MSS. 32,094.

might he resisted the summons of Parliament, refusing to trust that national feeling which, once the first shock had broken, was showing its reality in a swarm of volunteers for coast defence.

On this point he was beaten, and if England was saved, it was not by her ministers, but by her misused national energy and through the counsels of Holland. De Witt was convinced that peace was necessary, for the French conquests in Belgium threatened to make any future frontier impossible. The English, insolent and corrupt[1] as they were, must be made to drink the cup, and to peace he drove them with both weapons of his craft. Sword in one hand, he exhorted Cornelius to blockade London, to attempt Leith and Woolwich, to humour the dissenters, and to rescue General Lambert from his prison at Guernesy, while with the other he extended an olive branch at Breda. Even before the Chatham exploit mutual concessions had been made over the Navigation Act and commerce, and with that exploit at his back he felt able to intercept the dilatory pressure of the French and to accept more compromise. Accelerating the congress by a threat to raise their terms, the Dutch therefore made the most of the Swedes' good offices—agreed to postpone the vexed question of contraband to a later treaty, and to recall Valkenberg's proclamation of sovereignty in Guinea; on their side, the English accepted the Dutch rendering of the alternatives—that is, to make no claim to pre-war "pretensions" or to Pulo Run—and to compromise in the matter of rebels.[2] After long conference an

[1] Both French and Dutch accused Coventry, like Downing, of having a pecuniary interest in the "pretensions"; Colenbrander, i. 559, and D'Estrades, July 6, n.s.

[2] De Witt to Beuningen, June 13, Br. ii.; to Beverning, June 20, Fruin; Lionne to D'Estrades, July 5.

agreement was reached on the 30th June on questions of principle, but as the Dutch proposals involved, superficially at least, a breach of the Navigation Act, it was arranged that Coventry should return to England for the explicit sanction he and his colleagues had vainly asked.[1] "Long and controverted debates"[2] in Council on the 10th–11th July disposed of the points which went beyond our ambassadors' powers. The French would not yield on St. Eustatius and Tobago; as to St. Kitts, they had captured the English part of it by promising liberty to the slaves, to whom they now wished to leave an option of returning, or not, to their masters as they pleased. The Dutch stipulations went deeper. Contraband they would refer ultimately to a marine treaty, to be negotiated in England, but meantime they asked application of the relevant articles from their treaty of 1662 with France. They would promise no general amnesty to their own subjects, and refused to apply to English refugees for conscience' sake the penalties for rebels enacted in 1662. Finally, they asked the free transport of the commodities of Germany usually sent through Dutch ports, and would like, though they would not press, freedom to import the wines of France also.[3]

The Council there and then, apparently without dissent, decided on acceptance, and by the 17th Coventry was back at Breda. A few last struggles of the Courteen and Kievit interests could not delay the decision, and on the 21st July, despite a French effort to spin out proceedings, the treaty was signed. On the 26th John Coventry, whose nose an Act of Parliament has im-

[1] Holles and Coventry to Clarendon, June 10, Longleat.
[2] Anglesey to Ormonde, July 13, Carte MSS. 47.
[3] "Mr. H. Coventry's paper at his arrival from Breda, July 7, '67"—Carte MSS. 46, f. 502.

mortalized, reached England with the official news; none too soon, for Parliament had met on the previous day.[1]

Although on the controverted points the Dutch had, broadly speaking, got their way, it is still true that the three treaties[2] as a whole gave England much better terms than her administration deserved. That with Holland confirmed each Power in the territories it held on the preceding 10th May, and if on this test we lost West Africa (except Fort James and Cape Coast Castle), Pulo Run, and Surinam, we gained New York, New Jersey, and the Delaware. By the French treaty we renounced the Cromwellian conquest, or encroachment, in Acadia, but received instead, in virtue of the St. Albans agreement, the portion of St. Kitts we occupied at the beginning of 1665, together with Montserrat and Antigua. That with Denmark involved no territories and, save that it cancelled a small debt due to the English Hamburg Company, restored peace conditions without comment.

As to our vital differences of policy with Holland, there were, indeed, some important amendments made in the terms of 1662, as in those affecting rebels, the Navigation Act, or the "pretensions". But if the text of the treaty thus disposed of the immediate occasions of the last war, it left unsolved what had been the root causes of two wars and were to contribute to a third —those controversies affecting the rule of the sea, markets, and contraband, which by the English desire were referred to early treatment by special commissioners.

---

[1] Charles II to States-General, July 15, R.A. 12012; Aitzema, vi. 52; Fruin, iii. 331.

[2] Text in Dumont and Aitzema; see also "A Narrative of the Proceedings of Lord Holles and Coventry at Breda" (1667).

With the exchange of ratifications on the 14th
August the second war was officially over, but the
terms, if potentially good, seemed to surrender all for
which we had nominally taken up the sword,[1] and as
the Berks militia marched home ingloriously from the
Isle of Wight, they, like other Englishmen, meditated,
no doubt, upon this extorted peace. There were those
who still thought of revenge; in September the Duke
of York christened his infant son "Edgar", in token—
frail reminder for lost glory—that Britain ruled the
sea.[2]

While the French helped to prolong these three
months of negotiation at Breda, their armies had
pierced the Belgian frontier from Charleroi to Lille,
and menaced the sea front at Furnes. A cry went up
from all Europe against this "universal monarchy",
and was packed by Lisola's fierce pen into the famous
diatribe of the "Bouclier d'État et de Justice". Would
neutral Europe, and would defeated England, stand in
the breach of public law and avenge the infringement
of treaties?

[1] Downing's comment, Pepys, Sept. 8.   [2] Beaufort papers, 64.

CHAPTER VI

THE CHOICE OF SYSTEMS

BREDA TO AIX

WITHIN six months of concluding this inglorious war and this humiliating peace, the diplomacy of Charles II achieved, in the Triple Alliance and the Peace of Aix-la-Chapelle, its apex and its one reputed claim upon posterity, and at a moment when its every interest demanded tranquillity, faced the risk of a second and far more serious war.

Neutrality was the first thought of our government, which to neutrality was doubly committed by the St. Albans agreement at Paris and by the treaty, which we have still to see, lately signed by Sandwich at Madrid. To neutrality also other motives, more compelling than these ties of honour, impelled us; particularly the stricken field of our finance, and the civil troubles, styled by Arlington "no good counsellour", on which the French confidently counted to keep us quiet.[1]

Two years of continual disaster had raised the ghost of the Civil Wars, with the aspirations suppressed and the feuds only half buried by the Restoration. As if by black magic, the face of England changed; "I am in

[1] Meerman to de Witt, Nov. 19, Br.; Arlington to Sandwich, Aug. 8, Carte MSS. 75; Lionne's minute of Aug. 1 (Pagès, 172).

a strange country where I know nobody," wrote Clarendon, "and where are very few who do remember that they ever knew me".[1] Parliament, clamorously called for, was permitted to sit only four days in July before it was prorogued, but not before emitting growls against the new-raised regiments and vociferation (fomented by Lisola) for renewed war. All the normal symptoms appeared of the old Opposition; the "country" Peers met in force at Northumberland's house in Surrey, nonconformist preaching revived, pamphlets issued attacking the Papists. Nature herself turned unkind, for London was scourged by an epidemic of influenza.[2]

Upon the dismissal of Clarendon converged popular panic, political faction, and legitimate national wrath. All the summer long the young Cavaliers impressed on the King that this alone could mollify Parliament, and just before its abortive meeting the reappearance of Buckingham in favour focussed all opposition in one unscrupulous concert. On the 30th August Charles at length dropped the pilot of Restoration, and the tragedy[3] of his fall, flight, and impeachment cannot controvert the inexorable fact that it were better for his fame had the fall come a year before. As half of its root lay in foreign policy, so upon it Europe was divided. Lisola and Molina had contributed, and the article of impeachment, that he had betrayed secrets to the enemy, came perhaps from the Burgundian's inexhaustible quiver. Clarendon himself had hardly landed at Calais before he was appealing to Lionne to

[1] To Ormonde, Oct. 15, Carte 35, f. 762.
[2] Ranke; Pribram, 366, and Lisola's despatch of Aug. 13 (Klopp); Lindsey papers, 369.
[3] Lady Clarendon is "given over for dead; I believe griefe hath destroyed that lady"—Anglesey to Ormonde, Carte MSS. 217, Aug. 10.

work for his return, and it is hardly surprising that, even after the Triple Alliance, de Witt refused him passports.[1]

In other respects his removal imperilled his country in face of an international emergency. The Duke's position, hanging as it did upon his father-in law, was suddenly shaken, and with the revival of the Buckingham and Bristol groups revived also the gossip of legitimizing Monmouth or of divorcing the Queen.[2] Arlington, Buckingham, and William Coventry, in all else disunited, joined hands to find scapegoats for Parliament, and as the Chancellor suffered for a French policy, so Pett, the Navy commissioner, was imprisoned for the shame of Chatham, and Ashburnham expelled the House for taking French bribes. Through the autumn session the Commons faithfully scoured the dirty linen of the two past inglorious years; their committee of accounts made the reputation of Pepys without rehabilitating the Navy, Monk and Rupert appeared to explain the fatal division of the fleet, orders in Council menaced the Papists, Catholics were weeded out of the Guards and even recalled from service in Portugal. The changes rang on Dunkirk, on the loss of St. Kitts, on the lapse of our intelligence system, and on the price of coal, and while, to the New Year and beyond it, the pursuit continued, there was no hope of supply. Honest officials held up their hands in despair, and nervous souls like Father Patrick, the Queen's almoner, inquired as to the possibility of investment in Irish land.[3]

---

[1] Klopp, i. 389; D'Estrades, Sept. 17; Ruvigni to Lionne, Nov. 24 and Dec. 17, Fr. tr.; Clarendon to Lionne, Dec. 28, '67, *ibid.*; de Witt to Meerman, Feb. 24, '68, Br.; Temple to Arlington, Sept. 16, Courtenay.

[2] Conway to Ormonde, Nov. 5, Carte MSS. 36.

[3] Rawdon papers.

Yet to this distraught and discontented England all
Europe was looking for a lead, for the delicate specula-
tions of the closet had lost their value in war; whether
Temple's suggestion to let war rage till we intervened
with overwhelming force, or the Spaniards' hope that
the Breda peace would break down.[1]

One after another the vultures assembled in London:
Lisola in August, Ruvigni in September, in October
Meerman from Holland, in December the Prussian
Brandt. In one respect at least their reports agree, as to
the new ministry's deference to Parliament and a new
interest in foreign affairs, all of which bore fruit in a
social and financial competition among these ambassadors to win the legislature. We read of the left wing,
St. John or Wildman, entertaining Lisola, of others
cloaked to the eyes paying night calls on Ruvigni, and
the scanty Austrian purse was drained in efforts to expel
Clarendon, or to convert Arlington's followers to positive alliance. Through such channels every Power in
Europe was calling on us for mediation, help, or
neutrality, and if popular opinion was clearly against
France, Ruvigni derived some satisfaction from the
tittering in courtly circles at Meerman's cravats, or
from Molina's wretched display on the occasion of the
Empress' accouchement.[2]

It was by no means certain that any of these influences could move England from strict neutrality, and
to a Dutch project of joint mediation, conveyed through
Holles and Coventry at the end of August, we had
hitherto turned a deaf ear. As to talk of "honour and
glory", it came ill from those who had watched

[1] Temple to Arlington, May 27, Courtenay; Lonchay, 217, note.
[2] Carte, 47, f. 172; Ranke, iii. 463; Klopp, i. 198; Ruvigni, Nov. 14, Fr. tr.
Arlington to Sandwich, Nov. 14, Carte MSS. 75; Meerman, Nov. 13, Br. iv.

us, without raising a finger, while we struggled with three Powers, and Holland or Germany, who were more nearly affected, should "begin the dance", said Charles to Lisola and Meerman. It is thus to no popular opinion or pressure that we shall look for the cause of this considerable diplomatic revolution, which we find, as before and as we shall again, in the faction of Charles' counsels and in the position of his potential allies, Holland, Sweden, Germany, and Spain.[1]

It was from Spain, whose Belgian territories were being devastated, that the impulse should naturally come, and at Madrid, where, at the close of 1666, we left Sandwich clearing up Fanshawe's debris and contesting the Portuguese mulishness, the situation had improved. Throughout the following winter Sandwich with infinite patience put together the frame of a commercial treaty, and as we steadily refused to let the whole depend on the decision of Portugal, by March 1667 Madrid had almost agreed to a separate article of non-assistance to enemies. What the solemn warnings from Vienna failed to achieve followed upon news of the Franco-Portuguese alliance, signed on the 21st of this month, and on the 13th May, six days after Spain had received Louis' formal claim to Brabant, the treaty with England was completed.[2]

Forty articles, some of lasting value, related to commerce. We secured most-favoured-nation terms, and could henceforth re-export from Spain without paying additional duty. If on contraband we agreed to exclude

[1] Rec. Hollande, i. 207; Mignet, ii. 521; Arlington to Sandwich, Sept. 19, Carte MSS. 75; to Temple, Aug. 2 and Oct. 4; Brandt, Aug. 1; Pontalis, i. 443.

[2] Spain, 52, ff. 133 *et seq.*; Arlington to Sandwich, March 11, Carte MSS. 75; Leopold to Pötting, March 3; Sandwich to Arlington, April 11, H.I.

food-stuffs, our rule was recognized of "enemy ship, enemy goods", and while we dropped the notion of monopolizing the Spanish wool, our cloth was to be imported to Flanders on the footing of the ancient Burgundian treaties. A specially valuable concession allowed our colonial produce, including that certified by the East India Company, to enter all Spanish territories duty free, and finally, by avoiding mention of the treaty of 1630, Sandwich steered clear of ambiguities (like our title to Jamaica) in which Fanshawe had foundered.[1]

For our future commercial supremacy this part of the treaty was the more vital, but in 1667 larger significance attached to a new solution attempted for the dreary problem of Portugal. It was arranged that we should mediate on the basis of a forty-five years' truce with the "Corona Lusitanica", to whom should be offered all the commercial clauses concluded with Spain; a secret article provided that, whatever the Portuguese decision, the commercial treaty should stand, and that neither England nor Spain should assist the other's enemies. Portugal, that is, might be bribed, but in any case we were pledged no longer to help her against Spain.

Yet upon the creation of the Triple Alliance this important treaty had no bearing whatever, and that for two plain reasons. Through accidents of tide and warfare, getting the treaty to England exhausted nearly the four months allowed for ratification, and only in September did a third copy, smuggled by way of Vigo, Kinsale, and Milford Haven, reach the Cabinet. Moreover, while nothing but an end to the Portugal war

[1] For text and comment, see Dumont; Harris, ii. 102; and Cunningham, *English Industry and Commerce.*

could render Spain a useful ally, this was not achieved till February 1668, a month after the Triple Alliance was made at the Hague.[1]

Since the Portuguese rejection in November 1666 of Sandwich's first offers, a French Queen, French money, and the skill of St. Romain the French minister had demolished Castel Melhor's Anglophil system. Without funds he could not fight another year; the pay of the English contingent was eight months in arrears, and only a French diversion against Spain could save him. Thus forearmed, St. Romain outwitted Robert Southwell's campaign for delay, surmounted the national prejudice of Portugal, and on the 21st March 1667 triumphantly brought off his treaty. Louis promised to attack Spain as soon as he was at peace with England, or within thirty months at latest, and until such date Portugal was to receive abundant subsidies. France would mediate with Holland in regard to the Malabar coast, and French Companies should be put upon an equality with the English.[2]

For some months after this our double-jointed diplomacy between Lisbon and Madrid seems to have collapsed. Castel Melhor sent a mission to defend his action at London, and when Admiral Kempthorne seized French ships bound for the Tagus, raved against Southwell publicly in two languages; in July he rejected with contumely a project for a truce drafted by Sandwich. To make things worse, our envoys were at loggerheads, for Southwell complained of his Madrid

---

[1] Sandwich to Arlington, May 14, H.I.; Spain, 52, f. 209; Arl. ii. 235. Ratified in England on Sept. 12, Carte MSS. 75, f. 557.

[2] Southwell's narrative for Ormonde, June 10, Carte MSS. 35; Prestage, 96; Holland, 168, f. 24; Aitzema, iv. 170; Southwell to Arlington, March 12 and 25, Portugal, 8.

news "rather breaking through chinks than coming in at the window", and for five months on end did not hear from Sandwich at all.[1]

But the avenging gods outpace merely clever diplomacy, and the inhuman calculation of the French broke down on the human instruments they employed. Isabella of Nemours, so ambitious and so passionate, had found (in Southwell's words) a "total disappointment in her bed." and "a perfect insignificancy in the government", and indeed our language can scarcely comprehend the bestiality of her husband, Alfonso VI. From childhood he had been partly paralysed, and even now, a man of thirty-four, he could neither read nor write. His appetites were gross and to kill or to strike was his immediate instinct. Only among grooms and cavalry soldiers did he feel at ease; this hideous figure, wrapped in pistol-proof shawls, with a quill of tobacco in his nostril, covered with unclean sores, and encircled by a guard of mulattos, stalked the streets at night on his one sound leg, firing at passers-by. Tied by policy to this impotent monster, the Queen found herself by Melhor's predominance also deprived of power in council, and therefore turned to France, a force eager like her to see the fall of an Anglophil minister. Through French Jesuits she established contact with her brother-in-law, the comparatively virile Dom Pedro, and the normal stages of a *pronunciamento* followed. Gunshots in the capital, seditious songs, and ringing of bells ended on the 5th September with Melhor's dismissal, from which the conspirators proceeded towards their larger am-

---

[1] Southwell to Arlington, April 4 and 10, July 21, to Williamson, Jan. 25 and Dec. 3—Portugal, 8; to Sandwich, July 20, Add. MSS. 34,337; Sandwich to Arlington, Aug. 5, H.I.

bition of deposing Alfonso. St. Romain was active, Schomberg answered for the army, French ships were in the Tagus, and on the 11th November Isabella fled to a convent, at the gate of which the demented king was soon wildly battering. The mob rose, Pedro declared himself regent, and on the 13th deposed his brother.[1]

But the plot had gone too far; a cry for peace, within and without, was taken up in the streets and the pulpits, and the murder of Sande, head of the French party, testified to the people's will. By the 3rd December Pedro had given way, and through Spanish hostages and Southwell reopened conversations with Madrid, where a new peace move in earnest had, in fact, been launched in midsummer. News of the treaty of Breda at last speeded up the Spanish council, who on the 21st September pledged themselves to treat for a perpetual peace, as from King to King; this principle once settled, nothing remained but the powers to be given to Sandwich as mediator, and the detailed terms. In this, and in discussion of the *projet* he suggested, which in substance was the same as that put by Melhor two years earlier to the unhappy Fanshawe, two more months ebbed away, and not till the 25th November did Sandwich receive his commission, and not till the 12th January did he reach Lisbon. While in the royal barge he was rowing down the Tagus, in the cold rooms of the Hague Temple was perusing the perfected Latin of the Triple Alliance.[2]

Once more, then, that alliance owed nothing to our success in the Peninsula, and of this Sandwich's

[1] St. Romain's narrative, Mignet, ii. 265; D'Ablancourt, *op. cit.*; Southwell's account of Feb. 28, 1668, Add. MSS. 34,337; Southwell to Arlington, Nov. 5, Carte MSS. 35; to Williamson, Oct. 21, Portugal, 8; Prestage.

[2] Sandwich to Arlington, Sept. 25, Nov. 16, H.I.; Harris, ii. 125.

recall (dating from the 14th November) may be taken
as final proof. Castel Rodrigo's appeal for English
volunteers meant nothing in the absence of action
from Madrid, but for this Arlington watched in vain.
Medina, the staunchest of the anti-French party, did
indeed speak spasmodically of a defensive alliance, but
showed no serious purpose till the Breda treaty made
it clear that Spain must now bear the brunt of the
French attack. In the musical parties to which Sandwich (the patron of Pepys) took his violin, he had large
talk with Don Juan, the popular Infante. While Sandwich asked for an assiento and trade with Buenos
Ayres, the Spaniards hinted at subsidies for our ships
or a free port in the Indies, but to November nothing
encouraged us to accept their advances as serious,
their appeal to Papal mediation and their flaccid defensive in Flanders rather giving an impression that
they were ready to patch up with France. Other
negotiations, soon to be seen, suggested that they
might buy Dutch support by ceding strips of Belgium:
conferences in London early that month extorted an
admission from Molina that he was neither empowered
to make a league nor to give concessions in the Indies,
and of the Portuguese peace there was, as yet, not a
word.[1]

But by Molina's side was the great Lisola, giving
hopes that he could energize Austria to combat the
lethargy of Spain. It proved beyond his power. On the
day, in late July 1667, that he returned to London, the
Emperor was issuing instructions which made his own
participation in a league dependent on the adhesion of

[1] Carte MSS. 220, f. 270; Arlington to Sandwich, Sept. 5, *ibid.* 75; Spain, 53,
f. 55; Sandwich to Arlington, June 26 and Dec. 11, H.I.; Harris, ii. 113; Pötting,
i. 335; Arlington to Temple, Nov. 11; Queen of Spain to Gamarra, Dec. 22
(Lonchay).

Spain, and all the autumn long Leopold's undoubted
hostility to France withered under a cold sleet of faction
and corruption. His envoys' prolonged effort to get
from the Reichstag a guarantee for the circle of Bur-
gundy was a failure; on the contrary, the leading princes,
led by Mainz, issued a manifesto for peace upon the
status quo. This was not the worst, since the Catholic-
Rhenish group—Köln, Neuburg, and Münster—were
decided to resist by force of arms a march of German
troops to Flanders, and it was seen that the French
domination of Germany and its "liberties" was reaching a climax. The age of the Fürstenbergs had
arrived; one brother manipulated Köln and a second
Bavaria, while William, the third of the band, was the
hinge on which this French penetration turned. In him,
with his brilliant good looks, light morals, and distinguished intelligence, Lionne found his *alter ego*—to
him was due the serpentine moderation of the French
diplomatic campaign this winter, and this priest-lover
of the Comtesse De La Marck will be found to be one
author of the Triple Alliance. Even in the Protestant
group there were conflicting fears. The Brunswick
dukes were fearful that Sweden would try a *revanche*
for Bremen, and the Great Elector, though resisting
approaches from Köln, was convinced that the Hapsburgs were dealing in figments. Brandt had received
from Clarendon's lips the secret of our pledged neutrality to France,[1] from Brussels there was no hope
of subsidies, from Vienna no guarantee of support
in Belgium, nor recognition of Neuburg claims in
Poland.

We may say, in short, that even before the Breda
peace, all chance had vanished of Imperial resistance,

---

[1] Urk. xii. 656.

and date from June[1] the French decision to disarm it
by meeting it half-way. The Duke of Neuburg had
seventeen children to place, and jumped at Louis'
promise to recognize his claim to the Polish crown, a
move which simultaneously satisfied half the fears of
Berlin; the other half was placated by an announcement that French demands upon Belgium would be
limited, and that Spanish Gueldres might well fall to
Brandenburg. Sickened by Spanish *magnifica verba*,
and disappointed in his hope of allied money, on the
5th December the Elector signed a treaty with France
which pledged him to non-resistance in the Netherlands.[2]

Almost at the same time capitulated that other enemy
of France, the Emperor Leopold, less to French threats
in Hungary and on the Rhine than to despair of his
natural allies. He could hope for nothing from Germany,
his objurgations to Spain were all in vain,[3] while lack
of money and mutual distrust regarding Poland broke
off a long-drawn treaty with Sweden. In October his
envoy at Paris suggested, over the wine, to Fürstenberg that the partition scheme put forward in 1665
merited resurrection, while to Lobkowitz, that minister
of Leopold who saw in Spanish dominion the curse of
the Hapsburgs, Lionne transmitted the idea that Spain
must be treated with healing medicine "as a sick man".
By the 15th November Leopold had accepted the
principle of a partition in the event of the King of
Spain's death, on the understanding that France
would reduce her gains from the present war either
to Franche-Comté (or Luxemburg), with Douai and a

[1] Lionne to Louis, June 17, Pagès.
[2] Urk. xii. 747, 800; Pagès, 181; Mignet, ii. 279.
[3] "Ego moneo, increpo, obtestor, sed sine effectu"—to Pötting, Dec. 8.

few specified fortresses, or to her actual conquests of this campaign.[1]

The death, on the 3rd January 1668, of his infant son, and the doctors' verdict that the Empress could bear no more children, perhaps convinced Leopold; since his "dear angel" had slipped away to heaven, he would transact with mammon, admit the nullity of the French renunciation, and make sure of Spain, the Indies, and Italy in the event of Charles II's death. At two o'clock in the morning of the 10th January the treaty was signed, the vital clause for our purpose being Leopold's promise not to intervene in the existing war. Catholic Vienna was moved in its low and its high places, Auersperg was rubbing his hands at the cardinal's hat promised him by France, the Emperor was on his knees to St. Anthony and speaking of the Triple Alliance as a league of heretics.[2] The actual document was conveyed to France by seven of Louis' guards, to be locked away for a century from men's eyes,[3] but Lisola's talk of veteran troops tinkled so false and so empty, for the very reason that his master's embarrassed silence as to ways and means seemed to confirm the French boast he was in their hands.

In one corner only of the horizon could our government discern a faint glimmer, in the continued anti-French system of Sweden, who had used our friendship as a lever to make Holland cancel the hated "elucidations" of Elbing, had tried in the face of French objection to extend the Breda treaty to Brandenburg and Holstein, and was supporting Neuburg in Poland. Their

---

[1] Pomponne, i. 423; Legrelle, i. 129; Mignet, ii. 337; Wolf, 167.

[2] Pötting, i. 363; Legrelle, i. 139, note.

[3] *Ibid.* 140; add, not only that Louis revealed it to William III in 1698 (Gaedeke, i. 226), as did Torcy later to Bolingbroke (*Works*, ii. 265), but that it was known to the Prussians by March 1669—see Droysen, iii. 589.

representative at the Hague, Christopher Dohna, was impelling them to go further; ardently Calvinist, Orangist noble by birth, stout, Latinless, determined, he had excited the just suspicion of France, and in September was pressing on de Witt an armed mediation.[1]

Our envoy at Stockholm was Thomas Thynne, a nephew of the Coventries and best known for his patronage, in old age, of the saintly Ken. At this date he was young and mercurial, but in October he represented that no chance existed of Sweden taking the field against France. Even as he wrote, powers for Dohna to negotiate a league were on the way, but he was so far right in that for six months the Swedish decision vacillated, and that it came too late seriously to influence our policy. Pomponne and the Austrians were vying in offers of subsidies, the Bierenclau and La Gardie factions brandished their periwigs in senatorial snap-divisions, while a last touch was put to Swedish anarchy this summer by a flying visit from ex-Queen Christina, whose mass priests roused riot and protest as she reached the Baltic. Not till Christmas, when La Gardie, true to character, went off for a prolonged holiday, did the anti-French faction more or less get the upper hand, and even then, if subsidies alone could secure them, what could England do, with not £100 to spare?[2]

Sweden, Spain, Portugal, Austria, and Germany; from none of these, plainly, did the impulse to the Triple Alliance proceed, and we must look for it in Holland, with whom we had but just closed a vindictive war.

[1] Thynne to Clarendon, May 1, Lister; Carlson, iv. 498; Pomponne, i. 376, 442; Wicquefort, iii. 364; Pagès, 158; Beverning to de Witt, June 8, *Br. aan de Witt*, ii.; D'Estrades, July 3; Fruin, iii. 377; Aitzema, iii. 365.

[2] Clarendon to H. Coventry, Aug. 2, Add. MSS. 32,094; Thynne to Arlington, Aug. 14 and Oct. 9, Sweden, 6; Carlson, iv. 500; Pomponne, i. 455.

De Witt's life-work hitherto had rested on French friendship, and neither before nor after the Triple Alliance was he prepared to lose it.[1] As in 1663, so now, his hope was to dispose of the Belgian question in concert with France, and of him at any rate nothing could be more misleading than Temple's repeated message from Brussels that war, and war on the side of Spain, was the Dutch interest. It was, of course, a fact that de Witt was no autocrat any more than Charles II, that many Dutchmen—notably Beuningen—were more warlike than he, and several provinces more warlike than Holland; it was inevitable, too, that he should probe the possibilities of resistance to France in view of her exorbitant conquests, of German lassitude, and Münster's talk of a new war. But this will not be found to vitiate the main conclusion, that the Triple Alliance, in so far as it was designed to menace France with war, was not his work, though perhaps only precise dates will dispel a legend.[2]

Not till the last week of September 1667 did Temple's first unofficial visit to the Hague glean from de Witt a reprobation of Belgian partition and his desire for an English league. But much earlier, in mid-May, he had intimated to France the Dutch acquiescence in force being 'put on Spain to surrender Franche-Comté, with Arras, St. Omer, and much more, or an equivalent; in mid-July, though resisting recognition of all the "claims of the Queen", he was ready to "cantonize" Belgium if the young King died, and it was by the Dutch that the second alternative was put forward,

[1] For preliminary proof, see de Witt to Courtin, Aug. 31 (Combes); to Meerman, May 4 (Br.); and to Beuningen, May 31 (Fruin), 1668; Dohna's view of his Francophilism, Wicquefort, iii. 382; Japikse, *De Witt*, 259.

[2] Temple to Arlington, July 16, Flanders, 37; to Ormonde, Oct. 1, Carte MSS. 35; D'Estrades, Jan. 11, 1668.

which Louis accepted in September, of a peace on the footing of *uti possidetis*.[1]

There was, indeed, a short phase, culminating in early October, when he was exploring what resisting ground he could find to overcome what he disliked most in the French terms—their refusal of a long armistice or of express "renunciation", and their loyalty to Portugal. But that phase was short, and his terms were very high—nothing less, in fact, than that Spain should finance Prussian mercenaries and, in return for a loan, pledge Ostend and Bruges to Holland. Taught by Spanish delay and bankruptcy, he soon returned to his substantive policy, and by November had broken off conversations with Brussels and Germany, and reopened his discussion of partition with D'Estrades; on the 30th the States of Holland voted that Spain should be forced to the French terms, the Pensionary going so far as to guarantee France against attack by a third party, on condition that her future conquests were made outside the Low Countries.[2]

Anxious his position must be, but never had his measures been more determined; was this civilian, the French grumbled, an umpire to give law to Europe? He sped another arrow this autumn, not of good omen for England, for, seizing on the prestige won at Breda, he revived an earlier idea of divorcing the supreme military from the supreme civil power in Holland, and in August the States, going beyond his decisive moderation, passed the Perpetual Edict, to suppress for ever

---

[1] Temple to Arlington, Sept. 25 and Nov. 12, I. c.; Sec. Res., May 10; de Witt to D'Estrades, May 13, Combes; to Beuningen, July 11, Br.; Mignet ii. 488 *et seq.*; Louis XIV, ii. 326, 441; Aitzema, vi. 329.

[2] Dollot, 177; Urk. xii. *passim*; Pontalis, i. 430; Temple to Arlington, Oct. 15, Nov. 12 and 29, Flanders, 37; to Ormonde, Nov. 19, Carte MSS. 35; D'Estrades, Nov. 7; Japikse, *De Witt*, 262.

the office of Stadtholder in the province. Such were the ingredients of the European cauldron towards the end of 1667, and it was plain that Holland and France were the only two that mattered.

Of the new Foreign Committee who had to determine the rôle of England, Lord Keeper Bridgeman was anti-French,[1] and the "northern" secretary, Morrice, followed Monk, who in his turn usually said ditto to the King. The most uncertain factor was Buckingham, now in the heyday of a popularity which he enjoyed as much as, and identified with, power. He was bent on using Parliament, for whose cause many thought him a martyr, to destroy Clarendon and then Arlington, and would embroil foreign policy to the same end. He declared, in consequence, for a policy of action, at first on the side of Spain, but Ruvigni won him in October, made a tool of his secretary, the Catholic Ellis Leighton, and got the Duke added to the Foreign Committee. A war giving to France the land, but to England the sea, perhaps even a Belgian partition between them—such visions dropped from Buckingham's alcoholic fancy.[2]

Arlington on the other hand, so Ruvigni reported, was "not a friend". Neutrality was his first, and perhaps his last, wish, but neutrality might be made to pay, or "worth something", Williamson reports Charles as saying, "considering how the humour of his people runs to the contrary". Now, as five years before, over the Declaration of Indulgence, Arlington's eyes turned to Parliament, for he was engaged, Ruvigni saw, "on a parliamentary slope", and clear that the King "must

---

[1] Ruvigni, Oct. 27, Fr. tr.; de Witt to Meerman, Feb. 24, 1668, Br.; Temple to Bridgeman, Jan. 27.

[2] Ruvigni, Sept. 9 to Dec. 26, *loc. cit.*

settle his own affairs in my judgement before he meddles with his neighbours' ". His fear of a refusal of supply, and his hope that patriotism would make Parliament relent, certainly explain in part both his long hesitation and his final adoption of the Triple Alliance.[1]

Quite certainly the conduct of English diplomacy this autumn did not spell surrender to France. St. Albans had stimulated the sending of Ruvigni, but was politely elbowed out of the negotiation, while to French complaint of Southwell's activity at Lisbon, and a suggestion that we should break off Sandwich's treaty, we opposed silence or refusal. Thynne helped in the Swedish-Prussian *entente* in regard to Poland, and promised subsidies for the Swedish troops. The government did, indeed, allow the Papists dismissed from the Horse Guards to take French service, but it also allowed hundreds of volunteers to cross to Ostend.[2]

But these pin-pricks would not stop the French legions, and a nearer view of Dutch policy convinced us that no bare, or Spanish-inclined, neutrality could save the balance of power. Not until mid-November had both their envoys, Meerman and Boreel, arrived;[3] Meerman, the leader, was a close confidant of de Witt, but the French disagreed whether he was their friend. Their instructions were merely to press on the Marine treaty, particularly the amendment of the Navigation Act, and to offer a joint mediation in the war; beyond

[1] Ruvigni, Sept. 12, Oct. 10, Nov. 25, *loc. cit.*; Williamson's note of Nov. 14, France, 123; *E.H.R.* xliv. 290; Arlington to Ormonde, Aug. 31 and Jan. 21, Carte MSS. 46; to Sandwich, Oct. 31; to Temple, Feb. 14.

[2] Spain, 53, f. 166, intercepted; France, 123, ff. 163 *et seq.*; Ruvigni, Sept. 16 and Dec. 22–26; Pagès, 170; Beverning to de Witt, June 11 (Fruin, *Br. aan de Witt*); D'Estrades, June 11.

[3] Meerman arrived on Oct. 12—his Verbaal in R.A. Leg. 797; Boreel, before their first public audience on Nov. 15, Carte MSS. 217, f. 421.

that bitter pill and this generality their powers did not go, and the vagueness of their proposals deepened an initial distrust of Dutch intentions which Holles and Coventry had brought back from Breda.[1] Charles was deeply indignant at the contemplated mortgage of Belgian lands to Holland, and would agree only if Ghent and Nieuport fell to England, but this de Witt would not stomach, clinging as he still did to the hope of some acquisition in Spanish Gueldres. Till December Arlington still believed the French-Dutch understanding to be unbroken, and that Holland would rather "go in for their share of the prey" than help the Spaniard.[2]

At a series of conferences held late in November, Arlington, Buckingham, and Morrice tried to test the degree of reality behind the Dutch talk of a mediated peace and the plans for a league which de Witt had imparted to Temple. The envoys at first disclaimed knowledge of the fact that the States had agreed with France to force Spain to the "alternatives". Pressed whether they would compel France to disgorge her conquests, they replied, as individuals, that this meant everlasting war; asked, did they then mean to put force on Spain, they implied "yes, by refusing her subsidies". Peace at any price, they told the Hapsburg ministers, was Holland's interest; Spain must make a sacrifice, and all they were concerned with was to reduce it to a minimum.[3] Further conferences at Whitehall on the

---

[1] Ruvigni, Oct. 16; Rec. Hollande, ii. 208; Fruin, iii. 380; Verbaal, *loc. cit.*; Sec. Res., Sept. 24; interview of Arlington with Holles, Sept. 14, Carte MSS. 46, f. 550; Meerman to de Witt, Nov. 4, Br.

[2] Meerman to de Witt, Nov. 4, de Witt to Meerman, Dec. 6 and 27, Br.; Verbaal, Nov. 24; Wicquefort, iii. 337; Arlington to Temple, Sept. 26; to Ormonde, Dec. 7, Carte MSS. 46.

[3] Foreign Entry Book, 176, Nov. 21–30; Verbaal, Nov. 29; Meerman to de Witt, Dec. 1, Br.; Lisola, Dec. 6, Klopp.

6th and 7th December broke down the Dutch fencing
a little further, for Lisola and Molina took a hand.
Arlington and Buckingham protested that England
could not forsake Spain, who only three months ago was
joined to us by treaty, and a biting analysis from Lisola
showed that, while the Dutch scheme would make them
either the allies or the accomplices of France, it could
not in any event banish the necessity for a league to
guarantee whatever peace might be won. The English
urged joint action with Sweden and the Empire, and
supported Lisola's point-blank question—would Holland help England and the Hapsburgs if Spain
accepted, but France refused, the alternatives?[1] With
Meerman's halting reply that he believed so, but had
no authority to say so, our effort to commit Holland
through her envoys was abandoned; on the 25th November Arlington had drafted instructions for Temple
to proceed to the Hague with the project of an offensive
alliance, and a messenger detailed that day left England
(after long waiting for a packet) on the 5th December.[2]

This step did not proceed merely from a wish to get
to grips with Dutch policy, but formed part of a reaction from a negotiation simultaneously proceeding with
France, the sincerity of which we can only determine
when the period ending in the peace of Aix is reviewed
as a whole. But there were, notoriously, chords in
Charles' personal policy upon which an instrumentalist

[1] Verbaal, Dec. 17; Lisola, Dec. 17, Pribram.

[2] There is a mystery, important to determine the order of events, about this
matter. The instructions, dated Nov. 25, were brought to Temple at Brussels by
one Osborne on the night of Dec. 15. But Osborne was issued with a pass for
Holland on Nov. 25 and sailed on Dec. 5. As Arlington's letter of Nov. 25, warning Temple to expect instructions, reached Temple on Dec. 1, Osborne was clearly
carrying something more weighty. But could he take ten days *en route*? Possibly
Osborne's first mission was merely to order Temple to return to England, *via* the
Hague, which Temple knew by the 13th; if so, he could return and still catch the
second packet which left Harwich on Dec. 10 or 11.

less skilled than Ruvigni could play. He was not prepared to let his control of foreign affairs suffer through
the Clarendon shipwreck; he was inordinately jealous
of the Dutch fleet; and the Orange group, represented
by Sylvius, were urging that now was the chance to
punish de Witt. And if Ruvigni could measure the
French chances by Charles' professions, or by the
dinner parties he was asked to, he had ground for hope.[1]

Our doubt as to the real attitude of England turns
less on an absence of documents than on the incessant
feud between Buckingham and Arlington, and the in-
constancy of their influence with an inconstant master.
Arlington's anti-French bias was so strong that
Ruvigni asked his exclusion from council, and though
the King and Buckingham may have preferred the
French alliance to any other, pride in the navy and
love of popularity were strong cross-currents, and the
language of some of the Buckingham group in the
Commons inclines one to think that Ruvigni, like other
French ambassadors of this reign, was over-confident.[2]
If we may assume that neutrality was genuinely the
first idea of Charles and Arlington, their second was a
neutrality that could be made to pay, and that could
come only by agreement with France, who must be
made to rise to our expectations. Ruvigni had instructions to follow up D'Estrades' approaches of 1662
towards "closer union" and assistance against rebels,
but he could make little progress, finding instead
general complaints about the non-restoration of our
half of St. Kitts, Arlington demanding completion of
Holles' commercial treaty, and Charles peevish about

[1] Charles to Madame, Nov. 30, Ady; Meerman to de Witt, Oct. 27, Br.;
Arlington's note of Nov. 26, see Appendix.

[2] Ruvigni, Dec. 5, Barbour; Howard's speech, Nov. 11, Grey; Meerman to
de Witt, Nov. 9, Br.

the Flag. The King refused to repeat Lisola's conversation or the Spanish offers, and said plainly that only considerable assistance would enable him to overcome the hostility to France in Cabinet and Parliament. In fact, the conduct of this negotiation was far less personal than might be supposed, for Morrice was cognisant of the French endeavours, Manchester and Lauderdale were put on to the commercial treaty, while the final decision leading to the Triple Alliance was taken in the whole committee of Foreign Affairs.[1]

It is also noteworthy that the English demands upon France steadily rose in magnitude. To Louis' first suggestion of a share in the Indies and troops in case of disorder, Charles replied on the 7th October by asking money down, a share in conquests in Flanders, and a commercial treaty, and by the 29th he would only promise neutrality till the next March. On the 25th November—Temple's instructions being drafted that day—the ministers demanded admission of our supremacy at sea, and on the 1st December postulated a league, offensive and defensive, against Holland, and yet that we should keep, at least for the present, our neutrality in regard to Spain. In an evening conference of the 12th, Buckingham asked for Ostend and Nieuport, while Arlington's pencilled draft demanded an attack on Holland, no partition of Belgium in Dutch interests, and, as usual, his treaty of commerce. We asked much: France must promise, sooner or later, to attack Holland, while we would only pledge ourselves to war if Holland were the aggressor, and still refused to break with Spain.[2]

---

[1] Finch papers, i.; Barbour, 135, note.
[2] Arlington's memorandum, Dec. 1, appendix; Ruvigni, Sept. 16 to Dec. 13, *loc. cit.*; Mignet; Barbour.

A month later Temple was ordered to reveal the
French share in this discussion to de Witt, from which
it might be inferred that to blast any French-Dutch
understanding was throughout Charles' primary object.
The inference would, we think, be wrong—though not
perhaps in the case of Arlington; it was all in Charles'
character to exalt his own position, and his later complaint, that the French had played with him, rings
true. We can see from the protests of York and
Buckingham that Louis made the elementary mistake
of despising his enemies, for while his final reply
of the 21st December reserved to himself a liberty
of breaking with Holland or not, we were to promise
not to join Holland while the Spanish war lasted,
were to get a paltry 200,000 crowns a year to help
us in the Indies, and would receive only one port in
Flanders in return for an unconditional break with
Spain.[1]

Here, then, was the supreme danger and the deciding motive; if we stood wholly aside, the future of the
Spanish Netherlands, perhaps of the Spanish empire,
would be settled between France and Holland, or,
alternatively, by some loan-territorial arrangement,
highly disagreeable to ourselves, between Holland
and Spain. Yet, if we wished to take a hand, the
Hapsburgs still gave no sign of support, and from
prolonged conferences with Molina in the first fortnight of December it emerged that he was not empowered to subsidize the sixty ships and the troops
which we considered necessary to save Flanders. Our
government, therefore, while not wholly abandoning
approaches to Spain, turned to the one avenue still
not seriously explored, and sent off, presumably about

[1] French *projet*, dated Jan. 4, n.s., Mignet; Ruvigni, Jan. 2, n.s.

the 10th December, the instructions long drafted for Temple.[1]

Confirmed in his prepossessions by a particularly pompous harangue from Rodrigo, boasting of Austrian troops and Spanish gold, our envoy reached the Hague, icebound and steely, on the 20th. His first instruction was to ask whether Holland would make an alliance, offensive and defensive, to protect Belgium—"if the interests of both nations shall require it, then against France itself". This de Witt refused; they would keep their alliance with France unless she was false; their intention was to "oblige" France to stop fighting, to hold Louis to the alternatives already offered, and, if need be, compel Spain to the same. He blenched, however, at Temple's hint that by arrangement with France or with Spain we might get hold of the Flemish ports, and repeated more than once that a quick resolution from Charles to defend Flanders might change the Dutch view. They would, in any case, accept a purely defensive alliance, like that brought over by Beverweert in 1660.[2]

There is, in point of fact, a good deal to indicate that even before hearing Temple's report Charles had decided to accept the Dutch limited scheme of enforcing the alternatives. Temple had orders to avoid mention of the Orange question and to keep his distance from Molina when he reached England; Lisola recognized that the alternatives, and possibly the use of force against Spain, had become inevitable, and the

---

[1] Temple to Arlington, Nov. 19 and Dec. 10, Flanders, 37; Lisola to the same, Dec. 13, *ibid.*; Arlington to Sandwich, Nov. 28 and Dec. 5, Carte MSS. 75, Barbour, 131; Lisola, Dec. 14 (Pribram).

[2] Temple's instructions, Nov. 25, Add. MSS. 9796, printed in Courtenay; his report in Arl. i. 191; de Witt to Meerman, Dec. 29, Br.; Temple to Bridgeman, Jan. 17; Pribram, 399.

final decision was reached within forty-eight hours of Temple's arrival in London. In possession of his report, Charles met the Foreign Committee on the 1st January, and there new instructions were drafted, accepting in each detail de Witt's platform—armed mediation, an armistice, force against an obstinate Spain, a defensive alliance with Holland, and a guarantee of the peace when made. Temple, now envoy extraordinary, was impressed with the government's wish for speed, and ordered to conclude, if possible, without further reference home; even if he failed at the Hague, he was to proceed to Brussels, to urge on the Spaniards that England meant business, and to discover what Spain could provide. Parliament, it may be added, was adjourned on the 19th December, until February; peace with honour should open the purse-strings which they had hitherto tied so stonily tight. While, then, it would be dangerous to close all other avenues, and while Arlington produced new projects for the unsuspecting Ruvigni (who did not grasp for a fortnight that there had been a cabinet meeting at all), Temple was hastily coached in Arlington's cypher, packed on to a royal yacht, and by the 7th January was back at the Hague.[1]

Sir William was now to find something of the true metal of de Witt, "the plain steady man", "the sincere dealer", whose praises he had lately taken to singing. He had not been the only visitor to the Hague that December, nor the first; there had been Prussians, Mainz envoys, Count Waldeck, and two Fürstenbergs. The dangerous William Fürstenberg had, indeed, only left the day before Temple first arrived; his purpose had been to help D'Estrades terminate the acrimonious

---

[1] Instructions of Jan. 1, Add. MSS. 9796; Temple to his father, Jan. 2; Arlington to Ormonde, Dec. 31, 1667, Barbour; Ruvigni, Jan. 16.

correspondence between Paris and the Hague regarding Belgium, and his success had not been insignificant. They had canvassed the towns of Holland almost inch by inch, and had good ground for confidence in de Witt's intentions; he was certainly resolved to force Spain to speedy concessions, as was shown by his threat to seize the Indies.[1]

While Temple was on his return journey, the States of Holland took a decision (4th January) of fateful significance. Adopting Fürstenberg's project as their basis, they agreed not to press France in the matter of the "renunciation", or to view a French attack, in Portuguese interests, upon Spain itself or Italy, as prejudicial to the general peace, while if Spain refused the alternatives they would themselves invade Belgium. Compared with this, the threat to force Louis, if he defaulted, back to the Pyrenees treaty was hardly more than a pious aspiration, reflecting rather the acute differences of opinion between the Dutch provinces. For, as the use of force against Spain and a free hand for his pretensions if the young King died were precisely what Louis had been asking for six months, the resolution meant that, if he adhered to his last manifesto, Holland would get for him what he asked. A statement of the action proposed was circulated to the German princes, and de Witt told Meerman not to encourage English armaments.[2] It is, therefore, not surprising to discover that de Witt described the Triple Alliance to Fürstenberg as "your treaty", and this, taken with Lisola's simultaneous claim to be its

[1] Ruvigni, Jan. 13; Prussian despatch from Paris, Jan. 12, Urk. xii.; Lionne to D'Estrades, Jan. 6; Klopp, i. 210.

[2] French offers of Sept. 17 (Mignet) and Nov. 8 (D'Estrades); Fürstenberg's *projet*, Aitzema, vi. 339; de Witt to Fürstenberg, Jan. 13, Fruin, iii.; Sec. Res. ii. 616; de Witt to Meerman, Dec. 27, Br.

parent,[1] brings us to the conclusion that the real import
of this famous agreement lies not in its content but in
the manner of its making.

The speed of Temple's famous "five days", from the
8th to the 13th January, was thus less due to his skill
than to earlier preparation of the ground, for all Europe,
except Spain, was agreed that Spain must suffer, and
Charles' scruple at using the word "force" against
Spain melted in the formula of *moyens plus efficaces*.[2]
Yet the days and nights spent in de Witt's room and
Temple's lodging showed the sharp difference between
the high contracting parties. A majority of Dutch provinces would hear of nothing for Spain beyond the alternatives, while the English resolutely made a defensive
alliance the condition of any negotiation. It was only
after great pressure and for a high price, that de Witt
agreed, well knowing that it might reverse the whole
policy of Holland. Temple's revelation of Ruvigni's
discussion touching an attack on Holland, the steady
support given to Temple by Dohna, and the spectre of
provincial disagreement, all, no doubt, contributed, but
not so much, one suspects, as a concession made by
Temple in advance of, or beyond, his instructions—that
is, the insertion of the provisional commercial articles of
Breda in the body of the present treaty, and the pledging
of Charles' acceptance, which could not be received for
a week, by a confirmation of Breda in the new preamble.
Reading into Temple's sanguine pressure more good-
will than Temple's government owned,[3] the Pensionary
accepted what, on paper, must be an enormous gain

[1] Temple is to act "in conformità della pianta che qui habbiamo projettata"
—Lisola to Lobkowitz, Jan. 17, Pribram.

[2] "For the indecency of the word (force) I would willingly have it left out"—
Charles' marginal note on instructions of Jan. 1.

[3] See Williamson's hostile comment, Treaty Papers, 74.

for Dutch commerce, dispensed with the interminable delay of provincial ratification, and on the 13th January signed the treaties.[1]

As between England and Holland they were two-fold. The first, confirming the Breda treaty in all particulars, including those of commerce, was a perpetual defensive alliance, to be ratified within four weeks, whereby in case of aggression each party was to assist the other with forty ships and 6400 men.

The second shaped the mediation of the "alternatives". Following in detail the Dutch-Fürstenberg *projet*, it suggested the 31st May, instead of March as the French had offered, as the term of the armistice, and undertook to force Spain, if need be, to acquiesce; this force, however, was to be executed not by France but by the Allies, who, with the Emperor and other States so disposed, were to guarantee the eventual peace.

There followed three secret articles. The first provided that the "renunciation" should not be mentioned; the second disposed of the Portugal problem, though safeguarding the neutrality of Belgium; the third stated that, if France obstructed peace, the Allies would join Spain, and push the French frontiers back to the limits of the treaty of the Pyrenees.

Three days later an undertaking by Dohna brought in the third partner. His own relationship to the Orange house and his hatred of Catholic France impelled him to value English friendship and to suspect de Witt; the English faction at Stockholm had sent him powers to sign, and all the Swedish jealousy for the Baltic had lately been revived by the French-

[1] Temple to Arlington, Jan. 14, to Bridgeman, Jan. 17; Wicquefort to Lionne, Jan. 20; Japikse, *De Witt*, 266; Urk. xii. 756; Courtenay.

Prussian treaty signed on the 5th December. He therefore accepted the Allied offer to reserve a place for
Sweden and to mediate her differences with Austria,
the Dutch undertaking that their ministers at London
should concert with England, and with other Powers
affected, the payment for Swedish troops and all other
means to give the league "the substance as well as the
form" of a triple alliance. The same day Dohna left for
London, accompanying the text of the treaty carried
by Temple's brother Henry, who was back at the
Hague on the 23rd with the English ratification.[1]

The curtain descended in Allied rejoicing. "God be
thanked it is done", wrote Arlington, "and that both
the world abroad and at home understand it to be both
honourable and safe for His Majesty, and foretell we
shall find the parliament much better complexioned
for it". At the Hague de Witt and young Orange (of
whom, he told Temple, he was getting so fond) gave
Temple banquets, dancing, and tennis; Pepys' city
friends praised the treaty as the best thing done for
years; Ruvigni, said the exultant Lisola, seemed out
of his mind. But apprehensively our eye travels round
Europe.

In Vienna the Emperor on his knees before St.
Anthony; from Franche-Comté tidings that Condé,
the great captain at last forgiven, has fallen on the
province like a thunderbolt and captured it in a fortnight; in Flanders, Turenne urging the ease of victory;
in Madrid a weeping queen; on the turf at Barn Elms,
Lord Shrewsbury run through the body by Buckingham; could not France compound from these elements

---

[1] Text in Dumont, Aitzema, and Temple; Wicquefort, iii. 390; Urk. xii.
206, 755; Temple to Arlington, Jan. 16; Salvetti's despatch, Jan. 24, Add. MSS.
27,962, f. 197.

of crime and imbecility a draught which would slay
in its cradle the infant league?[1]

THE TREATY OF AIX

This infant was afflicted with at least one mortal
complaint, to wit, that neither France nor Spain, the
two belligerents, showed any intention of accepting its
programme. The first impression in France was not
unfavourable, letters from both Charles and the States
urging that the Triple Alliance only secured what
France herself had offered,[2] but the immediate disclosure[3] of the secret articles dispelled the charm.
Condé's triumphant procession in Franche-Comté,
planned though it was long before, came too oppor-
tunely not to appear as a defiance; Louis promised,
indeed, that his new conquest would not alter his demands, and offered to extend the period for Spanish
acceptance to the 15th May, but for three months the
Triple Alliance shuddered and nearly dissolved in fear
that the consciousness of power would break down Louis'
fidelity to his word. Sir John Trevor was sent to join
Beuningen at Paris and to explain that only despair of
"closer union" had driven England to these extremities,
but his reception was discouraging; Condé and Turenne
were advising the new Alexander to war *à l'outrance*.[4]

[1] Arlington to Ormonde, Jan. 21, Carte MSS. 46; Lisola, Jan. 25, Klopp.

[2] Charles to Madame, Jan. 23, Ady; to Louis XIV, Feb. 3, Dalrymple;
Ruvigni, Jan. 3; de Witt to Fürstenberg, Jan. 13, Fruin, iii.; States-General, Jan.
16, Aitzema; Rec. Hollande, ii. 210.

[3] By whom is uncertain. D'Estrades speaks of verbal communication; Meerman
hints at leakage in the English Cabinet; Arlington disclaimed responsibility,
Verbaal, Jan. 30, R.A.; for de Witt's nervousness see his letter to Beuningen,
March 1, n.s., Fruin, iii.

[4] Louis XIV to Charles II, Jan. 17 (copy), Carte MSS. 46; same to Gremonville, Jan. 27, Mignet; Arlington to Temple, Feb. 4; Trevor to Arlington, March
12; Beuningen, March 17, Van Dijk; Picavet, 183; Trevor's instructions, Feb. 2,
Rawl. MSS. A. 255.

As for the Hapsburgs, their rage was much deeper and even more natural; why, furiously asked Castel Rodrigo and Molina, should Spain be thus forced by two friendly states to surrender territory to an aggressor? It would be better to evacuate Belgium, and throw responsibility for its defence on these egoistic nations of shopkeepers. Lisola, still hoping against hope, saw in the Hague negotiation the nucleus of the great coalition for which he lived, and a lively means of embroiling us with France.

All depended, then, on good concert between England and Holland, and none as yet appeared. The sea, in every sense, still divided them. In January news came that Sir John Harman had recaptured Surinam, and though Charles promptly ordered its restoration, a weary controversy began, distorted in each detail by distance and suffering. Hardly were the two fleets again in the Channel before the two governments were again quarrelling about the Flag, a question enough in itself, de Witt told Temple, to destroy joint operations; once again we find Charles begging the Dutch to keep the peace in India. As to the commercial articles, Temple's stretch of his powers had only been condoned on his representation that the royal honour was pledged, and the reference of a final settlement to joint commissioners was to be pregnant with trouble, foreshadowed even when Temple's articles first appeared in print by a protest from our East India Company. Yet another cause of division, and a familiar one, reappeared, for so interlocked in this reign were England and Holland that domestic and foreign relations cannot be kept apart. A growing excitement over the Perpetual Edict, and the question of admitting Orange to the Council of State, together with the "Spanish"

sympathies of his party, revived the party strife in
Holland which always stirred a chord at Westminster,
and the previous refusal of our government to touch
the problem had changed by April into protest against
this treatment of the King's nephew.[1]

Not only were the Allies' permanent interests thus
conflicting, but they approached the peace from different angles. The English desired peace, but a peace of
prestige, strongly in the interests of Spain, and were
not prepared, like Holland, to keep peace with France
at almost any price. We were ready to take something
less than the terms of the Triple Alliance, but the
whole trend of our policy at the moment was emphatically anti-French. An inspired press campaign
in London exalted the treaty. Charles sent messages
to the lately widowed Great Elector, affecting to disbelieve his French treaty and the rumour that he
inclined to marry "that gendarme", the Grande Made-
moiselle. Temple was bidden to ask Castel Rodrigo for
£300,000 to equip an English fleet, and incessantly,
though in vain, we pressed on Holland the need of a
league with Spain. March and early April were the
climax of this policy of war; the Cabinet recommended
raising 4000 foot, with a possibility of more, and detailed Admiral Allin to watch the French and to put
his ships at war strength.[2] The personnel entrusted
with the negotiation—Arlington and Bridgeman,
Rupert and Monk—the proved sympathies of Trevor,

[1] Charles' letters of Jan. 25, R.A., and Jan. 29, Cal. Col.S.P; Meerman,
Verbaal, R.A.; de Witt to Meerman, April 24, Br.; Temple to Arlington, Feb. 2;
Khan, 125.

[2] Pepys, Feb. 10; Arlington to Temple, Feb. 28 and March 6; Brandt, Feb. 20,
Urk. xii.; instructions of Jan. 24, Add. MSS. 9796; de Witt to Temple, Feb. 15;
Meerman to de Witt, March 7, Br.; Treaty papers, *loc. cit.*; Arlington's note of
March 13, Appendix; *Memorial of English Affairs* (1729), Admiralty orders of
March 30 and April 7.

our plenipotentiary in France, reinforce the impression to be collected from the triple negotiation proceeding at Paris, London, and the Hague.[1]

But a familiar and irremediable weakness cursed this policy of would-be vigour, in that, despite drastic economies, Charles' government had no money. When Parliament reassembled on the 10th February, it plunged once more into the "miscarriages" of the Clarendon ministry, adding thereto the time-honoured and time-consuming subjects of Popery and toleration; not till the 26th was a bare £300,000 voted, and then another month went in discussion of ways and means. Arlington was conscious that the whole edifice of the alliance was shaking—"God knows what will become of this nation when France shall be master of Flanders and Holland submits to them".[2] Peace therefore hung rather on elements outside than within England.

By the 9th March, after a month of immense strain for Temple and Trevor, the situation reached as between Brussels and Paris was, briefly, that both belligerents accepted a truce till the 31st March, beyond which France would not prolong it; that Castel Rodrigo had accepted the "alternatives", without naming which he preferred; and that France offered to extend the period for accepting the terms (though not the truce) till the 15th May. On 16th March, to overcome the French scruples as to Castel Rodrigo's sincerity, Trevor and Beuningen guaranteed the intention of their masters to use force against a recalcitrant Spain.[3]

---

[1] Foreign Entry Book 176, *passim*; Barbour, 140; for Trevor, see Beùningen's view, Van Dijk, 13, note, and the whole tone of his correspondence with Temple in 1669, Sloane MSS. 1003.

[2] To Ormonde, Feb. 15, Carte MSS. 46.

[3] Temple; conferences of Lionne, Trevor, and Beuningen, Rawlinson MSS. A. 293, ff. 50 *seq*; memorial of March 16, Arl. i.

Here, for three weeks, progress stopped: and if already, when the truce was still in being, the French advanced guards threatened Brussels, what should be done in the dry season after the 31st March when it expired? Vast military alliances were contemplated at Paris, where (Trevor wrote) it was a "mortal sin" to whisper peace and Turenne was passionate for war. If further and ruinous concession were to be avoided, the Alliance must assert itself; but it was not yet in being.[1]

Immediately he reached London, Dohna put before Charles a draft scheme for a subsidy treaty in accord with his Hague agreement of 16th January, but three weary months of conference followed—conferences at Whitehall, conferences in Dohna's bedroom (for already he was a dying man), conferences interrupted by a squabble of Lords and Commons over privilege and embarrassed by Lady Arlington's attack of smallpox. The Swedish claims were high, including "compensation" for keeping troops under arms since October, as they alleged at the Allies' instigation, but the Dutch objection to them was more than pecuniary, for they viewed them as leading to a war which by agreement with France they meant to avoid, and not till the 20th March were their ministers empowered to negotiate on this question at all. Their own favoured scheme was still that of 1667, to lend Spain the subsidy money in return for a mortgage of slices of Belgium, and this project, on which England did not smile, they pushed at the Hague apart from the proceedings at London; as it was to lose validity if Spain refused the peace, or if France accepted a longer truce, the limitation to the Dutch view of the alliance is clear.

[1] Picavet, 199; Rousset, i. 148; Trevor to Arlington, March 2.

Instructed, then, to refuse larger commitments, their envoys would not listen to Charles' personal suggestion that they should pay Sweden direct, or the pressure from Arlington and Lisola for a wider league, and every discussion brought these hopeless differences more into the light. For Dohna had no powers to deal with Spain, Arlington did not want Sweden solely dependent on Holland, Lisola could give no guarantee of real help, and Molina, as usual, had no instructions at all.[1]

In this froth of negation the attitude of Arlington was comparatively constructive. For, overcoming the economic objections of his colleagues, he was ready to pay half the past expenses of Sweden, argued that Spain "wants power rather than good will", and ultimately found out, after ceaseless interviews, the solution, if such it can be called, that Sweden should join the alliance, but should be content, instead of cash down, with the Spanish promise for payment, backed by a guarantee from England and Holland. Reports from Stockholm showed an imminent probability of Sweden retracing her steps, if she were not quickly secured— better, the English argued, to make the framework at least of alliance, filling in the body and blood later. To extort a promise from Castel Rodrigo meant, as Temple found, waiting till Doomsday, but Molina was induced to undertake the responsibility of guaranteeing financial indemnity to the maritime Powers. On the 25th April the Triple Alliance at last achieved triplicity; England and Holland pledged payment of 480,000 crowns to Sweden, undertaking that, if Spain failed to implement

[1] Dohna to Arlington, Feb. 3 and March 7, Sweden, 6; Meerman to de Witt, March 15 and 16, Br.; Verbaal, R.A., March 13 and 21; Aitzema, vi. 405 *et seq.*, 795; Destrades, March 18; Fruin, iii.; Treaty papers, 74; Lisola to Arlington, March 29, Flanders, 38; Cabinet of March 23-4, Foreign Entry, 176; conference of March 16, Br. and Pribram, 430.

her ambassador's promise, they would withdraw the guarantee of the peace terms given to Castel Rodrigo, and wash their hands of the whole concern. Thus, resting on a promise of non-existent Spanish money, the alliance came into being; a future it might have, but its present value was nil, for the peace between France and Spain, which it was made to enforce, had been signed at Aix three days before.[1]

Peace was made, and it is a point of weight for the next phase of our policy, on the terms laid down between France and Holland. There were good reasons why Louis should hesitate to continue the war. It disturbed the system of German alliances which he found useful; the Spanish-Portuguese peace, which crowned Sandwich's labour on the 3rd February, might be a mortification to France in one sense, but also removed what to Louis' curious conscience had been an obstacle of honour; infinitely greater things were won by his secret understanding with the Emperor, while a peace such as Holland offered him—whereby Spain tacitly dropped the "renunciation", and actually infringed it by territorial cession—would be a long step on the road of destiny. And, if the Orange drum was throbbing, it would be well to meet de Witt half-way.

In fact, he had hardly to go so far. If de Witt found fault with the "Spanish tendencies" of Temple, most pro-Dutch of Englishmen, far more must he lose patience with their scruples about forcing Spain, the objective for which, he made bold to tell Paris, the Dutch armaments were being prepared. On the 17th March he decided to approach England with a more

[1] Cabinet note, March 13, appendix; Foreign Entry, 176; Meerman to de Witt, March 15, Br.; Thynne to Arlington, April 1, Sweden, 6; Arlington to Temple, May 1; Temple to Arlington, March 10, Flanders, 38; Van Dijk's account, 293 *et seq.*, and authorities there quoted; Louis XIV, ii. 367; D'Estrades, March 19.

drastic policy: if France accepted the truce till the 30th May, but Spain refused to warrant Castel Rodrigo's acceptance of the "alternatives", the Allies should at once attack her; if her resistance continued after the 30th June, they should, assisted by France, conquer for France the other "alternative", not chosen by Castel Rodrigo, that is Franche-Comté—and if after the 31st July, they should "cantonize" Belgium as a free republic, under the guarantee of France, England, and Holland. The old cat had leaped out of de Witt's bag; by these crescendo moves he might hope to win a stake which at the lowest would enable him to push the French frontier farther from Holland, and at best settle the Belgian question for ever on the lines so often discussed with France. Nor, probably, did he ignore the assurances at this time renewed of French benevolence to his cause as against Orange.[1]

Our reception of this cool scheme, particularly of the cantonizing project, was unfavourable, and Arlington freely voiced the suspicion that France and Holland had come to an understanding; but the Dutch stuck to their guns, even approaching Trevor direct, and, in fact, as Trevor's instructions and Arlington's letters show, we were faced with the old dilemma, that if we did not co-operate with Holland, they would fall back on their attitude of December, of "dividing the prey of the whole Low Countries with France".[2] Since, then, our allies declared any resistance impossible, since

---

[1] De Witt to Temple, Feb. 15, to Meerman, March 2, Br.; to Beuningen, March 5, Fruin; deputies at Brussels to de Witt, March 3, *Br. aan De Witt*, Meerman, Verbaal, March 6; Dutch resolution of March 17, Aitzema, vi. 683; Lionne to D'Estrades, March 20, Mignet. For the English view of the alternative chosen, contrast Temple's instructions of Jan. 1 with his own view to Bridgeman, March 13.

[2] Arlington to Temple, April 3 and 10; Trevor's instructions, Feb. 2, Rawl. MSS. A. 255.

Trevor and Beuningen reported that only thus could the larger truce be won, and since German opinion strongly supported this course, our government gave way. On the 5th April the preliminaries were signed at St. Germain, embodying the terms agreeable to France and Holland; if Spain resisted after the 30th May, the French would recover their liberty of manœuvre, though only south of the Maestricht-Ostend line; while, as for the stronger penalties due after the 31st July, a general clause promising "further expedients" replaced the barefaced threat of cantonization. In return for these advantages France extended the truce till the last day of May; the peace was in effect won, and our zeal for military preparations declined. The diplomatic victory of France was complete.[1]

While, then, at London the allied ministers still disputed the burden of the alliance, the Spanish government were goaded by Sandwich and the Austrians into sending full powers to Castel Rodrigo; on the 10th April Temple and the Dutch gave him a guarantee of the peace, and on the 17th Temple with twenty-nine persons in his train reached Aix. There, after a week of Spanish punctilios, swords drawn between Spaniard and Dutchman, and like amenities, peace was signed on the 22nd April 1668.

The cloud which had descended upon Europe was thus for a season rolled away, not least by English initiative, but every circumstance of the peace tokened a future war. The French gains—Charleroi, Ath, Douai, Tournai, Lille, Oudenarde, Armentières, and Furnes —severed Brussels from Flanders and reached the sea;

---

[1] Committee of Foreign Affairs, March 24 and April 8, Foreign Entry Book, 176; Meerman to de Witt, April 3 and 4, Br.; Arlington to Trevor, April 4, Treaty papers 74; conference ending March 19, Aitzema, vi. 693; Lionne to D'Estrades, March 20; Mignet, ii. 627; Pomponne, i. 541.

the "renunciation" given at the peace of the Pyrenees was held null and void; while the Dutch, trapped by their nervous pressure for a rapid settlement, could not now make France hear of any territorial exchange which would make a frontier less dangerous and absurd. The guarantee given by the Allies to Spain was still on paper, the money promised by Spain minted in El Dorado, the general league aspired to by Lisola still unfound, and Dohna, the one stalwart champion of this buckram alliance, dead and gone.[1]

[1] Aitzema, vi. 812; German States, 58, f. 37; Temple to de Witt, May 17; de Witt to Beuningen, May 21, Fruin; Arlington to Temple, Nov. 3, 1668, for Trevor's opinion as to the effect of this treaty on the "renunciation".

CHAPTER VII

THE FINAL CHOICE

THOUGH history is no science, the human beings that form it are obedient to natural laws. In their blood-stream rival corpuscles, good and evil, are struggling for mastery, and under the microscope we can see approaching the moments of equilibrium, crisis, or victory, and the flight of the vanquished. Such an epoch we have reached in the history of Charles II, a man of dual political personality, whose pride in his navy, his commerce, and his power, contended with older, perhaps deeper, motives of dynasty, sex, impulse, and religion. From the moment of Clarendon's downfall the King in person dominates the field, and it is the conflict of tendencies within him which explains the next five years of feverish diplomacy.

One distinction above all marks off, at least superficially, this period from those before and after—that is, the existence, on which so much has been said, of a "grand design" for the Catholicizing of England. Obviously the bare suspicion of such a scheme must destroy the internal harmony, and therefore the external power, of the nation, and, as compared with this, the precise degree of fact about it is largely irrelevant. Yet the story is so steeped in romance, so weighty in affecting our judgment of the actors,

267

that we must deal here with this aspect once and for all.

It is impossible, with our general knowledge of Restoration politics, to suppose any serious religious zeal in King or ministers. Throughout his political life Charles had been used to ask Rome for spiritual comfort when he wanted financial support, and the extraordinary candour with which, to foreigners and subjects,[1] he ridiculed the anarchy of Protestantism, almost in itself destroys the notion of a deep Machiavellian purpose. The tears he shed in January 1669 on confiding to York his religious fears had dried by June 1670, when he told Madame he was not yet satisfied of Catholic truth, and had disappeared when in 1675 he complained to Barillon that York's Popery had endangered the throne.[2]

Much the same seems to be true of Arlington, despite some purchase of Paris divinity for his library and an authentic death-bed conversion.[3] Quite plainly he looked at religion with the eye of a pure politician, was emphatically not a Catholic in 1672,[4] won the lasting hatred of the Jesuit circle, and as carefully guarded himself from suspicion in diplomatic corre-

[1] See his talk to Orange in 1670 (Burnet, i. 495), or to Edmund Warcup in 1679, *E.H.R.* xl. 245.

[2] James I, 442; Lingard, ix. 172.

[3] Authentic, in view of James II's categorical statement of 1688 in conversation with Bishop Francis Turner: see Add. MSS. 32,096. I owe this reference to the kindness of my pupil Mr. C. Emmott of Queen's College.

[4] "I hope to hear your answer of my last about the question which imports us to have answered, and I am sure you will judge it so, and consequently promise (?) me satisfaction. I shall need say nothing to you of myne in all your temporal blessings; my best offices shall be applyed to carry them up even to aeternal" —Abbé Montagu to Arlington, Aug. 17, 1672, France, 134; cf. Barbour, 156, 261. I have found no evidence stronger, for this period, than Montagu's letter; the language of an intimate like Bernard Gascoyne (Jan. 18, '71, German States, 59) appears to me incompatible with any idea that Arlington was known to be a Catholic.

spondence as he did by good offices as a patron of Anglican churches.[1]

Of the other signatories of the Treaty of Dover, the political influence of the Catholic Bellings and Arundell was slight, and only Clifford's case needs consideration. Here again, though strong claims[2] have been made, the evidence of Catholicism at the date of that treaty has strong facts to overcome. His son was in 1669 at a Protestant college in Oxford, in April 1670 he himself opposed a proviso to the Conventicle Act which would have exempted Peers' houses from search,[3] and in July 1671 the Protestant bishop of Exeter dedicated his private chapel.

Catholic zeal can, in truth, be discerned at that date in one only of the inner ring, the Duke of York. But the Catholic scheme was fully hatched before it was imparted to the Duke;[4] in 1669–70 the royal brothers were, politically, on bad terms, while the sore point dividing them was a projected divorce of the Queen, which must itself almost veto Catholic reunion.

Moreover, the character of our evidence and the extraordinary discrepancies of our leading witnesses alike suggest that Charles' secrecy was one of many degrees, imparted, as was his habit, to several different persons, each of whom could think his knowledge unique until indiscretion or some betraying sign disillusioned him. York thus assures us that Madame was not originally

---

[1] W. Godolphin to Arlington, April 14, 1674, H.I.; the charge that he is a Catholic is meant to "wound your Lordship"; *vide* also the Fitzherbert and Westmoreland papers, and appendix.

[2] Notably by his descendant the 6th Baron (G. Rose, *Diary*, ii. 340), that the Treasurer was converted during the exile.

[3] Grey, i. 265. The point is probably impossible to determine, but from James' description of Clifford as a recent convert, and some expressions of Colbert in March 1672, I should take the winter of 1671–72 as the date of his change.

[4] Charles to Madame, March 22, 1669, Ady; Ranke, iii. 495.

admitted to the secret,[1] yet Charles tells Madame that York has been brought into it "on the score of religion", nearly two months after the historic meeting of the 25th January 1669, for which James is our sole authority.[2] James declares that Arlington was ignorant of Buckingham's mission to Paris in August 1670, of which, in fact, Ralph Montagu kept him well informed; and the Jesuit papers, on which Lord Acton relied, say that Charles' Jesuit son was bidden, on arrival in England in 1668, to disclose his identity to the Queen Mother—who was not there.[3]

Apart, however, from questions of detail, profound insincerity or opportunism seems stamped on every move of our government. The language of Charles and Arlington was very different, before the treaty with the French money was secured, to what it became after; in 1668–69 we hear of the divisions among Protestants, the close relation of English High Churchmen to Rome, and the King's change of heart, but from the close of 1670 the tone has diminished to the lack of competent Catholics in this country, to Charles' hesitancy in doctrine, or the need of waiting for a new and more vigorous Pope;[4] and hopes of a Catholic party, when ostensibly founded on the chameleon Cromwellian Orrery, or the youthful Sunderland, are not more convincing than the staunch governors to whom, Charles told Madame, he was confiding his arsenals, when that list includes the Whig Bedford as governor of Plymouth.

Again, however satisfactory the evidence for Charles' sincerity in 1668–69, it is permissible to point out that

[1] Macpherson, i. 51.   [2] Dalrymple, ii. 22; James I, 442.
[3] Macpherson, loc. cit.; Acton, Historical Essays and Studies.
[4] Acton, loc. cit. 101; Charles to Madame, June 6; Colbert, Nov. 13, 1669, Oct. 23, Feb. 25, 1671; Forneron, 75; Pomponne, i. 490.

both he and Arlington were men of considerable ability, whom a very little investigation must convince that the chances for Catholicism were remote. Reports sent to Rome in those years paint the situation in gloomy colours; the converts made by the Capuchins were mostly women, the feud of Jesuit and secular had impeded the attempted toleration of 1662 and still dogged the faithful, and the English college at Douai was divided by faction. Nor could substantial support be counted on from the laity, for a future Secretary of State put the Catholics fit to bear arms in the province of Canterbury at under 5000 men. Most of all, the parliamentary action of the period demonstrated that only sheer force could convert the nation, and the ardour for the Conventicle Act of 1670 was followed by demands for execution of the recusancy law, by appointment of a Commons committee on the growth of Popery, and by attack on "Popish" counsellors.[1]

We have, again, to take account of the very curious relation of this "Catholic" conspiracy to the head of the Catholic Church. If the great secret was confided for political motives to the rulers of Spain and Tuscany, and known, it seems, to Queen Christina of Sweden, it was carefully concealed from the Papal nuncio who came from Brussels to visit Charles in November 1670.[2] In a negotiation conducted with Alexander VII through Bellings during the winter of 1662–63, Charles had stipulated for liberty to bring about conversion in his own time, for toleration to Protestants, and for some grave restrictions upon clerical celibacy and other Catholic practice, and he took precisely the same

---

[1] Roman transcripts; Acton, *loc. cit.*; All Souls MSS. (Jenkins) 205, f. 41; Wood ii. 181-2, for Ralph Sheldon's diary at Rome.
[2] Clifford MSS.; Barbour, 188; Ranke, iii. 503.

ground in this later stage. What messages, if any, were sent to Rome by Charles' eldest son, the mysterious Jesuit who appeared in England in 1668 and then vanished from tangible history, may never now be known, but the actual documents which survive from 1671–72 bear the same impression of caution: masses in English and communion under both kinds, Charles told the French, were essential. Some instructions drafted for an English envoy proceeding to Rome are even more minimizing, and not less important, though they were never, one supposes, sent. The envoy, they say—the superior of the Douai college is indicated, who, indeed, was in London in 1672—will be silent on the points of celibacy and reordination, and for the moment merely ask the Holy Father to send a sensible legate, and to grant a bull confirming the owners of church land.[1] Lastly, the declaration of indulgence given in March 1672, in confining Catholic worship to private houses, only legalized a state of things connived at for generations by successive governments. Other reasons will reinforce the conclusion that, if ever seriously purposed, "Catholicity" was abandoned by the year 1672, before the manifestation that the Dutch war was going to be long and doubtfully victorious, and before the parliamentary explosion of January 1673 showed that the "secret" was one no longer. The careful restrictions drawn up that February for the private worship of the proposed Austrian bride for York seem as incompatible with any formed Catholic scheme as the official appointments of 1672, whereby the liberal and Whiggish Essex replaced the perhaps

---

[1] Roman tr.; Clifford MSS., which also contain some proposals on doctrinal and liturgical matters, endorsed (in a later hand) as of April 1671 and as sent by Father Hugh Serenus Cressy.

half - Catholic Berkeley as Lord - Lieutenant and the exuberantly insular Henry Coventry joined Arlington as Secretary of State. In fact, a deciding date may be the last months of 1671, when the increasingly common appearance of Ormonde in Cabinet was immediately connected with the renewed persecution of Catholics.[1]

Yet the existence to this day of the actual treaty, signed by four English counsellors, reminds us that once, if only for a fleeting fantastic season, this ideal, perversion, or dream was literal fact, just as the remainder of Charles' reign, culminating in the Popish plot, was its nemesis. Granting that the two royal brothers were, in England, its only begetters, and that it was a personal policy, entered upon in sanguine mood and dropped through spiritual idleness or political discernment; yet were its effects so vast that the King's motives merit some consideration.

Incidental remarks show us that Charles was alive to Protestant weakness on the Continent, where a golden age of the Catholic faith seemed to have dawned. Two of his Palatine cousins were recent converts; in 1671 a third, Elizabeth, became the second Duchess of Orleans; the family into which a fourth, the Electress Sophia, had married, was itself divided by the lapse of John Frederick of Hanover. In 1668 the Jansenists formally submitted to Rome, and that October Bossuet had his greatest triumph in the conversion of Turenne. We must further recognize that religion was not yet hardened and encrusted with the prejudice or vested interest of centuries, that reunion of the Western Churches, which had engaged the mind of Charles I, was still a living question in the Germany contem-

[1] Instructions for B. Gascoyne, Stowe MSS. 191, f. 30; Miscell. Aul. 90; Essex papers, i. 23; Molina, March 6, 1671 (Simancas).

poraneous with Charles II, and that Stuart princes, who had bishops of Cosin's type or chaplains like Francis Turner, might be forgiven for underestimating the distance between Rome and Canterbury.

Again, if Charles was fully capable of feigning religion to deceive Louis XIV, it is difficult to get over his professions to his favourite sister in 1668-69, or his alleged urgency to keep a Jesuit son by his side. The personal influences which had long impelled him in that direction—and here that of Catharine of Braganza has probably been underestimated—were reinforced now by a convert in Lady Castlemaine, and it would be hard to find among his intimates one not a Catholic or a sceptic. But more probably neither religion nor affection moved a mind that ultimately responded only to political advantage, and what Charles conceived that to be is surely discoverable in the political circumstances of 1668-69. The fall of Clarendon, from which so much had been hoped, had left him worse off than ever. From fixed revenues, instead of £1,200,000 as estimated, he received only £649,000 in the eighteen months ending with Michaelmas 1669, and the total parliamentary supply for the three years 1669-72 was roughly £660,000—sums ridiculously insufficient for everyday needs of government. His fleet in 1669 was not even large enough for the protection of commerce; his serving soldiers, including Tangier, did not amount to over seven thousand men; the revived policy of administrative toleration had only led to new Commonwealth plots, even to religious dispute in the dockyards, while party and personal faction were so rampant that his ministers, divided on the point of dissolving Parliament, adjourned it for eighteen months in May 1668 for fear one of them should instigate it against the other. Such considerations, coupled with his declared gratitude for the loyalty of his Catholic subjects, presumably contributed to this speculation—to find a policy which would centre obedience in the Crown, enlist Catholics, Anglo-Catholics, and Dissenters in one tolerant scheme, and win the help of the model monarchy of Europe.

But whatever his grounds, we may provisionally assume that Charles' "Catholic" decision was an ephemeral adjunct to his policy, taken up not as principal but as subsidiary, and not seriously pursued when its political object had been achieved and its danger revealed. The dissolution of the Triple Alliance came, therefore, from other motives than Catholic zeal, motives more permanent and normal, and to their elucidation we return.

The five years separating the two Dutch wars of the reign were the climax of Arlington's power, which is marked on the English diplomatic structure. Trevor, fresh from making the peace at Paris, was in May 1668 made Secretary in place of Morrice, and his sympathies, like those of Lord-Keeper Bridgeman, were assuredly Dutch.[1] The return of Temple to the Hague in August as ambassador was a victory for this section in the Cabinet; William Godolphin took the Madrid embassy in 1669, Gascoyne and Werden taking charge meanwhile; Southwell returned to Lisbon in July; Thynne was still at Stockholm; Sylvius went in 1669 on a mission to Berlin; and Ralph Montagu got the important embassy at Paris.[2] All were Arlington's nominees, and most of them shared the policy he hitherto had championed—of reconciliation with Holland and an *entente* with the Hapsburgs. But if the Triple Alliance

---

[1] Colbert, July 7, 1670, and March 29, 1671.
[2] Spain, 53, f. 280; Add. MSS. 34,331, f. 20.

was to be made a reality, defensible and self-contained, everything was yet to be done.

Whatever their differences of opinion as to the proper treatment of Spain or the future disposition of her territories, both England and Holland alike were met on the threshold by one difficulty destructive of the alliance in any shape. By the London agreement, signed with Dohna on the 25th April 1668, they were pledged to get for Sweden 480,000 crowns from Spain, but in the first week of May Castel Rodrigo repudiated Molina's promise, refusing to hear of subsidies till the guarantee promised to him by Temple was in being. Remonstrances at Madrid and Brussels bounced as off a wall of stone, for the Spaniards hoped to drive part, at least, of the Allies into making the new defensive league so long desired by Lisola. To this the Dutch would not listen, and though, at the price of a contribution to our naval expenses, the English might have been more amenable, by the autumn Arlington was clearly growing more sceptical in view of the very shadowy backing behind Lisola's exhortation.[1]

The question thus arose how Spain could be induced to keep her bond. Holland and Sweden would force her by extending the guarantee of the peace to France also, but this the English refused, as a further and uncalled-for rebuff to Spain. In short, Arlington's wish seems to have been for a complete, but literal, loyalty to engagements. The clauses of the Triple Alliance were to be fulfilled neither more nor less, and, though extra expense must be avoided, we were ready to pay one-third of the Swedish subsidy if Holland and Spain did

---

[1] Van Dijk, 303; Gamarra's letter of June 1, Aitzema; Temple, May 12; Arlington to Temple, May 11 and Oct. 30; D'Estrades, April 20 and May 11; Pribram, 446; Boreel, Verbaal, August, R.A.; Werden to Arlington, Sept. 9, Spain, 53.

the rest, and to stretch the guarantee from Belgiu. the whole Spanish empire.[1]

On the other hand, the negative limitations to British policy were sharply brought out in the last three months of this year. On the 5th October representatives of the Allies, including Temple, drafted recommendations for submission to their principals, involving a guarantee, as asked by Spain, of the treaty of the Pyrenees, and an immediate "concert" in detail for their respective military liabilities. The reply from the English Cabinet was prompt and unanimous. It was imperative to avoid anything touching on the French "renunciation", which the treaty of Aix had implicitly declared void; the Pyrenees treaty embraced questions, like the status of Lorraine, in which we must not get entangled; it would frighten off other guarantors, and might well be taken by France as a *casus belli*. The immediate obligation to be honoured was that England and Holland were bound to give Spain a guarantee, but bound to nothing till she paid up subsidies; this minimum must be settled first, until which time the Swedish adhesion and the military "concert" could wait. It was hoped that a guarantee "to assist Spain, not only in Flanders but in all his estates and dominions", would induce some payment, and let us save "the money we have offered"; this done, we should be ready to ask other Powers to join, and to consider the "concert" for its execution.[2] The Dutch contention that the Aix peace had not nullified the *renonciation*,

[1] D'Estrades, May 20; Meerman's memorial, Cal.S.P.D. 504; Boreel to de Witt, Aug. 25, Br.; Boreel, Verbaal, Oct. 13, and Nov. 5; instructions for Temple, Aug. 10, Add. MSS. 9796; Arlington to Temple, Oct. 23.

[2] *Projet* of Oct. 5, Aitzema, viii. 862; Add. MSS. 9797, f. 123; Cabinet notes— (1) n.d. *ibid.* f. 12, (2) Nov. 10, Treaty papers, 74; Arlington to Temple, Oct. 23 and Nov. 3; Trevor to same, Oct. 8; Boreel, Verbaal, Oct. 13, Nov. 11; Werden to W. Godolphin, Aug. 26, Spain, 53.

and that it involved as much as the Pyrenees, was neither true in fact nor in accord with their attitude at the date of the treaty,[1] but then the "renunciation", for reasons daily more obvious, was far more vital to Holland than to Britain.

Apart from this important change in Dutch policy, which demands later discussion, our other allies were hopeless. Sweden would not hear of a reduction in the subsidy period, and if they were to guarantee the whole Spanish empire, asked punctual payment; they looked askance at a proposal for Denmark joining the circle of guarantors and, therefore, of beneficiaries ("many cooks spoil porridge", de la Gardie said), while large French offers were weakening the Allies' faction at Stockholm. A direct Swedish negotiation with Vienna had broken down, and Lisola's with Wrangel was unauthorized.[2]

The Brussels situation was worse still. Gamarra, the Spanish ambassador to Holland, was an important link but personally most unpopular, while Velasco, who had succeeded Castel Rodrigo as governor, was inexperienced, given over to women, and reputed pro-French. When Spain at last abandoned her demand that a "concert" should accompany the guarantee, and accepted her liability for the whole 480,000 crowns, her ministers still boggled at points of detail, and still clamoured for a defensive league; the Swedes still asked financial guarantees which Holland utterly, and England in part, rejected; Lisola was still dealing in visions.[3]

Our objections to coupling the "concert" with the guarantee were substantial enough. That it should

---

[1] De Witt to Fürstenberg, Jan. 13, 1668, Fruin, iii

[2] Carlisle to Arlington, April 15, 1669, Sweden, 7; Thynne, June 3, Oct. 19, and Nov. 25 to same, *ibid.*; de Groot to de Witt, March 6, 1669, Br.; Pribram, 455; Temple to Arlington, Sept. 7, 1669, Holland, 185.

[3] Additional instructions for Temple, Jan. 7, 1669, Add. MSS. 9796.

precede payment of subsidies was inconsistent with treaty; to postpone it would give Spain more time in which to find the money; if we had to find more, we should want more than Lisola's bond for reimbursement; the guarantee affected, and must be communicated to, the two parties, France and Spain, whereas the concert was a matter domestic to the Allies; finally, while Sweden and Holland would keep their contingents on foot in the ordinary way, in our case it would be a sheer addition to establishments.[1]

Rejecting this pressure from Holland and Sweden on one side, and on the other a French suggestion that the guarantee should be dropped entirely, our government in February 1669 approved an amended form drawn up at the Hague, and induced Sweden to accept payment by instalments. The instrument, at last signed on 29th April, guaranteed Spanish territories in any part of the world, and empowered the signatories, in the event of aggression, to concert military remedies; on ratification, Spain undertook to pay the Swedes 200,000 rix-dollars down, and another 280,000 in two eight-monthly instalments.[2]

Signs were not lacking, particularly with reference to the "concert",[3] that the French diplomatic offensive was already affecting English staunchness. It was not only, or mainly, a question of unusual courtesies between Arlington and Colbert, or the fact that we informed France of the terms of the guarantee;[4] influenced, we may believe, less by the King's "secret"

[1] Arlington to Temple, Feb. 16 and April 13; instructions for Werden, Oct. 11, 1669, *ibid.* 9797.

[2] Originals, Add. MSS. 9797, ff. 1-30; our ratification, f. 33; Dumont; Van Dijk, 314.

[3] "France does not desire it", Williamson's note, April 25, Foreign Entry, 176.

[4] Instructions to Montagu, Feb. 22, 1669, Add. MSS. 32,094.

than by Spanish backwardness and financial poverty, Arlington hoped to be able to defend Belgium, at least for a season, by the ways of peace. In February 1669 Louis XIV, anxious to prevent the Austrians yielding to Spanish pressure and joining the Allies, gave a solemn pledge to the Pope that throughout this year he would not attack Spain,[1] and offered to refer to arbitrators the unsettled dispute regarding Condé, Linck, and other "dependencies" of his Belgian conquests—a ground eagerly seized upon by the English as cause for putting off the "concert".

And yet every overt action of our government, and the testimony of enemy and friend, declare that for a year after the peace of Aix it still substantially followed a policy guided by Arlington and in consistency with the Triple Alliance. Thus Temple's self-drafted instructions of July 1668, revised by the Secretary, postulate the admission of the Swiss and the Protestants of the Empire, and though the Swiss project evaporated in pleasant talk from Bridgeman and Trevor, and in French intrigue among Catholic cantons, something solid was attempted in Germany and the North; more particularly with the Great Elector, who once more had lost patience with the French meddling in Poland.[2]

The long-planned [3] mission of Gabriel Sylvius was finally launched in April 1669, but his powers were ominously narrow, for he could only invite the German princes to sue at the Hague for entry to the circle of guarantors. He found the Hanoverians agreeable; so,

---

[1] Kent to Williamson, March 2, Italian States, 10; Mignet, iii. 185 *et seq.*

[2] Cal.S.P.D. 1668-69; instructions, Add. MSS. 9796, f. 106; Arlington to Temple, Nov. 3; Meerman to de Witt, June 16, Br.; Boreel, Verbaal, R.A., Aug. 20, 1668, February 1669; Pontalis, ii. 9; Brandt's audience, July 1668, Urk. xii. 272; Trevor to Temple, May 13, 1669, Sloane MSS. 1003.

[3] Ruvigni, May 31, 1668, Fr. tr.

too, his colleague Higgons, carrying the Garter, won
the Elector of Saxony; but Frederick William was a
harder proposition. Sylvius had orders to approach
him through de Witt, and this was unfortunate, for
the Elector still resented the Dutch attitude of 1667,
but the moment of negotiation was more unlucky still.
When Sylvius reached Berlin in June, the long-
intrigued Polish election was at length over; Condé
had failed, but so too had Neuburg, the German candidate, and the choice of the obscure Michael Wisniowiecki had left Frederick too indignant to think of
much else. His demand for regular subsidies indicated
his price, his question whether England was not treating with France showed his suspicion, and he very
plainly meant to keep a free hand, despite all Sylvius'
benevolent optimism.[1]

This eternal Polish question, the mercury of the
Northern system, was an element not easily controlled
even by a diplomacy with money to spare, and our
effort was, in fact, limited to economical reward and
tepid rebuke. Carlisle, Downing's peevish brother-in-
law, took the Garter to the young King of Sweden,
and pressed the claims of the Allies at Copenhagen;
Wych was detached to discourage Russian aggression on Sweden and to stimulate Polish resistance
to Russia, while Thynne, our resident at Stockholm,
worked in decent accord with the Dutch de Groot.[2]

A justifiable suspicion still reigned at Paris as to our
attitude in all quarters of Europe. Ruvigni accused

[1] Sylvius to Arlington, April 13, May 15, June 19; Higgons to same—April 3,
German States, 58, and April, Hamburg, 11, f. 153; instructions for Sylvius—
Nov. '68, Stowe, 191, and Jan. 17, '69, Foreign Entry, 176; Prussian protocol,
Urk. xii. 272, 899.

[2] Thynne to Arlington, Aug. 26, '68, Carlisle to same, April 15, '69, Yard to
Williamson, Oct. 13, Sweden, 7; de Groot to de Witt, Nov. 21, '68.

Arlington of dabbling in the plot of Roux de Marcilly, who in 1668 was organizing from Chandos Street a rising in southern France, with affiliations in Switzerland; Montagu had orders to represent the wrongs of the Huguenots; Charles was receiving from a spy sketches of Brest harbour. At Madrid was Godolphin, pressing the Swedish subsidy; Southwell was moving the anti-French party at Lisbon; while Temple was encouraged to arbitrate in the venerable Indian feud between Portugal and Holland. A testimony as strong as any was our care not to revive the Orange-Louvestein quarrel; Temple's orders were to get the Prince's revenue improved, but to steer clear of the stadtholdership, and to take no notice of Orange partisans in Zealand. But indeed, in all essentials, the official view of the alliance in England and Holland was still the same, for Holland even more emphatically than ourselves declined to consider the admission of the Hapsburgs as confederates.[1]

It is thus a parody of historical fact to represent de Witt, in 1668–69, as the enemy of France, or the champion of an expanding Triple Alliance. On the contrary, he viewed it only as a corrective or regulator to the tried friendship of Holland with France which, for reasons both external and domestic, he did not mean to abandon, and without which the "wonted insolence" of the English would dominate the sea. The ink was hardly dry on Temple's treaty before de Witt began conversations with France for a joint resistance to the English pretensions over the Flag; had not Allin already forced

[1] Ruvigni, May 29 and July, Fr. tr.; instructions for Montagu, Feb. 22, '69, *loc. cit.*; Arlington to Temple, July 9, '69; instructions to Godolphin, Feb. 24, '69, Rawlinson MSS. A. 225; Southwell to Arlington, Aug. 2, '68, Carte MSS. 36; instructions to Temple, Aug. 10, '68, *loc. cit.*; Cabinet note, Nov. 10, '68, Treaty papers, 74; Mignet, iii. 415; Lisola, 463.

a Dutch squadron to dip their pennants till he was out of sight?[1]

Towards Spain the Dutch attitude was one of acrimonious and egoistic hostility. They thought that she delayed her money payments with a view of involving them in another war, and old conflicts over Ostend pirates and religious bickering on the frontier kept the two Low Countries apart. The distribution of territories by the Aix settlement alarmed de Witt, who, even in June 1668, was still nibbling at the other "alternative" of Franche-Comté. He perceived that the Spanish future lay in darkness, and could see no light save in an arrangement with France. With D'Estrades, and from February 1669 with his successor Pomponne, he therefore renewed discussion of the partition or "cantonment" of Belgium, his projects ranging from arbitration between France and Austria back to the old idea of 1663 for a free Belgian republic. Not sharing the anti-French sentiment of Beuningen, just back from Paris, or of Amsterdam, now being harried by Colbert's edicts, his negotiation shows his rooted contempt for Spain and his old suspicion of the English. He spoke of partition as too favourable to England and, provided a Flanders barrier were assured, showed a supreme disinterestedness as to what happened to the rest of the Spanish empire. To him the Triple Alliance was not a league against France but a contribution to the balance of power, a balance of which Holland formed the tongue, giving her, as critics complained, the rôle of arbitrator or Areopagus.[2]

[1] De Witt to Beuningen, May 21, '68; to Temple, May 25, Fruin, iii.
[2] D'Estrades, May 14 and 21, '68; instructions for Colbert, Aug. '68, Fr. tr.; Aitzema, vi. 829; Mignet, iii. 572; Dollot, 191; Legrelle, i. 203; Van Dijk, 21; Rec. Hollande, 265; Lisola's criticism of de Witt, Pribram, 446, with which cf. Lionne's, in Legrelle, i. 204.

Until some such date, then, as the spring of 1669, or just about the signature of the Guarantee in May, the Triple Alliance stood intact or, more accurately, stood rooted in its original uncertainty. England had still concerted many measures hostile to France, and from France the Dutch had not yet, of their own volition, broken. The change of systems was to be accomplished in 1669–70, and was due primarily to two connected causes—the triumph of an anti-Dutch party in English counsels and the resolve of Louis XIV to revenge himself on Holland as the next necessary step to the Spanish succession.

There was, further, another cause, domestic to Holland, where de Witt's palmy day of supremacy was over. Now he had to meet a combination of dangers never before seen in such force and union—a renewed Orangist campaign gathering round a leader growing to precocious maturity, bitter personal enemies,[1] and the antagonism of Amsterdam. A blend of economy, self-confidence, provincial disputes, and lassitude seemed to afflict the Republic's policy, and while France laboured in every nook and cranny, the Dutch till late in 1670 were unrepresented at Paris and Madrid, and constantly refused the subsidies to which the Brunswickers and other potential allies aspired.[2]

Even if France had not existed the root of English-Dutch jealousy was still there, with its evil leafage and its bitter fruit. The commercial agreement annexed on the 7th February 1668 to the Triple Alliance dealt only in the vaguest terms of fair trading, leaving it to commissioners to meet at a later date to correct, expand, or

---

[1] "La pluralité des Césars ne peut pas vivre ensemble": D'Estrades, cited by Haje, *De geheime corr. van A. de Wicquefort met de Lionne*, 1901, p. 77.

[2] Fruin, iv. 62, 67; Japikse, *De Witt*, cap. xvii.

harmonize the articles into a marine treaty. But this procedure, originally the wish of the English, was dropped when they realized its rigidity and possibilities of friction, and the negotiation was entrusted to Temple at the Hague.[1]

The full seriousness of the problem can be seen, not in disputes of variable sincerity, such as flag or fisheries, but in the yet unresolved struggle for markets, in which the East India Company led the English van. The very method of our investigation, by a Cabinet committee in co-operation with the Company and the newly formed Council of Trade, is itself enough to show that the case was neither unsubstantiated nor vamped up by the Ministry. Our Company's demand was the same as in 1664, for "freedom of trade" with all that implied, and all the more important now because interlopers were challenging its monopoly. The issues were enormous, and larger than Whitehall realized, for the host of Dutch factories, and the scantier, more concentrated, English settlements, were caught up in the dying politics of the Mogul empire, meeting the thrust of Sivaji and the Mahrattas, or the ruthless Puritan Aurungzebe. The East, too, was the area of economic decision, for the Dutch still commanded the Baltic trade and we had the lion's share of the Levant.[2]

Directing British expansion in the East was as solid a body of merchant princes as in Venice at her prime, and the weight of the Childs, Houblons, and Papillons, in politics and society, was reflected in things deeper than their villas at Enfield and Epping, their glass coaches, and their daughters' marriages. Their loans to

[1] Instructions of Aug. 10, '68, *loc. cit.*; Arlington to Temple, Sept. 14, '68, and Jan. 22, '69.
[2] C. Bertie to Osborne, Lindsey papers; Mocenigo's *relazione* of 1671—Add. MSS. 10,171.

government in the late war, and their frequent gifts to
the King, enhanced the political importance acquired
by their growing trade, and while they ceaselessly
fought interlopers on their own preserves, their imports
of calicoes and silk hit hard the old clothing interest.
As they practised, so they preached the purest mercantilism—"foreign trade produces riches", wrote their
chairman Josiah Child, "riches produce power, power
preserves our trade and religion"—and from the period
of war depression they were emerging with flying
colours. Yet they had still far to go; while in 1669–70
their shares changed hands at prices from 108 to 130,
their rivals' stock at Amsterdam stood at over 500.[1]

Their protest had been immediate against accepting,
without more explanation, the articles of commerce
which Temple had signed, and in July 1668, after much
sifting by the Council of Trade, their petition was substantially adopted by Order in Council and annexed to
Temple's new instructions.[2] Our ministers took wide
and familiar ground: that "blockade" had yet to be
defined; that certificates regarding contraband were
useless in the East; monopoly contracts with natives
should be dropped; each party should respect the
other's passports in time of peace and abandon the
right of search; freedom of trade must not depend on the
consent of the native "sovereign"; lastly, that the mere
occupation of a fort by one Company should not bar the
other from access to its hinterland.

To find remedy for these things was the task committed to Temple, and one highly uncongenial to him.
His airy view that they came from a few prejudiced

[1] Khan, 190; Scott, i. 284.
[2] Instructions of Aug. 10, *loc. cit.*; report of Lords of Trade, April 10, Jenkins'
MSS. 205; Council order of July 15, Treaty papers, 47.

merchants is rebutted by the Company's fierce correspondence, and a year of wrangling conferences at
London and the Hague left agreement apparently
impossible on three major points. Our Company demanded that blockade be total, by land and sea, if
blockade was to be valid in bar of trade; to this the
Dutch provisionally agreed. The grievance of monopoly treaties was inflamed by a new case at Macassar,
where the Dutch ally had promised to evict both
English and Portuguese. And finally, on the moot
point of trade past fortified posts, the Dutch would
not budge, Beuningen arguing that such open trade,
whether in reach of their forts' guns or not, would
allow the English, for instance, to seize Ceylon, and
amount to "une bouleversement de toutes leurs esta-
blissements". On this business the Cabinet were solidly
behind our Company, which at their request tabulated
in 1669 a long list of Dutch forts, the hinterland of
which was to be regarded as open to both parties;
among others they named Calicut and Porcat, Macassar and the Moluccas, and if this, as their chairman
said, was their last word, no number of politicians
could have settled it. And so, in a quick rapid fire of
counter-claims from the tireless Beuningen, this conflict entered on 1670.[1]

In the East this struggle for the spoils of the oldest
world; in the West another, to appropriate a new, with
slaves and sugar as the fount of gold. Surinam, now
a corner of Dutch Guiana, was the creation of the
Willoughbies, and in the war of 1666 Francis Lord
Willoughby (who disappeared in the hurricane of that

[1] Jenkins' MSS. *loc. cit.*; Temple's narrative up to March 1669, Add. MSS.
28,093; Treaty papers, 47; Arlington to Temple, Jan. 1, '69; Cabinet note of Nov.
29, '68, Foreign Entry, 176; Trevor to Temple, May 13 and Aug. 17, '69,
Sloane MSS. 1003; Add. MSS. 9796, f. 18; E.I.C. 1668–70, ix.

July) made it a base of resistance. But the Dutch captured it on the 6th March 1667, and on those articles
of surrender their title turned, under the Breda treaty.
The terms allowed the English to migrate, if they
desired, to islands under their own government, but
to migrate with what belongings was the disputable
point, complicated threefold by a temporary English
recapture and proscription, lasting from October 1667
till a final surrender in March 1668. Our settlers,
though moved by little political sentiment except hostility to France, were some 4000 strong with their de-
pendents, and were not ready, treaty or no treaty, to
be dispossessed. They claimed, if they stayed, a bi-
lingual administration, their own ministers of religion,
and their privilege of "turtling" in the bay, and if they
went, the right of taking their slaves with them.[1] One
nation tried chicane, and the other violence; the new
Lord Willoughby claimed property which had fallen
to him between the two surrenders, and commissioned an adventurer, William Needham, against
the "Indians", while the Dutch seized on his agents,
and sent Needham and Bannister, the ex-governor, as
prisoners to Holland. For one moment there seemed a
chance of the Dutch reselling the colony,[2] but this was
resisted in Zealand, and though some concession was
made regarding the slaves, a settlement was still far
off in 1670; the released Bannister haunted Whitehall
"like a ghost daily", pressing the ruin of his estates
and the danger of his family, while our proposal that
he might return once to take off emigrants was rejected
by Holland.

[1] Boreel, Verbaal, R.A. 1668.
[2] "To be pressed as fast and as far as possible"—Cabinet order to Temple,
Feb. 14, '69, Foreign Entry, 176.

Where lay the rights in these old colonial disputes no amount of discussion in Europe could determine without mutual goodwill, but the element within the English Cabinet which was most favourable to Holland deplored the Surinam business as the worst blow. For it came at a time when, as Trevor wrote, "nothing but our faith and our amity can defend us from the greatest temptations that ever were applied to princes".[1]

In August 1668 Louis XIV, for the third time as he angrily noted, sent an ambassador to England empowered to discuss terms of "personal union"; to discover what reality there might be in Charles' talk of an understanding "de gentilhomme à gentilhomme", which since the Peace of Aix he had poured out to a rueful and mystified Ruvigni.[2] The new ambassador, Colbert de Croissy, was told by his famous brother that his task was the most vital in Europe, and his instructions show that this time Louis was bent on winning the English alliance in earnest. He was to make plain that France would gladly make it offensive, or in other words would drop her Dutch alliance of 1662, and was authorized to expose de Witt's partition scheme and his approaches to France about the Flag. But there must be no repetition of the English "promise" given in March 1667, and the Triple Alliance must be explicitly surrendered.[3]

Yet this official negotiation, conducted by Colbert at London and Montagu at Paris, was emphatically

[1] R.A. Leg. 799; Temple's narrative, March 5, '69, Foreign Entry, 175; Trevor to Temple, Sloane MSS. 1003, *passim*; Fruin, iv. 77; Wicquefort, iv. 52; Arlington and Temple letters.

[2] Ruvigni, May 11.

[3] Instructions, July 23, Fr. tr. and Rec. Angleterre, ii.; Colbert to Croissy, Sept. 4, Forneron. Croissy arrived on the 7th August.

a failure. The fault did not lie, primarily, with Colbert, though the English united to condemn[1] his "little understanding" and his irritability; for, if like others of his family he invited ridicule by pretensions to noble birth and danced strenuously to enhance them, he was both competent and industrious. The cause was deeper, and is the more significant because it was seriously to impede the secret negotiation also. One refrain rang without ceasing. Why was France laying down warships? Charles asked Colbert; commerce, he told Madame, was "nearest the heart of the nation", and must be reckoned with before anything deeper. Arlington insisted that Holles' treaty must be completed, and York complained of French incivility to the Flag. At Paris Montagu was presenting grievances touching French port dues and the exclusion of English traders in the French Leeward islands; there was suspicion of organized smuggling on a large scale, in which the Walloon colony at Canterbury and French *douanniers* took a hand. Colbert's aggressive policy had fairly roused the English Parliament, which this year convulsed Bordeaux by raising the duty on claret, while a committee, called during 1669 to advise the Cabinet—including the great merchants Child and Papillon—recommended reciprocity in regard to wines, silks, and woollens, and reduction of duties to the level existing before December 1664.[2]

What positive advantages could Colbert set against this permanent mercantile enmity? Apart from the incalculable element of the King, the political personnel

[1] Buckingham to Madame, Feb. 17, Mignet; Charles II to same, June 6, Ady; Montagu to Arlington, May 8 and 24, M.H. papers.

[2] Colbert, Aug. 20, Mignet, and Sept. 17, Fr. tr.; Charles to Madame, Sept. 14; M.H. papers; *Trans. R. Hist. Soc.* n.s. xv.; France, 128, f. 143; Clément, i. 297; Treaty papers, 13.

on whom he reckoned rather hated Holland than loved France. There was Downing, who had been disgusted by the treaty of Breda, and his colleagues in the Treasury, who, Temple thought, were goading on the East India Company. There was Clifford, conscientiously believing that we must revenge the last war, and notoriously[1] itching for the next. But their influence was secondary, and so was Lady Castlemaine's, though her excellent French sentiments were fed by French pin-money. The only big fish Colbert netted was Buckingham, for whom it was quite enough that the Triple Alliance was the work of Arlington. But to gamble on his driving Arlington from power was, by the end of 1668, demonstratably hopeless, and even if one conquered his idleness, he too was not immune from notions of English supremacy at sea and asked not less than a year for the conversion of public opinion. His childish and vain adoration of Madame made suspect any action, through her, of which he was not the manager, and he was on bad terms with the "Clarendonian" Duke of York. Indeed, in November 1668, his rascally agent Ellis Leighton went to Paris, ostensibly to patent a new carriage, but in fact to protest to Madame that Colbert was hopeless.

But while the French soothed and complimented Buckingham, his negotiation was revealed by Leighton to York, as Leighton's was by Montagu to Arlington, and the real steps were taken by those who wore the crowns—by Charles and Madame, Louis and York.[2]

---

[1] Temple to Sir J. Temple, July 22; cf. Ossory to Arlington, Oct. 12, '70 (Holland, 186); on board the *Henrietta* at Helvoetsluys, "If the Treasurer were here we might be capable of attempting a folly, for the forts here have not answered our salutes, and we are within twenty paces of the *Charles* and many of their best ships".

[2] Mignet; M.H. papers; Forneron; Macpherson.

If death-bed asseverations are true[1]—a large assumption—the initiative came from Madame, who in an evil hour, her rare talent thwarted and her character warped by a wretched state of married misery, turned to establish her brother, her Church, and her own prestige in France, on a foundation of rock. From her correspondence with Charles, those still waters on which we find ever-broadening ripples of publicity, we see that essentials were clearly agreed between them before they were imparted to York, or probably to Arlington, but no cipher was used till December 1668, which may therefore date the introduction of the religious element. From her later effort to postpone a Catholic pronouncement to the Dutch war, even Madame's religious passion must be taken as second to her political instinct, and the famous meeting of the 25th January 1669, for which York is our authority, was perhaps solely designed for overcoming his objection to a dangerous policy by an appeal to his faith.

The composition of that meeting—the Catholics York, Arundell, and possibly Bellasis, with Arlington and Clifford—suggests that the religious factor was now brought to the forefront, and the same inference follows from the choice of agents. Arundell led them, most loyal of Catholic Cavaliers and Master of the Horse to the Queen Mother, a man whose very remoteness from public politics marked the personal nature of the negotiation; Bellings, the man sent to Rome in 1662, was to assist him in drafting, and St. Albans joined them. Established on this basis of the throne and the altar, Arundell's mission carried no pledges as to a Dutch war, but put Catholicity and personal union in

---

[1] Charles to Madame, March 22; Montagu to Charles, July 5, '70 (Arl.).

the foreground and invited the French to suspend, for one year, their construction of warships.[1]

From Arundell's departure in early March to his return in June, there were comings and goings of St. Albans, conferences between Madame, Ruvigni, Lionne, and Turenne, with resultant letters from Charles to clear up the doubts on which France asked for more light. As for the Catholic declaration, it was promised within eight or ten months;[2] Charles was profuse with promises that he could answer for the event, that he was carefully fortifying Chatham and Portsmouth, and that holders of Church land could be satisfied. To the prompt demand whether he would attack Holland, he replied in affirmative, though more general, terms, glorying both to Madame and Colbert over his hopes of revenge for Chatham. Though firm enough on the guarantee given to Spain for the young King's lifetime, after Arundell's return Charles promised to assist Louis' pretensions in the event of the young King's death, in return for an undefined share in the profits; he dropped, also, his protests against French shipbuilding, and a Cabinet order issued that naval salutes would be neither given nor expected, so far as France was concerned, south of Finisterre. The great affair seemed to be sailing into smooth seas. Madame assured her confidants that Rome could refuse England nothing, while Louis, warm in gratitude for recognition of his Spanish claim, urged Charles to lose no time in approaching His Holiness.[3]

[1] Clifford MSS.

[2] Arundell's declaration of June 5, quoted by Colbert, Sept. 19, '70, Fr. tr.; Colbert to Louis, May 23, '69, *ibid*.

[3] Clifford MSS. (for two letters of Madame, *vide E.H.R.* xliii.); draft Cabinet order, Aug. 29, France, 127; Cosnac, i. 383; Louis to Charles, Aug. 31, Dalrymple.

Across this Eden fell only the shadow of Arlington —so rich, so timorous, so "cursed cunning", as York said. He it was but for whom, Louis wrote, the alliance would "make itself"—whom Lionne this February of 1669 called "devoted" to de Witt, and whom the Swede Puffendorf named the "midwife" of European peace.[1] From every French source of information in London reports came of his staunchness to Spain as the key to English commerce, and of his hostility to the new scheme. Presents and bribes for himself or his servant Williamson were declined, and Madame's advances ignored.[2] So late as September of this year, French accusations dogged him in all quarters: to Turin he was delated as opposing the English-Savoyard treaty of commerce; to Florence as instigating their Crown Prince, this year in England, to slight Colbert; while from Paris, Rome, the Hague, and Königsberg the Secretary was informed of a French campaign for his downfall at the meeting of Parliament, and of the Allies' concern.[3] His conversion, if such it can be called, would thus be of real import—conversion not to any Church, but to a policy he had spent his life in resisting. How far Charles was justified in his reiterated assurances to Madame that Arlington would obey orders implicitly, we can measure only by the event, but it was clearly to the minister's advantage to control the game proceeding between Madame and Buckingham, to get another bulwark against that eternal nightmare of a

[1] Instructions for Colbert, July '68, Mignet; Rec. Holland, i. 284: "tout le monde vous regarde comme la sage femme d'une alliance si nécessaire pour le repos de la Chrestienité"—Puffendorf to A., Feb. 15, '70, Holland, 186.

[2] Colbert, May 2 and 20, Fr. tr.; Lionne to Colbert, March 24, '69, Mignet; Forneron, 34.

[3] Tuscany, 10, ff. 225, 368; Fr. tr. 122; Kent to Williamson, Aug. 24, Italian States, 10; Temple, Oct. 8, Holland, 185; Montagu, July 16 and Aug. 27, M.H. papers; Prussian protocol, June 16, Urk. xii.

return of Clarendon, and to deepen his favour with the King by ending this half-feud with the sister dear to the King's heart. Harmony was therefore restored in courteous letters to and from Madame between June and September, each party insisting that England's interest and the King's order were their guide, and was sealed by a present of £500, exceedingly convenient to Madame, pressed as she was to redeem some jewels which she had pawned without telling Monsieur.[1]

Happenings of the autumn, in Paris and London, drew still nearer this triple alliance of Charles, his sister, and his trusted minister. Henrietta Maria died on the 31st August, entailing upon her children a good many pictures of Madonnas, a silver warming-pan, a deal of debt, and a nasty tussle with Monsieur for her belongings. Madame's grief was great and her physique exhausted; Monsieur's sordid vice and his jealousy of her political influence degraded and wore her down— her best friends were under a cloud, she was isolated, thrown upon her religious longings, and fighting for her political life. By December she was resolved on that journey to England so long urged by Charles and Buckingham.

This autumn, also, the private negotiation was extended, and in a sense blended with public diplomacy; for even the deadliest secret must find political expression, and the plan of keeping private and public policies in air-tight compartments inevitably broke down. In October Colbert de Croissy was told the whole secret, and on the 3rd Arundell was sent off again—this time not only as head of a commission to wind up the Queen Mother's affairs, but charged to

---

[1] Charles to Madame, May 6 to June 24, Ady; Arlington to Madame, June 20, Mignet; Madame to A. Sept. 14, *E.H.R. loc. cit.*

tell Louis that we would stave off, as long as possible, the military "concert" to which the Triple Alliance bound us.[1] And yet the essentials did not advance. Arlington had refused Lord Castlemaine leave to publish in English his bitter little history of the late Dutch war, and Colbert thought he meant to use "Catholicity", and an understanding with France, as two only among many levers, including the Triple Alliance, whereby to raise the power of the Crown. Charles did, indeed, boast of the ease of "Catholicity", yet not so convincingly that the French felt any confidence about getting more than his neutrality as against Holland.[2]

In fact, "the great design" was striking on the solid rocks of our national system and our parliamentary tradition, and we must go a good deal deeper than the despatches of the Frenchmen, who "know no more of England", Montagu said, "than they do of Persia", to find the real purpose of our government between the fateful meeting of January 1669 and the Dover treaty in May of the following year.

The session of November 1669 to April 1670 was unexpectedly favourable to the Crown,[3] some larger parliamentary grants putting Charles in a better bargaining position with the French. Yet a wine duty, to be paid in part by the King's new allies, would not pay for the fleet, and Lauderdale's subservient church and militia settlement in Scotland spurred the English Commons not to emulation but suspicion, heated as they were by a fiercer Conventicle Act and a report from the commission of accounts of missing millions.

[1] France, 128; Arundell's instructions, Clifford MSS.; Colbert to Louis, Nov. 3; Cal.S.P.D. 1669.
[2] *Ibid.* 488; Mignet, iii. 106, 117; Lionne's comment, Pagès, 227.
[3] Oñate, March 4, Simancas.

Worse still, from the French point of view, was the
bitter quarrelling between those councillors whose
unanimity was vital. Buckingham's feud with Ormonde
and the Cavaliers, like his support with Lauderdale
and Ashley of a divorce for the King, directly affronted
the Duke of York, and with York and Ormonde went,
for broad party purposes, Arlington.[1] The lines of
division in domestic and foreign policies did not,
therefore, correspond. Monk's death and Robartes'
departure to succeed Ormonde in Ireland weakened
the Dutch party, but the French group was split into
two cliques—Lauderdale, Ashley, and Buckingham,
as against York and Arlington. Meantime, the wildest
rumours and circumstantial reports of a French-
Popish treaty were current in London. St. Albans was
said to be offering Dunkirk and four millions, bets were
exchanged that mass would be said at the Abbey in
a twelvemonth, and Charles had to beg the French
for more silence and discretion. One section in the
Commons, led by a Spanish pensioner in Sir Robert
Howard, were not content with asking for prohibitive
duties on French imports, but were only dissuaded
from a solemn declaration on the Triple Alliance by
Arlington's reminder that treaties lay wholly in the
scope of the prerogative.[2]

The French, who had to digest Charles' hard driving
for money this winter, put it down to his consciousness
of more assured power, but we can probably ascribe
as much weight to the extreme uncertainty of the
international position. Was it yet sure, for instance,

[1] Colbert, Dec. 27, '70, Fr. tr.; Harris, ii. appendices. Marvell's remark (*Growth
of Popery*, etc.) that Trevor, Ormonde, and Bridgeman were now left out of the
Council is inaccurate.

[2] Marvell to Popple, March 21 and April 14; Cal.S.P.D. Dec. 17, '69; Boreel
to de Witt, Sept. 14, '68, Br.; Ranke; Oñate, March 4 to April 8, Simancas.

that the French-Dutch conversations had ceased
touching Belgian partition? Arlington had reason to
think not.[1] And, again, while we were exhorting
Spain to produce the subsidies which alone could keep
Belgium Spanish, the oddest stories were coming from
Madrid. Our old acquaintance Watteville had started,
even in 1668, a new hare for the exchange of Roussillon
against the Low Countries, which was urged by the
French, though vainly, at Vienna, and taken up more
seriously this winter. In December the intriguing
Monsieur Gourville, worthy client of the fallen Fouquet, reached Madrid with a blonde singer and some
excellent cooks; over that libretto flit light Mlle.
Jollivet, *modiste*, and even lighter Marquesa de la
Fuentes, but this light man was advancing, so Godolphin reported, a dangerously weighty idea that, if the
exchange of territories materialized, Anjou should be
recognised as heir to Spain, which with France should
attack Holland, and after Holland, England. In March
1670 he was followed by an official envoy in Bussy,
well known in Warsaw as attached to Madame
Sobieski, who was authorized to tell the Spaniards of
de Witt's partition talk and to dilate, if the territorial
exchange broke down, on the Catholic league, which
France had in fact refused to Austria but which always
dazzled certain eyes in Spain.[2] In allied countries the
alarm was great, if the interpretation various; Louis'
announcement, that at Easter he would "progress" in
his new conquests in Artois, was taken to mean that
he would thus drive home the exchange project, and
lugubrious messages from Lisola and the Dutch under-

[1] Arlington to W. Godolphin, Aug. 26, '69; Pontalis, ii. 43.
[2] Legrelle, i. 153; Pötting, ii. 16; Mignet, iii. 413; Gourville, Mém. (Petitot);
Lecestre in *Rev. des questions historiques*, lii.; Rec. Espagne, 231; Godolphin to
Arl. (cipher), Feb. 9, '70, Spain, 56; Van Dijk, 327.

lined the possibility that the Triple Alliance might lose its very *raison d'être*. Other expedients were in circulation, the product of optimism or despair; Temple and Lisola failed to convince Madrid that Belgium might be given with an archduchess to the Duke of Lorraine, and the Dutch were mumbling over the other "alternative" of Franche Comté for France.[1] If diplomatic reversals like these were possible, it is natural to find the English, even those in the secret, moving warily in their bargain with France, and it was not by leaps and bounds, nor without mature experience of its working, that the Triple Alliance was reversed.

Having made, against the French wishes, the guarantee of May 1669, there remained two consequential problems: the obligation thereby incurred, after Spain had paid Sweden for her "past" services, to frame a military "concert", and then the intense pressure, at first from Lisola and latterly from the Dutch, to admit the Emperor in some capacity or other to the alliance. From the position he took up in opening his decisive correspondence with Madame, that he meant to fulfil the guarantee to France and Spain alike, Charles showed no sign of retreat in spite of Louis' remonstrance, and in the Cabinet Arlington, Ormonde, and Bridgeman carried this point against York and Clifford, partly on the ground that Parliament must be humoured.[2]

Whatever the motive, the English attitude from

---

[1] Lisola, Oct. 8, Holland, 185; St. Maurice, Mém. ed. Lemoine, Jan. 7, '70; Montague to Arl. Jan. 1; Godolphin to Arl. Nov. 10, '69, Spain, 55; Temple to Lisola and to Arl., both Aug. 17, '69, Holland, 185; Perwich's reports, R.H. Soc. *loc. cit.*; Arl. to Godolphin, July 29, '69.

[2] Clifford MSS.; Foreign Entry Book, 176, Sept. 26 and Nov. 21; Louis to Charles, Oct. 17, Mignet.

November 1669 onwards was very remarkable in the circumstances. On the 22nd of that month Temple was ordered (reversing instructions of a month earlier) to drop the objection we had maintained for a year past, and to sign the "concert", whether Spain had paid up her first subsidy or not. Though Charles characteristically told the Spaniards that Temple had orders to sign, the ambassador's official limitations were that he must only sign if pressed, that no time limit must be set for our mobilization in case of a rupture, and that in no case whatever would we guarantee any payments beyond our quota.[1] But the last point, despite assurances to France, was dropped in the end, and the "concert", signed at the Hague on the 21st January 1670, bound us not only to send, if peace were broken, 6000 foot and forty ships as quickly as possible to help Spain, but pledged our credit to one quarter of the first three months' subsidy promised to Sweden in the event of war.[2]

Guarantee and "concert" were thus complete,[3] and with the actual payment by the Spaniards of the first instalment for the Swedish "services" given in 1667–1668, the Triple Alliance at last achieved a fleeting embodiment. Arlington's tone to Temple, particularly in regard to Holland, was now much more acrimonious, but the detail of his correspondence forbids us to claim him as even yet a convert to war. The disaster he sought to avoid was renewed warfare between France and Spain. Hence his incessant pressure for the Spanish

---

[1] Cf. instruction to Werden, Oct. 11, with those to Temple, Nov. 22, Add. MSS. 9797—drafted in cabinet (Trevor to Temple, Nov. 23, Sloane MSS. 1003); Temple to Trevor, Dec. 3; Arlington to Temple, Feb. 4; Colbert to Louis, Dec. 5, Mignet.

[2] Originals, Add. MSS. 9797, ff. 95, 112.

[3] Our ratification forwarded by Trevor, March 7, Sloane MSS. loc. cit.

subsidies, his conviction that the Triple Alliance was more necessary to the Allies than to Spain herself, and hence also his labour, against French suggestion, to keep its framework in being. Finance alone would forbid England entering upon "great schemes", and we must not get "praised into measures" we could not support, but the interest of Spain and Holland was, he recognised, against France; "honour" might place us by their side, but "without vigour to support that honour" it would not do — we must seek peace by mediation—"I would it were otherwise".[1] Was not he fighting in these "melancholy reflections", as Temple styled them, to stick to the old scheme, and is it not rather a case of an angel falling than of an *âme damnée*?

The "concert" being thus designed by the English to give "the same security" as that of Aix, though "in a more proper way",[2] and no more, we could have nothing to do with the ambitious plan of Lisola for a general league. Once that had been emphatically the Dutch attitude also, but now, under pressure of their fears, they were working with Lisola for a German *bloc* which should later be linked to the Alliance, and to this Arlington, in September 1669, agreed on condition that it was limited to the guarantee of Aix.[3] In December Spanish pressure at Vienna won a triumph in the fall of the French pensioner Auersperg, but Leopold's wretched vacillation still persisted, though its detail can have for us little interest, save as confirming Arlington's conviction that Lisola and Vienna were very different

---

[1] Arlington to Temple, July '69, Holland, 185, f. 74; Jan. 6 and Feb. 4, '70; to Godolphin, Feb. 7; Boreel to de Witt, Dec. 28, '69, *Br. aan De Witt*.
[2] Trevor to Temple, May 2, '70, Sloane MSS. 1003.
[3] Lisola to Arlington, Aug. 17 ("vous connoisez mieux que personne combien importe à la Triple Alliance d'avoir les flances couverts ou asseurés du côté de l'Allemagne") and Oct. 8, Holland, 185.

beings.[1] Enough, then, to say that between August 1669 and March 1670 Leopold twice gave Lisola power to conclude and twice revoked it, palpitating between the Spanish threat to cut him out of the succession and the French threat to combine a league of the Rhine, Hungary, and the Turk.

French threats succeeded, in fact, better at Vienna than in London, for while Leopold had by March promised not to enter the Alliance, and even weakened on the guarantee, Temple had orders to welcome proposals from any German prince. It is true that we rejected any wide defensive liability, as for instance for Breisach or the Turkish frontier, and that we asked "permission" of France thus to keep Austria quiet, but our pretexts were so transparent (such as, that it was important to lull the suspicions of Buckingham) that Colbert thought Arlington had himself manufactured Lisola's project merely to enhance the English claim for money. Yet short of gigantic subsidies it is hard to see what more could be done with Germany; the Great Elector had just signed a secret treaty with France, giving him a reversionary interest in Spanish Gueldres; both he and Mainz, though not anti-Dutch, viewed the Dutch activity as provocative; the Hanover dukes saw no hope of Dutch money, and were veering away.[2]

Preserving, then, the ghost of the Triple Alliance for bargaining uses, or future resurrection, the English turned to arbitration as the cheapest means whereby to

[1] Arlington to Temple, March 22; T. to A. July 5, and cf. Lobkowitz' humour —"que l'Isola n'était qu'une poupée donnée aux Espagnols pour les amuser" —Mignet, iii. 465.

[2] *Ibid.*, 157, 464; Colbert, Feb. 13 and March 27; Cabinet instructions for Temple, sent by Arlington and Trevor, March 22, Sloane MSS. *loc. cit.*; Urk. xii. 902; Droysen, iii. 223; Temple, Dec. 13, '69. Pribram's narrative and a comparison of dates seem to dispose of Klopp's thesis, that only English perfidy prevented Leopold entering the Triple Alliance.

save Spain, and made it an integral part of their secret negotiation with France. One implication of this step, recommended in February 1669 by the Dutch themselves,[1] was that an arbitrator could hardly contemplate war, and perhaps for this reason Louis had first offered the task to Leopold, who perhaps for that reason refused. In August Temple took part in a joint *démarche* against French infractions of the Aix peace, and this, though disavowed in London, was renewed by Montagu at Paris. Louis having accepted the principle, by December it was agreed to associate Sweden as co-arbitrator with ourselves—the better, perhaps, to detach her from Holland—and in January 1670 we received a formal French promise not for the space of one year to assert their pretensions by force. Lisola hailed it as a "grand coup", de Witt shrewdly concealed his disgust at the marked exclusion of Holland, Arlington urged Oñate to lose not a moment in getting the consent of his mistress. If the French ministers really meant peace, as much testimony showed, their war department were buying artillery horses, and Charles candidly advised Spain to look to her Flemish fortifications.[2]

Making this guarded use of defensive weapons, which on public grounds might be made to justify their secret policy, the English from December 1669 pushed home their long fencing bout with the French, on the 8th of that month presenting to Colbert a draft treaty which left him gasping. It declared that Charles' "Catholicity" must come about in his own discretion, but France must provide troops in the event of rebellion and pay

[1] Dutch memorial of Feb. 10, Williamson's journal.
[2] Montagu to Arlington, Oct. 9, M.H. papers; Colbert, Sept. 9, Fr. tr.; France, 129; Trevor to Temple, Jan. 28, '70, Sloane MSS. *loc. cit.*; Lisola to Arlington, Feb. 12, Holland, 186; St. Maurice, March 18; Oñate, Simancas, March 11 and April 18.

£200,000 before his declaration, within six months of
ratifying this treaty. Louis must keep intact the peace
of Aix, and yet leave Charles at liberty to preserve
the Guarantee; if the King of Spain died, the English
ambitions, long asserted,[1] were to be satisfied with nothing less than Ostend, Minorca, and Spanish America.
Both kings were to make war on Holland and Hamburg, England with all her naval forces and 6000 troops,
in return for which France should pay us £800,000
a year, the first £400,000 to accrue three months before the declaration of war. From the spoils of this war
England would take Walcheren, Sluys, and Cadsand,
and would ask a separate arrangement for the Prince of
Orange; the date of beginning war was left to France,
but it was to be after Charles had become Catholic and
had secured peace within England.[2]

The price asked of the French was immense—their
reward, the attack on Holland, was left in the air; it
was on this point, and not on York's religious ardour,
that they fastened in the long evening conferences,
now opened in the Whitehall lodgings of Father
Patrick, Arlington's favourite intermediary. As to the
Spanish succession, Charles showed some prophetic
instinct of what Louis would do—that is, try to harmonize the English claims with his direct pledge to
Austria of January 1668; conceding that this problem
should be left in general terms, he stipulated that
France should make no separate agreement with
Austria or with Don Juan, and refused explicitly to
proclaim Louis' right to "the succession of Spain".[3]

---

[1] See Trevor's conversation of March 17, '69, with Colbert—Legrelle,
i. 212.

[2] Mignet; Clifford MSS.; for other points in the minds of the English commissioners, see appendix.

[3] Colbert, Dec. 20, and Louis XIV, Feb. 6, Mignet; Legrelle, i. 216.

On the other hand he dropped, without more ado, the demand for a joint attack on Hamburg.

Thus acquiring some bargaining merit, Charles bade high in the question of Holland. That war, the English (pre-eminently Arlington) repeated, could only be to the interest of France, and till February they still put forward the old proposal of 1667, for English neutrality during the first year. Their arguments, pressed in midnight conclave at Father Patrick's, in low conversation at the Queen's drawing-room, in walks at Newmarket, throw a searchlight on the reality of the "great design" and the rôle of the "Catholic" conspirators. Clifford, who did most of the detailed revision, suspected in every point (Colbert tells us) a trap for England, while his colleagues and his master represented, with equal fluency, both the ease and the danger of their task. We had, they argued, to man the whole fleet, for experience proved the danger of opposing to Holland a mere defensive; we must have convoys out to protect our commerce, and cruisers to pick up the Dutch colonies. All this would cost much beyond the English means, but success need not be doubted; the King hoped to announce his conversion in the autumn session of 1670, and the French troops for England would never be required. But on one point there must be no misapprehension: English sailors could never take orders from a French admiral.

It was not till the 11th May, four days before Madame reached Dover, that the last preliminaries seemed to be adjusted. The French had begun by offering 500,000 *écus* a year for the war, but rose finally to three million livres for an English squadron limited to fifty ships, one half of the first annual payment to be made over before declaration of war; for

"Catholicity", they rose from 1,500,000 to 2,000,000 livres, and agreed that all payments should be in cash, at London or in French Channel ports. The treaty of commerce so long pondered was to be finished; York or some other Englishman should command the combined navies; declaration of war was to follow "Catholicity", the date of which was still undetermined when Madame arrived. Colbert's last orders were to follow Charles to Newmarket and conclude all, since Beuningen, the Dutchman most hostile and formidable to France, was coming to England.[1]

On the Dover cliffs bent the gaze of England and Europe, for what meant this stir on each side of the water? In Artois and Flanders the French Court viewing their latest conquest, from Arras to Douai and on to Lille; at Dover the whole English royal family; in what "family counsels"[2] were Charles and his sister engaged? There came the King and Queen, York and his duchess (now an avowed Catholic), Rupert and Monmouth, the ministers in the secret and those who knew it not, and the Dutch Boreel—who felt he was unwelcome—while Ruvigni and St. Evremond were expected to bring their popularity to help the unliked Colbert.[3] Oñate, the Spanish resident, came fresh from an angry interview with Arlington, news having arrived that Spain declined England and Sweden as sole arbiters of her difference with France; Spain, the Secretary vociferated, so basely ungrateful for the peace with Portugal and the settlement of Aix, should never drag England into war. But no politics, he insisted, would be dealt with in this quiet family

[1] Louis to Colbert, May 11; Trevor to Temple, April 23, Sloane MSS. 1003.
[2] Marvell to Popple, April 14.
[3] Boreel to de Witt, May 21, R.A. 2816, Holland.

reunion at Dover. At last, on Sunday the 15th May, Sandwich and St. Albans brought Madame over from Dunkirk, with Antony Hamilton, a Breton lady Louise de Queroalle, and some 230 other persons in her train.[1]

The detail of her negotiation is still hidden from us, as it was that week from York, who was sent back to town to prevent Puritan riots (and, in fact, the London parks were full of troops), or as it was from Trevor and Boreel, who were both emphatic that nothing serious had occurred. But even if the text of the treaty were lost, we could seize some incidental gleams that lighten up her frame of mind; graciousness itself to Oñate, she struck others as thin and feverish, declared aloud against the Dutch and Temple, and moved (though this was to be hidden from Arlington) that Turenne be sent for to map out a campaign. Her time was short, though the three days first allotted by Monsieur's jealousy were stretched out to sixteen, and she lost none of it in getting down to business, for the treaty was signed on the 22nd May.[2]

Its content shows the limited nature of her triumph. If the English gains from the Spanish succession were, like the French, left in a studied vagueness, Charles still privately spoke of Ostend and the Indies; she had failed to persuade him to let the Dutch war precede "Catholicity",[3] the date of which was still left wholly to his discretion, but the money for which was to be paid in full within six months of ratification. For the rest, the treaty proceeded on lines which Colbert had

[1] Oñate, May 6 and 21, Simancas; Cosnac, i. 415. By August Hamilton was bound for Rome, Tuscany, 11, f. 409.

[2] Boreel to de Witt, June 7, R.A.; Trevor to Essex, "Of that which hath alarmed the world, I see nóthing and believe as little", June 1, Sloane MSS. *loc. cit.*; Ady, 330; Colbert, May 20, Fr. tr.; Oñate, May 21.

[3] Louis XIV to Gremonville, June 7, Mignet; contrast the text of the treaty with York's assertions in Macpherson.

already accepted; he himself immediately took one
original to France, the other was consigned, perhaps,
to Clifford's despatch-box, where it now reposes, and
on the 4th June Charles fixed his secret seal to the
ratification, carefully countersigned "Arlington, by
His Majesty's command".

Ten days passed in feasting and ceremonial—one at
Canterbury, where the Garter knights attended the
service of the Church their master had promised to
destroy, a second there in ballets and archery, a third
at Dover with John Caryll's *Cautious Coxcomb* as the
command performance (a Caryll of East Grinstead, we
think, with whom Father Serenus Cressy had found
refuge), and a fourth in the King's yacht on a visit to the
fleet. Madame was all sunshine and quicksilver, happy
to have reconciled Arlington and Buckingham, as to
have won Charles' promise to raise the Secretary and
Clifford to new honours.

On the 2nd June she crossed to France, more Eng-
lish-hearted than she had ever been, in expectation, no
question, of more work for her cause, and on the 28th
was singing an English song and writing to Clifford
her first English letter. Early on the 30th she died,
protesting to Ralph Montagu that she had done this
work for her dear brother's good.

So was cut down and withered this brief flower of
courtesy, wit, and ambition; tortured, bled, and dis-
sected that frail body; "Vanitas vanitatum" was the
text of Bossuet's sermon that ushered it to the grave—
Bossuet, to whom went her last word, that she loved
God with all her heart. At London there were cold
rumours of poison, voiced by Rupert and Trevor,
Buckingham called for instant war, the mob demonstrated against Colbert.

But neither piety nor wit, anger nor evil report, could touch Madame further or cancel what was writ; somewhere, signed and sealed by four English names, whether at Whitehall or already in a deep valley of Dartmoor, the secret treaty was concealed which put England at the mercy of Louis XIV.

CHAPTER VIII

THE EVE OF WAR: 1670–1672

THE tragedy of Madame was not, as the French at one time feared, to make an end of her great design. Charles' grief was sincere, and broke out in execration against the villainy of Monsieur, but he assuaged it, he wrote, by "thinking of other things". Among such must be the French subsidies, some of which would fall to him automatically within six months, whether he were a declared Catholic or no, and more again if he made the Dutch war. The problems of the next year and a half were to carry the whole government into his secret policy, and so to isolate Holland that we need not thereby wreck our whole diplomatic structure.

At this stage we begin to see most instructively the working of alien and naked principles in the complex, dense, and pervasive atmosphere of the English State. Secrecy, Popery, and despotism are plunged, as it were, in this strong colouring matter of administrative routine and practical politics, to emerge, if they emerge at all, as draggled linsey-woolsey remnants of ideals. Publicity and Protestantism had been for over a century the conditions of English life, and from their potency no hidden policy could be immune.

It thus proved a dangerous slope when Charles decided to enlarge the number of his confidants.

Already Madame had disclosed the coming onslaught upon Holland to our representative at Paris, Ralph Montagu; and this was important, for though, as later history proved, Montagu was a covetous scoundrel, he took a lofty view of English power, much disliked Buckingham, and never ceased to represent that Colbert was ruining our trade. It was more momentous that in July Buckingham's group were brought into this part of the secret also. Charles had always meant to tell the duke, whom he found it hard to keep at a distance, and boasted that, though he could not keep a secret, his obedience could be relied on, even up to Popery, while the process was easier because Madame's visit and death so fired Buckingham to his old French proclivities that he himself took the initiative. There followed the smooth acquisition of Lauderdale, whose pace was ever the King's, and that of Ashley was only a little more deliberate; his passion for trade made him anti-Dutch, and by July's close he, with Clifford, was added to the commissioners dealing with Beuningen, to see that Trevor "did no harm".[1]

This transaction's effects were far-reaching, and not least its first purpose, the second or *traité simulé*; a treaty, that is, if we look from both sides, for which the "Protestant" councillors could take the credit, but for which they should also be made to shoulder the responsibility, if things went awry. Naturally the French were not averse, since the new scheme must involve the postponement of "Catholicity" to the Dutch war, the object they long had sought but in which they still found Arlington cold, and again because the new confidants must in their own interest support the French

[1] Arl. i. 440, 444; M.H. papers; Colbert, July 4, Mignet, and July 20, Fr. tr.

cause in Parliament.[1] Buckingham was therefore given a royal reception when in August he proceeded to Paris, was inoculated (when he could be dragged from his tailor) with the portions of the Dover treaty which it was judged in England he might know, and promised the command of the English auxiliary troops. In September he returned to goad on his colleagues, whom he found so dilatory, to attack Holland in the spring.

This matter of a date for the outbreak of war was a dilemma on which the parties nearly split. Catholicity, the *sine qua non* of the Dover chronology, seemed far distant; York was ardent enough, but Arlington complained that Charles kept him in the dark, while Charles himself inundated Colbert with pretexts. He must wait for the Pope's sanction, but then the Pope was so old—he was obliged for the offer of the Bishop of Laon, but would prefer an English emissary, and the right Englishman was still abroad.[2] Yet, if the war was given priority, as it must be if Buckingham and company were to be humoured, a date must be fixed.

Other differences involved in the enlightenment of the "Protestant" ministers delayed the negotiation during October and December, for they asked the islands of Goree and Woorne in addition to the conquests indoctrinated into them from the Dover clauses, and made more of our sole command in the Channel. But the real blow fell when Louis announced that, in deference to his German allies, he could not fight before the spring of 1672, and suggested that his subsidy for "Catholicity" be suspended till Charles officially announced his change of faith.

Parliament was now sitting—it must sit, Arlington implied, if Louis did not offer better terms—and from

---

[1] Colbert, July 4, Sept. 18 and 19, Fr. tr.   [2] *Ibid.* Oct. 23.

its existence the English extracted all the pressure they could put upon France. A month earlier Charles and Arlington had been saying that finance made war impossible in 1671, and now with equal facility they declared it would prohibit the delay till 1672 which Louis suggested. Had they not manned the fleet, the expense of which they must recoup? And having appealed to Parliament for help in the menacing state of Europe, it would be difficult to resist Parliament in its anti-French temper. Arlington could not believe that Louis would contemplate such a breach of the Dover treaty; was he unaware of the pressure put on Charles by Holland and Lorraine, or was it possible that he was intriguing with the Dutch?[1] Colbert reported that everything was near shipwreck, and Louis gave way; the English at least should get the money, the question on which they felt strongest.

The treaty signed on the 21st December 1670 by the whole Cabal therefore accumulated the two million livres pledged for "Catholicity" at Dover to the three million subsidy now promised for the first year of the Dutch war, which was to begin in May 1672 at latest, and provided that two millions of the five should be paid within three and a half months of ratification; Goree and Woorne should be added to Sluys, Cadsand, and Walcheren; on the Spanish succession there was silence, but a promise was given that Louis would "never" break the peace he had made with Spain. It was perhaps on this ground, as much as to stop more financial juggling, that Louis extorted from a most unwilling Charles a secret agreement to the effect that the first two millions were given for the Catholic purpose, that he would claim no further assistance on the score

[1] Fr. tr.; Mignet; Dalrymple.

of Goree and Woorne, and that the Dover treaty stood in every detail.

France, then, had Charles' promise for a Dutch war, unclogged by the embarrassing piety of a religious revolution which Louis knew would estrange his German Protestant allies. But much might happen in a year, and meantime Charles' book-keeping had transferred 2,000,000 livres from a payment for Catholicity, which he meant to evade, into a cash subsidy, due by the end of March, in anticipation of a war that might never be fought.

By the spring of 1671 still other consequences of this enlargement of the treaty were exposed. The session of parliament which then closed had brought foreign affairs into an undesirable publicity. Bridgeman's oratory, innocent or strategic, appealed to the King's prestige in Europe, to his treaties with Spain, Savoy, and Portugal, as to the trade agreements under negotiation with France and Holland, and asked for a strong navy to meet emergency; France was arming, our quota in the Triple Alliance must be assured, Louis was hourly expected at Dunkirk. Buckingham could resist no chance of winning a little popularity; and while denouncing Arlington to France as "Dutch", he insisted to Parliament that he was "French", and allowed his friends Orrery and Trevor to spread rumours of a French treaty. Again, proposals were forthcoming that supply should be earmarked for the Triple Alliance, French competition to the London silk stocking industry was mooted in Council, a French and an anti-French faction bickered as to impositions on French "trinkets" and brandy. To members of Parliament the Dutch circulated their project for an extended league, and it was with Spanish encouragement that the Commons partly paid off the royal debts. In April the session closed, not only with detailed complaint as to the growth of Popery but in a full-dress financial dispute between Lords and Commons, in which Buckingham and Ashley backed the Lords and the Plantations, as against Arlington in the triple rôle of champion of the Commons, the King's revenues, and the sugar refiners.[1] From this blazing hatred between the factions it followed, of course, that Arlington tried to enlist wider support against a policy he detested; in May his group broke the secret of the coming war to Rupert and Ormonde, though Ormonde was, with Trevor, working for accommodation with Holland, though his son Ossory was notoriously anti-French, and though Rupert was definitely "Spanish"; by August Henry Coventry was fully instructed also.[2]

Every day it became more obvious that our policy had changed, and the secrecy of the secret treaties oozed away. In France a large circle were initiated; not only leaders like Lionne, Turenne, Colbert, and Pomponne, but Abbé Montagu who translated for Arundell, Cosnac who deciphered for Madame, and Ralph Montagu to whom Lionne showed the second treaty.[3] From Paris or London circumstantial rumours reached the Hague. When Temple returned home in September 1670, he retailed to the Cabinet the news he had from de Witt, to the effect that France offered five millions for our neutrality; *"tacitus prudens"* ran

[1] Marvell, Oct. 25, onwards; Molina, Simancas, Dec. 18 and 22; Colbert, Fr. tr. Dec.–Feb.; Barbour, 178-9; Harris, ii. app. J; France, 129, Nov. 9, '70. I venture to doubt Bridgeman's "innocence"; it is Buckingham whom we find (Barbour, 179) trying to oust him from Cabinet.

[2] Colbert, March 19 and May 18; Oñate, March 11, Simancas; Arlington to Coventry, Sept. 10, Longleat MSS. lxv.

[3] Pomponne, i. 480; Picavet, 262; Cosnac; Clifford MSS.; Montagu to Arlington, Jan. 7, '71.

the motto on Temple's seal, but did the wise man keep silence on his violent interview, this November, with Clifford, when the Treasurer denounced his excessive patience with the rascally Dutch, and the ambassador answered, "in the name of God, what he thought a man could do more"? Certainly by May 1671 de Witt heard that French troops were to be used in England to set up Popery and crush Parliament, while that autumn the French money payments were bandied about in private correspondence.[1]

Incidentally the enlargement and increasing publicity of the negotiation enhanced, as Colbert ruefully complained, the "honorarium" rate for English politicians. The government had bought off or persuaded some Opposition leaders of the last session, like Oñate's counsellor Robert Howard, and Oñate's pocket, judging by his debts, had felt the strain. The Spanish were offering pearls and diamonds to Lady Bridgeman and Lady Trevor, and Buckingham, while thankfully taking a French pension for Lady Shrewsbury, depicted the great sums offered him by Spain and Holland. This particular pension was suggested to Colbert by Arlington, who himself seemed still detached, for thrice after the Dover treaty he declined gifts and pensions. Was this symptomatic of a possible change? In that light we can take up the diplomatic threads which ran parallel, from May 1670 to April 1671, with the great design.[2]

Towards Holland our tone was agressive, curt, and sullen. Madame's visit had startled them into sending

---

[1] Temple's audience, Sept. 25, '70, Foreign Entry, 176; Fruin, iv. 59; Groot, 26, 37; Hatton Correspondence, i. 72; Magrath, *The Flemings at Oxford*, i. 189.

[2] Oñate, March 21, '70, to de la Torre, Molina, Nov. 20, Simancas; Arlington to Godolphin, Jan. 1, '73; Colbert to Louis, Sept. 22 and Dec. 22, Buckingham to same, Oct. 3, '70, Fr. tr. and Dalrymple; Barbour, 169; Colbert to Louis, May 31, '71.

Van Beuningen[1] on a special mission—Beuningen, the leader of Amsterdam, rival of de Witt, since 1667 the declared enemy of France, verbose, masterful, and profligate. Never were conferences more sterile, for we refused to mention Austrian adherence to the alliance till satisfied as to Surinam and the Indies, while they, though yielding a point for the woeful Major Banister, would not face the problem of trade monopoly in India. While this was going on in London, Temple received a last and most uncongenial order, perhaps to be taken as a first drop in "filling up the cup"; he was to obtain the extradition of Cornet Joyce, once so forceful to Charles I at Holmby and now suspect of murderous conspiracy against Charles II. De Witt gave all the help he could, knowing (he said) that the King's death would mean the fall of Arlington, but the Rotterdam magistrates connived, not unnaturally, at the Cornet's escape.[2] Such things as this, and Buckingham's trip to Paris, troubled the Pensionary less than the sudden recall of Temple in September; the forms were decently observed, for Temple's house was left standing, but taking this with the "hot skirmishes" over Surinam and Arlington's solicitude for the Spanish arbitration, de Witt concluded that we had agreed to make Holland the sacrifice on condition that Spain were saved. He had gone to great lengths in trying to soothe us; he had protested that the States could not answer for every piece of tapestry, embroidered with the burning of Chatham, exported to Japan, and promised that the *Royal Charles* (falsely alleged to be now a floating restaurant in the Maas) should have a change of name.

---

[1] Reached London, June 7, '70, Fruin, iv.; conference, July 21, with the Secretaries, Ashley, and Clifford (Spain, 57, cf. 47).

[2] Temple to Trevor, Aug. 2 and 5; Fruin, iv. 79.

But complaisance failed, nor did menace seem to promise better, the old threat that Holland would strike up terms with France falling unaccountably flat.[1]

He decided by a last determined effort to break down this icy, captious hostility, and in pursuance of a suggestion to Temple,[2] instructed Beuningen in October to propose an extension of the defensive treaty of 1668. As this stood, it committed England only to supply an auxiliary force, without necessarily involving rupture with any Power attacking Holland, and yet entitled her to send in a bill for expenses when peace was renewed. The model now put forward was the Dutch-French alliance of 1662.

Such hopes, partly based on enlisting parliamentary support, quickly vanished. When Beuningen departed in December, it fell to the cloudy and credulous John Boreel to conduct the case with Arlington, Clifford, Trevor, and Ashley, but these commissioners were not appointed till March 1671 and all our procedure was deliberately prolonged. When they had done boggling at Boreel's powers, they reintroduced the *Charles* or a new complaint of Dutch intrigue at Madrid, and finally intimated, as Charles did himself, that we expected large concessions. There were murmurs of an indemnity, and even of the surrender of Brill and Flushing. But any such humiliation de Witt was determined to avoid, for experience had shown that English goodwill was never won by danegeld. He bade Boreel break off; silence might bring England to her senses.[3]

---

[1] De Witt to Beuningen, Sept. 16 and Nov. 4, Fruin; Wicquefort, iv. 109; de Witt to Temple, Oct. 11.

[2] Foreign Entry Book, 13 (Sept. '70).

[3] De Witt to Beuningen, Oct. 21, to Boreel, Feb. 10–April 21, Fruin; to Beverning, March 9, n.s. Van Dijk; Boreel to Fagel, Add. MSS 35,852 (copies); Pontalis, 133; Colbert, March, Fr. tr.

His ardour in this matter had, possibly, been increased by the visit to England during this winter of 1670–71 of the young Orange. Though the clause of the Dover treaty, promising William "his advantages" in the war, was entirely vague, Charles had kept a place open for his nephew, and originally tried to make his visit coincide with Madame's, as a step to weaken Holland further. But the Prince's journey was postponed for the very reason that Holland was, by intestine division, weakening herself. Zealand, the nobles, the clergy, and de Witt's rivals at Amsterdam saw their opportunity in the advancement of Orange, who was now twenty years old and openly ambitious of his ancestors' prerogative. While Madame was at Dover, his followers clinched a victory in the States-General by getting him admitted to the Council of State without conditions, the Perpetual Edict itself was threatened, Madame Buat moved between Paris and Holland bent on revenge, and even the province of Holland was slipping from de Witt's control. Still his resistance, though courteous, was adamant, and he had opposed a proposal that William should see the English despatches. Whether Charles concluded that William, in this mood, might safely be entrusted with "the grand design", or what passed in the intervals of those interminable gaieties, we shall presumably never know, but if he, defying Louis' advice, told the Prince his religious plans, as Burnet testifies, the history of the next ten years shows it was worse than in vain.[1]

Yet it would be hard to prove that at this date our decision to fight was irrevocable. Ossory, brother-in-law both to Arlington and to William's friend Odyk,

---

[1] Japikse, "De Witt"; Pontalis; Louis to Colbert, Oct. 23, Mignet; Burnet, i. 494, and cf. Colbert's explicit declaration of Nov. 24 in Dalrymple.

pressed de Witt to reconcile England by concession to Orange, and that Ossory spoke thus of his own volition is most improbable. The theory of pure "deception" on our part, if pushed thus far back, is weakened again by the long-drawn interviews given by Charles to Boreel, and by Beuningen's report that, though Arlington seemed changed, all was not yet lost.[1]

Here and there, in other countries, incidents of 1670–1671 support this feeling that our final decision must be put later than is usually assumed, and that our own economic interests still outweighed any other motive in the policy of Charles II. One may be found in Fauconburg's mission to the anti-French Duke of Savoy, and his report on the possibilities of Genoa as an *entrepôt* for our Indian goods.[2] A second occurs in Denmark, a state for whose neutrality as a minimum the Dover signatories had agreed to work, and whose brooding annoyance over the shame of Bergen was deepened by disputes in Iceland and by others touching the Sound dues. In 1669 Frederick III made a new claim of parity for the Danish flag, but Charles, after hearing Philip Meadowes, the Cromwellian Baltic expert, refused to give up our ancient privilege, and the crisis drew near when early in 1670 the young King Christian succeeded, full of large ideas and military ambition, and arrived when his governor at Cronenburg fired on Essex, our ambassador. With Essex' refusal to strike his flag and Charles' delight thereat, with the Danish senators, their potations of cherry brandy, and their effort to make Essex land in a rowing boat, we need not dally; the relevant point is the treaty of commerce signed in July, which included a promise to give France no monopoly

1. Wicquefort, iv. 123.
2. See his report of 1670, Sloane MSS. 2752.

of Norwegian naval supplies and no preference on her salt and wines.[1]

Even in our feeble policy of saving Belgium by means of peace, a few glints shone of a policy hostile or suspect to the French. Whether the English knew of Louis' betrayal to the Emperor of our ambitions on the Spanish heritage, we do not know, but they had reason to fear, even in 1671, that he was still proposing the Belgian exchange as the basis of a direct deal with Madrid.[2] In Germany, where Frenchmen swarmed, we had at this time no agent, but Colbert tells us how Arlington wished Brandenburg to be entrusted with the secret of the war and encouraged to lull Holland asleep by negotiation. Simultaneously we hear that English diplomacy is urging Leopold to come to terms with the middle group of Mainz and Trier, who were trying to form a German *bloc*, much like the league of the Rhine, to save Lorraine from France and the Empire from Austrian monopoly. Not the least common method of checking too strong an ally is to enlarge the alliance to contain him, but if this was in the English mind they were disappointed. When in August 1670 the French, resolving to intimidate this group into passivity, invaded Lorraine and drove its duke into exile, the aged spiritual Electors did not move, nor till the January following do we get a mild British protest.[3]

If even for the Mainz school the key lay with the Hapsburgs, much more was it so for England, and here were two interconnected questions, left outstanding at the time of Madame's visit: the Spanish view of

[1] Denmark, 8; Urk. xvii. 63 *seq.*; Burnet, ii. 108; Charles Bertie's letters in *Retrospective Review*, 1828: Admiral Allin's evidence, Tanner MSS. 293, f. 1.
[2] Mignet, iii. 473; Legrelle, i. 215; Molina (Simancas), Dec. 22, '70.
[3] Ermansdörffer, i. 535: Colbert to Louis, July 4, '70, and Jan. 2, '71; Leopold to Pötting, June 8, '70.

the arbitration and the admission of Leopold to the Triple Alliance, which Holland now pressed for and which we had so far refused. In April 1670, when Louis was "in the stirrup going to the frontiers"[1] and Madame to England, we heard that Spain rejected England and Sweden unless she could name two other arbiters, and by subsequent correspondence of May and June she insisted at least on adding Holland. Arlington feared that Louis would take his pretext— he did, indeed, threaten to denounce the promised year of peace—and exerted himself to prevent what he thought the crowning calamity. On one side we suspended negotiation with Lisola, telling Leopold that Spanish submission was the condition of treating with him, and on the other we asked France, though in vain, to let Spain have her way. This second step, connected no doubt with our pressure on France for more money, was perhaps not meant to do more; the Dutch, at any rate, suppressed their indignation in hope of keeping the peace, and Leopold also urged Spain to yield. With this assistance England and Sweden in January 1671 persuaded Louis to extend the arbitrage period for yet another year,[2] and Spain to submit her list of counter-pretensions to the arbitrators.

From the summer of 1670 onwards Europe was thus in an uproar, for the invasion of Lorraine, the multiplying incidents over Belgian frontier posts, over Amsterdam or Ostend privateers, and the Bishop of Münster's collection of funds, ostensibly "for a uni-

---

[1] Arlington to Temple, April 12.

[2] Trevor to Temple, April 12, Sloane MSS. 1003; Colbert, April 14, Fr. tr.; Arlington to Godolphin, May 9 and July 6; Temple to Arlington, July 18, Holland, 186; Montagu to same, Jan. 26–July 13; de Groot to de Witt, Jan. 13, '71 (Van Dijk); Godolphin to Arlington, June 14, Spain, 56; Oñate, May 6, and Molina, May 15 (Simancas).

versity", all betokened war. The Emperor, unable to
disregard the indignation of Germany and Spain,
made a real advance, and in September communicated
to us his readiness to enter the Aix guarantee, without
imposing any reciprocal burden of defending Austria.[1]
But a request from Arlington in November to make
his proposal more specific revealed that de Witt and
Lisola still meant to tack on a mutual warranty of
defence, and that Vienna and the Hague were not
agreed as to Leopold's obligations. The project presented to Charles by Molina in December bound England to defend all Austrian territories and the German
princes to defend not only Spain but Holland, and was
promptly condemned, it is vital to say, by Leopold
as well as by England: Temple himself argued that
Austria offered too few troops, and Sweden would not
join in any project which England refused. Yet if the
French succeeded in getting Lisola disavowed, they
had to bear with the Austrian and English persistence
in shielding Spain, and the main English attitude remained constant; the fifth article of the Triple Alliance
invited the Emperor to guarantee the Aix settlement
—let him make a declaration to that effect, stating the
troops he could contribute—no further negotiation was
necessary, and Germany was too remote for us to
think of reciprocity.[2]

Our final reply was issued on the 20th January 1671,
without communication to Sweden or Holland, and its
content showed that this separation was its very *raison*

[1] Lisola's mémoire, n.d., endorsed by Temple, Add. 9797, f. 54.
[2] Lisola to Arlington, Aug. 28, '70, Holland, 186, and Jan. 31, '71, *ibid.* 187;
Colbert, Aug. 29–Jan. 19, Fr. tr.; Arlington to Lisola, Nov. 18, Archives, 100,
and Jan. 20, Foreign Entry, 175; de Witt to Boreel and Beuningen, Dec. 9, Fruin,
iv.; Boreel to Fagel, Feb. 1, Add. MSS. 35,852; Molina, Dec. 22, '70 (Simancas);
Pribram, in *Mitteil. Inst. Österr. Gesch.* vol. xxx. (1909), for Lisola's despatches
of 1669–71.

d'être; it invited Austria simply to guarantee assistance to all Spanish territories, cutting out any notion of reciprocity between Austria and the Allies. It coincided with the extortion from France of the second year of grace, and with French assurances to Vienna that they asked only a pledge of non-assistance to Holland. In conversation with Boreel Charles jeered at Lisola's inability to produce his full powers, and the detailed facts seem to warrant the English, as against de Witt, that the notion of Austria warring with France was a baseless fabric of Lisola's noble dream. In April Leopold decided to drop the whole negotiations.[1]

If, with this narrative before us, we would reconstruct the mind of the English ministry this winter, we must conclude that it was still marking time, and exploring all quarters for possible counterbalancings before finally burning their boats in the grave undertaking of a Dutch war.

Whether we take the Austrian view of Arlington's long consideration and amendments to Lisola's projects—that he was raising his price with France—or the French view, that he was trying to placate Parliament—is less important than the conclusion, that he was still fencing with the future.[2] We thus told Colbert in September 1670 that Downing would be sent to the Hague to make the war, yet the decision finally to recall Temple was taken only in the following July. If France was determined in any case to attack Holland, as all the evidence showed, Charles was no question resolved to share in the profits, unless—and here was

---

[1] *Ibid.* pp. 475-94; Arlington to Godolphin, Oct. 27, '70; Charles' interview with Boreel, March 1, Add. MSS. *loc. cit.*; de Witt to Boreel, March 6, n.s.

[2] See Lisola's remarkable despatch of Feb. 6, '71, Pribram, *loc. cit.*

the point of the matter we have examined—the enemies of France could outbid her. But this was proving to be impossible; Austria was paralysed, the Mainz schemes were going up in smoke, and neither Holland nor Spain, as Arlington candidly put it, "charm us with any propositions that may either better our present condition or alleviate the future one of the war". Launched on his piratic craft of pure egoism, Charles was drifting down-stream at ease, though all the time towards the rapids he had promised to pass; meantime, what fixed point, de Witt asked bitterly, could be found in a King and a nation rooted only in instability?[1]

There was, in fact, one such point, a determination to keep Belgium intact and Spain our friend, and we claimed after the event to have looked after Belgium like an English child.[2] But Spain realized that in certain circumstances she might have to choose between her English and her Dutch guarantor, and as it happened, Anglo-Spanish relations were inflamed by other causes when that decision drew near. Spaniards felt as an affront the compulsion put upon them to submit to arbitration, and when Molina returned in September 1670, his old intimacy with Arlington was not renewed. Among the grievances he had to allege was the permission given to France to recruit in Scotland and Ireland for the Douglas and Roscommon regiments, and he reproached Charles to his face with swelling the enemy army destined to ravage the very cities of Flanders where he had once found a kindly refuge.[3] A

---

[1] Arlington to Godolphin, Jan. 26 and May 31, '71; de Witt to Beverning, April 11, '71 (Van Dijk).

[2] Meerman and Boreel, Verbaal, March 14, '72; R.A. Leg. 800.

[3] Instructions for Godolphin, Feb. 24, '69, Rawl. MSS. A. 255; Godolphin to Arlington, Feb. 22, '71, Spain, 58; Molina, July 2, Simancas.

far more vital controversy arose over the Indies. In
July 1670 Godolphin carried to completion a year of
toil in a new treaty of commerce, which settled old
"pretensions", supplemented Sandwich's work in detail, and for the first time admitted our legal title to
Jamaica.   It was hoped to devise measures in common
against the scourge of the West, the buccaneers, and our
government gave an earnest of its sincerity in ordering
the recall of the governor, Modyford, who was suspected
of connivance. It was in vain; at that distance the arm
of government could not so quickly uproot a deep-
seated disease, and so desperate was the condition of
trade that City firms thought of chartering warships on
their own account, and there was talk of sending out
Sandwich as viceroy with extraordinary powers. While
Godolphin was putting the last touches to the peace, the
famous Henry Morgan took Porto Bello, and in January 1671 proceeded to sack Panama. By June all this
was known in Europe, and it was "impossible to paint",
Godolphin wrote, the Spanish wrath. The few English
adventurers who were captured were sent in irons to
Europe in the Seville *Flota*; our merchants in Seville
dare not leave their houses; reprisals began on our log-
wood-cutters in Campeachy and threatened to spread
nearer home.[1]

Late in 1670 Beverning, whom we last met at Cleves
in 1666, was persuaded to return to his country's service,
and in February 1671 reached Madrid. His instructions were sweeping; he was to ask a defensive alliance,
rapid provision of subsidies for Sweden, and, if possible, for the Brunswickers also, he was to represent the

[1] Godolphin to Arlington, July 17, '70, Spain, 57; Godolphin to Charles
II, July 19, '70; to Arlington, June 14, '71, *ibid.* 58; Arlington to Modyford,
June 11, '70, *ibid.*; Haring, 143 *seq.*; Oñate, March 4 and 11; Molina, July 27.

defencelessness of Belgium, protected as it was by some 14,000 unpaid brigands mistermed soldiers, and to offer large credits in Amsterdam against transmission of silver to Batavia.[1]

When he left Spain in June, he had secured little specifically of this huge programme, but he took away the vital promise that negotiations should be opened at Brussels with the new and fiery governor, Monterey. Of this a first-fruit was the threat to prohibit, like Holland, the entry of French staple goods to Belgium, and the usual portents appeared of war in the Low Countries—in the tearing down of French douanes, the closing of roads on the frontier, and Dutch mobilization at Maestricht.

It was not till the autumn that our government awoke to the danger that Spain was slipping out of our system, for Godolphin was prostrated by illness most of the year, and his despatches confirmed a prevailing impression that Spain would, at the worst, be neutral.[2] Yet neither Charles nor Arlington had ground either for surprise or for complaint of Spanish concealment. If England and Sweden could not be relied on, only Holland was left to Spain, of which Boreel gave Charles early warning, while to Charles' asseveration that he would protect Belgium with the last drop of his blood, Molina and Oñate gave the obvious but displeasing answer, that England was for one thing too weak and, for another, loathed his policy. All too late, then, came Arlington's frenzied activity from October onwards. Southwell was hurried off to Brussels to tell Monterey that France promised to extend the truce till the end of

---

[1] Summarized by Van Dijk, 372, 478.
[2] Godolphin to Arlington, March 8, Spain, 58; Montagu to Coventry, Nov. 13, Longleat; Arlington to Godolphin, Dec. 11·

1672, that Holland was merely fanning the flames between France and Spain, and that Sunderland (whom
we shall meet there) was going as envoy extraordinary
to Madrid. Too late; for when on the 29th November
Godolphin memorialized the Spanish government,
demanding no ratification till Sunderland could be
heard, this considerable diplomatic revolution was, in
effect, completed, the Spanish and Dutch commissioners signing at Brussels on the 7th December.[1]

The English government long struggled to avoid
what proved to be inevitable, a break with Spain, and
delayed for that reason the declaration of war; there
were, too, other indications that part of the grand design
was now otiose, while from other parts Charles would be
glad to escape. "Catholicity" seemed to be laid aside;
though the "instructions" were ready for the messenger to Rome, Charles announced he must postpone acting upon them, and rumour alleged sharp differences
of opinion between Catholic extremists and the old
Catholic families.[2] Moreover, if war had to come, the
King more clearly than ever meant France to foot the
bill. In September Louis relieved him of the obligation
to maintain six thousand auxiliary troops—much to
Buckingham's annoyance, who had hoped to command
them—and twice he asked, though in vain, for another
four million livres wherewith to equip a Mediterranean
squadron. At the same time a new intense pressure
began over the everlasting treaty of commerce. A
Cabinet subcommittee (Arlington, Clifford, and Ashley) represented that French tariffs, particularly on

---

[1] Van Dijk; Pontalis; Fruin, iv. 176; Godolphin's memorial, Spain, 59, f. 62;
Arlington to Coventry, Nov. 3 (Longleat); Molina, Sept. 18 and Oct. 22,
Oñate, Jan. 8 (Simancas); instructions to Southwell, Oct. 26, Rawl. MSS.
A. 255.

[2] Colbert, Feb. 1671, Dalrymple; Christie, ii. app. xxxvii.; Clifford MSS.

cloth, must be cut to the levels of May 1660, that merchants domiciled in France must not be harried by Colbert's inspectors, and that Parliament would certainly retaliate, failing a remedy.[1]

On the other hand, we see from midsummer the growing predominance in the Cabinet of a war party, into which, as into all questions, the ceaseless Arlington-Buckingham rivalry must enter, and which must turn largely on the life or death of Parliament. It was, then, a decisive step when the long prorogation, already stretched from April 1671 till the next March, was in September further prolonged till October 1672; it was attributed by the French to York and Buckingham, whose increasing weight in council the Spaniards also reported. And a new influence in Charles' horoscope, where Venus conjoined with Mars, may have counted in directing him towards war, for in November 1670 Louise de Queroalle, whose refined babyishness had caught his eye at Dover, reached our shores, to be launched, if report be true, by Madame Colbert and Lady Arlington on her long and not insignificant career. In July 1671 Temple was finally recalled, *un méchant signe* in itself, as Orange saw it, but infinitely worse were the experiences of Temple's wife and children. The captain of the royal yacht *Merlin*, sent to bring them from Holland, had orders, communicated to France, to fire if the whole Dutch fleet did not strike their flag; he found his pretext, with some difficulty, on the return journey, and Dorothy Osborne might well have gone to the bottom, like the Triple Alliance. But this manufactured provocation was to be used to the hilt, and the man to use it was provided in (to

[1] Mignet, iii. 654; Montagu to Arlington, Sept. 16–Feb. 11; Treaty papers, Jan. 13, 1672.

repeat Arlington) "the rougher hand" of Sir George Downing.[1]

Early in December Downing left for the Hague, and Charles published in Council the principle of the war; in January 1672 Colbert's son Seignelay arrived to discuss naval detail with Sandwich; on the 2nd February a third treaty was signed with France, repeating that of December 1670 for the benefit of the councillors to whom, with "silence absolutely enjoined",[2] it was read on the 18th. Before that date the first instalment of French war subsidy had reached us, nine carts escorted by sixty cavalry taking it from the port of disembarkation to the Tower.[3]

Leaving the final controversy with Holland in those experienced hands, we can hear in other negotiations the gathering momentum to war, and glean the nature of the war which the English government designed. On the side of France preparations were early completed, for Mainz, Münster, and Cologne were paid allies, Leopold was newly pledged to neutrality,[4] Brunswick was detached, and only Brandenburg and Sweden caused some anxiety. A long dispute between the Lionne and the Louvois views of northern politics delayed action till August 1671; then Coventry and Pomponne, old rivals in 1666, were simultaneously sent off to co-operate at Stockholm, where French and Dutch concessionaires were already competing for copper and ordnance. The Swedes' mercenary appetite towards the Triple Alliance had first been maddened

[1] Colbert to Louis, July 4; Molina, Oct. 2, and Fonseca, Feb. 19; Orange to (?) Arlington, July 14, Holland, 187; Temple to Sir J. Temple, Sept. 14; Arlington to Godolphin, July 7 and Oct. 9.

[2] Present: King, Duke, Monmouth, Rupert, Bridgeman, Buckingham, Ormonde, Arlington, Ashley, Clifford, Trevor—Foreign Entry, 176.

[3] Mignet, iii. 701; Colenbrander, ii. 47, 81; Fonseca, Feb. 15 (Simancas).

[4] By the treaty of November 1671; see Pribram.

by Spanish delay, and then sated by the only gold they could expect from Spanish poverty, and Bierenclau, the prop of the Allies' party, had just died. But their Protestantism still existed, and they dreaded a war in the Empire; if the English part was changed, the other elements were much the same as in 1666, Sweden still asking insurance against Russia and the Austrians still refusing to outbid the French.[1]

Henry Coventry, gouty as ever, reached Stockholm late in September, to find that the old Alliance party, disorganized though it was, had yet been strong enough to postpone decision till he came. His original instructions were curiously limited; for while he was to exhort France to pay Sweden plentiful subsidies, and to offer our service as guarantor of a French-Swedish treaty, he was not (till February) authorized to disclose our own French alliance, was to ask for a Swedish envoy who could deal with the Spanish arbitrage, and must keep on good terms with the Hapsburg representatives.[2]

His difficulties were very great, and in particular to make Sweden believe that we meant war at all. The Dutch-Spanish agreement had made a deep impression, adroitly emphasized by Arlington's old friend Nunez. German envoys, and above all the Prussians, beat the Protestant drum; Coventry had to persuade them that we had no intention of swallowing Holland whole, to coax Pomponne into offering more, and Sweden into less suspicion of Richmond's mission to Copenhagen. When Pomponne left in November, nothing determinate was yet done, Sweden declining

---

[1] Werden to Arlington, July 8, to Williamson, Aug. 16, Sweden, 7; Colbert to Louis, July 31, Fr. tr.; Pötting, ii. 205; Coventry to Arlington, Oct. 4, Longleat MSS. lxv., whence the following pages are largely derived.

[2] Coventry to Arlington, Sept. 11, Sweden, 7; additional instructions, Aug. 26, Longleat; Carlson, iv. 551.

to sell even her neutrality except for a price to which France would not ascend. As regards ourselves there were two special obstructions: first, that the Swedes again demanded that fertile source of friction, a marine treaty, and, further, that they asked a guarantee during the war against attack from any third party—which might mean Spain.[1]

It was not till the eve of war, in March, that Arlington was fully aware of Coventry's progress. To the guarantee suggested he was firmly opposed, preferring either an offensive alliance or the old defensive clauses of 1661; for the first we would offer the hand of the Princess Mary to the young King.[2] In vain the net was spread, and not even for much enhanced subsidies would Sweden abandon neutrality as regards Holland. The gist of the treaties signed by Courtin and Coventry in April was the Swedes' promise to stop any interference from the Empire, though this police obligation was restricted to a period of three years, and to keep for this end an army of observation in Bremen and Pomerania. The English came off lightly; we cancelled a debt from Sweden of 200,000 dollars, but we paid no subsidy, staved off the marine treaty, and limited our guarantee to a break with any German prince who attacked Sweden on the single ground that she was preventing him helping Holland.[3]

In May Coventry was ordered to Copenhagen to help Richmond. Besides pressing Denmark to close the Sound to the Dutch, they were to urge the desirability of an attack upon Hamburg, which had given

[1] Urk. xvii.; Mignet; Longleat MSS. *loc. cit. passim.*

[2] Arlington to Coventry (cipher), March 22; Coventry to Arlington, April 17, Sweden, 8.

[3] Coventry to Arlington, March 26 and April 3, *ibid.*; April 6, Longleat; Arlington to Coventry, March 1, *ibid.*; Carlson.

offence in 1666 by permitting a Dutch attack on our
shipping in the Elbe, and would, it was believed, break
our blockade of Holland by "colouring" Dutch goods.
This hopeful scheme was characteristic of the prevalent
obsession in the English war-party of a quick and
lucrative war, even if it involved a distinct breach of a
promise to the French. Happily, it was rapidly ex-
tinguished by opposition from our own Hamburg company, and by receipt of some compensation for our
damages.[1] As to the Danes, they had old scores with
Hamburg and even more with Holstein, but until
Sweden and Brandenburg moved nothing would make
them budge.

Of the other members of that Quadruple Alliance
which in 1666 had so much embarrassed us, French
bribes and Dutch parsimony had accounted for Brunswick, and there remained only the all-important Great
Elector. But he was fired, in part by Lisola's pamphlets, into Lisola's view that Germany, and not Holland,
was the French objective; he was well aware of Louis'
aspiration to the throne of the Empire, and saw with
loathing the swelling power of Popery. The name of the
British envoy detailed to overcome his scruples was
significant of the wider scope which our government
now hoped to impart to the war; it was the very considerable William Lockhart, who had held his own
in Cromwell's dealing with Mazarin, and was now
brought again into business by Lauderdale. His instructions were to go first to Paris, there to extract more
money for the German princes, thence to the Hanover
dukes, giving special heed to the advice of the
Electress Sophia, and last to Berlin, to represent (as

---

[1] Arlington to Coventry (cipher), April 12, Longleat; Foreign Entry Book, 64,
for Richmond's instructions; Hamburg, 11, ff. 212 *seq.*; Urk. xvii. 96.

Downing had already to the Prussians at the Hague) the enormity of the Dutchmen's sins and Frederick's chance to profit by their fall. He failed in every particular, and above all at Berlin, where a treaty with Holland, begun after receiving news of his mission, was completed (26th April) the day after his first audience. The Elector, more than ordinarily curt and vague, criticized our attack on the Smyrna fleet, and on the 2nd May dismissed Lockhart, with a message to Charles deploring these "extremities" and offering his mediation to end this reproach to "Christianity".[1] Once more, as in 1665–66, the North had spurned our wooing; this would impede us, but a rebuff from Spain might mean destruction.

The Spanish-Dutch agreement had not yet been signed when Sunderland left England in November 1671, and his first letter from Madrid[2] maintained that what "we so much feared at London is not yet done". France was better informed, and before his arrival Villars made known the great concessions he could offer for Spanish neutrality; that is, the integrity of their dominions during the King's minority, the dropping of the "dependencies" claim, and placing the Low Countries under the guarantee of England, Austria, and Sweden. (Such promises, Condé and Louvois confided to each other, would never lack a pretext to break them, if need be). And if Spain would only join in, she should share the conquests and reopen the Scheldt.[3]

In these propositions Sunderland was to co-operate, but he had two points to mention on our own behalf. He was to bespeak Spanish assistance at Vienna to get the

[1] Draft instructions, German States, 59, f. 142; Foreign Entry, 64, March 14; Charles' letter of credit, Urk. xvii.; Pagès, 291; Droysen, iii. 600.

[2] Arrived, Dec. 30; first conference, Jan. 22; to Arlington, Jan. 3, Spain, 59.

[3] Mignet, iii. 665, seq.; Arlington to Coventry, Nov. 23, Longleat.

Archduchess Claudia Felicitas of the Innsbruck line as wife for the Duke of York, a scheme mooted by Arlington within a month of Anne Hyde's death.[1] And probably Sunderland, whose Catholic leanings were affirmed to Colbert, was entrusted with a second message equally unwelcome, we know, to the French, but designed to conciliate the orthodoxy of Spain; for by February at latest the Queen was informed of Charles' Catholic design.[2]

The Spain to which he was accredited was still much the same country as that with which Fanshawe and Sandwich had wrestled. Don Juan had made his bid and ousted Nithard, only to find the Jesuit succeeded in the Queen's favour by the base-born Valenzuela, a species of Neapolitan Piers Gaveston, and was now himself relegated to another ten years of exile, honorific, sullen, and watchful, in Aragon. In Madrid, while the troops starved, office was bought and sold by nobles whose palaces were full of Mexican silver-work and brocades, and Maria Anna's favourite dwarf trafficked in the government of Flanders and the Indies. Within the Junta the succession to the throne still provided a pretext for faction; Peneranda, with his peculiar hatred of Lisola, still supported France, and Castel Rodrigo had replaced the old Aytona as leader of the "Austrians". Yet an unceasing optimism ("altijd vol hoop, etiam in rebus desperatis", wrote Beverning's successor[3]) tinged with a certain grandeur the disordered counsels of Spain. Their pride had been lately wounded by the impertinences of the French embassy, they were con-

[1] Colbert, April 3, '71, Fr. tr.; Pötting, ii. 215; Valckenier, Dec. 27, Van Dijk.
[2] Clifford MSS. Valckenier, *loc. cit.*, speaks of it in January. I conjecture that the ecclesiastic whom Colbert named as Charles' messenger (Mignet, iii. 703) worked, if he existed, through Sunderland; but cf. Barbour, 188.
[3] Kramer, 53.

vinced of Louis' wholesale insincerity, and perhaps
cognisant of his new treaty with Portugal, and it was
Peneranda himself who led the conferences from January to March, in which Sunderland had to endure language rarely meted out to an English minister. The
Innsbruck match they approved, and Peneranda was
presumably as sympathetic now to Charles' Catholic bias
as he was a year later,[1] while to Sunderland personally
they were all courtesy, providing him with royal apart-
ments, endless cooks, carvers, and liqueurs. But on the
vital matter they were as iron. The Queen acknow-
ledged Charles' religious confidences with a cold expression of her interest, while Peneranda enlarged on
their surprise at finding England ready to attack her
ally, bluntly accused us of "selling" them, and refused
to hear of neutrality.

When we appealed to the mutual-assistance clause in
Sandwich's agreement of 1667, they retorted effectively
with Aix-la-Chapelle and the Hague, and furiously
resented Sunderland's threat of war; William Godolphin was noted to be cooler, and almost certainly disliked the whole venture as much as he did his colleague.
But even Sunderland could appreciate the gravity of
Peneranda's prediction that our scheme could only last
till the reassembly of Parliament, or his threat of an embargo on our goods, and before February he was telling
his wife that her jaunt to Madrid must be postponed.[2]

Hitherto the Spanish representatives in England
had not been of a calibre to impress the King. Oñate
had been on good terms with Arlington, but that alone
sealed his enmity with Molina, while both were plunged

---

[1] Kramer, 152; cf. the Venetian report, dating from the same period, in
Barozzie Berchet, ser. i. Spagna, vol. ii. 425.

[2] Sunderland and Godolphin to Arlington, Jan. 24, H.I.; March 6 and 20,
Spain, 59; Mignet, iii. 680; Kramer, 48; Valckenier, Jan. 24, Van Dijk.

in debt and both put too much trust in lobbying members of Parliament. But del Fresno, who arrived on the 2nd March, spoke with authority as Peneranda's brother-in-law, and with a natural dignity of his own. He made it clear that our new system involved nothing less than the loss of our best market and the end of Arlington's diplomatic scheme. For though it was believed that Spain was merely committed to lending Holland some auxiliaries, to which the anxious Arlington thought France might turn a blind eye, one "incident" in the Channel might turn this limited hostility into open war, the very rumour of which was already defeating our hope of winning Sweden. For the moment nothing could be done, and on the 1st April Sunderland was sent his letter of revocation. Yet our intention to avoid a break still held good, and when in the next few days Sidney Godolphin left England to act *en liaison* with the French army, he carried orders urgently to represent to Louis that he must not ask us to sacrifice our customs revenue from the Spanish trade.[1]

Yet the Spaniards, too, were disappointed in the hope that their Dutch agreement would frighten England into abandoning France or recalling Parliament; before Sunderland and Lockhart had so egregiously failed, and before Coventry had achieved his petty success,[2] our government issued, on the 17th March, its declaration of war.

The reasons given in that belated document—

---

[1] Spain, 59, f. 188; Coventry to Arlington, March 20, Longleat; Fresno, March 3 and 28, Simancas; Cabinet of March 6, Foreign Entry, 177; Williamson's note of March 28, Treaty papers, 47; Godolphin's instructions, April 2, Stowe MSS. 191.

[2] Coventry's despatch with the treaty reached England on May 12 (*Misc. Aul.*).

belated, because four days earlier Admiral Holmes fired
without warning on the Dutch Levant convoy—represented, with perhaps one exception, rather the pretexts than the real causes. Nine-tenths of it dealt with
the Flag, the offensive medals, Surinam, or the marine
treaty; but one charge rings deeper, that Holland had
long attempted to make France return to the old anti-
English *entente*. Constant repetition perhaps made
Charles (like George IV with Waterloo) believe it;
this was the reason confided to Coventry in September,
hurled at Boreel in audience during January, and reiterated in Council,[1] and if from Charles it comes with
singular ill-grace, it was not so wholly devoid of substance but that one section in this vacillating Cabinet
might use it with effect. In June de Witt had suggested
to Pomponne that France, together with the Triple
Alliance, might dispose of Spain, if Spain gratuitously
attacked France or if the young King died, and he
continued after that to appeal for restoration of the
"ancient confidence" and a lowering of tariffs.[2] His
candid explanations to England became less candid
from December, when the major controversy of his
life, the power of the Prince of Orange, reached a new
climax. To make William captain-general for life
would, he argued, shatter the work of twenty years
and be a remedy worse than the disease, and he asked
whether France would not save Holland from an
Orange-English control.[3]

[1] Arlington to Coventry, September, Longleat: "that the great reason why he
made so much haste to France was the assurance he had upon more than bare
conjecture that if he had not done it, Holland had been there before him"; Boreel
(secret), Jan. 13, R.A.; council, Dec. 10, '71 (Foreign Entry, 176), and September
'72, *E.H.R.* xlv.

[2] Pomponne to Louis XIV, June 22; de Witt to Pomponne, Sept. 15; States-
General, Nov. 30, to Louis.

[3] De Witt to de Groot, Nov. 30 and Dec. 21, Fruin, iv.

Of this correspondence the English had at least an inkling, though they distorted it into a *carte blanche* to Paris for an offensive alliance, and the old hopes of Orange agitation, with the old fear of de Witt patching up with France, reappear in Arlington's correspondence. Yet this bogey, though it may have influenced the making, did not make the war. Nor, as the bare dates show, did the last mission of Downing, which terminated three days after the signature of the treaty with France on 3rd February.[1] Whether war was settled before that mission began, is another question.

Sir George and Lady Downing reached the Hague on the 18th December, six years after their last departure, and the ambassador maintained his continuity in a prompt claim for exemption of his wine from the Customs. The French were suspicious of this mission, but allayed by assurances that Downing was only the *agent provocateur* and that he would cement English union for war. His first instructions[2] were to demand instant and ample satisfaction for the Flag, the punishment of the guilty Admiral Van Ghent, reparation for the infamous medals and pictures, and a reply to the English complaint of August touching Surinam; others followed him, to the effect that if he got no reply on the Flag in a fortnight, he should send in another memorial, and if that lay unanswered for a week, he was to leave without warning. Boreel had written that if the Flag were settled, there would be no war, and had spoken vaguely of an indemnity.[3]

Downing's first memorial was given in on the 2nd

---

[1] Wicquefort, iv. 246; Arlington to Sunderland, Jan. 18 and 25.

[2] Nov. 5, Foreign Entry, 175; additional instructions, Dec. 24, Holland, 187.

[3] De Witt to Boreel, Jan. 2, Fruin; Holland, 187, ff. 173 *seq.*; Colbert to Louis, Oct. 26, Mignet, and Feb. 1, Fr. tr.; Boreel, R.A. Dec. 2; Fonseca, Feb. 1 and 19, Simancas.

January, and not till the 24th did he receive a formal answer; this he refused to accept, declaring (falsely) that he had received his recall; a furious letter from Arlington[1] failed to check his speed, and he was back in London on the 6th February, before other despatches could catch him. Was he afraid, as some said, of being lynched by the mob, or had he heard of the French money arriving and feared to be caught a second time by an outbreak of war?[2]

At any rate, here was Sir George home again, as Trevor had said he would be,[3] "sitting again like a publican at the receipt of custom", and his precipitancy had much embarrassed his government; for, if it were war, he had given Holland a pretext to seize our merchantmen, and if peace were still possible, he had made it more difficult. He was therefore at once sent to the Tower, for the reasons concisely, and probably truly, put by Arlington, "to gain us some time, as to punish his impertinence".[4]

Meanwhile, the memorial which he had refused to consider was, slightly amended, sent to Boreel. On the formal matter of the Flag nothing could be more conciliatory, the Dutch agreeing that the salute should be rendered, if need be, by their whole fleet to a single British ship. But this must not be extended to a sea-sovereignty infringing freedom of trade, and was made conditional on our honouring the defensive clause of the Triple Alliance.

In a written reply Charles refused this as insufficient, and in the audiences he gave to Boreel harped upon de

---

[1] Jan. 27: "you continue to misunderstand the orders that are sent to you, how intelligible and plain soever they be", Add. MSS. 22,920; cf. Arlington to Sunderland, Feb. 8.

[2] Boreel, Feb. 9 and 10, R.A.   [3] To Coventry, Jan. 30, Longleat.

[4] Arlington to the same, Feb. 9, cipher, *ibid.*; Colbert, Feb. 8, Mignet.

Witt's opposition to Orange, the medals, and Macassar, declaring that he was affronted in East Indies, West Indies, and every sea. Boreel, hearing talk of "revenge for Chatham",[1] was at last losing his optimism, and asked his masters to send an ambassador-extraordinary as the forlorn hope. From one circumstance only did he glean any comfort, the appointment of Orange on the 14th February to be captain-general, which might affect some English opinion; indeed, Sylvius had already come from the Prince to ask what terms Charles would accept.[2]

Meerman, well known from days of 1667, was the envoy selected, but by the time he reached London on the 8th March[3] we may reckon that hope of peace was gone. In a decisive Cabinet on the 11th the section led by Arlington made one effort to give notice of an embargo on Dutch shipping, knowing as they did that de Witt's resistance on the Flag and impassioned refusal of an indemnity were not universally commended by de Witt's countrymen. But if this was a last stand for peace, it was overcome, Lauderdale, York, and Rupert carrying the resolution, which resulted forty-eight hours later in Holmes' piratical plunge into war.[4] There were many and pressing reasons for a decision one way or the other. Arlington himself was inoculating the Spaniards with the pernicious argument which Clarendon had used in 1665—that now money was voted, the fleet must be used—adding, in almost as many words, that the French subsidy must be

---

[1] Jan. 9, R.A.   [2] Colbert, Feb. 1, Fr. tr.; Boreel, Feb. 23, R.A.
[3] Arlington to Coventry, March 8, Longleat; audience that day, Pontalis; interview with commissioners on 11th, Foreign Entry, 177.
[4] Where, as Arlington said in his detached way, he "had like to have caught a Tartar"; to Coventry, March 22. On de Witt, see Dumoulin's well-informed account in *England's Appeal from the Cabal at Whitehall*, 1673.

employed to satisfy the King's "honour". In January payment from the Exchequer to the goldsmiths was "stopped" for a year, and only action would extinguish the clamour in the City. A peace party (Ormonde, it seems predominantly) hoped to make use of the mediation ardently pressed by del Fresno. There was, finally, the agitation in Puritan circles which invariably followed the prospect of a Dutch war; some members of Parliament were counted upon by Lisola and the Dutch, and veteran soldiers were offering themselves for Dutch service.[1]

Charles himself, so far as we can ascertain his personal opinion, was momentarily quite decided; he spoke with pride of the fact that he this time, and not Louis, was the principal, declared that he would have the Flag and the fishery dues granted, as his Exchequer books showed, to his ancestors, and perhaps dreamed of all Zealand as his own. From March onwards a new spurt of "Catholicity" indicated his wish to get more French money, Colbert forwarding his time-honoured request for that *rara avis*, a theologian who was likewise a chemist.[2]

Taking, then, the Cabinet decisions from 6th to 11th March—to secure domestic peace by the Declaration suspending the penal laws against Protestant dissenters, but to make war certain by attacking the Dutch convoy—we must conclude that Meerman arrived too late by a week, and perhaps by more. Presumably he found it useless to offer Charles the money, up to £100,000, which he was authorized to dangle, while del Fresno would not look at the still larger scheme he

[1] Ranke, iii. 524; Boreel to Fagel, Nov. 4, '71, Add. MSS. 35,852; Coventry to Arlington, March 13, Longleat; Fresno, March 14.

[2] Boreel, Feb. 9; Meerman, Verbaal, and March 20, R.A.; Treaty papers, 47; Colbert, March 11.

tried at the last—that Spain should make up, with
Holland, the full amount of the French "secret" subsidies. Charles, alleging that Holland only approached
him after failing to settle with France direct, demanded
a "positive" reply to his last memorial; our commissioners, Arlington and Lauderdale, brushed aside the
promise to dismiss Van Ghent and the promotion held
out for Orange, asked indemnity for the events of
August, alleged that the Smyrna fleet had not struck,
and reported that Meerman only produced "chicanes
and delays". A final meeting on the 17th March, the
day war was declared, passed only in recrimination,
and on the 22nd Meerman took leave of the King; the
Thames was already garnished with batteries, and a
fast in the churches had invoked God's blessing on the
war.[1]

The war party knew, no doubt, that quick success
was imperative. Holmes' act of piracy had, indeed,
made war certain, but had begun it with a failure, and
the numbers of wounded, in an action of which the
chief actors were ashamed, proclaimed the scandal and
the danger of the government. Trevor reported the
"ill-will of the people" as open against France, the
pressgang was working under great difficulties, and
del Fresno, who had been greeted as he sailed up the
Thames with "Long live the Spanish ambassador",
could tell Arlington that any troops we sent to France
would have to be sent in handcuffs. Clifford was insistent that war must begin by seizing a port among
those assigned to Britain, and Louis was reminded of
his promise to keep troops in his coast-towns to assist

---

[1] Barbour, 184; Dalrymple, ii. 93; Verbaal, R.A., March 11–22; de Witt to
Meerman, March 19, Fruin; Arlington to Coventry, March 8 and 15, Trevor to
same (Longleat); del Fresno, March 28.

attack on the Dutch harbours. With friend and foe a curiously universal impression prevailed that we meant to force Holland to drastic concessions, but not to overwhelm her, and that, more likely than not, we should leave France in the lurch. Our policy seemed to be, in short, that expressed by Arlington to his friend Gascoyne, now at Innsbruck about a Hapsburg marriage for the Duke, that England must have "a short war".[1]

[1] Colbert, Jan. 4 and 11, Fr. tr.; instructions for Godolphin, April 2, Stowe MSS. 191; Trevor to Coventry, April 2 and 12, Longleat; del Fresno, March 3 and 14.

CHAPTER IX

EPILOGUE: 1672–1674

CHARLES had thus made his choice, and one from which in the deepest sense he was never to escape. "Catholicity", by ceasing to be secret, finally divorced him from his people, and enveloped even his spasms of independence and national pride in a vicious circle of suspicion, which made both King and Parliament the victims of Louis XIV, paralysed our policy by the Popish plot, and for ten years set France on a peak of insolent aggression. By his own doing Charles had lost the most precious instrument of policy, the power of the initiative, and so became the sport of stronger forces—of France and the Duke of York, of the Whig Opposition and William of Orange. A new phase opens in his foreign affairs with which this volume is not concerned, and here we sketch only the process, dictated by those new forces, leading to the peace of 1674; which, though an epilogue to the twelve years we have described, was intrinsically rather the prelude to a new act.

The battle of Solebay, fought on the 28th May 1672, was already enough to dispel the vision of "a short war", for if de Ruyter had been too late to stop the junction of the French and English fleets, he so damaged the English that they abandoned the strategic scheme of that year, an invasion of Holland from the sea, with the result that York was told to avoid more fighting unless he had an overwhelming advantage.[1] But even more devastating than the enemy success at sea was our ally's triumphant progress on the land. With 120,000 men Louis, Condé, and Turenne swept down the Meuse, seized the Rhine fortresses which guarded Holland on the east, turned the Yssel line, flooded with their armies five Dutch provinces, and by 12th June had reached Utrecht. Sidney Godolphin, our representative with the armies, wrote that France threatened to swallow the whole country, and called for some one with plenipotentiary power to insist that we should get our share, for Louis was already objecting to our acquisition of Dutch seaports.[2] Partly for such reasons it was, by the 10th June, decided to send out Halifax as special envoy, not only to assure the French of our loyalty, but to investigate the chance of Zealand accepting our rule and to consult with Godolphin on the French design.[3]

But his instructions were not complete before the arrival of a Dutch mission crystallized the doubt and dilemma of our government, and resulted in his rapid supersession by the despatch to the Continent of Charles' two principal ministers, Arlington and Buckingham. Their orders, finally revised by a council meeting on James' flagship, were to try to stop the French winning all Holland, but to press upon Holland the highest possible terms. "Cautionary" towns were to be handed over "for ever", there must be an indemnity and an annual Fisheries payment, Orange must be

[1] June 21, Foreign Entry, 64.
[2] Godolphin to Arlington, June 13 and 18, France, 134, "I have no opinion of their sincerity to us from the moment that our interests begin to be separate"; Louis to Colbert, June 13, Mignet
[3] Cabinet of June 11, Foreign Entry, 177; instructions, June 14, Foxcroft.

made sovereign or at least hereditary stadtholder, and there must be a satisfactory arrangement for the Indies, including, so said Clifford's following letter, half the spice trade.[1] Clifford being empowered to act as secretary in Arlington's absence,[2] the ambassadors set forth on the 22nd June.

Few things better expose than this mission the wretched morale and factiousness of our diplomacy. We find Buckingham hurling himself, as ever, from one extreme to another; on June 19th his emissary treats, at the Red Lion Inn, Brentford, with the Dutch envoys for renewal of the Triple Alliance, on the 25th in Orange's camp he is a fervent convert, but pass on another forty-eight hours to the French quarters at Utrecht, and Buckingham is demanding all Zealand in perpetual sovereignty, and this he maintains when he returns to England in July.[3] While he was false and fleeting, Charles himself seems this summer to have lost all sense of proportion; left to himself he would apparently have refused to treat with Holland at all, was only prevented by his ministers from making over to France his claim to Sluys and Cadsand, and allowed Colbert to refuse any progress with the commercial treaty.[4]

Only in Arlington's cautious craft can we find anything approximating to a policy. The conditions of the moment had been altered in a direction more consonant with his old prepossessions by the fierce revolution which, just as he reached the Hague, had demolished de Witt's power and committed Holland to Orange, had set Orange flags flying on the church steeples and

[1] June 21, Foreign Entry, 64; June 22, *ibid.* 176.
[2] Original warrant, Clifford MSS.
[3] William Howard's negotiation, Carte MSS. 37, ff. 702 *seq.*; Archives, 101, f. 51; Treaty papers, 47; Foxcroft, i. 92.
[4] *Ibid.* 94, note; Lockhart to Coventry, cipher, Sept. 16, '74, Longleat.

wild cries in the streets of "Up with Orange and England—down with France". Not Arlington only, with
his strong Orange leaning, but all England must be
drawn by every motive to isolate the cause of Orange
from that of Holland at large, and to check through an
Orangist Holland the supremacy of France; again we
discern the old fear of a French-Dutch deal behind our
back, and French patronage of a revived Dutch republican party.[1]

It was then inevitably Arlington's purpose to moderate the terms on either side. To the Dutch he admitted
that his master would not treat apart from France, but
suggested that the cautionary towns should be cautionary indeed—held, that is, by England only until the
treaty terms were fulfilled; to Louvois he insisted that
France must modify her terms in the interests of peace.
From conversation with Orange's followers he was confident that the Prince, tempted by a real sovereignty,
would make our path easy, and in this sense he and
Buckingham reported to the Cabinet on their return in
late July.[2]

But the next two months dealt one blow upon
another. Inspired by the brutal Louvois, Louis im-
periously refused to lower demands which would have
made Holland a vassal and Belgium a certain prey;
terms of which Orange said, that he would "perish
rather than submit".[3] And while Charles was newly
pledged by a treaty signed on the 6th July[4] to make no
peace without France, his own negotiation with Orange

---

[1] Charles' audience to Brandt, Oct. 28, Urk. xvii.; Pontalis, ii. 472.
[2] Arlington and Buckingham to Clifford, June 28, Holland, 189; Arlington to
Louvois, July 10, *ibid*. 190; to Clifford, July 11, Archives, 101; Barbour, 199;
Foreign Entry, 177, July 22.
[3] Godolphin to Arlington, July 12, Holland, 190.
[4] Archives, 101, f. 26.

was sticking fast. Messages begun by Sylvius even in February were continued by him again from June to September, by the Prince's servant Frederick Van Reede, and his physician Dr. Rumff. In vain the King brandished expressions of affection, declaimed against the republicans, or suggested that even for Orange's own safety some English garrisons were advisable; between Arlington's demands of June and the case put by Sylvius to the Cabinet on the 29th July yawned a great gulf, for instead of a million indemnity the Dutch would offer only £400,000, while for territory they would only surrender Sluys in temporary pledge.[1] Charles reproachfully replied that this was "infinitely short of what I expected", but on Arlington's advice reduced his demand to two towns for a ten-year term, and invited Orange to send his envoys to a congress at Dunkirk. But the murder of de Witt did not have the effect for which the English hoped; two months passed in a silence they found hard to endure, and when Van Reede appeared again at the end of September with no concessions they broke out in petulant rage. Charles told him that he would be "a beast or a fool" if he abandoned France, and Arlington was unwise enough to hint that Orange might draw on himself the hideous fate of de Witt.[2]

Only despair could make Charles and Arlington bad-tempered, and despairing their policy was proving to be. Money was running short, though the French had produced one credit of £20,000, but they refused

<hr>

[1] Williamson's Journal, Cal.S.P.D.; Schotel, *Briefen tusschen Karel II. en Wilhelm III.*, Bijd. Vd. Geschied. 2nd series iv.; Koervezee, *ibid.* 6th series vii.; Foreign Entry, 177, July 29; Fruin, *Versp. geschr.* iv. 339 *seq.*

[2] Charles to Orange, July 8, July 31, Aug. 20, Holland, 190, and Koervezee, *loc. cit.*; Orange to Arlington, Oct. 7, Schotel, *loc. cit.*; Cabinet of July 31, Foreign Entry, 177.

to meet a new call for "Catholicity" or Charles' extraordinary demand in September for the loan of another
million. Our alternative policies for Zealand, to get up
a "spontaneous" rising there or to land from the sea
and make it a desert, had both failed.[1] Interviews between Arlington and Monterey at Brussels had cast
an even deeper shadow, for though some counsellors
like Shaftesbury thought that if Spain and France
were at war we could "capture the trade of both",
what would happen if Spain broke with us also? The
Parliament which, in absence of French money, must
some day reassemble must be confronted with some
policy, and this none knew better than Orange, whose
agents put it about that England could, if she wished,
drop the French, and whose ambassadors were dis-
tributing pamphlets for the benefit of members. This
effort to force peace upon us from within was resented,
and was not at this time bringing peace any nearer;
Henry Coventry declared that the Dutch, "wanting
good men to defend their own country, hope there will
be found bad here to destroy their own".[2]

Dealing with Charles II and the Cabal, it is not
surprising to find that they agreed to compromise.
Arlington's warning in Council, that Parliament would
have something to say to those backward in the cause
of peace, was so far met that we professed our readiness for a truce, but Charles would only make it conditional upon French assent; while those who argued
that Parliament must be shown some tangible fruits of
the war got an extended prorogation from October to

[1] Colenbrander, ii. 122; Colbert, May 28, Christie, and Sept. 5, Barbour;
Arlington to Godolphin, July 14, and report of July 22, Treaty papers,
47.

[2] Arlington to Clifford, July 9, Holland, 190; Cabinet, Nov. 25, Foreign Entry,
177; Koorvezee, 243; Coventry, Jan. 13, '73, Add. MSS. 21,122.

February.[1] By that time, Charles hoped, Holland might have been persuaded to take part in a general negotiation. Meantime, though he sharply refused an offer from Brandenburg, he accepted mediation from Sweden, and occupied the winter in argument whether the consequent congress should meet at Dunkirk, as he wished, or in a "neutral" city like Aix or Cologne.

This sort of optimism found full expression in our relations during this year with the Hapsburgs. Arlington had sent Gascoyne off on the very eve of our declaration of war to ask the hand of the Archduchess Claudia for the Duke of York, the Spanish support was presupposed,[2] and it was thought possible to entertain this Austrian marriage together with our French policy. By November the parties were agreed as to Imperial money for the lady's *dot*, guarded precautions for her religious liberties, and parliamentary approval of the contract; but Leopold still demanded his political price—inclusion in any peace with Holland, a reconfirmation of the terms of Aix, and a defensive alliance. On the last the English resistance was as firm as it had been before, and was still maintained when, in March 1673, the Empress Margaret died and the widower claimed York's bride for his own. Not that the negotiation could, probably, in any case have materialized, since Leopold would only proceed with the approval of Spain, and that each day grew more improbable.[3]

Yet the international balance was still indeterminate enough in the first half of 1673 to leave intact all

---

[1] Foreign Entry, August and Oct. 27; Charles' speech of Sept. 17, *E.H.R.* xlv.

[2] Gascoyne's instructions, Feb. 72, Stowe MSS. 191, f. 30.

[3] Gascoyne to Arlington, April 12 to June 30, '72, Empire, 12; marriage project, Oct. 2, Jenkins MSS. 239, f. 113, copy; Arlington to Gascoyne, Nov. 11, '72–May 26, '73 (recall), *Misc. Aul.*; Leopold's correspondence, Pötting, ii. 222 *seq.*

Charles' hopes. Monterey might send troops to help Holland, but the Spanish Dutch treaty was not yet a reality; Lisola had brought off a subsidy treaty between Holland and the Emperor, but it made a slow, difficult passage through French ultimatums, Spanish dribbling-out of funds, and a Dutch peace party, while by the new year Leopold's army had retreated over the Rhine and Turenne was left master of Westphalia. The Great Elector's first impulse was ebbing, partly on account of a new collapse of Poland before the Turk, and in April he signed a suspension of arms.

Nor was the much-dreaded parliamentary session of February 1673 immediately or directly fatal to the continuance of the war, for which, in fact, the Commons provided £1,200,000; its victims were rather "Catholicity" and the cohesion, such as it was, of the Cabinet. The Cavalier majority made their grant conditional on the revocation of the Declaration of Indulgence, a step repugnant equally to the liberal Shaftesbury, the Catholic York and Clifford, and the despot Lauderdale. Two forces seem to have extorted Charles' reluctant consent, and precisely those to whom "Catholicity" was secondary or uncongenial—the French, to whom it was as nothing compared with the war, and Arlington, who weighed it lightly as compared with supply. But the division of the ministry had begun before Parliament met at all, with a deep cleavage on the point of peace or war, with a struggle for the Treasury staff between Arlington and Clifford, and with the instinctive response of Shaftesbury and Buckingham to what they felt to be a swelling hostile opinion. What the Test Act did was to fix these fissures; it is enough to add that York and Clifford resigned upon it, that Shaftesbury worked for it, and that Arlington acquiesced in its results

But though the Secretary was convinced that the "great design" must go, and for his part only adhered to war as a means of winning an advantageous peace, war and the French alliance was still the policy of the government as a whole, even when at midsummer it was reconstructed on more popular lines. Coventry was emphatic that though we wanted peace, we could not "buy an ill one by a breach of faith", and Ormonde, we hear from Arlington, would never advise "so dishonourable and imprudent an act". We consequently refused the Dutch offer of a year's cessation by sea, and instructed our plenipotentiaries at Cologne to insist on two Dutch seaports; while Rupert, now commander at sea, had orders to offer to Zealand (though without telling the French) the privileges of English citizenship, religious liberty, and representation in Parliament.[1]

The real period of decision came, rather, between the two sessions of February and October. Not till June did the Test Act reap its dramatic triumph in the fall of the Catholic ministers, and by that time all England was reading *England's Appeal from the Private Cabal at Whitehall*. This famous pamphlet, showing on every page a detailed knowledge of our diplomacy since 1668, graved on the public mind the transformation of our policy since that happy year, charged the ministers in general with extruding sound Protestants from the council and Arlington in particular with taking French gold, and declared that his embassy of 1672 had finally sacrificed us to French ambition. Its author was one Pierre Du Moulin, once employed in our Paris embassy, more recently under the Committee of Trade and

[1] Coventry to Jenkins, July 11, Add. MSS. 25,122; Arlington to Jenkins and Williamson, July 25, Archives, 221; to Williamson, cipher, June 26, German States, 60; Treaty papers, 47, Feb. 21, '73; Foreign Entry, 64, May 27; Coventry papers, iii. Longleat, Council minutes, n.d.

Plantations, and finally dismissed for intrigue with Dutch envoys. This little man was now used by Orange to knit up his relation with the English opposition; revenge, he told his friends, was the passion of great natures, and at Cologne this summer his pen was steeping in venom the Dutch state papers, while Dutch and German translations of his work elaborated the charge of despotism and Popery.[1]

All the rumours which had accompanied Clarendon's fall now reappeared in more panic-stricken form; they were not assuaged by the appointment of the anti-French Danby as Treasurer or by Ormonde's revived power, and were only accentuated by the choice of Schomburg, a Huguenot but a Frenchman, to command the army for Zealand. By one step in particular they were greatly inflamed, by the extraordinarily precipitate and ill-timed marriage of York to the Catholic Mary of Modena. Lord Peterborough had left in March for Innsbruck, but, when hope of that archduchess faded, was quickly diverted to inspect other eligible princesses. The Neuburg claimant was one of thirteen children, but her plainness outweighed that hopeful quality, and in August Charles adopted the Modena scheme independently put forward by the French, who offered a *dot* of 400,000 crowns and undertook to smooth Mary's exit from her convent to a more transitory crown. On the last day of September she was married to York by proxy, so anticipating by some three weeks the first possible protest from the House of Commons.[2] The storm that broke out was only checked by an immediate

[1] Barbour, 211 *seq.*; De Vic to Southwell, April 4, '73, Add. MSS. 34,342; de Groot to Wicquefort, Oct. 16; De Beer, *E.H.R.* 1924; Fruin, *Versp. geschrift.* v. 38, note.
[2] Arlington to Gascoyne, March 7, *Misc. Aul.*; Add. MS. 34,342, ff. 111 *seq.*; Peterborough to Arlington, Aug. 15, Italian States, 11; Pomponne, i. 515; Ranke.

prorogation to January, but that one week's debate
reminded elderly men of troubles long forgotten—the
same long silences in which seventeenth - century
Houses of Commons looked grimly on each other, the
locked doors, and the vote against "evil counsellors" as
Black Rod knocked for admission. The Arlington
group did their best to keep the new Duchess abroad,
and even suggested that the Duke should leave
London.

Not that this marriage alone provoked such signs of
revolution; that, it is surely almost certain, was due to
disclosure of the "grand design". If, as there is reason to
hold, Buckingham had got wind of it, we need scarcely
probe further for the source; but however it came out,
the open allusions in debate, pamphlets, and correspondence to the secret treaty, to Clifford's conversion, to
Arundell and Father Patrick as active agents, show that
the essentials of "Catholicity" had become public property. All chance consequently vanished of realizing
Arlington's first hope that Parliament could be induced
to support an "honourable" peace; Shaftesbury, on
whom he had counted, ostentatiously joined the rising
cause, and the Commons, well led by William Coventry,
refused supply unless Dutch obstinacy made peace
untenable. Moreover, a bitter feud between Arlington
and Danby, the new aspiring minister, made it certain
that one group or the other would look for support in
an understanding with the Dutch.[1]

In short, even by November an early peace was
practically assured, and all that was left to dispute were
its terms, high or low, in concert with France or without her. In the decision one ruling factor was the failure

[1] Christie, ii. 86, and app. xxiii.; Temple to Essex, Dec. 25; Grey, ii. 152,
200.

of this summer's sea fighting, with its political consequence that Rupert, who had always opposed the
alliance with France, ended as her strenuous enemy.
The drawn, elusive skirmishes of May and June were
extinguished in August at the fierce battle of the Texel,
where Destrées by disobedience to Rupert's signal lost,
in Rupert's words, "the plainest and greatest opportunity was ever lost at sea", as if (a member said in
that autumn's debates) "English and Dutch had been
gladiators for the French spectators". We thus find a
demoralized navy, the army at Yarmouth disbanded,
and the French requested to take their ships home.
Overseas, the Dutch retook New York and the Delaware, Virginia was raided, and St. Helena lost; near
home, a first serious opposition attacked Lauderdale in
Scotland.

From midsummer the European system, a matter
more vital to Charles, was steadily turning into a coalition against France. Louis' aggression and perjury
were at last reaping their reward; he had marched and
ravaged on German territory, seized towns in Alsace,
invaded Treves, betrayed to Spain his secret treaty of
1668 with Leopold, and instigated Portugal against
her. In the last days of August a bundle of treaties
bound together Austria, Spain, Holland, and Lorraine
to secure a fair peace by common assent, the crux from
our point of view being a Spanish promise to Holland
that she would attack England if her mediation were
refused. In September Gremonville, the French minister long all-powerful at Vienna, received his passports, in October France declared war on Spain, and
in early November Austrian and Spanish troops joined
the Prince of Orange at the siege of Bonn.

How fateful the war was becoming to England was

revealed, meantime, at the Congress of Cologne; yet
how little Charles meant to make of the congress
emerged in the very name of our envoys. The nominal
leader, Sunderland, was ill in France when, in June,
twenty-six waggons of baggage, soap, sugar, and
other necessaries rolled into Cologne before our active
representatives, Jenkins and Williamson.[1] Good Sir
Leoline Jenkins was only an honest civilian, meant
to do the drudgery, and the King's wishes were communicated to Williamson, Arlington's deputy and suc
cessor. Yet Sir Joseph was not a man who would be
trusted with an initiative, being, in fact, a poor thing,
easily flattered by the brilliant Courtin, captivated by
the dashing Fürstenberg, and writing reminiscently
afterwards to the Swedish Sparr of "la belle troupe"
and "la belle comtesse", who had adorned his musical
parties and comedies.

Constant revision of their instructions registered, as
on a weather-glass, our government's unhappy fluc-
tuations, which gradually set to storm. In May their
orders were to get the Flag, a million indemnity (to
be reduced to £600,000 at a pinch), a marine treaty,
£12,000 a year for the fisheries, free migration for the
English in Surinam, Orange's hereditary title, and two
treaty ports for a term of years.[2] The last was the sticking point, not merely because Charles' pride forbade
him to lose hope of winning towns while France won
provinces, or because Orange was adamant, but since
Sweden openly and France more covertly opposed

[1] "Intrusted with his Majesty's most interior thoughts and resolutions", Arlington to Sunderland, May 26, German States, 60; his despatches sometimes concealed from the Cabinet, Add. MS. 25,122, f. 114; de Groot, 202.
[2] Brill and Goree, or Sluys and Goree, or Flushing and Rammekens; Foreign
Entry, 64; Williamson's journal, June 12, Archives, 229; Williamson to Arlington,
June 13, German States, *loc. cit.*; Foreign Entry, 177, March 31.

a plan which would plant England on both sides of the Channel. Neither on this matter nor on the East Indian grievances could our envoys get any French support.[1]

But the French alliance being still our basis, our government tried to make the best blend of an impossible combination, tried with little success to make Louis lower his terms, and constantly readjusted our own. On the 14th July Arlington asked two towns for seven years, but on the 28th dropped this *in toto*, observing that Orange's title would be a better safeguard, and asking instead the entire surrender of Surinam. Keeping pace with a slightly improved offer from the French, our envoys in August announced these terms to the mediators, but in vain; the Dutch, fired by naval and diplomatic success, refused to hear of an indemnity, asked that India might be referred to separate negotiation, and would not treat apart from their allies. Vainly we tried every combination of motives, vainly offered to waive Orange's title, or to reduce our figure to £300,000. The Dutch were bent on forcing us to a separate peace, and their message of the 15th October, composed by Du Moulin, was actually, what Charles' angry reply called it, not an offer but a manifesto, appealing to English public opinion and menacing us with a European league.[2]

In the rapid change from this recriminatory deadlock to the peace of February 1674, there were four chief actors; the Prince of Orange, Spain, Arlington,

[1] Coventry to Jenkins, July, Add. MSS. 25,122; Rec. Hollande, i. 318; Terlon to Feuquières, April 12 (Lettres de F. 1845, ii.); Rec. Suède, 137; Rousset, i. 467.

[2] Archives, 221, July 14 and 28; Williamson to Essex, Aug. 4 and 10, Stowe MS. 203; journal, Oct. 12; Rec. Hollande, ii. 301; instructions of Nov. 14, Foreign Entry, 64; Sylvius, i. 684; Charles to States-General, Nov. 7, R.A. 7332; Wicquefort, iv. 580.

and the House of Commons. The Prince had one bond
with our government, and one never far away from all
his history, that is, a well-grounded fear, that France
might patch up a separate peace with Holland through
a revived party of republicans, and in November Van
Reede again appeared to emphasize this danger. But
Charles, no doubt with reason, felt assured of French
arrogance alienating any section in Holland, and the
really decisive pressure upon him came much less from
Orange than from Spain.[1]

Till the summer of 1673 we continued our tone of
bluster to the Spanish government—in May formally
withdrawing our guarantee of the treaty of Aix and
in July rejecting an offer of mediation brought over
by Salinas. But in September Arlington heard of
a secret article signed at the Hague, whereby Spain
undertook to present a three-flanged ultimatum, giving
us the Flag, reciprocal restitution outside Europe, and
a small indemnity, with war if we refused; while in
October the ambassador del Fresno was cognisant of the
Dutch "manifesto".[2] The crisis was thus near; indeed,
Spanish intervention was in more ways than one decisive, for while our government in all its phases refused
to face a war with Spain, they realized that Spain for
her part dreaded new trouble in the Indies and was
therefore ready to extract better terms from Holland.[3]

Its effect can be seen in the improved tone of the
next Dutch approach, and on the 10th December del
Fresno's memorial gave the English an opening for a
bargain; for though formally he could offer only the

[1] Koorvezee, *loc. cit.*; Arlington to envoys, June 26, Archives, *loc. cit.*; Mignet,
iv. 149.

[2] Godolphin's memorial, May 12, Mignet; Archives, 221, f. 81; Foreign Entry,
177, April 13; Arlington to Godolphin, Sept. 25; Klopp, i. 359.

[3] Foreign Entry, 177, February, 73; Krämer, 138.

three terms stipulated by the Dutch-Spanish treaty, he was notoriously a friend to peace, and that treaty was not yet ratified. The ensuing week may therefore be taken as critical; Charles let Colbert see that a loan of 100,000 livres was a drop in the ocean of a naval deficit of a million and a half sterling, while Arlington suggested that France should restore both the Dutch towns and Lorraine. On the 16th the King's decision seemed to be made. Accepting with mild reproaches del Fresno's proposition, he asked that three more articles be added—a marine treaty for the East, free migration in Surinam, and a system of Fishery licences; all six points were to be adjusted through Cologne, and our envoys should be instructed to confer on that basis.[1]

But the hiatus between any cup and Charles' lip was always a long one, and the Spanish pressure had to be reinforced. A Dutch memorial of December gave new offence by attacking Charles' counsellors, and since it was in print before it reached the government, was plainly in the nature of an appeal to Parliament. Their offer of the 14th January 1674 did, indeed, make a substantial stride forward, for it met us on the matters of Surinam and restitution, promised the honour of the Flag even to a single British warship, and offered an early meeting of commissioners to settle Indian trade. But they were not themselves yet sure of Spanish sincerity, and at Cologne the English were bickering with "the old fox" Beverning about Indian forts.[2]

Peace, in fact, drew not only its name, but its final reality, from Westminster. It was on the 7th January

[1] Williamson to Essex, Jan. 1; Arlington to envoys, Dec. 17, Archives; Sylvius, i. 708; Colbert, Dec. 11–15, Mignet.

[2] Coventry to Jenkins, Jan. 9, '74, Add. MSS. 25, 123; to Essex, Jan. 13, Stowe MSS. 204; Kramer, 140 seq.; Sylvius, ii. 14; Williamson, journal, Jan. 13, Archives, 222.

that Parliament met again; two months had elapsed
since they attacked the Duke's marriage and threatened Lauderdale, and the King seems to have hoped
that with this cooling interval he could induce them to
arm him, either for peace or war. He declined the
French notion of a longer prorogation, and in his opening speech appealed for national confidence; hinting at
his desire to satisfy them in matters of religion, he declared the Dutch projects were meant only to "amuse",
and promised to show them the whole content (here,
one observer noticed, he "fumbled") of the treaties,
so strangely misconstrued, which he had made with
France.

That vacillating mind was, in fact, turning on a new
wheel, and to complete the story of the peace we must
for the last time penetrate into the factions of his council.
Clifford was dead and Lauderdale falling, Shaftesbury had been dismissed in November, but the sempi-
ternal hatred between Arlington and Buckingham
infested the last hours of the Cabal, as it had ushered in
its birth. In one sense the Duke had triumphed, in that
two of the new triumvirate, Danby and Seymour, had
begun life as his clients, but the third, Finch, was drifting towards Arlington, who could count, at least in this,
on Ormonde and Coventry. Between these groups lay
the unscrupulous vitality of Shaftesbury, and outside
them the French, like them in doubt whether with King
or Parliament lay the deciding power and which were
easier to win.

On the advice, it seems, of Buckingham and Danby,
Charles submitted to Parliament the treaty of Decem-
ber 1670, and asked their support for a spirited policy.
Their motives, we may believe, were various, for while
Danby took this course to keep the King's humour and

advocated candour as the surest means of killing the secret alliance, Buckingham was again, as in 1667, the agent of the French, by whose means he would recover power and prove to Charles for ever the pusillanimity of his rival. His first idea had been to dissolve Parliament or to bribe it, but these proving impracticable he would lead it astray.

But the Commons had hardly broken into their rehearsal of grievances before Buckingham, by a final blunder, threw away any cards that he held. On the 13th January he volunteered a statement, for two days exasperated the House by a rambling tissue of self-glorification, and lost Charles' favour by disclosing Cabinet discussion, while by placing on the dead Clifford and the hated Arlington an incredible monopoly of evil counsel he simply set up a reaction. From that day onwards all was lost. The Commons asked the King to remove Buckingham and Lauderdale, to disband the army, and to embody the train bands against the Papists, while the Lords were framing Bills for Protestant education of the royal house and exclusion from the succession of those who married Catholics. Against this passion nothing which the French could do availed. To dispel the association of his alliance with Popery, Louis had sent the Huguenot Ruvigni to replace Colbert, but the £10,000 he put at Shaftesbury's disposal was declined, and after some hesitations that ruthless figure cast himself into the front of opposition. Only peace with Holland could save Charles from anarchy or a new and more violent Parliament, and on the 24th January he asked the Houses' advice on the terms tendered by del Fresno.

The Commons, who thus demolished the Cabal, rejected by 166 votes to 127 an address for Arlington's removal; his speech of two hours in defence, Coventry tells us, "charmed the House"—an effect incalculable from the half light of our cloudy reports of the debate, but proceeding from a common impression that Arlington "broke the French alliance".[1] His timidity and love of power could not, perhaps, in the long run uproot his considered policy and his proved sensitiveness to parliamentary opinion, nor need his obsequious conversations deceive us as they did Colbert. As in July, so in November, he had urged that peace should be made before the session; his secret conferences with del Fresno, his anxiety that Portugal should not embarrass Spain, his new cordiality to Temple, the settled conviction of the French and Dutch that on the peace he had staked his fortunes, Charles' remark that Arlington had "wearied" him into it, the subsequent concentration of Catholic anger on his head—all the evidence is the same, that the policy in which Arlington had always at heart believed, he now forced on Charles as an urgent necessity.[2]

It was on the 23rd January, when the charges against him had gone to a committee, that the Cabinet resolved, without telling Ruvigni, to take the Dutch terms to Parliament next day, and on the 27th that the Commons advised the King to proceed in a treaty. A last effort of Buckingham's in the Lords, and protests from Ruvigni and the Swedes, broke down; Charles promised to leave his envoys at Cologne, and not to recall his troops from France, but more he could not do; for, besides

[1] Coventry to Jenkins, Jan. 16, Add. 25, 123; Conway to Essex, Jan. 27, Essex papers.

[2] Arlington to the envoys, July 28, Archives, 221; to Godolphin, Oct. 23; Colbert, Nov. 10, Mignet; Kramer, 148; Burnet, ii. 46, *seq.*; Pomponne, i. 492; Sylvius, March 13, Holland, 196; Westmoreland papers, H.MSS. comm.; Barbour; Grey.

Arlington, Danby was now an open, as he had perhaps been always a secret, champion of peace. On the 2nd February a Dutch messenger, with the news that Orange had been given his hereditary title, asked a suspension of arms and passports for their ambassadors; on the 5th they superseded both this and Charles' proposal to send Temple to them by a second message giving full powers to del Fresno; by the 7th Temple and del Fresno had threshed out a project for our commissioners; on Monday, the 9th, at Arlington's office, the Peace was signed.[1]

As its articles could not represent the essential meaning of the war, so they did little more than embody an honourable retreat for the King, who spent that evening in expatiating to Ruvigni on the dishonour thrust upon him. The Dutch conceded the Flag in terms more ample than those of Breda, promised redress in Surinam, gave an indemnity of 800,000 crowns, agreed that New York and conquests on each side be restored, and prolonged for nine months the commercial articles of 1668, pending an early settlement by commissioners meeting in London—as meet they did, indeed, in July, to argue with a now ageing Downing on the well-worn matter of forts and blockade.[2] A secret article, insisted on by del Fresno at the last minute and to be the subject of intense prevarication,[3] provided that neither party should give assistance, direct or indirect, to the other's enemies. On the 10th February Charles announced the conclusion to the States-General; on the 24th,

---

[1] Archives, 222, Jan. 3 and 23; Ruvigni, Jan. 29, Mignet; Temple to Sir J. Temple, March 27.

[2] Stowe MS. 204, ff. 139, 158; Temple, *Memorials*; Beuningen to S. G. Dec. 1, '74, and Jan. 29, '75, R.A.; Holland, 196, ff. 131, *seq.*

[3] Temple's version in his works; Charles', in Ruvigni's despatch of Feb. 10; his expostulation to the Dutch, R.A. 7332 and S.G. 6928; Ossory's interview with Orange, Nov. 4, Carte, 220, f. 470.

without warning to the Cabinet, he prorogued Parliament; and on the 28th peace was proclaimed in London.[1]

With which ended the veritable Odyssey of King Charles, who would go no more on his travels, but would seek in a pensionary peace the profits he had hoped to extract from war. The country which he had once followed, and once led, against Holland had turned definitely against France, and the European coalition was in being, and in his despite, which he and Arlington had tried to use as counters in their game. He had reaped little from the policy of Madame. Parliament had refused or detected his aspirations and turned out his ministers, and in place of the easily persuaded Clarendon or of Arlington, his friend, there were tougher men and harder times; Danby, Orange, and that sermonizing Temple, the religious *sottise* of York, which endangered the monarchy, a new Shaftesbury instinct with old republican ambition, and a new Arlington intimidated into Whigdom and Orangery. But Arlington would keep counsel on what was past, that wild Clifford was dead, and the most Christian King would surely not prejudice the Faith by allowing any indiscretion.

Henceforward he would call a truce to the opposed temptations ever dangled before him—to "Catholicity" on one side and, on the other, to divorcing his wife or legitimizing that delightful, illiterate Monmouth. Let come what might come, he would keep the throne, which his father had lost by excess of zeal, for his own life and his brother's. There was profit to be won by a King of England who stood between a European coalition and

---

[1] "Vostre bien bon amy, Charles R"—original, R.A. 6923, S.G.; Coventry to Sylvius, Feb. 24, Add. MSS. 25,123; Christie, ii. 192.

his rich (and to-be-hoped discreet) cousin of France; Minette was in her grave, but the world held other women, not so dear but in their own way affording some compensation for the inexhaustible folly of politicians.

APPENDICES

I

Arlington to Downing, at the Hague, 14 *July* 1665;
draft; Holland 177, *f.* 92

"HAMPTON COURT.

SIR,—I have yours of the seventh, and seen what you wrote
to my Lord Chancellor of the same date; particularly how you
press him, and with reason (as I said in my last) to enable you
to say something reasonable on our parts towards an accommodation, without which you will never be able to draw out
anything from them. And my Lord Chancellor hath promised
me that by the next weeke we shall be able to say something
effectually to you upon this point.

But for feare the difficulty of resolving in it, as we should
doe, should take up too much time, I have his Majesty's leave,
and my Lord Chancellor's approbation, to mind you that this
is the criticall minute whenever the French and Hollanders
are agreeing, and to our prejudice, which agreement it is not
in our power to unlose or interrupt otherwise than by making
some advance ourselves to the Hollander, which if you can
dexterously doe, the effect of it will certainly be the retarding
their agreement. So that whatever you can devise of this
nature by playing well the ambassador's part, his Majesty
recommends the performance of it to you, with all the dex-
terity and skill you have.

In the meane time, despairing now of understanding ourselves well with France, wee have turned ourselves with such
a warmth towards Spaine that wee doubt not of closing well

with them. And the French themselves begin to plucke off the maske; for, two days since, the 3 Ambassadors were with the King, declaring to him that if the Bishop of Munster stirred, the King their master would enter his country with 20,000 men, and that they should have their passage free through Flanders—which the Spanish ambassador doubts. With this pretence they will certainly begin their succour to Holland, or to say better, take their posts for the conquest of Flanders, which is the only jealous point now betwixt the Hollander and them, and may be much improved, if you can helpe to distract them by making a fair advance on our side—with whom they certainly had much rather treate.

And effectively wee would not be sorry to doe it, so wee saw them fairly disposed to aggree with us. But of this you shall heare more in my next; without which, you must fall to worke presently, that no time be lost, to begett this amusement in them."

II

THE BERGEN AFFAIR

The Governor of Bergen to Sir Thomas Clifford,
7 August 1665; autograph; Clifford MS.

"Monsieur,—Si le defunct Milord Montague eust voulu suivre mes advis, nous n'aurions pas subject de plaindre la glorieuse mort d'un si brave seigneur. Je vous envoye la presente escritte du Chevallier Talbot, la quelle je viens de recevoir un heure apres que ce porteur est retourne icy. Le dict Chevallier m'envoye une copie, la quelle est accompagne d'une ordre de mon Roi de mesme teneur. Vous la presenterez a Monsr l'Admiral s'il vous plaist, avec la circonspection deue dans une affaire de telle consequence, & apres l'avoir bien entendu vous pourriez traicter avec ce gentilhomme, pour moyenner une entrevèue entre nous deux, puis que Mons l'Admiral & moi ne nous attendons pas l'un l'autre.

Ce gentilhomme a faict un nouveau serment de secretesse

& circonspection; c'est pourquoi, Monsieur, vous vous pourriez entierement fier sur sa parole. Plust a Dieu que nous eussions eues plutost notres ordres, le tout ne sera pas arrivee.

Il me tarde grandement d'avoir l'honneur de vous voir, mais je vous supplie tres humblement que ce soit de nuict, & encore en habit deguise, puis que il y va grandment de l'interest des notres Roys. Ce present gentilhomme vous en monstrera un lieu convenable, ou nous pourrions conferer sans estre veue de personne.

& en vous attendant je suis de tout mon cœur, Monsieur, Vostre tres humble tres fidel serviteur,

ARLLFELLDT.

Il est fort necessaire que mons l'admiral œvre la lettre de monsieur Talbot a Monsieur le Comte Sandwich; puis que cette lettre vous donnera tout l'eclaircissement de tout l'affaire.

adu.
a 7me d'Aust 1665."

III

Sir William Temple to Ormonde, 5 Dec. 1665; original; Bodl. Carte MS. 47, f. 268

"I finde our state with the German princes is this. Brandenbergh leans to the Hollander by his inclination, or rather by the instigation of his wife, being very uxorious, but by His Majesty's negotiations, awe of the Swede in his northern territorys, and respect to the House of Austria, I believe he will grow so far retained as to continue his neutrality. More at present we are not to expect from Nieubergh, beeing awed and influenced by the French, though his inclinations are warme to the Munster quarrel, and his devotion not lesse to his Majesty's person and service. The two Luneburgh brothers are so far engaged with the Dutch, that Count Waldeck is now in the head of a force, which is at least crackt up to eight thousand, designing to join the Dutch and French troops.

The Lady Landgravine of Hesse is governed wholly by the counsels and actions of her brother of Brandeburgh. The Elector of Maintz is a good Austrician at this time in his heart, and not onely friend but confidant to our Bishop of Munster; but (being in his nature coverd enough) has not any desire at present that either of them should be thought. The Emperor interposes hitherto in this matter onely by way of mediation, which hee has offred to the States by his Ministers' memorial at the Hague, pressing them very much not onely to accomodation with Munster, but to a peace with England, as an affaire wherein the whole Empire is concerned."

IV

Arlington to Sandwich, 14 September 1666; draft (extract); Spain 52, f. 32

"To conclude. If the King and Counsell of Spayne are soe well satisfied in the sincerity of France, as that during the minority of his Catholique Majty it will set no pretence on foot to the prejudice of the House of Austria, his Majty cannot expect that in contemplation of him they shall in any degree offend so potent an ally. But if by their observation or experience they find cause to apprehend that they may have occasion to use their friends' assistance upon any accident that may fall out, His Majty doth againe, as hee hath heretofore done, offer them his friendship, which he will apply inviolably to the support of that house, and to the obstruction of all machinations their enemyes shall contrive against them. And if this franke overture from his Majty shall meet with noe other reception than it hath hitherto done, he shall hold himself absolved before the world if he shall henceforward pursue those councells which will be attended with more present conveniences to his owne interest."

V

Arlington to Ormonde, 12 *Feb.* 1667—*original.*
Bodl. Carte MS. 46, *f.* 450

"Yesterday morning we received an expresse from my lord
of St Albans, giving an account of the sincere intentions of
that court towards a peace; promising their effecting it with
Hollande if His Majesty would sign in a letter to the Queen in
his owne hande, that hee was not yet in, nor would not in the
space of one whole yeare to come, make any ligue with any
prince or potentate to the prejudice of France, and in the
meane time treate with that King such a strict union as he hath
often promised; who would withall restore to the King our
master all the places he hath taken from him in America. This
letter His Majesty hath signed this evening, and to-morrow the
courier is returning with it. I must likewise observe to your
Grace, that when France did conceive this ouverture, they
could not imagine wee would sende to treate in the Hague;
soe that if the knowledge of that make noe alteration in them,
we may hope the peace will be made. This faire and easy disposition in France makes us conclude they doe not meane to
suspend any longer their breaking with Spaine, and perhaps
they saw it was not any longer in their power to keepe Hollande from treting with us".

VI

Arlington's Note of Discussions with Ruvigni, Nov.–Dec. 1667.
Foreign Entry Book, 176—*Extracts*

(*a*) [Undated, save "Thursday 26"] Ruvigni reports the
"alternatives": "During this discourse we asked what France
would doe to meet Englande in case it would joine with them.
Monsieur De Ruvigny sayd, any thing wee would desire; continue the warre, or make the Peace at our [?] Wee sayd France
must thinke well to gratify the interests of the Nation, not

much inclined to them, if they would winne us. Hee answered, they would in any thing we would propose. Wee sayd they could not doe it in a more essential point than in cesing to assist a stronger at sea. Ruvigny sayd hee was confident that for the satisfaction of England his master would gratify us in that, and tooke his [?] to digest this proposition, promising to write in it by the next post".

(b) "December 1, Sunday. Qn. for Mosr. de Ruvigny.

Will his master enter into a league offensive and defensive against Hollande, and contente himselfe with the King our Masters neutrality as to Flanders, this later to bee wavd upon his demande of the contrary".

VII

Arlington's Note for Committee of Foreign Affairs
(autograph—Foreign Entry Book, 176)

"March 13, 67/8. Questions for the private Committee.

Where the treaty with Sweden sticks and my expedient for their conclusion.

Send to Elector of Brandenburgh to engage him to take part with those that desire peace, and against those that oppose it.

Power to Sir William Temple to goe to Aix in case of necessity and the character.

The preparations for the warre by sea and lande. Name the officers of both, especially the land, for 4000 foote.

Sir Robert Southwell's Instruction.

Send to the Emperor.

Resolved to the 1st point.

That I goe to the respective ambassadors. See what the Spanish ambassador will doe for the past as well as future satisfaction of the Swedish troopes.

Presse Holland ambassadors to come into their quota for the past: in the worst, answer for the whole. Spanish secure the future monies and their quota for the past. Upon the whole reported to Count de Dhona, and got him to accept it, declaring, this goes for the execution of His Majesty's former promises. Swedes march upon the agreement, anon, before the ratification".

VIII

Note on Draft Secret Treaty in the Clifford Papers at Ugbrooke

This paper, apparently a copy in English for the use of the "Catholic" counsellors, but undated, has on it some marginal notes which are of interest.

(1) On the words, "being resolved to declare himself a Catholic"; "Q. the terme Catholick, whether Roman added".

(2) "What to be done with Dutch colonies?"

(3) "Q. what conditions to be made in case K. of Spn dye before the war against Holland be declared, or that the K. hath declared himself a Catholick.

R. we must presently enter into the war upon the death of the King of Spain—the charge will be defrayed and America his Maties".

These remarks are in two different hands, and neither is Arlington's.

IX

Sir William Godolphin to Arlington, 28 June 1671
(Spain, 58—autograph postscript)

"I do not wonder that the newes of my death was so currant, since it had an author of so much authority as the Conde de Molina, who I find receives as false newes as he writes, My brother, Sir John Go, having written to me that he reported not only my passing to the other world, but also to another faith, and without doubt he believed the former and would never have scandalized me with the latter. I thank God I want many of that Conde's good qualities, and among others his religion.

Wch I have thought fit to mention lest any such report should have made any wrong impression on your Lordships mind".

X

1671, *octubre*, 16, *Londres.*   *Simancas.—Estado, leg°* 2546
El Conde de Molina a la Reina Gobernadora. (*Descifrado*)

SEÑORA,—Siendo tan dificil como ariesgado e inçierto el asegurar resoluçion de este gobierno que no preçeda el veerse executada, diré a V. Mgᵈ que asentada ya la guerra contra la Olanda se dize publicamente que la Françia contribuyra con el coste que tendra esta flota y que sera de quarenta mil hombres; añadiendo dos circunstançias muy sensibles al pueblo y nobleza, que son, el que el pagamento de dicha flota ha de correr por comisarios nombrados por la Françia, y el otro, que para disimular la remision del dinero se supondrá la venta de algunos nauios. Persona de quien tengo comprobada la berdad de sus notiçias me dijo ser çierto que pocos dias antes de la prorrogaçion del Parlamento se le ohió (*sic*) deçir al embaxador Colbert en vn discurso que tubo con este Rey que debia al suyo el poder deçir que lo hera de sus vasallos pues con la resoluçion que hauia tomado no neçesitaria ya de la soberania tiranica de sus parlamentarios con que hauiendo conseguido que lo ayan entendido algunos de entrambas salas no se puede creer lo que se a aumentado su aborrecimiento con vno de los mas confidentes de Milord Arlinton causado de algun fin particular v desengañado de lo que le hauian contribuydo, cada dia son mayores los agasajos que me repite, me dijo ayer que hauiendo estado en su casa de campo hablando muy despaçio sobre la postura en que se hallaban vna y otra corona le pidió que me dijese no holuidase ni dudase lo que me hauia confiado del animo en que estaba su amo de no permitir la menor infracçion en los estados de Flandes y que esperaba que conprobaria ser el dicho Arlinton menos françes de lo que me hauian dicho; a que añadire no pedir menor admiraçion que hauiendo dias que no me hauia visitado el Duque de Boquingan dos noches antes que salió con el Rey me bino a veer y al despedirse me dijo casi lo mismo, y que a su buelta del viaje me hablaria mas despacio; siendo la que mas puede persuadirme a ser lo referido lo que tienen determinado al presente hauerme hablado en la misma conformidad Don Roberto Aobartd, que no obstante hallarse muy en la graçia deste Rey y con el puesto de mayor manejo y valor del reyno y sauidor de los secretos del gabinete me conserba la misma amistad que siempre; y en el sentir de los mas experimentados de ser dificil el dejarse de reconoçer muy presto considerables nobedades. Dios et cetera.

XI

1672, marzo, 28, Londres.   Simancas.—Estado, leg° 2547
El Marques del Fresno a la Reina Gobernadora. (Original)

SEÑORA,—En medio de las perturbaçiones que se ofrezen y los disturbios y ynquietudes con que nos amenaza el rigor de la guerra ocassionando el desconsuelo que en la real piedad de V. Mg^d caua la consideraçion de que la padezca la Christiandad, llega el consuelo de que los perseguidos catolicos deste pais que a V. Mg^d han deuido tanto cuidado, como el que me encarga en el primer capitulo de mi ynstrucçion, logren mas ensanche y liuertad por la que este Rey ha conçedido en la deliberaçion que manifiesta el papel yncluso, traduçido en nuestra lengua, que pongo en las reales manos de V. Mg^d, de que en su real nombre me antiçipare a dar gracias confirmando lo que en despacho de 14 deste referi a V. Mg^d,[1] *del afecto con que el Rey y Duque de Yorc atienden a nuestra santa fee procurando por este medio estenderla, aunque el discurso no deja de prebenir que esta demonstraçion sera con mira a la razon de estado pues por ella puede adquirir las voluntades de los parlamentarios ocultos catholicos para hazerse señor absoluto del Parlamento que apruebe sus maximas siendo esta vn motibo de asegurarnos en la duda y desconfianza que del y de su gouierno tenemos para con mayor seguridad lograr las operaçiones premeditadas,*[1] de que mas dilatadamente doy quenta a V. Mg^d en despacho de este dia. Guarde Dios la C. R. P. de V. Mg^d, como la Christiandad ha menester. Londres 28 de Marzo de 1672.

EL MARQUES DEL FRESNO.   (Rubricado.)

[1] Cipher.

INDEX

INDEX

180; Spain and France and the
Triple Alliance (1666-70), 232-266,
276, 280, 283, 301, 322, 325; the
peace of Aix-la-Chapelle, 263; the
Spanish-Dutch alliance (1671), 326-
328, 331, 333-338, 352, 359, 360
Stanhope, Lady, 87
Stuyvesant, Peter, 124
Sunderland, Robert Spencer, Earl of,
270, 328, 334-337, 357
Surinam, 204, 226, 258, 287, 289, 317,
339, 357, 358, 360, 364
Sweden, 183, 240, 241, 299, 372; and the
Dutch war, 155, 157-159, 161, 163,
168; England negotiates with (1664-
1666), 184-195, 220, 223; her relations with Holland and France, 190,
192-194; and the Triple Alliance,
247, 255, 262, 276-279, 300, 323,
330, 331; and the second Dutch war,
326, 327, 330-333, 337, 351
Sylvius, Gabriel, 88, 91, 197, 199, 200,
275, 280, 341, 349

Talbot, Sir Gilbert, 184-189, 368
Talbot, Father Peter, 53
Talbot, Richard, 54
Tangier, 39-41, 45, 48-50, 59, 116, 172,
173, 179
Temple, Henry, 256
Temple, Lady, 152, 329
Temple, Sir William, 21, 77, 116, 145,
154, 211, 231, 242, 282, 286, 299,
307, 317, 318, 363-365, 372; and the
Dutch war, 148, 155, 157, 162, 196,
197, 369; his career and character,
152-154; his pamphlet, *The Lon-
don Merchant's Letter to him of
Amsterdam*, 209; and the Triple
Alliance, 247, 249-256, 258-260,
262, 263, 265, 276, 277, 280, 285,
299, 301, 302, 315, 323; returns to
the Hague, 275; recalled, 317, 324,
329
Terlon, French diplomat, 186
Terron, Colbert de, 160
Test Act, 352, 353
Texel, battle of, 356
Thurloe, John, 3, 6, 31, 56, 58, 94,
96, 99
Thynne, Thomas, 241, 245, 275, 281
Tobago, 136, 222, 225
Tortuga, 72

Trevor, Lady, 316
Trevor, Sir John, 20, 257, 259-261,
264, 265, 275, 280, 307, 308, 311,
314, 315, 318, 343
Trier, 321
Triple Alliance, the, 228-266, 275-289,
296, 297, 299-304, 314, 318, 322,
323, 347
Turenne, 47, 57, 207, 214, 256, 257,
261, 273, 293, 307, 315, 346, 352
Turkey — Anglo - Turkish relations
(1663), 75; and Austria, 117, 121

Valencia, 116
Valenzuela, Fernando de, 335
Vane, Sir Walter, 154, 160, 161, 197,
198
Vasvar, Peace of, 140
Verneuil, Duc de, 142
Villars, 334
Virginia, 123, 356

Waldeck, George Frederick of, 155,
252, 369
Watteville, Baron, 37-39, 42-44, 46,
57, 298
Weiman, Daniel, 91
Werden, Sir John, 275
West India Company (Dutch), 124,
132, 133, 135
West India Company (French), 73
West Indies, 71, 125, 210, 217
William II, Prince of Orange, 86,
89
William III, King of England
(Prince of Orange), 85-92, 198, 319,
338, 341, 345-348, 358, 364, 365
Williamson, Sir Joseph, 21, 26, 77, 78,
207, 244, 294, 357
Willoughby, Francis, Lord, 71, 204,
287, 288
Winchilsea, Earl of, *see* Finch,
Heneage
Wisniowiecki, Michael, 281
Witt, John de, *see* De Witt
Woorne, 312-314
Wrangel, General, 194, 278
Wreden, Baron von, 151

York, Duke of, *see* James II

Zealand, 347, 350, 353
Zulestein, governor to William of
Orange, 88, 89, 198